Technology
NOW

Your Companion to SAM Computer Concepts

Corinne Hoisington

CENGAGE
Learning·

Australia • Brazil • Mexico • Singapore • United Kingdom • United States

CENGAGE
Learning·

Technology Now: Your Companion to SAM Computer Concepts, Second Edition
Corinne Hoisington

SVP, GM Science, Technology & Math: Balraj S. Kalsi

Senior Product Director: Kathleen McMahon

Product Manager: Amanda Lyons

Senior Director, Development: Julia Caballero

Senior Product Development Manager:
Leigh Hefferon

Senior Content Developer: Marjorie Hunt

Contributing Authors: Rachel Biheller Bunin,
Barbara Clemens, Lisa Ruffolo

Developmental Editors: Rachel Biheller Bunin,
Barbara Clemens, Lisa Ruffolo

Product Assistant: Cara Suriyamongkol

Marketing Director: Michele McTighe

Marketing Managers: Stephanie Albracht,
Jeffrey Tousignant

Marketing Coordinator: Cassie Cloutier

Senior Production Director: Wendy Troeger

Production Director: Patty Stephan

Senior Content Project Manager:
Jennifer Feltri-George

Content Digitization Project Manager:
Laura Ruschman

Senior Digital Production Project Manager:
Noah Vincelette

Manufacturing Planner: Fola Orekoya

Composition: Lumina Datamatics, Inc.

Cover Designer: Diana Graham

Cover image: Melpomene/Shutterstock.com

Text Designer: GEX Publishing Services

Art Director: Diana Graham

> For product information and technology assistance, contact us at
> **Cengage Learning Customer & Sales Support, 1-800-354-9706**
>
> For permission to use material from this text or product, submit all
> Requests online at www.cengage.com/permissions
> Further permissions questions can be emailed to
> **permissionsrequest@cengage.com**

Some of the product names and company names used in this book have been used for identification purposes only and may be trademarks or registered trademarks of their respective manufacturers and sellers.

Windows® is a registered trademark of Microsoft Corporation.
© 2012 Microsoft.

Microsoft and the Office logo are either registered trademarks or trademarks of Microsoft Corporation in the United States and/or other countries. Cengage Learning is an independent entity from Microsoft Corporation and not affiliated with Microsoft in any manner.

Disclaimer: Any fictional data related to persons or companies or URLs used throughout this text is intended for instructional purposes only. At the time this text was published, any such data was fictional and not belonging to any real persons or companies.

Microsoft product screenshots used with permission from Microsoft Corporation.

Library of Congress Control Number: 2017930058

Softbound Edition:
ISBN: 978-1-305-67011-2

Loose-leaf Edition:
ISBN: 978-1-337-56311-6

Cengage Learning
20 Channel Center Street
Boston, MA 02210
USA

Cengage Learning is a leading provider of customized learning solutions with employees residing in nearly 40 different countries and sales in more than 125 countries around the world. Find your local representative at www.cengage.com.

Cengage Learning products are represented in Canada by Nelson Education, Ltd. To learn more about Cengage Learning, visit
www.cengage.com

Purchase any of our products at your local college store or at our preferred online store **www.cengagebrain.com**

Printed in the United States of America
Print Number: 01   Print Year: 2017

Brief Contents

Contents

Chapter glossaries of all key terms are available for download on cengagebrain.com and on the Instructor Resource site.

Enhance the learning experience with
Technology Now, 2e

Technology Now, Second Edition: Your Companion to SAM Computer Concepts makes it easy for students to learn computer concepts essential for success on the job and in today's digital world. Fully updated to cover the latest technology and featuring accessible content aligned with the updated Computer Concepts tasks in SAM (Skills Assessment Manager), *Technology Now, 2e* offers a streamlined learning experience for all students, no matter what their learning style or level of expertise. (Available in print or as a fully digital solution in SAM or MindTap.)

Aligns with SAM Computer Concepts tasks: The content in each chapter corresponds to the Computer Concepts tasks in SAM, Cengage Learning's robust training and assessment system. Using this book with SAM keeps students engaged and encourages them to work independently as they read and study, watch videos, and take SAM exams within the SAM system. The updated SAM Computer Concepts tasks feature new videos and content to reflect state-of-the-art technology all designed to involve and inspire students.

SAM (Skills Assessment Manager) is a robust assessment, training, and project-based system where students are active participants in learning essential computer concepts and Microsoft Office skills.

The MindTap Reader version of *Technology Now, 2e: Your Companion to SAM Computer Concepts* works within the SAM environment to teach Office and computer concepts skills. Let SAM be an integral part of your students' learning experience! For more information, please visit *cengage.com/sam*.

Available as fully digital course: You can use this book as a 100% digital solution in SAM or in a MindTap course that contains reading activities integrated with SAM Computer Concepts training videos, SAM exams, quizzing, and more, all delivered in a customizable learning path.

MINDTAP
From Cengage

Typical courses often require students to manage a variety of print and digital resources, platforms, access codes, logins, and homework systems. Now all of those resources are available in one personal learning experience called MindTap. MindTap is a complete cloud-based, interactive, and customizable online course. More than an e-book, each MindTap course is built upon authoritative Cengage Learning content, accessible anytime, anywhere. The MindTap course for *Technology Now, 2e* includes the e-book, flashcards and other study tools, SAM training videos, SAM exams, quizzes, and more, all in a learning path you can customize to suit your course.

- *Customizable to fit your needs:* Choose the print chapters you want to meet your course learning outcomes, and set up SAM or your MindTap course to contain only the SAM tasks or topics covered in the custom book.
- *Updated content covers IC3 digital literacy certification objectives:* All topics in *Technology Now, 2e* have been revised to cover cutting-edge technologies, including augmented and virtual reality headsets, wearable devices, advanced cellular connectivity, state-of-the-art hardware, Office 365 & Windows 10, mobile apps, and more. The content corresponds to the updated SAM Computer Concepts tasks, including those that meet IC3 certification objectives.
- *Elevates learning with hands-on activities that engage and inspire students:* A wide variety of end-of-chapter hands-on activities including critical thinking exercises, team projects, and ethics scenarios engage students in meaningful and relevant ways to reinforce key concepts and inspire them to use technology at school, on the job, and in their daily lives.
- *Designed for today's students:* Content is presented efficiently for today's visual learners with concise, accessible text and appealing graphics. Tips on emerging technologies ("Hot Technology Now"), careers ("On the Job Now"), and relevant statistics ("By the Numbers Now"), plus a Twitter-type message feed with a hashtag for each chapter, speak to the interests of today's students to keep them interested and motivated.
- *Follow the @SAMTechNow Twitter feed:* Stay current with the latest trends and news in technology. Monitored and updated frequently by the book's author, Corinne Hoisington, this Twitter feed will keep students engaged throughout the semester!

About the Author

Courtesy of Corinne Hoisington

Corinne Hoisington is a full-time professor of Information Systems Technology at Central Virginia Community College in Lynchburg, Virginia, with more than 25 years of teaching experience. Professor Hoisington travels over 200,000 miles a year delivering keynote addresses to college and university professors and K-12 educators in over 70 cities worldwide for customers such as the Microsoft Corporation, Microsoft Camp 21 International Events, Cengage Learning, Capital One International Bank, Executive LIVE 2017 in London, and the international South by Southwest event in Austin, Texas. Professor Hoisington is the recipient of the Microsoft Most Valuable Professional award in Computer Programming. She has authored over 20 textbooks with Cengage Learning/National Geographic on topics such as Android Studio Boot Camp, Dreamweaver Creative Cloud, Outlook 2016, Office 2016, Microsoft Windows, and Visual Basic 2017.

Instructor Resources

Instructor support materials are available for this product. These include:

- PowerPoint presentations
- Instructor manual
- Test banks

You can access these resources with your instructor account at login.cengage.com.

Getting Started

Learning computer concepts with immediate feedback provides Emily with confidence in learning technology skills.

Emily is focused on her first week of classes. She just signed into SAM to get started on her computer literacy course.

SAM helps Emily learn in the kind of interactive, immediate environment she's grown up with.

Alexander Image/Shutterstock.com

Emily is excited to use SAM (Skills Assessment Manager) so she can learn more about computers. She likes SAM because it's self-paced and personalized, allowing her to reinforce the information she already knows and explore and learn technology topics that are new to her. SAM builds her confidence with engaging activities that prepare her for life after graduation.

Getting Started with Computing

computer | data | hardware | software | information | computer literacy | digital literacy | computer concepts

Throughout a typical day, you might use a computer to complete a course assignment, compare prices on a pair of shoes or new headphones, exchange text messages with a friend you're meeting for lunch, and listen to music as you walk to class. As you gain computer skills and knowledge, you enhance these experiences and prepare yourself for new ones. Learning and applying computer knowledge makes you computer literate, an essential requirement for a career in today's economy.

Computer Literacy Basics

To be successful on the job and make the most of your personal life, you need to be comfortable and proficient at using a computer. At the most basic level, a **computer** is an electronic device that receives data (input), processes and stores the data, and then produces a result (output). **Data** is a raw fact, such as text or numbers.

A computer includes hardware and software. See **Figure 1**. **Hardware** is the device itself and its components, such as cases, wires, switches, and electronic circuits. **Software** consists of programs that instruct the computer to perform tasks. Software processes data into meaningful **information**.

Figure 1: Computers include hardware and software

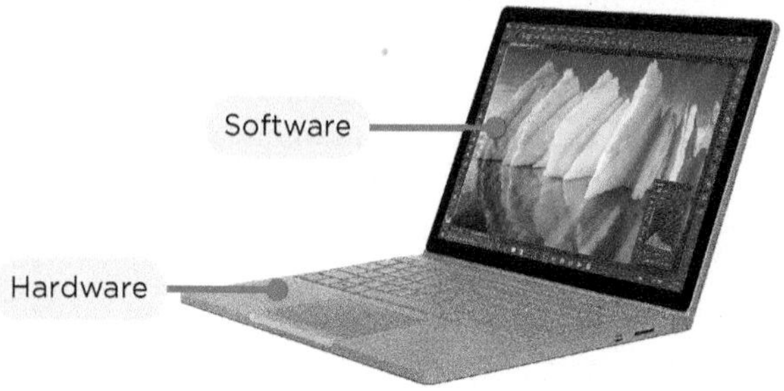

Software

Hardware

Since the computer was invented, computer technology continues to change rapidly. To keep pace with these changes, you need to be computer literate. **Computer literacy** (also called **digital literacy**) is the knowledge you need to understand and use computers and related technology effectively. In general, this knowledge includes the basics of computer technology, known as **computer concepts**, and software skills. More specifically, you should be able to do the following:

- Identify the differences among types of computers, such as desktops, laptops, tablets, smartphones, and servers.
- Describe electronic devices such as digital cameras, portable media players, global positioning systems, and e-book readers.
- Identify types of input devices (such as keyboards, pointing devices, and cameras), output devices (such as displays, speakers, headphones, and printers), and storage devices (such as hard drives, cloud storage, and USB drives).
- Explain the purpose of computer components such as the processor and memory.
- Define a network and explain the difference between the Internet and the web.
- Describe how to use a browser, view websites, and open webpages.
- Define system software and application software.
- Understand the purpose of an operating system and use it to manage files.
- Use productivity apps such as those in Microsoft Office.
- Identify risks in using computers and networks.
- Communicate using digital technology such as email, messaging, and social networks.
- Describe types of digital media such as graphics, video, and audio.

If any of this is confusing or unfamiliar to you, you have the right tool. SAM helps you achieve computer literacy so you can succeed in a career, keep in touch with people around the world, and participate as an active, contributing member of contemporary society.

Getting Started with Technology Now, 2e

screenshot | tweet | follow | timeline | hashtag

To use *Technology Now, 2e: Your Companion to SAM Computer Concepts* effectively, you should understand the structure of the book and its features.

Figure 2: *Technology Now, 2e* features

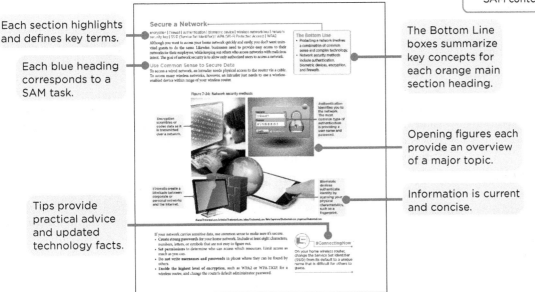

Each section highlights and defines key terms.

Each blue heading corresponds to a SAM task.

Tips provide practical advice and updated technology facts.

The Bottom Line boxes summarize key concepts for each orange main section heading.

Opening figures each provide an overview of a major topic.

Information is current and concise.

Navigate a Chapter

The chapters in this book contain the following sections and features:

- **Chapter opener**: The opening page displays a photo and a scenario that set the context for the chapter, showing how the contents are related to daily life. A table of contents lists the main topics in the chapter.
- **Key terms list**: The key terms discussed in each section or task are listed in order of their appearance below the main heading of the section.
- **The Bottom Line**: This box summarizes why the section topic matters.
- **Subheadings**: These blue headings correspond to SAM computer concepts tasks so you can use the book as you work with SAM or as a reference for later study.
- **Figures**: Figures illustrate the concepts being discussed.
- **Tables**: Tables compare and condense chapter content.
- **Tips**: Four types of tips appear in the margins throughout the book.
- **End-of-chapter activities**: Each chapter concludes with a robust selection of activities to use for homework and assessment.
  - **Chapter Review** provides questions organized for each section that help you review what you've learned.
  - **Test Your Knowledge Now** provides multiple-choice questions and a labeling exercise to assess your comprehension of the material.
  - **Try This Now**, **Ethical Issues Now**, **Critical Thinking Now**, and **Team Up Now** are hands-on activities and projects.
  - **Key terms list** is the alphabetical listing of key terms for each chapter.

#getstarted

Twitter-style messages provide practical information about the chapter topic. The titles vary depending on the chapter content. For example, the tips for Chapter 4, Application Software, are titled #appsoftware.

Hot Technology Now

Hot Technology Now tips highlight emerging technologies.

On the Job Now

On the Job Now tips focus on careers in technology fields.

By the Numbers Now

By the Numbers Now tips summarize statistics in a meaningful way.

#getstarted

For complete information on using Twitter, see the Twitter Help Center at support.twitter.com.

Take Screenshots

Some end-of-chapter activities guide you to explore new technologies and websites, and then ask you to take screenshots of what you explored. A **screenshot** is an image of the content on your computer screen that you can save as a graphics file or insert in a document. You can take screenshots as follows:

1. On the computer screen, display the images to include in the screenshot.
2. To capture the full screen, press the **Print Screen** key. On a Mac, press **Shift+ Command+3** to store the screenshot as a file on the desktop.
   On a Windows computer, the screenshot is stored on the Clipboard, an area in your computer's memory.
3. In Microsoft Word on a Mac, insert the screenshot as a picture. In Windows, paste the screenshot in an open document.
4. Save the document containing the screenshot.

Follow @SAMTechNow on Twitter

Corinne Hoisington, the author of this book, keeps up with trends and topics in contemporary technology, which change rapidly. She tweets at the Twitter account for this book, which has the account name @SAMTechNow.

To follow @SAMTechNow on Twitter:

1. Go to twitter.com and sign into your account.
2. In the search box at the top of your homepage, enter **@SAMTechNow**.
3. Click **@SAMTechNow**, in the list below the search box, to display the @SAMTechNow homepage.
4. Click the **Follow** button to start following @SAMTechNow. To **follow** Twitter users means to subscribe to their tweets, which appear in your **timeline**, or the home page of your Twitter account.
5. Click the **Home** button on the navigation bar to return to your homepage, and then click the **Following** link below your profile picture to verify that you are following @SAMTechNow. See Figure 3.

Figure 3: Tweeting and retweeting

Source: Twitter

Computer Hardware

...earing an augmented
...R) head-mounted
... visualize the design
...round.

Using AR, Olivia can superimpose computer-generated images of a structure onto a real location before building on the site.

iStockphoto.com/jeangill

Olivia Grady is an intern at an architectural firm this semester. During her internship orientation, the architecture instructor provided an overview of the computer hardware devices that designers rely on to build realistic 3-D modeling projects such as playgrounds and buildings. Architects wear an augmented reality (AR) head-mounted display to create a real-time visualization that shows clients how the design of their building project would look in a particular space.

Review a Brief History of Computers

vacuum tube | transistor | integrated circuit | microprocessor | personal computer (PC)

People have used tools and machines to count and manipulate numbers for thousands of years, ranging from the abacus in ancient times and the first computing machines in the mid-nineteenth century to handheld, powerful devices such as contemporary smartphones.

The first generation of computers used **vacuum tubes**, cylindrical glass tubes that controlled the flow of electrons, which can be set to one of two states: on or off. Vacuum tube computers such as the ENIAC and UNIVAC were expensive and limited, used a lot of power, ran very hot, and wore out quickly.

Figure 1-1: Computers in history

Apple introduced the first computer for personal use, but IBM popularized the PC.

Apple iPhones

Windows 2-in-1 laptop

Chromebook

The trend in modern computers is to streamline the physical design while increasing processing capacity.

iStockphoto.com/Franck-Boston, Source: Apple Computer, Source: Google

The next generation of computers replaced vacuum tubes with **transistors**, which were smaller, cheaper, and more reliable. These computers contained many components still in use today, including tape and disk storage, memory, operating systems, and stored programs.

In the 1960s, computer engineers developed **integrated circuits**, which packed the equivalent of thousands of vacuum tubes or transistors into a miniature silicon chip. In 1971, Ted Hoff and a team of engineers at IBM introduced the **microprocessor**, which was even faster, smaller, and less expensive than earlier integrated circuits.

Trace the Rise of Modern Personal Computers

In the 1970s and 1980s, computers meant for personal use started to gain popularity. In 1978, Steve Jobs and Steve Wozniak of Apple Computer Corporation introduced the Apple II, a preassembled computer with color graphics and the popular spreadsheet software called VisiCalc.

Figure 1-2: Using more than one computing device

Dragon Images/Shutterstock.com

IBM followed Apple's lead in 1981, introducing its own machine, dubbed a **personal computer (PC)**. Other manufacturers began making less expensive clones of IBM PCs to capture a share of the growing market. Since 1981, the number of PCs in use grew to 1 billion in 2008 and 2 billion in 2016, according to Forrester Research. However, worldwide sales of PCs have been falling recently as many people use tablets and smartphones instead of or in addition to PCs. See **Figure 1-2.**

Modern computing devices are still based on microprocessors, which have become ever smaller in size but larger in processing capacity.

Describe Types of Computers

desktop computer | monitor | system unit | all-in-one desktop | laptop | tablet | stylus | slate | 2-in-1 device | mobile device | smartphone | wearable device | activity tracker | smartwatch | Internet of Things (IoT)

Computers are so much a part of our world that you might not even realize when you're using one. Chances are, though, that you use computers every day.

Figure 1-3: Types of computers

When purchasing a computer today, most people choose a laptop or tablet.

A 2-in-1 device combines the features of a laptop and a tablet.

Smartphones, portable music players, and e-book readers are types of modern computers.

Uber Images/Shutterstock.com, Supapun Narknimitrung/Shutterstock.com, pathdoc/Shutterstock.com, MAStock/Shutterstock.com

Identify Desktop Computers

The first type of PC was the **desktop computer**, which consists of a system unit, a **monitor** (the display screen), a keyboard, and a mouse. The **system unit** contains most of the electronic circuitry in the computer. In a traditional setup, the system unit can lie flat on the desk or, if it's a tower unit, placed under the desk or on the floor.

Sales of traditional desktop computers are declining, though they remain popular with serious gamers and business users, especially those in design or scientific fields.

Another type of desktop computer combines the system unit with the monitor to create an **all-in-one desktop**. Because they take up less space than traditional desktop computers, all-in-one desktop computers are a logical choice for home users and anyone else who wants to use a large display screen without the extra hardware of a system unit. See **Figure 1-4**.

However, an all-in-one computer is not as easy to carry as a laptop, and it does not allow as much room for hardware upgrades as a traditional desktop computer.

Describe Laptops

Laptops are as powerful as many desktop computers. They are lightweight, small, and portable because they can run on a rechargeable battery. See **Figure 1-5** on the next page. Laptops are popular computers for work, education, and personal use.

You can attach a mouse to a laptop, but you often don't need to because laptops include touchpads or other pointing devices that perform the same functions as a mouse.

A laptop usually includes one or more USB ports for connecting printers, headsets, cameras, external hard drives, and other devices. Laptops also include built-in cameras and microphones and depend on wireless connectivity for

Figure 1-4: All-in-one desktop computer

The system unit is located behind the display screen in an all-in-one desktop such as the iMac.

Source: Apple Computer

Figure 1-5: Laptop

Laptops contain the system unit, the display screen, and the keyboard in a foldable case.

Touchpad

iStockphoto.com/Cesare Andrea Ferrari

other functions. For example, you can connect to the Internet to back up files in the cloud. In fact, Chromebooks primarily are designed to be used when you are connected to the Internet and do not include much storage space for software or personal files.

Describe Tablets

A **tablet** is a small, flat computer with a touch-sensitive screen that accepts input from a digital pen, a **stylus**, or your fingertips. You can use a tablet as a writing or drawing pad, making it convenient for people who need to use their computers as they would a pad of paper or a sketch book and yet take advantage of the tablet's power to access data, perform calculations, and search the web.

The standard one-piece rigid tablet, also called a **slate**, has a display built into the front of the tablet case. The iPad and Samsung Galaxy Tab are popular slates. Slates often include a touch screen keyboard that lets you tap the screen to type. A **2-in-1 device** combines the touch screen of a tablet with a keyboard that you can fold away or detach. The Surface Pro is an example of a 2-in-1 device. See **Figure 1-6**.

By the Numbers Now

According to StatCounter, most active computers are PCs running a Windows operating system. Other popular computers include MacBooks (9%), Linux PCs (2%), and Chromebooks (1%).

Figure 1-6: Slate and 2-in-1 device

Slate with touch screen keyboard

2-in-1 tablet with a detachable keyboard

Mygate/Shutterstock.com, Source: Apple Computer

By the Numbers Now

The average laptop battery lasts 6 hours, while the average tablet battery lasts almost 10 hours, depending on your task. Some laptop and tablet batteries provide up to 17 hours of power.

Identify Smartphones

Tablets and smartphones are types of **mobile devices**, portable computers that weigh up to about 2 pounds. A mobile device often accepts input through your fingertips, a digital pen, or a stylus. Many mobile devices also accept voice commands and provide a keyboard for entering data. In addition, these devices have features that mobile users need, such as hardware for connecting to Wi-Fi networks or navigating with a GPS.

A mobile device has a mobile operating system, such as Android, iOS, or Windows 10 Mobile. It can also run applications, or apps. Typical apps on mobile devices include those that provide access to the web, let you text and video chat, take photos and videos, play music, find directions, as well as manage email, appointments, contacts, and other personal information. A **smartphone** includes these features in addition to tools that let you make phone calls through cellular networks. Other types of mobile devices include portable media players, e-book readers, and game consoles.

#introhardware

One way to classify computers is to group them into PCs (desktops and laptops), mobile devices (tablets and smartphones), and servers, which provide access to software, services, and data for a group of users. Businesses and other organizations often use servers to centralize data and software.

Many people use a PC for some tasks and a mobile device for others. Because of their physical keyboards, storage capacities, and processors, PCs are well-suited to productivity tasks. Because of their size, weight, and battery life, mobile devices are ideal for consumption tasks, such as watching videos, visiting websites, checking email, and playing games.

Describe Wearable Devices

A **wearable device**, or wearable for short, is a small mobile computing device designed to be worn by people. Examples include smartwatches and activity trackers.

Figure 1-7: Apple Watch

A smartwatch can receive and send messages, access the web, track fitness, and make electronic payments.

Activity trackers contain smart sensors to monitor your vital signs such as your heart rate, count the steps you take, track your sleep patterns, and collect information about other physical indicators and movements. Activity trackers can take the form of a watch, wristband, jewelry, or clothing. They connect wirelessly to smartphones so you can store, analyze, and share the activity data.

Smartwatches such as Apple Watch shown in **Figure 1-7** are wristwatches with a computing chip and a touch screen. In addition to telling the date and time, they communicate with a smartphone to make and answer phone calls, send and receive messages, track fitness activities, display notifications, and perform other tasks suitable to mobile users.

Wearable devices are part of the **Internet of Things (IoT)**, a network of objects that contain software, sensors, and connectivity technology to independently exchange data with other computing devices through the Internet.

Hot Technology Now

You can use a free app and website named Glympse (glympse.com) to detect your location by using the closest cell phone tower. Many companies use Glympse to track the position of taxis, mail trucks, trash collection trucks, and delivery vans.

Define Input Devices

keyboard | touchpad | mouse | scroll wheel | trackball | graphics tablet | stylus | digital pen | smartpen | touch screen | gesture | multitouch screen | webcam | scanner | 3-D scanner | microphone | headset | voice input | voice recognition software | speech recognition software | MIDI | game controller | joystick | gamepad | virtual reality (VR) gaming device | biometric technology | biometric input device | fingerprint reader | facial recognition system

Imagine that you receive a computer as a gift. You set it up, sit down at your desk, press the power button, and wait for something to happen. The computer starts up and displays the operating system on the display screen . . . and then what? Without an input device, you are stuck; you cannot do anything. You need an input device to put the computer to work—to communicate instructions or commands.

The Bottom Line

- For many types of computers, a touchpad and keyboard are the most common input devices. A touchpad and a mouse are examples of pointing devices, which move the on-screen pointer.
- Instead of a pointing device, mobile devices use a touch screen, which accepts input from fingertips or a stylus.
- Computers of all sizes include microphones to accept voice commands as input.

Figure 1-8: Input devices

Keyboard
Mouse
Touch screen
Touchpad
Stylus
Voice input

JIPEN/Shutterstock.com, iStockphoto.com/shironosov, Source: Samsung, iStockphoto.com/baranozdemir

Figure 1-9: Backlit keyboard

A backlit keyboard makes it easy to work in a dimly lit place.

Use Keyboards

A **keyboard** is an input device you use by pressing keys for letters, numbers, and symbols to enter data into the computer. Most English keyboards are organized in the standard QWERTY layout, named for the letter keys on the second row. Countries outside the United States use different keyboards configured to their alphabet and numerical system.

Desktops and laptops generally use physical keyboards, some with special features such as backlighting. See **Figure 1-9**. Tablets and smartphones have keyboards as well, which can be built-in, detachable, or on-screen. Virtual keyboards are software controlled and often use formats other than QWERTY to accommodate their smaller size and fewer keys.

Use Pointing Devices

The most common pointing device is a **touchpad**, a flat surface usually built into laptop keyboards, though mobile devices such as portable music players also provide smaller touchpads on their case. You glide your finger across the pad to move the pointer across the screen and tap the pad to enter commands. On a laptop, a touchpad includes buttons or areas for clicking and right-clicking.

A **mouse** is a pointing device that fits under your hand. As you move the mouse, its movements are mirrored by the pointer on the screen. You click a mouse button to enter a command. A mouse might include a **scroll wheel** or touch-sensitive surface for scrolling the display. You can also use the touch-sensitive area on some mice to move the pointer and change the magnification of the screen content.

A **trackball** is an older pointing device with a ball anchored inside a casing. The trackball device is stationary; you roll the ball with your fingers to move the pointer.

On the Job Now

Instead of using pointing devices or keyboards, doctors often enter medical orders and patient information as voice input that is immediately converted into text.

Use Pen Input Devices

You use a pen input device such as a stylus or digital pen to write, draw, or make selections on a touch screen or graphics tablet. (A **graphics tablet** is a flat, pressure-sensitive pad that you draw on to create lines and shapes.) A **stylus** is a small plastic or metal device shaped like a pen that you use to draw freehand, tap icons, or press keys on an on-screen keyboard.

A **digital pen** or **smartpen** is more powerful than a stylus because it can include an electronic eraser or programmable buttons. A digital pen can also capture your handwriting or pen strokes as you drag the tip of the pen on a screen or special paper. See **Figure 1-10**.

Figure 1-10: Digital pen

Write or draw with a digital pen on paper and convert it to digital text.

Source: Livescribe

Hot Technology Now

Recent versions of Windows and Office apps use Windows Ink technology, while Mac apps use Apple Pencil technology to convert handwriting and drawings to digital text and images.

#introhardware

Touch screens provide a quick, intuitive way to navigate and make selections as long as the on-screen objects are large and easy to touch. Small buttons and links, for example, can be difficult to select, making touch screens frustrating for some to use.

Use Touch Screens

A **touch screen** is a visual display that responds to the touch of your finger, hand, stylus, or digital pen to enter data and commands. Tablets, kiosks, and smartphones commonly use touch screens. You interact with a touch screen by making a motion, called a **gesture**, to issue a command. For example, you tap to open an app, slide or swipe to scroll, and pinch or stretch your fingers to zoom. Screens that can recognize input from more than one finger at a time are called **multitouch screens**.

Use Cameras and Scanners

Cameras and smartphones serve as input devices when you transfer their pictures or video to a computer. You can transfer digital video or image files directly from your camera wirelessly using a Bluetooth or infrared connection, via a USB port, or using a memory card.

Most computers come with built-in digital video cameras called **webcams**, which you use for video conferencing or chatting. They convert your image to a digital format and enter the data as input to your device. That data appears as output on a display screen.

An input device called a **scanner** converts printed material into digital format. A scan head moves across a physical page to read and capture information and then creates an image file. A scanner can be connected to a computer via a cable or USB port, or it can be wireless. The bar code reader that a cashier uses to record a purchase is another kind of scanner. It reads the bar code and enters item and price data into the cash register's computer.

People in fields such as medicine and business use **3-D scanners** to scan an object or person in three dimensions, and then print the item on a 3-D printer. See **Figure 1-11**.

Figure 1-11: 3-D scanner

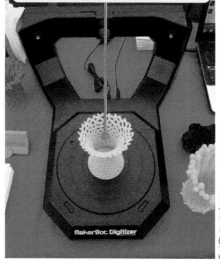

When a 3-D scanner scans an object, it stores data a 3-D printer can use to print a replica of the object.

MakerBot Digitizer

Tinxi/Shutterstock.com

Hot Technology Now

Instead of using a bulky scanner, business travelers and students use a free Microsoft app called Office Lens, which behaves like a scanner on a smartphone or tablet. Office Lens takes pictures of items such as business cards, restaurant menus, receipts, and notes on whiteboards or blackboards and makes them readable. You can save the pictures to the cloud and open them in an app.

Use Microphones

You use a **microphone** to enter voice or sound data into a computer. A microphone is usually internal, though it can be connected to your computer wirelessly or via a wire to a microphone jack or a USB cable to a USB port. Most webcams include microphones you can use to chat. A wired or wireless **headset**, which consists of a microphone built into a headphone set, is a convenient way to use an external microphone during an online conversation.

You can add music and other sounds to a computer by connecting an external device, such as a guitar, into MIDI and other compatible computer ports. **MIDI**, short for Musical Instrument Digital Interface, is a system for creating and storing synthesized music, and includes a standard for connecting electronic musical devices to computers.

Provide Voice Input

When you use a microphone to ask Siri for directions on an iPhone or speak to another type of device, you are providing **voice input**, which uses the human voice to give commands to a computer. The computer must have **voice recognition** or **speech recognition software** installed so it can accept the voice input and interpret it as computer commands.

Use Game Controllers

A **game controller** is an input device you use when playing a video game. Control your actions on the screen with one of the following types of game controllers:

- A **joystick** is a vertical stick or lever that pivots in a 360-degree range of motion.
- Steering wheel controllers simulate on-screen driving.
- A **gamepad** is a handheld console with buttons and other controls you typically press with your thumbs to play a game.
- Motion-sensing controllers let you control game play by gesturing and moving your body or the controller itself. Dance boards and balance boards record your movement on the board and then feed it to the device.
- A **virtual reality (VR) gaming device** is usually a headset or head-mounted display that generates a realistic environment you can explore and control physically. As with motion-sensing controllers, a VR gaming device records your interactions and supplies them to the main game console.

Hot Technology Now

Activate Cortana, the digital assistant in Windows 10, with your voice to set reminders and track and find information using any of your digital devices. For example, you can ask Cortana on your PC to remind you to pick up a new charger cord when you drive near an electronics store. Using the GPS on your smartphone, Cortana can detect when you are near the store and remind you about the charger cord.

Provide Biometric Input

Biometric technology analyzes a person's unique physical characteristics, such as fingerprints or voice patterns, to confirm identity and grant access to restricted spaces or devices. A **biometric input device** collects data that creates a digital imprint of a physical characteristic, and then transfers that information to a host system for review.

Fingerprint readers, also called fingerprint scanners, are the most common biometric devices. They are relatively inexpensive, with some models costing less than $100, and are often built into devices including laptops and smartphones. See **Figure 1-12**.

Figure 1-12: iPhone Touch ID fingerprint reader

Place your finger on the fingerprint reader to identify yourself.

ymgerman/Shutterstock.com

Windows 10 has a **facial recognition system** called Windows Hello, which verifies a user's identity using the device's built-in camera. Airport security and law enforcement officials use a similar technology to scan the faces of people trying to board airplanes or enter sensitive areas. They can compare these facial scans with database pictures of known criminals. Other biometric input devices create and transfer imprints of your hands, voice, eyes, or signature.

Use Keyboards

typing keypad | navigation keypad | numeric keypad | function key | Internet control key | media control key | modifier key

The keyboard is the most common input device for entering text. The layout of a typical desktop keyboard has areas for the kinds of keys described in **Table 1-1**.

Table 1-1: Parts of a keyboard

Keyboard area	Purpose
Typing keypad	Includes numbers, letters, punctuation marks, and symbols such as $ or %
Navigation keypad	Contains arrow keys and other navigation keys such as the Home key for moving the insertion point and scrolling the screen
Numeric keypad	Includes keys for numbers and symbols for addition, subtraction, multiplication, and division when the NUMLOCK key is selected
Function keys	Includes keys beginning with the letter "F" such as F1 or F10 for issuing commands such as Help or Refresh
Internet control keys	On some keyboards, these keys navigate webpages, open a list of favorite websites, check email, and display the home page.
Media control keys	Control the playback of digital music or video; might also include keys for controlling the volume and screen brightness
Modifier keys	Keys such as SHIFT, CTRL, and ALT that you use with other keys to issue a command, type symbols, or create uppercase letters

Figure 1-13: Smartphone with physical keyboard

This keyboard slides out from behind the screen.

Some smartphones come with a physical keyboard.

To conserve space, most laptops include only some of these keyboard areas, such as the typing keypad, navigation keypad, and function keys, but not a numeric keypad or special keys. If a device does not have a built-in numeric keypad, you can use an external keypad that plugs into a USB port.

Use Mobile Device Keyboards

To use the touch screen keyboards of mobile devices, you press the image of a key with your finger, a digital pen, or a stylus. Many of the keys have more than one purpose, providing similar functionality to standard keyboards. Some mobile devices show letters on the first keyboard screen and then, after you tap a button, numbers and symbols on another screen. In this way, on-screen keyboards can provide a full range of characters used in computer input. However, if you need to enter a lot of text, such as when you are writing a report, switching from one on-screen keyboard to another can be inefficient.

Mobile devices can also have mini keyboards with real keys rather than touch screen keys. They have fewer keys and less functionality than the keyboard on a laptop or desktop computer because they are not designed for document creation, but for short messages and notes. See **Figure 1-13.**

Hot Technology Now

Windows touch devices include an on-screen keyboard that you can switch to different layouts such as a thumb keyboard or handwriting keyboard, which you can use with a stylus or fingertip.

#introhardware

Some physical keyboards designed for desktop computers include connectors for tablets and smartphones so you can use a single keyboard with many devices.

> **The Bottom Line**
> - Pointing device actions include clicking, double-clicking, right-clicking, selecting, scrolling, dragging, and dropping.
> - On a touch-sensitive pointing device, you tap instead of click and use gestures such as swiping and stretching.

Use Pointing Devices

point | click | double-click | right-click | drag | gesture | tap | double-tap | swipe | pinch | stretch

You use a pointing device to move the pointer on a display screen. A pointer can be in the shape of an arrow, an I-beam, a bar, or other shape or image.

Use the Mouse

A computer mouse can be wireless, or it can be connected to the computer via a wire or cable. Most wired mice connect through a USB port. You use a mouse to interact with objects on the display screen. **Table 1-2** summarizes the actions you can perform with a mouse.

Table 1-2: Mouse actions

Action	Description	Use it to
Point	Move the mouse.	Move the on-screen pointer.
Click	Press and release the left mouse button.	Select an object.
Double-click	Press and release the left mouse button twice in quick succession.	Start an app or select an object.
Right-click	Press and release the right mouse button.	Display a shortcut menu.
Drag	Press and hold a mouse button and then move the mouse.	Move an object.

Use Gestures

Touch screens and some touchpads let you use your fingers to select, move, and change the size of windows or objects. Any finger motion you perform is called a **gesture**. **Table 1-3** on the next page lists touch input gestures and describes them.

#introhardware

Gestures can vary depending on the software and device. For example, a tablet may use different gestures from a smartphone screen.

Table 1-3: Touch input gestures

Gesture	Description	Use it to
Tap	Touch and release an object quickly.	Select an object. Press a button.
Double-tap	Touch and release an object two times.	Start an app.
Press and hold	Touch and hold an object.	Display a shortcut menu.
Drag	Touch and hold an object and then move it with a fingertip.	Move an object.
Swipe	Touch one side of the screen and then slide your fingertip horizontally or vertically.	Scroll a window or screen.
Pinch	Move two fingers together.	Zoom out.
Stretch	Move two fingers apart.	Zoom in.

Define Output Devices

head-mounted display (HMD) | flat panel display | liquid crystal display (LCD) | light-emitting diode (LED) | resolution | printer | ink-jet printer | laser printer | toner | multifunction device (MFD) | mobile printer | plotter | 3-D printer | headphone | earbud | headset | projector | HDMI (high-definition multimedia interface) | pico projector | pocket projector | voice synthesizer | text-to-speech technology | voice recognition software | closed caption

Without output devices, you wouldn't be able to see or hear anything on your computer or print anything from the computer.

Figure 1-14: Output devices

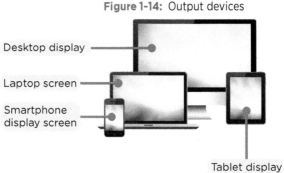

Desktop display

Laptop screen

Smartphone display screen

Tablet display screen

Color output from a printer

iStockphoto.com/Nik_Merkulov, Maksym Dykha/Shutterstock.com

On the Job Now

Some retail stores provide HoloLens augmented reality (AR) goggles to let shoppers see design or product options. At some large home improvement stores, shoppers can upload digital images of their kitchens to view a hologram showing details such as countertops and appliances in a 3-D image.

Describe Display Devices

All PC have a display device that shows text and images as computer output on a screen. These include touch screens, plasma screens, and LCD and LED displays. Untraditional display devices include wearable goggles, also called **head-mounted displays (HMDs)** that project a computer-generated VR and let users explore a 3-D environment to play games, attend a virtual yoga class, or test a product before buying it. See **Figure 1-15**.

Figure 1-15: Virtual reality goggles

The Oculus Rift is a set of virtual reality goggles that works with a gaming device.

iStockphoto.com/br-photo

Most computers have a **flat panel display**, which is a thin, flat screen that uses either **liquid crystal display (LCD)** or **light-emitting diode (LED)** technology. The **resolution** of a screen indicates the number of horizontal and vertical pixels (picture elements, or single points of light) in a display. A high resolution such as 1366 × 768 uses millions of pixels and produces a smooth, sharp, and clear image.

Display devices labeled 1080p or 1080i show images and video in high definition (HD), which has a resolution of 1920 × 1080; these displays let you watch HDTV on your computer. A display with Ultra HD (4K) resolution has the highest resolution currently available for commercial use. Some 4K display devices are thin and curved, providing a wider field of view and an immersive viewing experience. HD and 4K displays are more common in home entertainment and video production than everyday computing.

To save power without sacrificing clarity, many mobile devices use a display technology that lets you view high-quality images from all angles while consuming less power. For example, the Nexus One uses an active-matrix organic LED (AMOLED) display and Apple mobile devices use Retina Display.

Identify Types of Printers

A **printer** creates hard copy output on paper, film, photo paper, and other media. The most common printers are laser and ink-jet. The speed of these printers is measured in pages per minute (ppm). A printer can be connected to a computer or network by cable through a printer port, using a print server, through a USB port, or wirelessly using a Wi-Fi or Bluetooth network.

Ink-jet printers print by spraying small dots of colored ink onto paper. **Laser printers** use a laser beam and toner to print on paper and are faster than ink-jet printers. **Toner** is a fine powder that is sealed when heated on the page. Color laser printers can print a full range of colors. Other laser printers print only in black and shades of gray.

A **multifunction device (MFD)**, or all-in-one printer, can serve as an input device by copying and scanning documents and as an output device by sending faxes and printing.

A **mobile printer** is a small, lightweight printer that is built into or attached to a mobile device for on-the-go printing. External mobile printers often work with Bluetooth wireless technology. Mobile printers are battery-powered and use ink-jet or thermal technology to print. Thermal technology uses wax-based ink or burns dots onto coated paper to print. See **Figure 1-16**.

Because a mobile printer is so small, it fits easily into the case of a mobile device. The small size, however, prevents some mobile printers from using standard 8-1/2 × 11 inch paper; instead, they print on smaller, sometimes odd-sized, papers.

A large-format printer can print on very large sheets of paper. Some large-format printers called **plotters** use charged wires to produce high-quality drawings for professional applications such as architectural blueprints. Graphic artists and designers use large-format ink-jet printers to print large drawings, posters, and photographs.

Instead of printing text and images on paper, you can use a **3-D printer** to create objects based on computer models. These printers use special plastics and other materials to generate objects. See **Figure 1-17**.

To use a 3-D printer, you start by creating an electronic design of an object using a 3-D scanner or a 3-D modeling app. The printer reads the file containing the design and creates the object in an additive process, which means producing successive layers of material. Each layer is a thin cross-section of the object.

Because 3-D printing reduces energy consumption and waste, easily allows for customization, and increases the speed of production, it is changing industry worldwide. Manufacturers use 3-D printers for rapid prototyping, allowing them to quickly progress from ideas to scale models of products, buildings, custom parts, and other objects.

On the Job Now

Some companies require employees to cover their computer displays with a privacy screen to prevent others from viewing sensitive, confidential information.

#introhardware

You can attach an additional display device to a laptop through a VGA (Video Graphics Array), DVI (Digital Visual Interface), or HDMI connector. Check the back or sides of the computer for ports that allow these types of connectors.

Figure 1-16: Mobile printer

Some mobile printers such as the HP Sprocket are built into mobile devices including smartphones and cameras.

Source: HP

Figure 1-17: 3-D printer

A 3-D printer uses plastic and other materials to create objects based on computer models.

Source: MakerBot

Figure 1-18: 3-D printed car

The manufacturer used a 3-D printer to produce all the parts of this car, called the Blade Supercar.

Source: Divergent Microfactories

They can then use the 3-D printers to create the final products, including engine parts, lightweight airplane parts, aerodynamic car bodies, and custom prosthetic devices. In fact, Divergent Microfactories, an American automotive company, recently introduced the world's first 3-D printed car. See **Figure 1-18**.

Use Speakers and Headphones

Audio output includes recorded music, spoken voice, sound tracks for movies or video, computer-generated music, and other sounds, such as the beeps a computer emits if you make an error. Speakers are usually built into a computer, smartphone, or tablet. You can also add wired or wireless external speakers to a system to enhance sound. (You plug wired speakers into the audio output jack, which is usually on the back of a PC.) Some portable speakers are small enough to fit into your pocket.

Headphones let you listen to sound in a public space. They consist of a pair of small listening devices that fit into a band placed over your ears. Many computers, mobile phones, and digital music players have jacks for headphones or **earbuds**, which are speakers small enough to place in your ears. They can be connected via a USB or other cable, or can be wireless. See **Figure 1-19**.

If you want to video chat or use your computer for phone calls over the web, a **headset** is a good option. Headsets include one or more headphones (for output) and a microphone (for input).

#introhardware

Noise-cancelling headphones tune out ambient noise to allow you to focus on your work or listen to music.

Figure 1-19: Wireless earbuds

AirPods are wireless earbuds introduced with the iPhone 7.

Source: Apple Computer

Produce Voice Output

A **voice synthesizer** is an audio output device that converts text to speech. When you contact 411 for directory assistance, for example, the call is answered by a synthesized voice. **Text-to-speech technology** uses digitized voice files that can be interpreted by a computer.

Some operating systems have built-in voice synthesizers. For example, Windows has a tool called Narrator that can read screen contents. This feature narrates text displayed on-screen so that people with visual or cognitive impairments can use the computer.

Voice recognition software converts speech to text, which is especially helpful for those who have hearing impairments. Voice recognition systems such as Alexa for Amazon, Siri for Apple, Cortana for Microsoft, and Google Voice respond to commands with synthesized speech. See **Figure 1-20**.

Many videos include the option to turn on subtitles, or **closed captions**, so that users can watch the action on the screen and read what is being said in the voice-over.

Figure 1-20: Cortana digital personal assistant

Digital personal assistants such as Cortana use voice recognition technology.

ymgerman/Shutterstock.com

Use Projectors

Projectors, sometimes referred to as data or video projectors, let you display computer output on a wall or projection screen. Many projectors work with dual screens so you can view a slightly different output on your computer, such as a presentation with speaker notes, while your audience sees only the presentation.

Projectors can be connected to a computer wirelessly or via a cable. Many connect using HDMI cables to display output in high definition, and some work with 3-D imagery to project holograms of 3-D objects. **HDMI (high-definition multimedia interface)** cables transfer uncompressed video data and digital audio data among HDMI-compliant devices. Projectors can also include a dock so that you can share any video stored on a portable media device or smartphone with a wider audience. Newer projectors called **pico projectors** or **pocket projectors** can be very small—even built into a smartphone, tablet, or laptop. They display the information from the mobile device on a large screen.

On the Job Now

If your presentation to an audience demands two views on two monitors; you need to connect to external and extended monitors. Typically you connect the monitors using HDMI cables through a USB port on the back of your computer to get the best audio and video quality.

Define the Central Processing Unit

central processing unit (CPU) | microprocessor | processor | integrated circuit | chip | motherboard | circuit board | core | multicore processor | control unit | arithmetic logic unit (ALU) | register | machine cycle | clock speed | megahertz (MHz) | gigahertz (GHz) | cycle | bus | data bus | address bus | bus width | word size | cache | processor cache | Level 1 (L1) cache | Level 2 (L2) cache | Level 3 (L3) cache | benchmark

The **central processing unit (CPU)** is the brain of a computer. The CPU is often called a **microprocessor** or a **processor**. It is an **integrated circuit**, or **chip**, and can contain millions of electronic parts and circuits. The CPU is built into the **motherboard**, which is the main **circuit board** that houses much of a computer's electronics.

The Bottom Line
- The CPU processes all instructions that make it possible for you to operate a computer.
- The performance of a CPU is determined by many factors, including clock speed, bus speed, and cache.

Figure 1-21: Central processing units

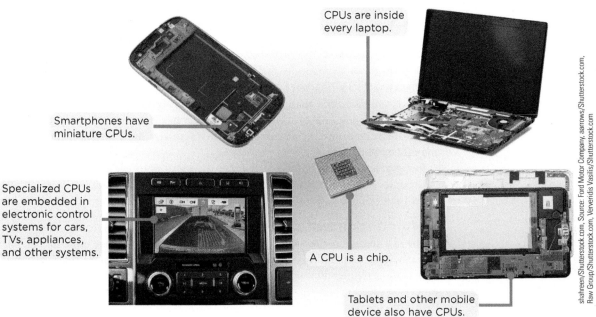

CPUs are inside every laptop.

Smartphones have miniature CPUs.

Specialized CPUs are embedded in electronic control systems for cars, TVs, appliances, and other systems.

A CPU is a chip.

Tablets and other mobile device also have CPUs.

shahreen/Shutterstock.com, Source: Ford Motor Company, aarrows/Shutterstock.com, Raw Group/Shutterstock.com, Ververidis Vasilis/Shutterstock.com

Define Processor Cores

One of the most important factors to consider in purchasing a computer is CPU performance. The more powerful the processor, the faster and better the computer will make calculations, format pages, load and stream video, and more. Processor performance is determined in part by the number of **cores**, or processor units, on a CPU. The more cores, the more processing power. The first processors were single core, but processors today can be dual core (two cores) or multicore, such as quad-core processors (four cores).

#introhardware

Intel and AMD are popular CPU manufacturers for desktops, laptops, and servers.

A **multicore processor** generally is faster and more powerful than a single-core processor. Multicore processors are particularly valuable when you run multiple programs at once or work with programs that require a lot of power, such as games, graphics, and video apps. However, all that power generates heat, which can make the chip fail or malfunction. The challenge for processor manufacturers is to reduce the heat without sacrificing power. For example, Intel produces a processor called the Core M, which has low power consumption and low heat generation. Because the Core M doesn't need a fan to stay cool, computer manufacturers can use the chip to build laptops that are thinner than ever.

Describe Processor Logic and the Machine Cycle

CPUs have different parts or functions. Two of the most important are the **control unit** and the **arithmetic logic unit (ALU)**. The control unit is like a traffic cop, directing the flow of instructions throughout the processor. The ALU performs arithmetic operations, such as addition and subtraction, and comparison operations such as comparing two numbers to see if they are the same. The ALU temporarily holds data, such as two numbers to add, in **registers**, or small storage locations within the CPU.

Every instruction to the computer goes through a four-step process in the CPU called the **machine cycle**: fetch, decode, execute, and store. Some parts of the machine cycle are performed by the control unit, and others are performed by the ALU. See **Figure 1-22**.

Figure 1-22: Machine cycle

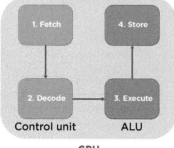

Measure Clock Speed

The processor clock sets the speed at which the CPU executes instructions. **Clock speed** is measured in Hertz. **Megahertz (MHz)** specifies millions of cycles per second, and **gigahertz (GHz)** specifies billions of cycles per second.

A **cycle** is the smallest unit of time a process can measure. Processors with faster clocks can execute more instructions per second than processors with slower clocks. The clock speed is one factor that affects a computer's performance overall. Other factors include the type of processor, bus speed and width, amount of cache, and memory speed.

Measure Bus Speed and Width

A **bus** is an electronic channel that allows the CPU and various devices inside or attached to a computer to communicate. A bus has two parts: the **data bus**, which transfers the data, and the **address bus**, which transfers the information about where the data exists in memory.

Bus width, measured in bits, determines the speed at which data travels. The wider the bus, the more data that can travel on it. For example, a 64-bit bus transfers data faster than a 32-bit bus. Bus width is also called **word size**.

Define Processor Cache

Cache is a storage space for recently or frequently used data in a place that is quick and easy to access. You may have heard of browser cache or disk cache. A **processor cache** stores frequently used data and instructions next to the processor. It improves processor speed because it's easier and faster to retrieve information from the cache than from the processor itself.

Level 1 (L1), **Level 2 (L2)**, and **Level 3 (L3)** are three types of cache. L1 and L2 cache are built into the processor chip. L3 cache resides on a separate chip. It takes a processor less time to retrieve data from L1 or L2 cache than from L3 cache.

Describe Benchmarking

A **benchmark** is a test run by a laboratory or other organization to determine processor speed and other performance factors.

Although you can look at individual factors such as clock speed, bus speed, and cache level, many other factors determine the performance of a processor. It is best to research how various processors perform on benchmark tests. You can find this information on the web and in articles published by computer magazines.

On the Job Now

If your company builds a mobile app or website, the app should be validated with benchmark tests to confirm that it can handle heavy Internet traffic.

Describe How Computers Represent Data

binary number system | bit | byte | ASCII | Unicode | sampling | pixel

The **binary number system** consists of only two digits: 0 and 1. Computers are binary machines because they are electronic devices, and electricity has two states: on and off.

Figure 1-23: Digital data

The binary number system consists of only two digits: 0 and 1.

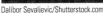

Dalibor Sevaljevic/Shutterstock.com

Bit is short for "binary digit," the smallest unit of information handled by a computer and the basis of today's computer processing. A bit can have the value of 0 or 1.

Bits appear in groups of eight. A group of 8 bits is called a **byte**. Bytes can represent letters, symbols, and numbers. Bytes are the basic building blocks of digitally representing sounds and colors.

Describe How Computers Represent Text

When you press a key on your keyboard, the computer translates the character into bits and bytes using a text coding scheme. Text coding schemes use groups of bits to represent characters. **ASCII** is an 8-bit coding scheme, with different binary codes representing each uppercase letter, lowercase letter, mathematical operator, and logical operation. For example, **Figure 1-24** shows part of an ASCII table with the binary codes for the lowercase letters "d," "o," and "g."

Entering the binary code for "dog" requires quite a bit of typing. Your computer translates your keystrokes into binary digits, however, so you can simply type the three letters.

ASCII doesn't include characters for languages such as Chinese or Arabic. **Unicode**, a 16-bit coding scheme, is an extension of ASCII that can create over 65,000 symbols and characters in many languages.

Describe How Computers Represent Sound

The human ear hears sound, such as music and speech, as sound waves that continually change. To digitize sound, a process called **sampling** takes samples of sound waves a specified number of times per second. Each sample is stored as a binary number. The more samples per second, the more accurate the representation of the sound. However, a higher sampling rate also requires a larger file to store the data.

Describe How Computers Represent Images

Computers also use bits to represent images. Each color is assigned a binary number, such as 0000 for black and 1111 for white. To digitize an image, the image is treated as a series of colored dots, or **pixels**. To a computer, an image is a list of the color numbers for all the pixels it contains.

Measure File Size

The amount of binary information in a file determines its file size. All files are measured in bytes, though the terms used to express file size vary to make it easier to describe the files. **Table 1-4** on the next page lists and defines terms for measuring file size. In the

Figure 1-24: Binary codes

Character	Binary
d	01100100
o	01101111
g	01100111

Hot Technology Now

Streaming music is the continuous flow of music to a device without needing to store it on your hard drive. The most popular streaming music sites include Pandora, Spotify, Google Play Music, Jango, SoundCloud, Groovesharks, Last.fm, and Slacker.

Table 1-4: File size units

Term	Abbreviation	Approx. number of bytes
Byte	B	1
Kilobyte	KB	1 thousand
Megabyte	MB	1 million
Gigabyte	GB	1 billion
Terabyte	TB	1 trillion
Petabyte	PB	1 quadrillion (1 million gigabytes)
Exabyte	EB	1 quintillion (1 billion gigabytes)
Zettabyte	ZB	1 sextillion (1 trillion gigabytes)
Yottabyte	YB	1 septillion (1 trillion terabytes)

#introhardware

Many email service providers set a size limit such as 25 MB for files you attach to an email message. To avoid this limitation, you can share much larger files from your cloud storage location.

ASCII coding scheme, each character you type is 1 byte. In a plain text file, the word "dog" takes up 3 bytes of the total file size. When you add coding for formatting and graphics, the file size increases substantially. Sound and video files tend to be much larger than text files and take longer to download. A high-speed Internet connection is required to download movies and high-definition video.

Describe Computer Memory

random access memory (RAM) | memory chip | memory module | volatile | dynamic RAM (DRAM) | static RAM (SRAM) | magnetoresistive RAM (MRAM) | read-only memory (ROM) | BIOS | power-on self-test (POST) | firmware | boot | programmable read-only memory (PROM) | electrically erasable programmable memory (EEPROM) | flash memory | nonvolatile | virtual memory | swap file | page

Computer memory holds data and programs as they are being processed by the CPU. Memory stores three kinds of information: instructions to be processed, data necessary to complete the instructions, and the results of the data processing operation.

The Bottom Line

- Some memory is volatile, which means that when the computer is shut down, the information in volatile memory is erased. Other memory is nonvolatile. It stores data even when a computer has been powered off.
- Memory types include random access memory (RAM), read-only memory (ROM), virtual memory, and programmable memory.

Figure 1-25: Computer memory

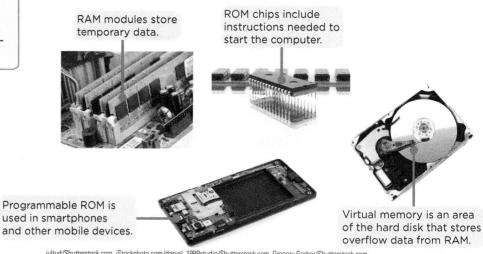

RAM modules store temporary data.

ROM chips include instructions needed to start the computer.

Programmable ROM is used in smartphones and other mobile devices.

Virtual memory is an area of the hard disk that stores overflow data from RAM.

jultud/Shutterstock.com, iStockphoto.com/darval, 1989studio/Shutterstock.com, Gregory Gerber/Shutterstock.com

Define Random Access Memory

Random access memory (RAM) is stored on a set of chips called a **memory chip** or a **memory module**, which is a small circuit board that slides into a slot on the motherboard.

When you start an app, its instructions are loaded from the hard drive, or internal storage, into RAM so that the app opens. When you interact with the app, such as by saving a file, you are copying it from RAM onto a disk or another permanent storage location.

Most RAM is **volatile**. That is, if your computer loses power, any data stored in RAM is lost. RAM capacity is measured in gigabytes. Today's PCs generally need 4–16 GB of RAM.

Identify Types of Random Access Memory

RAM comes in three basic types: **Dynamic RAM (DRAM)** chips need to be recharged constantly or they lose their data. This means that the slightest interruption of power results in data loss. However, DRAM chips are the least expensive of the three types.

Static RAM (SRAM) chips are faster, more reliable, and don't need to be recharged as frequently, but they are more expensive than DRAM chips. **Magnetoresistive RAM (MRAM)** chips use magnetic charges instead of electrical charges to store data. They have greater storage capacity and use less power. They also store data and instructions even after a computer has been turned off. In other words, they are nonvolatile—but more expensive.

Define Read-Only Memory

Read-only memory (ROM) is the memory permanently installed on your system when your computer is manufactured. The ROM chip is attached to the motherboard and contains the **BIOS**, or basic input/output system. The BIOS includes the instructions for starting up your computer as it performs the **power-on self-test (POST)**, which tests the CPU, storage devices, and many other components. After ROM has tested the hardware on the system, it loads the operating system and provides the interface between the operating system and the hardware.

Instructions on a ROM chip are called **firmware**. Your computer's start-up, or **boot**, instructions are an example of firmware. They tell the CPU how to use the hardware in your system.

Describe Types of Programmable Memory

Programmable read-only memory (PROM), **electrically erasable programmable memory (EEPROM)**, and **flash memory** are types of programmable ROM. Like other ROM, they are **nonvolatile**, meaning they keep their contents even if the computer is powered off.

A chip with PROM is a blank ROM chip on which a programmer can write code. Once a PROM chip is programmed, it cannot be changed. PROM is used in cell phones, video game consoles, RFID tags, and other electronics as a simple programming tool.

EEPROM is like PROM except it can be programmed more than once. Flash memory is a type of programmable memory that can be electrically erased and reprogrammed. Flash memory is faster and cheaper than traditional EEPROM. Most BIOS chips now use flash memory. Flash memory cards also store programs and data on many digital electronics devices.

Describe Virtual Memory

When an operating system uses **virtual memory**, it swaps files between RAM and the hard disk to avoid running out of RAM. The part of the hard disk used by virtual memory is called a **swap file**. The amount of data and instructions that can be swapped at any given time is called a **page**.

Virtual memory is especially useful when you have many applications open at the same time. Information from an idle running app is swapped to the hard drive while you're working in another app. However, overuse of virtual memory can slow your computer because retrieving data from a hard drive is much slower than getting it from RAM.

Store Digital Data

hard disk | hard drive | magnetic hard drive | platter | solid state drive (SSD) |
external hard drive | optical media | solid state storage | cloud storage

Figure 1-26: Storage devices

Internal hard drive for a laptop **External hard drive** **Memory cards** **USB flash drive**

Chalermchai Chamnanyon/Shutterstock.com, Be Good/Shutterstock.com, iStockphoto.com/stlee000, Source: SanDisk

Figure 1-27: Internal magnetic hard drive

A hard disk is a storage medium.

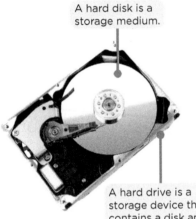

A hard drive is a storage device that contains a disk and other moving parts.

Gregory Gerber/Shutterstock.com

By the Numbers Now

The first hard disk drive that could hold up to 5 MB of data was introduced by Seagate in 1979.

Store Data on Internal Hard Drives

The main storage medium on a PC is the **hard disk**, which is contained in a storage device called the hard disk drive (HDD) or **hard drive**. See **Figure 1-27**. Most hard drives use magnetic storage, though some use solid state storage.

Most desktop and laptop hard drives use magnetic technology. A **magnetic hard drive** is made up of one or more disks called **platters** that spin on a spindle, and read/write heads that move over the surface of the disks to save and retrieve data. The disks and heads are stored in a protective case. (When you see the term HDD in a computer ad, it refers to an internal magnetic hard drive.)

Platters use magnetized particles to store data as bits. Depending on its orientation, a particle represents either a 0 bit or a 1 bit. To change the data on a disk, the orientation of the particles is changed.

Hard drives offer fast access to your data and large storage capacity, making them a good option as the main storage device for a PC. Hard drive capacities today range from 320 GB to 4 TB or more. On the downside, magnetic hard drives are easily damaged by impact and foreign particles. You need to protect your hard drive from excessive movement and contaminants such as dust. **Solid state drives (SSDs)** are more durable than magnetic drives, so they are particularly useful for portable devices such as tablets.

Use an External Hard Drive

You can add storage capacity to your computer relatively easily and inexpensively by attaching an **external hard drive** via a USB cable or a Firewire cable. Many people use external hard drives to back up data so it is protected in case their computer or internal hard drive fails. Because you can detach an external hard drive from your system and lock it away, your data is safe should your computer be hacked or damaged.

You can also use external hard drives to transfer large files from one system to another. To transfer data, you save it to the external hard drive, and then attach the drive to the computer to which you want to copy the data.

Store Data on Optical Media

Optical media include CDs, DVDs, and Blu-ray discs (BDs), though their use as storage media is declining. They store data as light and dark spots on a disc. When you store data on an optical disc, you "burn" the disc. Storage capacities for optical discs vary, with prices rising accordingly. CDs generally hold up to 1 GB of data, DVDs can store up to 17 GB of data, and more expensive BDs can store 100 GB of data.

Optical storage devices have two benefits over magnetic storage. First, they are easy to store and transport. Second, they are less susceptible to damage, although you do need to keep the discs free from scratches and dust.

Store Data on Solid State Drives

Solid state storage uses nonmagnetic technology and can be removable, such as flash drives and memory cards, or contained in a device, such as a solid state hard drive. Solid-state storage drives have no moving parts and are sealed, making them more reliable and less subject to harm from physical contact and foreign objects. Solid state storage is often the choice for cameras, smartphones, media players, and other portable devices. See **Figure 1-28**. Solid state devices store data as electrical charges.

Figure 1-28: Solid state hard drive

Solid state hard drives have no moving parts.

Source: SanDisk

Unlike magnetic disk drives, solid state drives have no moving parts, so they aren't vulnerable to mechanical failure or damage if dropped. They also require less power than magnetic drives, and are not susceptible to data loss due to power interruptions. On the other hand, the storage capacity of solid state technology doesn't yet match that of magnetic drives, and it costs more per gigabyte of storage.

Store Data in the Cloud

Storing data on servers over the Internet, or "in the cloud," is a popular and economical way to store data. **Cloud storage** lets you store your data remotely and access it with any device connected to the Internet, reducing the amount of space you need on your hard disk for files. Instead, cloud storage providers save your information and programs on servers, which have data storage capacities many times larger than a PC.

You might use cloud storage to add storage capacity to your system or to back up data, so that even if your system is damaged, your files will remain intact. People use cloud storage to access their data from Internet-connected devices wherever they are. For example, the Apple iCloud service allows you to access your media files from your phone, tablet, or PC.

With services such as Google Drive, Microsoft OneDrive, iCloud, and Dropbox, you can also use cloud storage to collaborate on documents and projects with others all over the world.

Cloud storage has some disadvantages. If you lose power or your Internet connection, you cannot access your data. If your cloud provider goes out of business, you might lose your data. In addition, whenever your data is transferred to a third party, you need to consider security and privacy issues. Moving data across the Internet increases opportunities for theft or manipulation and makes you dependent on technology you don't own or control.

#introhardware

Any mobile device that contains a solid state hard drive is not hot on the bottom because an SSD does not create heat like a laptop with a magnetic drive.

Hot Technology Now

Cloud storage services such as Google Drive, iCloud, and One-Drive allow you to store contacts, calendars, photos, music, books, apps, and more in the cloud and access them on all your devices. It can be safer to store your data on the cloud instead of on your local hard drive.

#introhardware

Go to twitter.com, search for @SAMTechNow, the book's Twitter account, and then follow @SAMTechNow to get tweets on your home page.

Chapter Review

Review a Brief History of Computers

1. Describe the general trend in computer hardware innovation.

2. How does a microprocessor compare to an integrated circuit?

Describe Types of Computers

3. Describe a 2-in-1 device.

4. Identify an example of a wearable device and describe how you might use it.

Define Input Devices

5. Name three types of pointing devices.

6. What is a biometric input device?

Use Keyboards

7. What can you use to enter numbers if your computer does not have a built-in numeric keypad?

8. Describe how on-screen keyboards can provide a full range of characters used in computer input.

Use Pointing Devices

9. Explain when you would use five types of mouse actions.

10. Describe four touch input gestures and what each does.

Define Output Devices

11. Name four types of output devices.

12. What is a voice synthesizer?

Define the Central Processing Unit

13. What role does the CPU play in a computer?

14. Name two factors to use when comparing CPUs.

Describe How Computers Represent Data

15. Why are computers considered binary machines?

16. Name five units for measuring file size and explain what each means.

Describe Computer Memory

17. Describe the difference between volatile and nonvolatile memory.

18. How does a computer use virtual memory?

Store Digital Data

19. What are the advantages and disadvantages of using a magnetic hard drive to store data?

20. What are the advantages and disadvantages of using cloud storage?

Test Your Knowledge Now

1. Modern computers are based on _____, which have become ever smaller in size but larger in processing capacity.
   a. transistors
   b. ENIACs
   c. microprocessors
   d. solid state technology

2. When IBM introduced computers for personal use, it called them _____.
   a. personal computers (PCs)
   b. Apple computers (ACs)
   c. clones
   d. VisiCalcs

3. A standard one-piece rigid tablet, also called a(n) _____, has a display built into the top of the tablet case.
   a. e-book reader
   b. slate
   c. tower
   d. all-in-one desktop

4. Types of _____ include smartphones, portable media players, and game consoles.
   a. mobile devices
   b. tablets
   c. wearable devices
   d. 2-in-1 devices

5. You interact with a touch screen by making a motion called a _____ to issue a command.
   a. click
   b. signal
   c. flip
   d. gesture

6. A fingerprint reader is an example of a _____ device.
   a. biological
   b. touch-sensitive
   c. facial recognition
   d. biometric

7. A(n) _____ can capture your handwriting or pen strokes as you drag the tip on a screen or special paper.
   a. electronic stylus
   b. digital pen
   c. joystick
   d. biometric scanner

8. Physical mobile device keyboards are designed for _____.
   a. creating documents
   b. drawing
   c. writing short messages and notes
   d. controlling music playback

9. You press and hold an object on a touch screen to _____.
   a. display a shortcut menu
   b. zoom out
   c. scroll the screen
   d. zoom in

10. A(n) _____ printer uses special plastics and other materials to create objects based on computer models.
    a. ink-jet
    b. 3-D
    c. laser
    d. dot matrix

11. To have a video chat, you can use a(n) _____, which includes one or more headphones and a microphone.
    a. earbud
    b. micro headphone
    c. headset
    d. portable speaker

12. The _____ is an integrated circuit, or chip, and is often called the brain of the computer.
    a. RAM module
    b. ROM chip
    c. BIOS
    d. central processing unit (CPU)

13. The CPU is built into _____, which is the main circuit board that houses much of a computer's electronics.
    a. the data bus
    b. the motherboard
    c. volatile memory
    d. nonvolatile memory

14. The number of _____ in a CPU determines the CPU's processing power.
    a. control units
    b. caches
    c. cores
    d. ALUs

15. A _____ is a group of 8 bits and can represent letters, symbols, and numbers.
    a. byte
    b. bit
    c. megabyte
    d. kilobyte

16. _____ is a 16-bit coding scheme, an extension of ASCII that can be used to create over 65,000 symbols and characters in many languages.
    a. ASCII plus
    b. Unicode
    c. Extended code
    d. ASCII 16

17. Most RAM is _____ because if your computer loses power, any data stored in RAM is lost.
    a. unnecessary
    b. inaccessible
    c. nonvolatile
    d. volatile

18. _____ is the memory that contains programs permanently installed on your system when your computer is manufactured.
    a. RAM
    b. ROM
    c. BIOS
    d. POST

19. The main storage medium on a PC is the hard disk, which is contained in a storage device called the _____.
    a. platter
    b. hard drive
    c. optical drive
    d. cloud

20. _____ storage uses nonmagnetic technology, and it can be contained in a device or can be easily removed, such as flash drives and memory cards.
    a. Magnetic
    b. Solid state
    c. Virtual
    d. Tape

21. In the space next to each term below, write the letter of the phrase that defines it.
    a. provides a way to add storage capacity to your computer or to back up data
    b. nonvolatile memory
    c. 1 billion bytes of data
    d. the four-step process that every instruction to the computer goes through
    e. small, flat computer with a touch-sensitive screen that accepts input from your fingertips

    _____ ROM   _____ gigabyte
    _____ external hard drive   _____ machine cycle
    _____ tablet

Try This Now

1: Laptop, Tablet, or 2-in-1—The College Student Decision

You need a new computer for college. You ride public transit to your college each day and take a full load of classes. Your budget is limited, but you need a decent computer.

    a. Research popular laptops, tablets, and 2-in-1s at CNET.com (an unbiased technology site). Create three tables with the specifications of the laptop, tablet, and 2-in-1 device that you would recommend.

    b. Research and document at least five advantages a laptop offers a college student.

    c. Research and document at least five advantages a tablet offers a college student.

    d. In your opinion, would you recommend a laptop, tablet, or 2-in-1 device? Explain why in one written paragraph.

2: 3-D Printers Changing the Proof of Concept for Inventors

The 3-D printer is changing the time is takes to develop an invention. After an inventor develops a drawing of a new product, printing the design on a 3-D printer provides a quick proof of concept. Proof of concept models "prove out" that an idea or design approach is feasible and demonstrate details such as range of motion, mechanics, and architecture. Research the use of 3-D printers in developing new products today and in the future.

    a. Write 100 words or more on at least five uses of 3-D printers in for inventors.

    b. Research and document the cost and specifications for a 3-D home printer. Share the link of the 3-D printer you researched.

    c. Name three types of media or materials used within the 3-D printer to create products.

3-D Printer

iStockphoto.com/vgajic

3: Using Voice Input on a Mobile Device

Note: This assignment requires a smartphone.

You can download a free app named Cortana, which uses artificial intelligence (AI), to any modern smartphone, or use Siri on your iPhone. Research the capabilities that Cortana or Siri provides for your personal and business use.

    a. Write a paragraph describing an example of how you could use a digital assistant with voice recognition in your future job.

    b. Ask Cortana or Siri five questions that you found in your Internet research. List the five questions with the digital assistant's responses.

    c. Research how you can use Uber's ride-sharing and location-based services with Cortana or Siri. Write a paragraph explaining how Cortana or Siri assists with Uber and location-based services such as by reminding you to pick up an item at a store.

Critical Thinking Now

1: Investigate Head-Mounted Displays

You have been hired as a summer intern for a cosmetics company in New York City. The cosmetics company provides men's and women's skincare, hair color, makeup, and perfume products. Your boss asked you to investigate three head-mounted displays that the company could use to display a new virtual or augmented reality app. The app brings skin-care and hair color products to life by producing a video or photo simulating how the products will look on the consumer. Create a table illustrating the specifications of three head-mounted displays that includes the name of the device, cost, size, and other specifications. Compare and contrast the three devices in a document of 200 words or more. Be sure to use your own words and your opinion on how the app might work.

2: Local File Storage vs. Cloud File Storage

When you save a file, you can save it locally to your computer or in a cloud storage location. In a Word document of 150 words or more, compare and contrast saving a file locally to saving it in the cloud. Be sure to use your own words explaining the security of the file, storage space, and accessibility. Share your opinion after your comparison.

3: Compare i3, i5, and i7 Processors

When you buy a laptop computer, you typically choose one with an i3, i5, or i7 processor. Research these three types of processors, select one that suits your needs, and then write two paragraphs about your findings. The first paragraph should discuss the specifications of the processor you would buy, and the second paragraph should discuss the features and cost of the processor.

Ethical Issues Now

You can use apps such as GPS PhoneTracker, Glympse, or FindMyPhone to recover lost or stolen smartphones by determining their GPS position. In fact, you can find the location of any phone as long as you have the permission of the owner. Consider the following ethical questions regarding GPS tracking.

a. If you were a parent, how would you feel about placing a GPS tracking app on your young teenager's phone for safety issues to determine his or her exact location? Write a paragraph stating your opinion.

b. Your best friend recently got engaged and seems concerned about the whereabouts of her fiancé at times. She asked you to install a tracking app on a pay-as-you-go phone and place it in the trunk of the fiancé's vehicle to track his location. How would you handle this ethical dilemma? Write a paragraph stating your opinion.

c. Many companies use remote tracking apps to locate their delivery trucks and personnel. For example, trash truck drivers use tracking apps to approximate their time of trash pick-up. Write a paragraph explaining two other business uses of tracking apps and whether they pose ethical obstacles.

Team Up Now—Biometrics in Your Career

Employers are adopting biometrics to secure their data and to restrict access to specific areas in the workplace. Fingerprint, iris, and facial recognition is replacing the use of complicated, ever-changing passwords. As a team, research how biometrics provide employee authentication.

a. Create a combined document describing the accuracy of different types of biometrics. Each team member should write 150 words on this topic.

b. Create a bulleted list of 10 reasons that replacing passwords with biometrics is a positive step in security.

c. As a team, compile your own opinions of how biometrics could be used by a college or university. List and explain four possibilities.

d. Identify three YouTube videos that describe the use of different types of biometrics.

Key Terms

2-in-1 device
3-D printer
3-D scanner
activity tracker
address bus
all-in-one desktop
arithmetic logic unit (ALU)
ASCII
benchmark
binary number system
biometric input device
biometric technology
BIOS
bit
boot
bus
bus width
byte
cache
central processing unit (CPU)
chip
circuit board
click
clock speed
closed caption
cloud storage
control unit
core
cycle
data bus
desktop computer
digital pen
double-click
double-tap
drag
dynamic RAM (DRAM)
earbud
electrically erasable programmable
  memory (EEPROM)
external hard drive
facial recognition system
fingerprint reader
firmware
flash memory
flat panel display
function key
game controller
gamepad
gesture
gigahertz (GHz)
graphics tablet

hard disk
hard drive
HDMI (high-definition multimedia
  interface)
head-mounted display (HMD)
headphone
headset
ink-jet printer
integrated circuit
Internet control key
Internet of Things (IoT)
joystick
keyboard
laptop
laser printer
Level 1 (L1) cache
Level 2 (L2) cache
Level 3 (L3) cache
light-emitting diode (LED)
liquid crystal display (LCD)
machine cycle
magnetic hard drive
magnetoresistive RAM (MRAM)
media control key
megahertz (MHz)
memory chip
memory module
microphone
microprocessor
MIDI (Musical Instrument Digital
  Interface)
mobile device
mobile printer
modifier key
monitor
motherboard
mouse
multicore processor
multifunction device (MFD)
multitouch screen
navigation keypad
nonvolatile
numeric keypad
optical media
page
personal computer (PC)
pico projector
pinch
pixel
platter
plotter

point
pocket projector
power-on self-test (POST)
printer
processor
processor cache
programmable read-only memory
  (PROM)
projector
random access memory (RAM)
read-only memory (ROM)
register
resolution
right-click
sampling
scanner
scroll wheel
slate
smartpen
smartphone
smartwatch
solid state drive (SSD)
solid state storage
speech recognition software
static RAM (SRAM)
stretch
stylus
swap file
swipe
system unit
tablet
tap
text-to-speech technology
toner
touch screen
touchpad
trackball
transistor
typing keypad
Unicode
vacuum tube
virtual memory
virtual reality (VR)
  gaming device
voice input
voice recognition software
voice synthesizer
volatile
wearable device
webcam
word size

Introduction to Software and Apps

...dical student, Karen
...nutrition and knows
...ortance of exercise
...g healthy.

Karen uses the Charity Miles app to track her workout statistics and see her real-world charitable impact each time she goes for a run, walk, or bike ride.

iStockphoto.com/andresr

Karen Franklin, a medical student, has been assigned a project in her nutrition class that uses fitness tracking apps to log her workouts and count calories. The project uses the app called Charity Miles, which tracks workouts, such as runs, walks, and bicycle rides, and donates money for every mile she completes. Corporate sponsors make donations on her behalf.

What Is Software?

software program | program | output | app | system software | application software | software developer | programmer | programming language | software publisher | graphical user interface (GUI) | instructions | input | preinstalled software | operating system | utility program | productivity software | Software as a Service (SaaS) | web app | load | uninstall | software update | upgrade

The Bottom Line

- You use system and application software to interact with your computer and to perform tasks.
- Some software programs are preinstalled on your computer; others you install.
- You can update software to improve performance and upgrade software to obtain new features.

Every time you click an icon on your desktop, tap commands on a touch screen, or follow a link on your tablet, you are using software. Software is what makes computers so useful in our everyday lives. It interacts with computer hardware to turn machines into invaluable tools that help us perform tasks throughout the day.

Figure 2-1: Creating and using software

iStockphoto.com/LuckyBusiness, isak55 /Shutterstock.com, Scanrail1/Shutterstock.com, Konstantin Faraktinov /Shutterstock.com

Define Software

Software, also called a **software program** or simply a **program**, is a set of instructions that tells a computer what to do, how to do it, and where to send the results, or **output**. The two types of software are system software and application software, or **apps**. See **Figure 2-2**.

Figure 2-2: System software and application software

Application software (also called an app) performs specific tasks.

System software controls a computer and its peripherals, such as its keyboard and pointing device.

MacBook Pro

Source: Apple Computer

Software is written by **software developers**, or **programmers**, using computer-readable code, called a **programming language**. Software is produced and distributed by **software publishers**, who either sell it or give it away. Some well-known software publishers include Microsoft, Oracle, Apple, and Google. Most software uses a **graphical user interface (GUI)**, which lets users interact with the computer by tapping, clicking, or pressing buttons, menus, icons, and links, rather than typing commands.

Describe How Software Works

Software interacts with computer hardware and other software in an organized chain of events; each link in the chain relays **instructions** along the chain until the job at hand is successfully completed.

When you type on a keyboard, select a menu option, press a button, or interact with a touch screen, you issue a command to the computer—you give it **input**. For example, when you click the Print button in a word processing program, you're entering the command to print the current document. Then a series of events occur, as shown in **Figure 2-3**:

1. The word processing software tells the system software that you want to print.

2. The system software relays the command to the printer software.

3. The printer software instructs the hardware, or printer, to print the document.

4. Finally, the printer produces the printed document as output.

Figure 2-3: Issuing the Print command

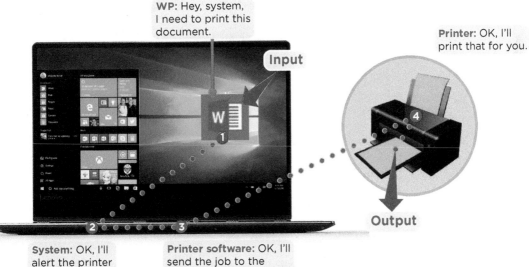

WP: Hey, system, I need to print this document.

Printer: OK, I'll print that for you.

Input

Output

System: OK, I'll alert the printer software.

Printer software: OK, I'll send the job to the printer.

Use Preinstalled Software

Computers come with **preinstalled software**, software that is already on the machine. Most important is the system software that allows you to use the computer the first time you turn it on. Preinstalled software typically includes an **operating system** and **utility programs** that run and maintain the computer. **Figure 2-4** shows some preinstalled programs that come with Windows 10.

Manufacturers preinstall additional programs, or apps, as part of marketing agreements with software companies. These might include games, more utility programs, and trial versions of **productivity software** that let you create documents, such as Microsoft Office. Preinstalled programs also take up memory and storage space. Consider uninstalling any software you don't intend to use.

Install Software

For tablets and smartphones, you usually download and install applications, or apps, to your device's internal memory from an online app store. On laptop or desktop computers, you typically install software on your computer's hard drive. Laptop and desktop

Figure 2-4: Some preinstalled Windows 10 programs

Quick Assist

Remote Desktop Connection

Snipping Tool

Steps Recorder

Windows Fax and Scan

WordPad — Windows accessories

XPS Viewer

Windows Admini— Cortana personal assistant

Ask me anything

software is most often made available online (see **Figure 2-5**), although it was originally supplied on CDs or DVDs.

Figure 2-5: Downloading and installing an app from the Windows Store

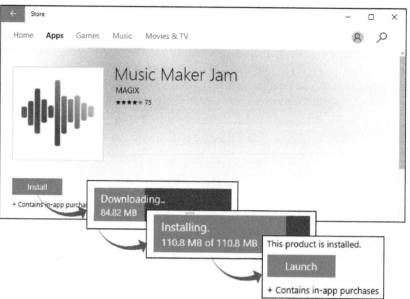

After downloading, follow any on-screen instructions to install the software. You'll probably have to agree to the conditions of a software license to continue. On a laptop or desktop, you might be asked to choose between a standard or custom installation.

You can now purchase the use of many apps by paying a monthly subscription fee instead of paying for the entire product all at once. This arrangement is known as **SaaS**, which stands for **Software as a Service**. For example, Microsoft Office 365 is the subscription version of Microsoft Office.

Increasingly, software publishers are creating **web apps**, which you can use without installing them. You'll learn more about web apps in the Purchasing Software section of this chapter.

Run Software

Once software is installed, you run it so you can use it. Some software runs automatically when you start your computer; other software you need to start yourself. Most programs are represented by an icon on your desktop, Start menu, or home screen. You can also find programs by opening their folders on your hard drive. To start a program, click or double-click the program icon or filename.

When you run a program or app, your computer or mobile device **loads**, or reads and transfers it, into memory so that you can use it. When you finish working with a program, you should save any files you want to keep and then close the program to free memory.

Uninstall Software

If you no longer use certain software, or if your computer came with software you don't need, you can remove, or **uninstall**, the unwanted programs. Operating systems provide ways to safely remove software. In Windows 10, you uninstall a program in the Settings app (System > Apps & features) or by right-clicking the program's name in the Start menu. In macOS, you move the program icon from the Applications window to the Trash.

On smartphones and tablets, you may need to use different methods to uninstall a program. In any case, an uninstall program removes the unwanted software and all of its related files from your computer or device.

#introsoftware

Some Microsoft Office 365 licenses allow users to install multiple copies of the software on 5–15 personal computers and devices.

By the Numbers Now

According to SurveyMonkey, the top downloaded apps include Messenger, Snapchat, Facebook, Instagram, and Color Switch.

If you try to remove unwanted Windows software by dragging a program icon to the Recycle Bin, you may remove the file that runs the program, but not its associated files. Be sure to use the uninstall method appropriate for your computer or device.

Update Software

Software publishers periodically update their programs to fix problems, enhance features, and improve performance. **Software updates** replace sections of existing code with the new, improved code. It's a good idea to install updates as they become available. In most cases, you check for updates, then download and install them from the publisher's website. See **Figure 2-6**.

Figure 2-6: Downloading and installing a software update in Windows 10

In addition to updates, software publishers periodically introduce new versions, or **upgrades**, of their software products with new features. If you own the current version, you can upgrade to the newer version for less than it would cost to buy the software outright. Upgrades are less time sensitive than updates, so you can wait until you're sure you need the newer version.

Identify Types of Software

computer software | system software | operating system (OS) software | platform | utility software | device driver | application software | mobile app | productivity software | vertical market software | horizontal market software |

Computer software manages the functions of computers and many other devices. Computers use several types of software, such as system software and application software. Other types of devices, such as refrigerators, cameras, and cars, use software to control their operation. See **Figure 2-7** on the next page.

Define System Software

System software performs computer-related operations and maintenance. System software falls into two categories: operating system software and utility programs. **Operating system software**, also called **OS software** or a **platform**, manages computer hardware and software. For example, it allocates memory and starts applications. Microsoft Windows and macOS are examples of operating systems. An OS is typically preinstalled on your computer's hard drive or embedded in smaller devices.

> **The Bottom Line**
> - Software is classified into several types, depending on its purpose, location, and use.
> - Software is already installed on some devices when you buy them; for other devices, you can choose to install software for a particular purpose.

Figure 2-7: Types of software

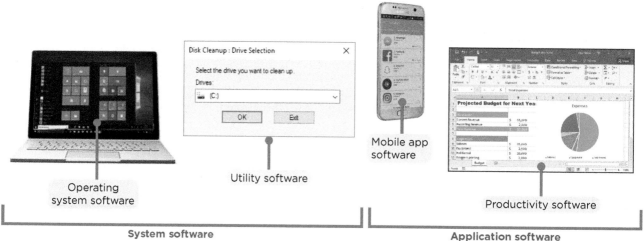

Mobile app software

Operating system software

Utility software

Productivity software

System software

Application software

Source: Samsung, Source: Google

#introsoftware

Mac operating systems use code names such as Sierra, El Capitan, Yosemite, Mavericks, Mountain Lion, Lion, Snow Leopard, Leopard, Tiger, Panther, Jaguar, Puma, Cheetah, and Kodiak.

Hot Technology Now

Google Translate is a free app that translates text in over 90 languages on menus and signs, speech, or real-time video.

Hot Technology Now

Self-driving cars, trucks, and Uber services are controlled by high-resolution maps and software that senses pedestrians, cyclists, and vehicles to safely drive around them. Cities may not need parking lots for long!

Utility software is system software that performs maintenance-related tasks on computers, such as searching, antivirus, file management, and diagnostic utilities. **Device drivers** are utility programs that control peripheral devices such as a keyboards, printers, or scanners.

Define Application Software

While system software gives you tools to interact with your computer, **application software** (also called apps) lets you perform specific tasks, such as writing documents, analyzing a set of numbers, or preparing presentations. Types of application software include word processing (such as Microsoft Word), spreadsheet software (such as Microsoft Excel), as well as educational, social networking, and entertainment apps.

Application software can be installed on laptops, tablets, and smartphones. **Mobile apps** are programs designed specifically for mobile devices such as smartphones and tablets. **Figure 2-8** shows the OneNote notetaking app on a smartphone.

Figure 2-8: OneNote smartphone app

Use Productivity Software

Productivity software is application software that makes people more productive by automating common or repetitive tasks. Word processing and spreadsheet applications are productivity software applications. **Figure 2-9** shows the Microsoft Office productivity suite.

Other types of productivity software include **vertical market software** that is customized for specific industries. For example, schools use student information software to process course registrations and track attendance and grades. **Horizontal market software** performs tasks that are common across industries. Examples include payroll processing, accounting, and project management.

Hot Technology Now

The Amazon Echo Dot device is a personal assistant that uses the Alexa voice service. It can play your favorite music, read the news, answer questions, provide sports scores, control light switches, and even order pizza.

Figure 2-9: Microsoft Office productivity suite

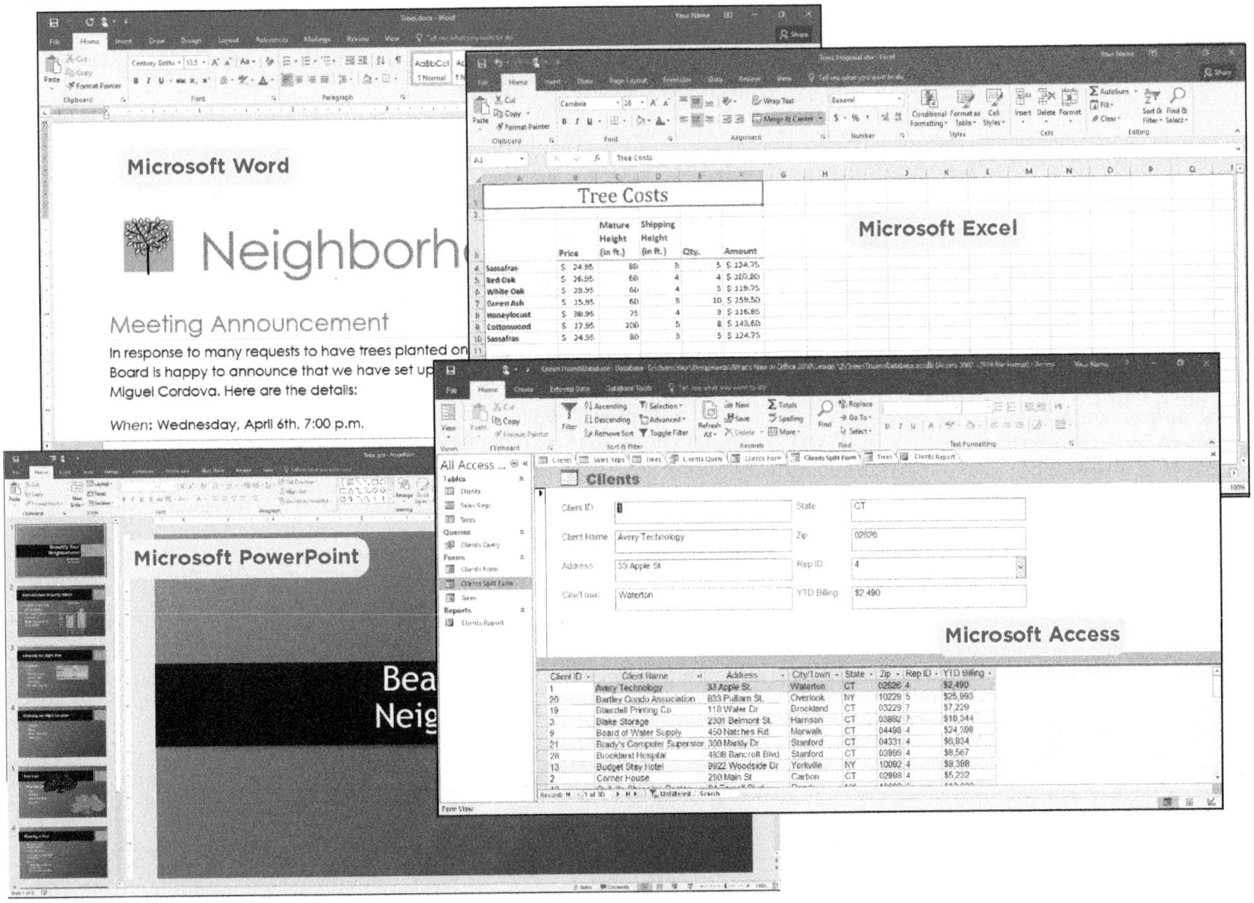

Software Design and Development

software development | programming | computer programmer | developer | algorithm | machine language | binary code | assembly language | source code | low-level language | high-level language | software development methodology | predictive methodology | agile | adaptive | extreme programming model | text editor | program editor | compiler | interpreter | assembler | debugger | code library | Integrated Development Environment (IDE) | software development kit (SDK) | comment | debugging tool | beta | quality assurance (QA)

The process of creating software is called **software development** or **programming**. The people who write software programs are called **computer programmers** or **developers**. Software programs are based on **algorithms**, which are step-by-step procedures for solving specific problems. Programmers write coded instructions using special programming languages and program development tools.

The Bottom Line

- Computer programmers write software code using programming languages.
- Programmers use multiple programming tools to write, document, and test program code.

Figure 2-10: Developing software

Andrey_Popov/Shutterstock.com, kimberrywood/Shutterstock.com, Source: Uber.com, Source: Uber.com, Sashkin/Shutterstock.com

On the Job Now

The Bureau of Labor Statistics projects a 19 percent employment growth for software developers, which is much faster than the average for all occupations.

Design and Develop Software

All software applications must be designed so that they meet user needs and wants. Successful software apps should be:

- **Task oriented**: Apps should be designed to address tasks that users need to perform, and in a way that helps them complete those tasks.
- **Personalized**: Apps should address the majority of users' experiences, behaviors, characteristics, and situations.
- **Provide an excellent user experience**: Apps should be enjoyable to use, with features that are easy to find and understand.
- **Scalable**: Apps should run equally well on a variety of platforms and devices, such as laptops, tablets, and smartphones.

Many of the conveniences we have today are in some way the result of programmers doing their jobs. The software development process involves a series of steps, shown in **Figure 2-11**.

Figure 2-11: Software development process

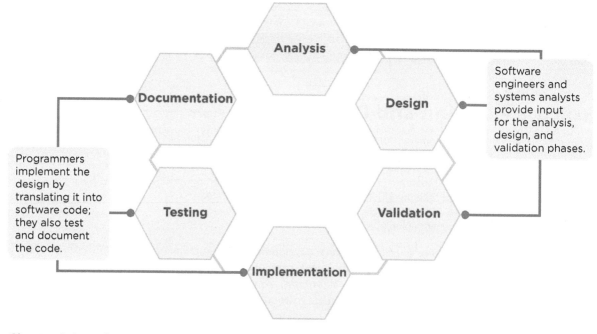

Software engineers and systems analysts provide input for the analysis, design, and validation phases.

Programmers implement the design by translating it into software code; they also test and document the code.

Analysis
Documentation
Design
Testing
Validation
Implementation

Use Programming Languages

Programmers use special languages that contain words, abbreviations, punctuation, and symbols to communicate specific instructions to the computer. Hundreds of programming languages exist today. Figure 2-12 shows examples of machine, assembly, and high-level languages.

Figure 2-12: Machine, assembly, and high-level languages

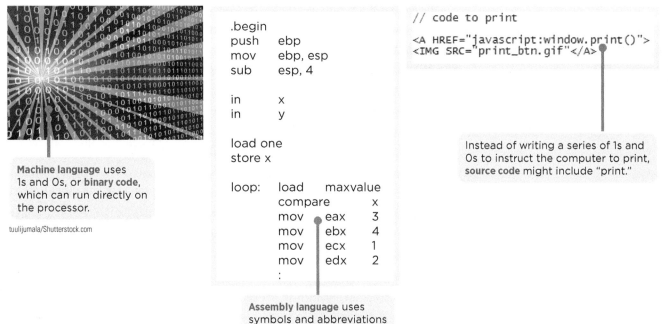

Machine language uses 1s and 0s, or **binary code**, which can run directly on the processor.

tuulijumala/Shutterstock.com

```
.begin
push    ebp
mov     ebp, esp
sub     esp, 4

in      x
in      y

load one
store x

loop:   load    maxvalue
        compare         x
        mov     eax     3
        mov     ebx     4
        mov     ecx     1
        mov     edx     2
        :
```

Assembly language uses symbols and abbreviations known as "op codes."

```
// code to print

<A HREF="javascript:window.print()">
<IMG SRC="print_btn.gif"</A>
```

Instead of writing a series of 1s and 0s to instruct the computer to print, **source code** might include "print."

Low-level languages include machine and assembly languages. Low-level languages are fast and don't use a lot of computer memory, but they are technically difficult and time-consuming to write. **High-level languages** create **source code** using words and structures similar to spoken language. High-level languages make programming easier; however, they must be translated from source code into machine code before a computer can read them.

Most business and scientific applications are written in high-level languages such as C#, Visual Basic, PHP, and Java. Java is a popular high-level language for web-based programming. For mobile apps, developers might use Swift, Java, JavaScript, or HTML5.

Identify Development Methodologies

A **software development methodology** provides a framework for designing, writing, and testing software. Two important methodologies are predictive and agile; each methodology has a number of different models. The **predictive methodology** focuses on planning and preparation to minimize changes later in the development process. Predictive programming is useful for large-scale development projects using many programmers across multiple locations. For example, in the waterfall predictive model, development progresses sequentially from one phase to the next. Only when one phase is finished does the next phase begin.

The **agile**, or **adaptive**, programming methodology focuses on flexibility; program designs and specifications change and evolve as a project moves forward. Agile programming works well for projects with small development teams working closely together. For example, the **extreme programming model** relies on short development cycles and continual feedback to drive design and coding. Changes can be made to the design and software code throughout the development process.

Hot Technology Now

To program an app on an Android phone, a free program named Android Studio provides an Android emulator that displays the results of the Java source code. To program an app on an iPhone, a programmer would use a programming language named Swift, which is similar to the Objective-C language.

Use Programming Tools

Programming tools are applications that programmers use to write other software programs. Common programming tools are shown in **Table 2-1**.

Table 2-1: Programming tools

Programming tools	What they do
Text editors Program editors	Let programmers write code using a word processing-like interface that often includes features such as AutoCorrect and AutoComplete.
Compilers Interpreters	Translate source code from high-level languages into machine code so it can be understood by the processor.
Assemblers	Translate assembly language into machine code.
Debuggers	Examine software code line by line to identify errors or "bugs," such as incorrect formulas or logic errors.

Code libraries contain modules of customizable code for common functions such as accessing files or issuing the Print command.

Most programmers today get their tools from **Integrated Development Environments (IDEs)** such as Visual Studio, or from **software development kits (SDKs)**, which are collections of programming tools designed for specific types of applications or programming languages.

Test and Document Software

Programmers document and test software before releasing it for distribution. When coding software, programmers write **comments** to give other programmers an overview of the program and identify the purpose of each section of code. See **Figure 2-13**.

#introsoftware

Some elementary schools are teaching an introductory programming language to third through fifth graders. Students learn how to create animations, computer games, and interactive projects using Scratch, a graphical programming language developed at the Massachusetts Institute of Technology.

Figure 2-13: Comment in code

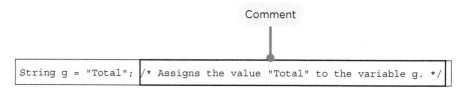

```
String g = "Total";   /* Assigns the value "Total" to the variable g. */
```

To test for errors, programmers use **debugging tools**; compilers and interpreters often identify coding errors as well. Programmers also run programs with test data to identify potential problems.

Software publishers often distribute **beta**, or test, versions of their software to selected users so they can help identify problems and even request new features before final software is released.

Finally, a **quality assurance (QA)** team usually tests an application thoroughly to confirm that it works as advertised. The QA process can involve back-and-forth communication between the QA testers and the programmers as bugs are found and then fixed.

The Bottom Line

- Purchased software may be packaged in collections called suites and purchased from the web or, less frequently, from a physical store; it can be proprietary or open source.
- Custom software is specially developed for a company's specific needs, but can be expensive.
- Web apps are programs you access over the web; they are often free to use, but may require payment for special features.

Purchase Software

packaged software | suite | download | app | app store | in-app purchase | custom software | web app | perpetual software | proprietary software | open source software | Linux operating system | monetize

You can purchase packaged software, download software from the Internet, or subscribe to a web application. Many software applications are sold commercially, but others are free. Still others make their source code available to the public so users can customize it. Make sure the software you acquire meets your needs and your computer's system requirements.

Figure 2-14: Packaged software

The Microsoft Store offers several versions of the Microsoft Office suite.

The Apple App Store lets you download free or paid apps.

Download.com offers over 150,000 free downloadable software applications.

Source: Download.com, Source: Apple Computer

Purchase Packaged Software

The term **packaged software** refers to software that is mass produced and appeals to a wide range of users. Packaged software is generally copyrighted and has many features. Popular packaged software programs include Microsoft Word and Adobe Photoshop. Packaged software can also refer to a group of programs having similar features and sold together, known as a **suite**. The Microsoft Office suite combines word processing, spreadsheet, database, and presentation software.

You can purchase packaged software from websites, catalogs, or retail stores. Packaged software purchased in a store typically includes a card containing a key code, which lets you **download**, or electronically copy, the software from the Internet.

More commonly, you purchase and download applications, or **apps**, directly from software publishers' websites or online **app stores**, using your computer or mobile device. To buy an app, you must create an account. You can pay for app store purchases with a credit card. Three popular app stores are listed in **Table 2-2**.

By the Numbers Now

More than 2 million apps are available in the Apple App Store for devices running iOS, such as iPhones and iPads.

Table 2-2: Online app stores

Online store	To open
Windows Store	Select the Store icon on the taskbar, Start menu, or screen of a Windows device.
App Store	Select the App Store icon on an Apple device.
Google Play	Select the Play Store icon on the Apps screen of an Android device.

To use an app store, you sign in and locate the app you want, either by viewing app categories or by searching. Select the app, examine its description, features, system requirements, and any available reviews or ratings, and make sure it's compatible with your device. Note if it requires purchases as you use the software, known as **in-app purchases**. When you are ready to buy, click the Buy (or other relevant) button, enter your payment information, and then download and install the software.

Acquire Custom Software

Unlike packaged software, which is designed to meet the needs of many, **custom software** is designed to meet the unique needs of an organization or business. Companies either hire outside programmers to write custom software or use their own internal developers.

Acquiring custom software is more time consuming and expensive than purchasing packaged software, because developers must go through the entire development process: analyzing needs, creating a software design, and then developing, testing, and documenting that design before the software is ready to use. See Figure 2-15.

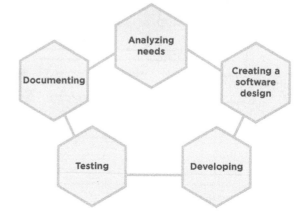

Figure 2-15: Developing custom software

On the other hand, custom software matches the users' needs exactly and can be modified if those needs change.

Access Web Apps

Web applications, or **web apps**, are applications you access over the Internet using a computer or mobile device with an Internet connection. Web apps are available for common applications such as email, games, mapping, photo sharing, and more. With web apps, you always have access to the most up-to-date version of the software without paying for an upgrade. In contrast to **perpetual software**, which you install on your computer to use indefinitely, web apps reside on a host computer, so you also save space on your hard drive.

Web apps, such as Word Online (see Figure 2-16), G Suite, and web mail, don't require users to install software on their own computers. Instead, the software runs on the host computer.

Figure 2-16: Word Online web app

Word Online document open in browser window

Some web applications are free. Others require a one-time registration fee or a periodic subscription charge.

Web apps also have risks. If you lose your Internet connection, if the host computer is out of service, or if the web app company fails, you lose access to the software and any data you haven't saved locally.

Use Open Source Software

Most software is **proprietary**, meaning that is owned by a company or individual, and the source code is kept secret. **Open source software** is copyrighted software whose source code is "open," meaning that it is available to the public. Users can copy, modify, and customize the software with certain restrictions. The concept of open source software was introduced in 1991 by Linus Torvalds, who created and then shared the **Linux operating system** with the world. Besides Linux, popular open source programs include Firefox, Audacity, and the OpenOffice productivity suite.

Open source software is typically distributed for free and requires less disk space and memory than many commercial programs. The software can be customized and has usually been tested by a wide range of programmers and users. A disadvantage to open source software is that it lacks the customer support you find with commercial software and can cause compatibility issues with other software.

Realize the Cost of Free Apps

Many web apps and downloaded apps are initially free of charge to the user. However, developers may **monetize** their apps to gain income through advertisements or special features. For example, a game app might require an **in-app purchase** to move to a higher level. Developers may form partnerships with other brands that target similar users and offer links to the other company's products. In other words, free apps are not always free to use.

License Software

intellectual property | copyright | software license | authentication technologies | license | single-user license | end-user license agreement (EULA) | multiple-user license | site license | Software as a Service (SaaS) | piracy | Digital Rights Management (DRM) | authentication | two-factor authentication | encryption | encryption key | digital watermark | copy protection technology

Define Intellectual Property

Intellectual property is the legal term for ownership of intangible assets such as ideas, art, music, movies, and software. Many of these assets are easy to copy, making them vulnerable to unauthorized use. Copyright protections and license agreements set rules for how intellectual property can be legally used, copied, and distributed, and by whom.

Define Copyright

A **copyright** is the legal right to copy, distribute, modify, and sell an original work, including computer software. The copyright belongs exclusively to the creator of the work, such as the software developer or publisher. Without the permission of the copyright holder, no one else can legally copy, modify, or distribute the software, because it is the intellectual property of the creator.

The Bottom Line
- Copyrighted software belongs to the author or publisher; when you buy copyrighted software, you can use it, but cannot copy, change, or distribute it.
- Software is protected by license agreements that specify how it can be used.
- Software publishers protect their products against piracy, or unauthorized use, by authentication, encryption, digital watermarks, and copy protection.

Figure 2-17: Some methods of protecting intellectual property

U.S. copyright law protects **Intellectual property** from illegal copying and distribution.

A **software license** grants a user rights to use of the software in specified ways.

CARBONITE

Carbonite Login

Please log in to your account. If you don't have an account sign up for a free trial.

Email   Your_Name@outlook.com

Password   ••••••••••

☐ I'm not a robot

☑ Remember me

Carbonite Login   Forgot Email   Forgot Password

Authentication technologies grant access to web-based software.

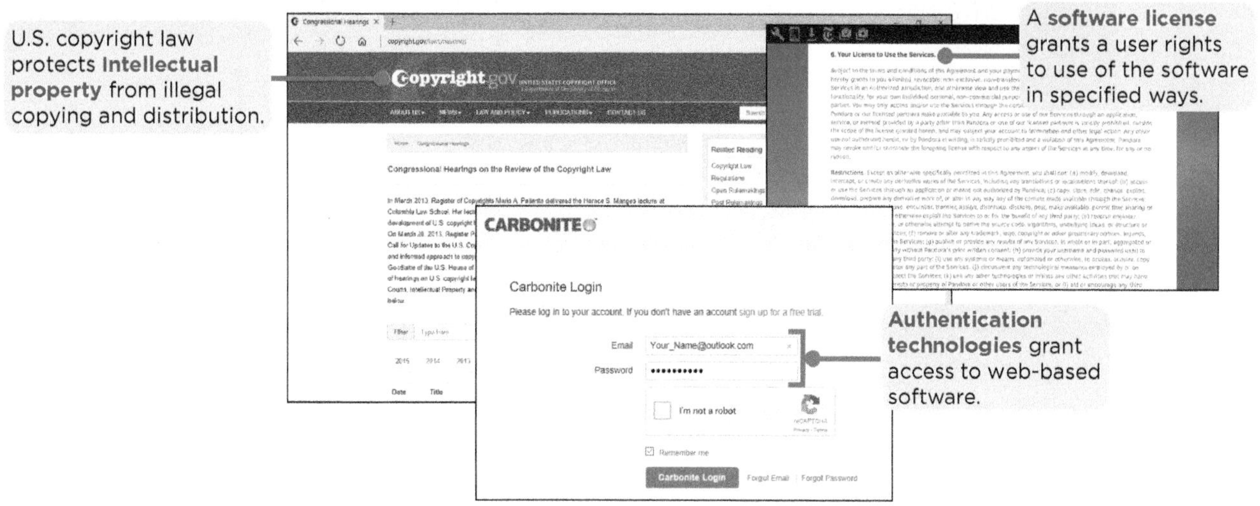

Copyright.gov, Source: Pandora.com, Source: Carbonite.com

A copyright is denoted either by the word "Copyright" or by a copyright symbol, which is the letter C inside a circle: ©. Even if there isn't a visible copyright notice, copyright protections automatically apply to software programs and other original works.

When you purchase copyrighted software, the copyright protection remains in effect. You have paid for the right to use the product, but all other rights remain with the copyright holder.

Use Software Licenses

When you purchase software, you are purchasing a **license** to use the software under the terms specified in the license agreement, which might include how many computers the software can be installed on and whether the license has an expiration date.

A **single-user license**, also called an **end-user license agreement (EULA)**, grants one user the right to use the software. Many students and home users buy single-user licenses. A **multiple-user license**, used by organizations and schools, lets many people use the software; the number of users and the price vary by license. A **site license** allows an organization to install software on all computers at a site, either locally or through a network. Site licenses are generally priced at a flat rate per site.

Use Software Subscription Services

Rather than selling a software package at a fixed, one-time price, software publishers are now offering products you can obtain by paying a monthly subscription fee for a given number of licenses. This arrangement is known as **SaaS**, which stands for **Software as a Service**. For example, Microsoft Office 365 is the subscription version of Microsoft Office. The Adobe Creative Cloud suite and many other applications are now available by subscription.

Subscription-based software offers advantages such as automatic software updates, the flexibility to install and license the programs they need for as long as necessary, and a lower initial cost. Users can be licensed to install the software on multiple computers.

Microsoft Office 365 lets users access and collaborate on files over the web ("in the cloud") using OneDrive online storage and the Office Online products. It also allows users to access the SharePoint document management system and the Azure computing and data storage system. Users can manage their Office 365 licenses online using the Office 365 portal, shown in **Figure 2-18**.

Figure 2-18: Microsoft Office 365 portal

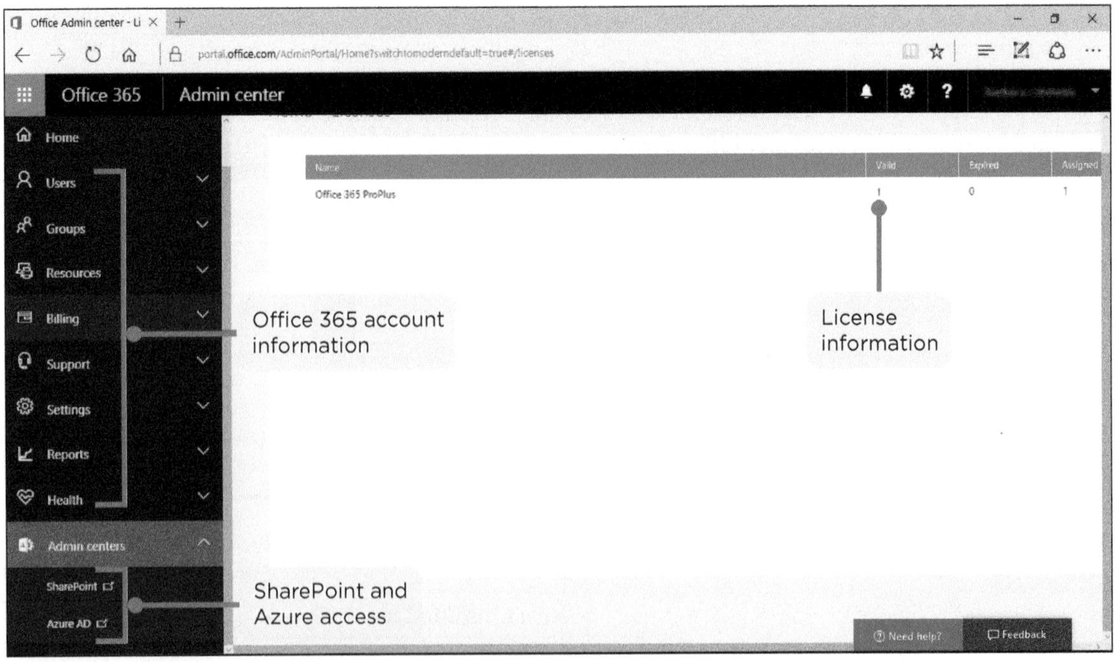

Office 365 account information

License information

SharePoint and Azure access

Use License Agreements

A **software license** is a contract between the software publisher and the user. Because users can't actually "sign" license agreements, publishers use other methods for validating them. For downloaded software from app stores or obtained via subscriptions, the details of the license may appear on the screen during installation, and users may have to click "Agree" or "Accept" before the software is installed. In other cases, the license agreement appears in the program settings. No matter what method you use to accept a license agreement, it is a legal contract, and you are bound by its terms.

Combat Software Piracy

Piracy, the illegal copying and distribution of copyrighted digital content, is a widespread problem for software and media publishers. Although software piracy has been greatly reduced by current operating systems and subscription-based software, billions of dollars' worth of software is still copied illegally worldwide. The United States has a piracy rate of under 20 percent; China's is a staggering 70 percent. Globally, nearly 40 percent of installed software is unlicensed.

Aside from reducing software publishers' revenues, unlicensed software can compromise the security of computer networks by making them vulnerable to malware and cyberattacks. However, some operating systems such as Windows 10 can now help defend networks by disabling computers that have illegal software copies installed.

If your employer has a software license that covers usage only at the work site, it would be a violation of the license to install that software on your home computer. Users also engage in software piracy by illegally sharing email and passwords to subscription services such as Netflix streaming media or Pandora Internet radio. While not all media companies prosecute such cases, password sharing is technically a federal crime.

Describe Digital Rights Management

Increasingly, software publishers and trade groups use **Digital Rights Management (DRM)** technologies to fight software piracy and prevent unauthorized copying of digital content. DRM technologies include:

- **Authentication** technologies require users to sign in with a valid user ID and password to access web-based content such as software programs or e-books. **Two-factor authentication** requires an additional verification method, such as requiring users to enter a code sent to their mobile phone (see **Figure 2-19**), to provide additional security.
- **Encryption** makes digital content unreadable unless viewed with a valid **encryption key** or authorized hardware device.
- A **digital watermark** is a hidden pattern or signal inserted into digital content to identify the copyright holder. Watermarks can also regulate and track who makes copies of the content and how often.
- **Copy protection technologies** prevent consumers from copying digital content or limit the number of copies they can make.

Figure 2-19: Authentication codes sent to a mobile phone

Source: Android

Identify Software Problems

application Help | user manual | on-screen Help | web-based Help | malware | security software | antivirus software | antispyware | spyware | antispam software | spam | firewall software | security suite | crash | rebooting | cold boot | warm boot | backed up | replicate | restore | restore point | reset

You rely on software every day to perform all kinds of tasks, but sometimes you need help figuring out how to use your software more effectively. Other times software doesn't work properly. Software publishers and other sources offer tools that can help you address software problems when you encounter them.

Access Help for Using Apps

Applications help you create reports, spreadsheets, presentations, and more. The more you know about an application, the more you can do with it. Most software applications

The Bottom Line
- To learn how to use software and to solve problems, you can use a user manual, on-screen Help, or web-based Help (see **Figure 2-20** on the next page).
- Software publishers fix software bugs by issuing updates.
- You can protect your computer from malware using several types of security software.
- If your computer stops working, you can often recover by rebooting it.

Figure 2-20: On-screen Help

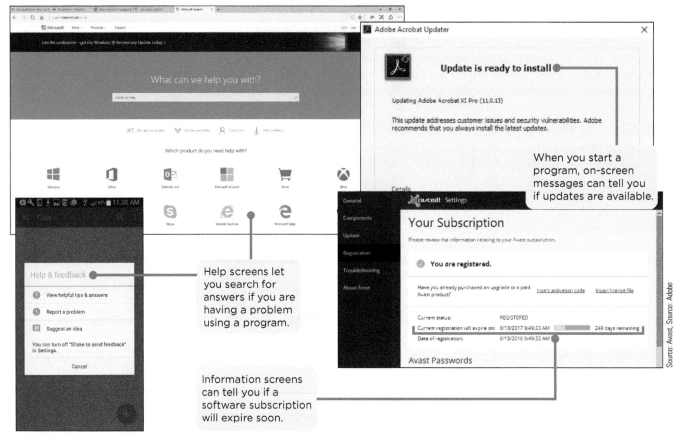

Help screens let you search for answers if you are having a problem using a program.

When you start a program, on-screen messages can tell you if updates are available.

Information screens can tell you if a software subscription will expire soon.

Source: Avast; Source: Adobe

include one or more forms of Help. **Application Help** includes user manuals, on-screen Help, and web-based resources.

- A **user manual** gives instructions on using the program's features and troubleshooting common problems. You usually download user manuals from the software publisher's website.
- **On-screen Help** is an electronic user manual with additional benefits, such as the ability to search for specific topics or click links to online resources. You can access on-screen Help from almost every window or dialog box in a program.
- **Web-based Help** can be found on a software publisher's website, blog, or another software-related site. You can chat with a customer support representative, step through a tutorial, watch a training video, or follow a discussion board.

Define Updates and Upgrades

Software updates and upgrades help to address software problems because they fix bugs, enhance features, and improve security. Software publishers number updates and upgrades sequentially using decimal places. For example, an update might change your software from version 3.0 to version 3.0.1. An upgrade might change the version from 3.0.7 to 4.0. Software upgrades, such as a change from version 1.0 to 2.0, are cumulative, containing all smaller changes made to a program to date.

Today, software publishers release updates online so they can deliver them more frequently and conveniently. You can choose to automatically download and install updates as they become available, or you can periodically check for updates yourself and install only those you want.

Identify Types of Security Software

Malware, malicious software written by hackers, poses a significant threat to your computer and its contents. You can install several types of **security software** to protect your computer from harm.

- **Antivirus software** finds and removes malware from your computer and scans incoming and outgoing email messages to identify threats. You should run antivirus software frequently, keep it running in the background at all times, and schedule periodic scans of your entire system. See Figure 2-21.

Figure 2-21: Results of a Windows Defender security scan

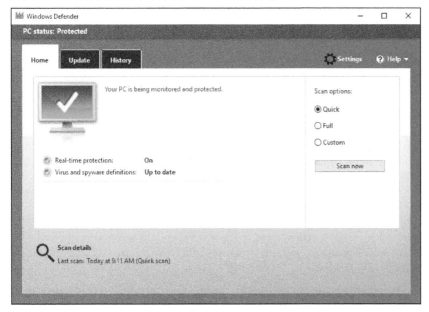

- **Antispyware** prevents **spyware**, a type of malware that secretly gathers personal information, from installing itself on your computer and removes any existing spyware.
- **Antispam software** blocks **spam**, or electronic junk mail, from your email inbox.
- **Firewall software** creates a personal security zone around your computer by monitoring all incoming and outgoing traffic and blocking any suspicious activity. Windows 10 features Windows Firewall to handle these tasks. You can enable it in the System and Security category of the Control Panel.

You can buy security software programs individually, but you can also find them bundled together in a security suite. **Security suites** typically contain antivirus, antispam, antispyware, and firewall software. Some offer additional features such as parental controls and network monitoring. Security suites cost less than standalone security programs and give you a consistent user interface. When you install a security suite, you need to uninstall any security software currently on your computer. As a general rule, you should update all security software regularly so you will be protected from current threats.

Recover from Software Crashes

When a computer program stops functioning properly—for example, if it freezes or won't start—it is said to **crash**. See Table 2-3 on the next page for possible causes and solutions.

Rebooting is the process of restarting your computer, either from a powered-down state (**cold boot**), or with the power on (**warm boot**).

You should reboot after installing new programs or updates or after encountering a problem that freezes your computer. A warm boot uses the operating system to restart your computer; processes and programs are closed properly, and most work is saved. To perform a warm boot, use the Restart command on your PC or Mac. (Newer computers may not have a Restart command.) With some computers, you can quickly press and release the power button to perform a warm boot. On a smartphone, you can turn the phone off and on, as well as delete the app and reinstall it.

Hot Technology Now

Windows 10 provides a free security program named Windows Defender, which protects against malware. To check if it is running, type Defender in the Search box and press the Enter key. If a check mark is displayed in the Windows Defender dialog box, your PC is being monitored and protected.

By the Numbers Now

Windows 10 typically reboots in a matter of seconds.

Table 2-3: Program crash problems and solutions

Problem	Possible cause	Solution
Program won't launch	Incorrect installation	• Check validation codes • Uninstall the program and reinstall it • Contact Customer Service
Program freezes	Bug, virus, or corrupted files	• **Windows**: Press the CTRL, ALT, and DELETE keys together • **Mac**: Open Activity Monitor, select and close program • Shut down and restart computer • Install latest updates • Run security scan to check for viruses • Run disk cleanup and repair utilities

If you are forced to shut your computer down completely after a crash, you have to perform a cold boot. First, turn off the computer, if necessary, by pressing and holding the power button, or unplugging the device from its power source. To reboot, reconnect the power source and press the power button.

Troubleshoot Software Problems

You may experience a variety of software problems as you use your computer. You might see an error message on the screen, or the software might respond in unusual ways. If you have such a problem, you can perform some basic troubleshooting techniques to try and find a solution:

1. **Stop and think**: Remain calm and consider the situation. Randomly pressing keys or clicking could make matters worse. Taking a thoughtful, organized approach can help solve the problem.

2. **Save and back up**: Save any open documents if possible, and verify that your work is backed up (copied) to an external drive or online location.

3. **Gather information**: Write down the problem, including the exact text and numbers in any error messages. What were you doing when it occurred? Can you replicate (reproduce) it? What steps did you take to replicate it? Note the time and date, and any other programs that were running. Write down your computer model, operating system version, and application program versions.

4. **Research possible solutions**: Have you recently installed any software or hardware? Is your antivirus software up to date? Have you recently downloaded anything from the Internet that may have introduced a virus? Does a virus scan reveal any problems? Search the Internet using a short problem description. Check the software manufacturer's technical support website, as well as forums and newsgroups. For Microsoft products, search the online Microsoft Community, shown in **Figure 2-22**. Other people may have had the same problem. If you test possible solutions, try only one solution at a time, and write down what happens.

5. **Contact Technical Support**: If necessary, contact the manufacturer's Technical Support department, with your notes in front of you, so you can answer any questions they might ask. Click an email or contact link, or choose from telephone or live chat support.

#introsoftware

Go to twitter.com, search for @SAMTechNow, the book's Twitter account, and then follow @SAMTechNow, to get tweets on your home page.

Restore or Reset an Operating System

When your device does not respond to common recovery techniques, or if you have a problem that has occurred since a particular driver or app installation, you may need to restore your operating system to a previous version. Your files will be preserved, but drivers, apps, and updates that you installed since the last restore point created by your system will be removed.

Figure 2-22: Searching the Microsoft Community

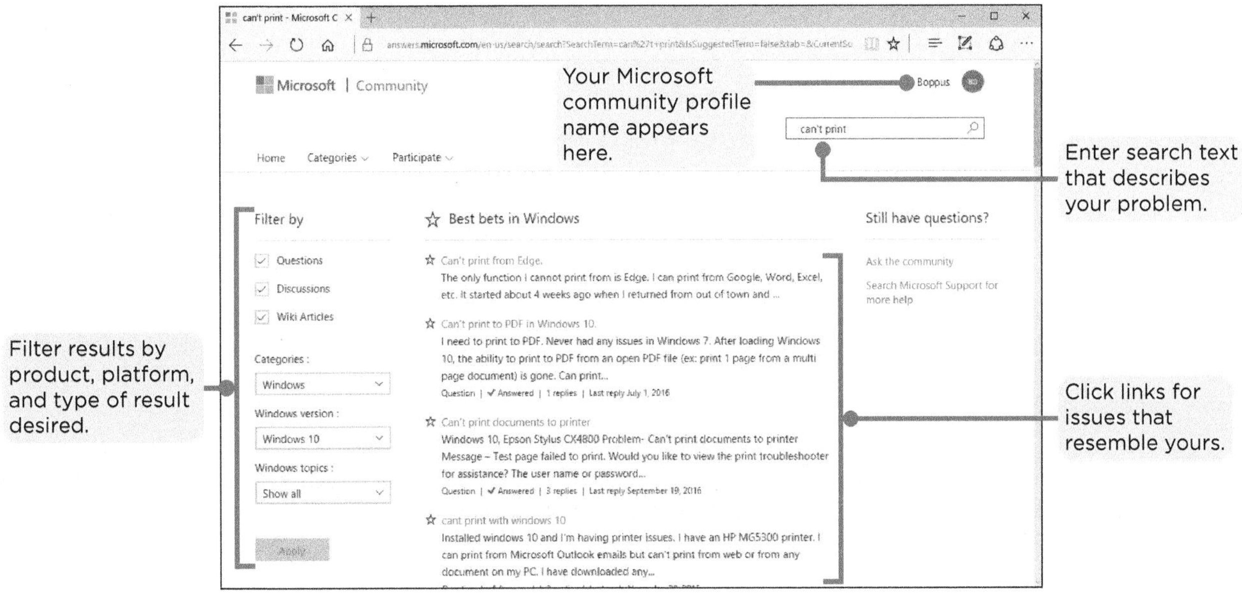

Your Microsoft community profile name appears here.

Enter search text that describes your problem.

Filter results by product, platform, and type of result desired.

Click links for issues that resemble yours.

In extreme cases, you may need to **reset** your device to its original factory settings. You can usually choose to preserve or delete your files when you reset. Each computer, tablet, and smartphone has a different method for storing or resetting, so check the device manufacturer's support information before you begin. If you do not have backup copies of your work files, be sure to preserve them before restoring or resetting your device, so that you don't lose your important information.

Chapter Review

What Is Software?

1. What are the two main types of software?
2. What do you call apps that you can use without installing them?
3. What are the two types of preinstalled software?

Identify Types of Software

4. Briefly describe the function of operating system software, and name two common operating systems.
5. What is the purpose of utility software? Name two common types of utility programs.
6. Name and briefly describe three types of productivity software.

Software Design and Development

7. Describe an advantage of high-level programming languages, and give two examples.
8. What are the two important types of software development methodologies? Briefly describe each one.
9. Name three common tools that programmers use and briefly describe each one.

Purchase Software

10. Name two popular online stores you might use to purchase software.
11. What is custom software? Name an advantage and a disadvantage of custom software.
12. Describe the purpose of open source software and give two examples.

License Software

13. What is a copyright, and who owns the copyright to a product?
14. What are two types of software licenses? Briefly describe each one.
15. What are three advantages of Software as a Service (SaaS)?

Identify Software Problems

16. If you have a software problem, what are three kinds of application Help that are available to you?
17. Name and briefly describe three types of security software.
18. Briefly describe the main steps you should perform to troubleshoot a software problem.

Test Your Knowledge Now

1. Software that lets users interact with the computer by tapping, clicking, or pressing buttons, menus, icons, and links has:
   a. a graphical user interface.
   b. preinstalled software.
   c. a compiler.
   d. a code library.

2. Software that you can pay for with a monthly subscription fee is called:
   a. a web app.
   b. productivity software.
   c. a software update.
   d. Software as a Service (SaaS).

3. The preinstalled software that runs your computer is called:
   a. an operating system.
   b. an app.
   c. productivity software.
   d. a programming language.

4. Which of the following translate source code from high-level languages into machine code?
   a. assemblers
   b. compilers
   c. debuggers
   d. program editors

5. Machine and assembly programming languages are examples of:
   a. high-level languages.
   b. debuggers.
   c. low-level languages.
   d. program editors.

6. The software development methodology that focuses on planning and preparation to minimize changes later on is called:
   a. extreme programming model.
   b. adaptive methodology.
   c. predictive methodology.
   d. agile methodology.

7. Which of the following allocates computer memory and starts applications?
   a. platform
   b. operating system software
   c. malware
   d. application program

8. What kind of software performs maintenance-related tasks?
   a. utility software
   b. application software
   c. operating system software
   d. a platform

9. What type of software is customized for specific industries?
   a. horizontal market software
   b. vertical market software
   c. operating system software
   d. application software

10. Mass-produced software that appeals to a wide range of users is called:
    a. custom software.
    b. web apps.
    c. packaged software.
    d. open source software.

11. Web apps are:
    a. designed to meet the unique needs of an organization or business.
    b. a form of packaged software.
    c. programs you access over the Internet with a computer or mobile device.
    d. public domain software.

12. The Linux operating system is an example of:
    a. shareware.
    b. a web app.
    c. open source software.
    d. custom software.

```
1  <!DOCTYPE html><html lang="en"><head><meta cha
   type="image/x-icon" href="/images/favicon.ico"
   href="/stylesheets/main.css"><script nonce="d8
2      var dce = document.createElement;
3      window.nonce = document.querySelector('scrip
4      document.createElement = function (a) {
5        var e = dce.apply(this, arguments);
```

13. Copyright is intended to protect:
    a. encryption.
    b. intellectual property.
    c. end-user licenses.
    d. digital rights management.

14. The legal right to copy, distribute, modify, and sell an original work is called a(n):
    a. license.
    b. copyright.
    c. digital rights management.
    d. authentication.

15. Which of the following DRM technologies makes digital content unreadable unless viewed with a valid key?
    a. digital watermark
    b. certificate of authenticity
    c. encryption
    d. copy protection

16. Which of the following is *not* a type of application Help?
    a. a software publisher's website
    b. on-screen link
    c. update
    d. user manual

17. What type of software monitors incoming and outgoing traffic and blocks suspicious activity?
    a. operating system software
    b. antivirus software
    c. firewall software
    d. software updates

18. If you encounter a software problem, you should determine if you can _____ it.
    a. crash
    b. update
    c. replicate
    d. reboot

19. In the space next to each image below, write the letter of the phrase that describes it.
    a. authentication
    b. Microsoft Excel application software
    c. utility software
    d. source code
    e. web app

Try This Now

1: Microsoft Online Apps

Microsoft Online apps provide a free way to create, edit, and share Word, Excel, PowerPoint, and OneNote files from any browser. If necessary, create a free Microsoft account at outlook.com. Click the **Waffle icon** in the corner. Select the **PowerPoint Online** app.

    a. Create a four-slide presentation explaining the features of Microsoft OneDrive. (Research OneDrive online as necessary.)

    b. Add appropriate images to each slide in the presentation.

    c. Save and share the presentation with your instructor using the Share feature.

2: Google Drive G Suite

Google Drive is the home of G Suite, a free office suite of productivity applications that offer collaborative editing on documents, spreadsheets, and presentations. If necessary, open a browser and create a free Google account at google.com. Sign in to your account, and then go to drive.google.com.

    a. Select the **New** button and then select **Google Docs**. Research using Google Drive for online storage, and then use the Google Docs word processor to write at least 100 words describing this feature.

    b. Select **File** and then select **Publish to Web**. Share the link of this document with your instructor.

3: macOS vs. Windows PC Operating Systems

Before you purchase a computer, you should read unbiased reviews, compare prices, and understand specifications to improve your purchasing experience. Research the newest macOS and Windows PC operating systems.

    a. List and explain five unique features in the latest macOS.

    b. List and explain five unique features in the latest update of Windows.

    c. What is your favorite operating system? Write a paragraph highlighting three reasons for your selection.

Operating Systems

iStockphoto.com/mediaphotos

Critical Thinking Now

1: Grocery Store Online Shopping with Office 365

You are employed part-time by a local grocery store chain. Your duties include assisting with the new online system for ordering items and picking them up at the store. The chain uses Microsoft Office in all the grocery stores to keep track of the online orders. Your boss requested that you research new Office 365 business subscriptions at office365.com.

    a. Which plans are available in the Office 365 business subscription?

    b. How much would your business pay for each employee per month to use Office 365 installed on five of their home computers on each plan?

    c. What are the advantages of subscription-based software compared to traditional perpetual software? Name at least three advantages.

    d. What are the disadvantages of subscription-based software in comparison to traditional perpetual software? Name at least three disadvantages.

2: Windows Virus Protection

You recently purchased a Windows gaming computer, which comes equipped with free antivirus software called Windows Defender. Research and determine if this antivirus software provides enough coverage for personal usage. Write at least 200 words explaining your conclusions.

3: Note-Taking Apps

Your school has received a grant that provides all students with an Android tablet. You plan to use the tablet to take notes in your classes. Open the webpage https://play.google.com. Search for the three best-rated note-taking apps. Write a paragraph on at least five advantages and cost of each one, for a total of three paragraphs.

Ethical Issues Now

Subscription-based services such as the Netflix app typically allow two users to stream the services on their devices at once on a minimal plan.

Subscription-Based Software

iStockphoto.com/luismmolina

a. Research the Netflix password-sharing policy. Write at least 50 words on whether it is against the law to share your passwords.

b. Two roommates share a single Netflix account in their apartment. One roommate shares their user name and password with the college soccer team. What can the other roommate do when they try to connect and get the message that too many people are using the account right now? Write a 100-word paragraph describing at least two options in your own words.

c. Would you prefer buying software outright or paying for a subscription plan? Write at least 150 words on the pros and cons of purchasing software or paying for a subscription.

Team Up Now—VideoNotes Web App and Virtual Reality

Google Drive includes a web app named VideoNotes, which is a tool for taking notes while watching videos. VideoNotes allows you to play any YouTube video on the left side of your screen as you make notes on a notepad on the right side of the screen. VideoNotes integrates with your Google Drive account. All the notes you type are synchronized with the video. Later, if you select a line in your notes, the video begins to play from the corresponding location. You'll use VideoNotes to interact with your team in this exercise.

a. Research and identify three YouTube videos that describe different virtual reality apps.

b. Share the links of the three YouTube videos with each member of your team.

c. Sign in to google.com, and then open the drive.google.com page. Select the **New** button and then select **VideoNotes**. (You might need to select More, and then select Connect more apps to display the VideoNotes app.) Each team member should open the three YouTube videos and take detailed notes as the video plays.

d. Share your VideoNotes link with each team member and your instructor using Google Drive.

Key Terms

adaptive
agile
algorithm
antispam software
antispyware
antivirus software
app
app store
application Help
application software
assembler
assembly language
authentication
authentication technologies
backed up
beta
binary code
code library
cold boot
comment
compiler
computer programmer
computer software
copy protection technology
copyright
crash
custom software
debugger
debugging tool
developer
device driver
Digital Rights Management (DRM)
digital watermark
download
encryption
encryption key
end-user license agreement (EULA)

extreme programming model
firewall software
graphical user interface (GUI)
high-level language
horizontal market software
in-app purchase
input
instructions
Integrated Development Environment
  (IDE)
intellectual property
interpreter
license
Linux operating system
load
low-level language
machine language
malware
mobile app
monetize
multiple-user license
on-screen Help
open source software
operating system
operating system (OS) software
output
packaged software
perpetual software
piracy
platform
predictive methodology
preinstalled software
productivity software
program
program editor
programmer
programming

programming language
proprietary software
quality assurance (QA)
rebooting
replicate
reset
restore
restore point
security software
security suite
single-user license
site license
Software as a Service (SaaS)
software developer
software development
software development kit (SDK)
software development methodology
software license
software program
software publisher
software update
source code
spam
spyware
suite
system software
text editor
two-factor authentication
uninstall
upgrade
user manual
utility program
utility software
vertical market software
warm boot
web app
web-based Help

System Software

Colin loves his new laptop with the latest Windows system software. He can store his e-books, assignments, messages, and course information in folders and read them anywhere without being confined to a desk.

Colin taps tiles on his touch screen to share files on his cloud computing drive, take photos, listen to music, get directions, and connect to friends.

iStockphoto.com/YinYang

Colin Yang is enjoying the campus quad as he reads *The Innocents Abroad* by Mark Twain for his freshman English class. Because he uses Windows system software on his laptop, he can take notes, search for files, and research information on the web using the Cortana virtual assistant. He also chooses to back up his documents in the cloud to protect his work.

Identify System Software

system software | operating system (OS) | platform | Software as a Service (Saas) | update | utility software | file management utility | disk cleanup software | search utility | file compression utility

The Bottom Line

- System software is the software that runs a computer, and includes the operating system and utility programs.
- You need to keep your operating system up to date to keep your computer running smoothly and to protect against security threats.

What makes computers so versatile and capable of performing so many tasks? Is it a blazing fast processor? Souped-up hard drive? Dazzling monitor? No, it's the system software. Without system software, a computer is just a collection of electronic components in a case.

Define System Software

System software is the software that makes it possible for you to use a computer. The operating system and utility programs are system software that control behind-the-scene operations so you can use the computer productively. Table 3-1 compares system software and application software.

Figure 3-1: System software

Microsoft Windows Start menu

Microsoft Windows desktop

WinZip file compression program for iOS

Apple iOS on an iPad and iPhone

Cortana search utility built into Windows

Source: WinZip, Source: Apple Computer

Table 3-1: System software and application software

	System software	Application software
Purpose	Runs a computer	Lets you perform work or personal tasks
How it runs	Starts when you turn on the power to a computer, and then runs in the background.	Starts at your request
Typical tasks	Keeps track of files, prints documents, connects to networks, manages hardware and other software.	Provides tools for creating, editing, and viewing files such as documents, photos, and webpages

Identify an Operating System

The most critical piece of software on a computer is the **operating system (OS)**, a set of programs that manages and coordinates all the activities in a computer.

As system software, the OS runs mostly in the background as you perform other tasks. It makes it possible for you to run two or more programs at the same time, for example, or connect your computer to a network. Suppose you are writing a report and want to save the document on your hard drive. Table 3-2 shows the role the operating system plays as you perform these tasks.

Table 3-2: Role of the operating system

Your task	Role of the operating system
Start a word processing program and then open the document.	• Starts the word processing program • Provides a way for you to access the document
Add information to the document.	• Manages memory so the program can run • Stores your unsaved work in temporary memory
Save the document on the hard drive.	• Finds the hard drive on the computer • Makes sure the hard drive has enough space for the document • Saves the document on the hard drive • Stores the name and location of the saved document so you can find it later

To completely identify an operating system, also called a **platform**, you typically state its name and version. For example, in Windows 10, Windows is the name of the OS and 10 is the version. Some software companies, including Microsoft, are dropping version numbers as they move to a more flexible **Software as a Service (SaaS)** approach. For example, the current strategy is that Microsoft does not plan to release Windows 11, but will continue developing the current version of Windows through software updates. An **update** is a collection of software changes to fix bugs, improve security, and enhance features.

Most operating systems include a feature that automatically downloads updates using an Internet connection and then installs them. Automatic updates help to keep your system running smoothly and to protect against security threats.

Identify Utility Software

Utility software performs a specific, limited task, usually related to managing or maintaining a computer system. Some utility programs are included with the operating system, such as the following:

- **File management utilities** such as File Explorer (for Windows 10) and Finder (for macOS) let you copy, move, rename, and delete files and folders.
- **Search utilities** help you find files stored on the computer. For example, on a Windows 10 computer, you can ask Cortana to search for a file using natural language commands you write or speak, such as "What Word file did I create today?"
- **Disk cleanup software** deletes unnecessary files. File optimization utilities work to free up disk space by consolidating data.
- **File compression utilities** reduce the size of files.

Other utility programs are available separate from the operating system. For example, you can install a collection of security utilities to protect your computer and its data.

On the Job Now

Many companies are building Windows 10 holographic experiences using HoloLens. The Kennedy Space Center Visitor Complex opened a new exhibit called Destination Mars, which provides visitors the opportunity to experience what it would be like to walk around the red planet.

#syssoftware

Siri (Apple), Google Now (Google), Cortana (Microsoft), and Alexa (Amazon) are four leading digital assistants providing voice-activated help to users through smartphones, tablets, and personal computers.

Define Operating Systems

operating system (OS) | boot process | user interface | process | multitasking | multithreading | multiprocessing | parallel processing | random access memory (RAM) | personal computer (PC) operating system | server OS | network OS | mobile OS | embedded OS | General Public License (GPL) | web app | web server

Is your computer usually reliable and quick to respond to your instructions? Can you use the same types of controls and tools in any program you start? Or do you have to learn a new way of working with software when you work with a new program? The answers to these questions depend on your **operating system (OS)**, the set of programs that manages and coordinates all the activities on your computer.

Describe the Purpose of an Operating System

The OS is responsible for coordinating the resources and activities on a computer and is loaded into memory during the **boot process**, which is a series of events that begins when you turn on the computer.

After it starts, the OS is the go-between for you and the computer, accepting your instructions and data, and providing information from the system. You interact with the OS through the **user interface**, which controls how you enter and receive information.

The OS is also the go-between for software and hardware. For example, if you want to print a flyer you created in your word processing program, the OS guides the flyer document to the printer and lets other software know the printer is busy until it's finished printing the document. Along the way, it uses internal components such as the processor, RAM, and storage space to manage and complete the task.

Figure 3-2: Operating system responsibilities

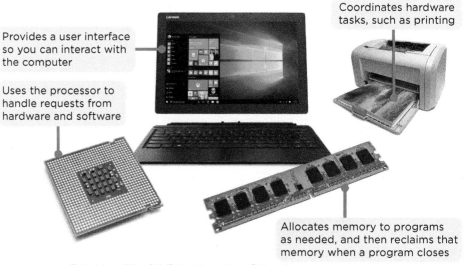

Provides a user interface so you can interact with the computer

Coordinates hardware tasks, such as printing

Uses the processor to handle requests from hardware and software

Allocates memory to programs as needed, and then reclaims that memory when a program closes

aarrows/Shutterstock.com, Maksym Dykha/Shutterstock.com, Jr images/Shutterstock.com

Describe Processing Techniques

As you work with a computer, many activities, or **processes**, are competing for the attention of your operating system. Applications request action, the pointing device and keyboard send data, and webpages arrive from your Internet connection and wait to be displayed on your screen.

In response, the OS uses one or more of the following processing techniques to handle and prioritize these requests efficiently and improve the performance of a computer:

- **Multitasking**: Most operating systems use multitasking to perform many tasks simultaneously, such as running two or more programs at the same time.

- **Multithreading:** The OS uses multithreading to process many parts, or threads, of a single program. Multithreading helps programs run faster and more efficiently.
- **Multiprocessing:** Most computers have multiple processors, such as dual-core or quad-core processors, which means the OS can use multiprocessing to split tasks among the processors.
- **Parallel processing:** Many operating systems also can use parallel processing to divide one task among many processors so that parts of the task are completed simultaneously, or in parallel. For example, gaming computers with quad-core processors use parallel processing to enhance the speed and realism of a computer game.

Describe How an OS Manages Memory

One key task that operating systems perform is memory management, which involves using **random access memory (RAM)** efficiently.

Every program needs RAM to run, including the operating system. Each additional program you run or window you open requires RAM. The more RAM a device has, the more efficient the operating system. If you are using a device with a low amount of RAM, the operating system slows if you open many folder windows, for example, or run an app that uses a lot of RAM, such as Microsoft Excel or Adobe Photoshop.

In addition to RAM, the performance of an operating system depends on the computer's processor and storage space. See **Figure 3-3**.

By the Numbers Now

Top gaming computers such as Alienware have 64 GB of RAM with a closed-loop liquid cooling system for high performance play.

Figure 3-3: Operating system performance

Top-of-the-line dual-core processor means fast CPU processing performance.

Windows 10 Laptop
- 15.6" display
- Intel dual-core i7
- 16 GB RAM
- 1 TB
☆☆☆☆☆

Good amount of RAM lets you run many apps and open many browser tabs at once.

High hard disk capacity lets you install apps and store data efficiently.

Identify Types of Operating Systems

You can classify operating systems in different ways, including the following:
- The user interface might require you to type commands or to interact with graphical representations of objects.
- Operating systems installed on a single computer are called **personal computer (PC) operating systems** or desktop operating systems. Most are single-user operating systems because one user interacts with the OS at a time.
- A **server OS** or **network OS** is a multiuser OS because it controls a single, centralized computer that supports many users on networked computers. It also controls access to network resources such as network printers.
- You use a **mobile OS** such as Android or iOS on a smartphone, tablet, or other mobile device.
- Motor vehicles and electronic devices, such as card readers, medical equipment, and robots, use **embedded OSs**, usually those that let them participate in the Internet of Things (IoT).

#syssoftware

The operating system for Mac PCs was called Mac OS X or OS X until the release of Sierra in 2016, when Apple introduced the name macOS.

#syssoftware

The term "PC" once referred only to personal computers that ran Windows. Now "PC operating system" refers to the OS on a desktop computer or laptop, which is different from a mobile OS that runs on a tablet or smartphone.

By the Numbers Now

According to Statista, Apple Computer is focused on mobile devices and mobile operating systems because more than 69% of the company's revenue comes from sales of the iPhone.

By the Numbers Now

Gartner states that 79% of the worldwide smartphone market is running the Android operating system. iOS phones are responsible for a 18% share and the remaining percentage is split among Windows and others.

Identify PC Operating Systems

The PC operating system you prefer—for example, Windows, macOS, Chrome OS, or Linux—usually determines the type of PC you buy. See Table 3-3.

Table 3-3: PC operating systems

OS	Type of computer	Notable features
Windows	Desktop computers, laptops, and some tablets	Supports the Cortana virtual assistant, touch screen input, HoloLens headsets, and built-in apps such as the Microsoft Edge browser
macOS	Macintosh desktop computers and laptops	Includes the Siri virtual assistant, coordination with Apple mobile devices, and cloud file storage
Linux	Desktop computers, laptops, and tablets	Distributed under the terms of a **General Public License (GPL)**, which allows you to copy the OS for your own use, to give to others, or to sell
Chrome OS	Chromebook laptops	Based on Linux, it uses the Google Chrome browser as its user interface and primarily runs **web apps** (applications you run in a browser)

Identify Server Operating Systems

A server OS resides on a server computer and runs to manage a network. The following are three popular server operating systems:

- **Windows Server** is the server version of Windows. It includes advanced security tools and a set of programs called Internet Information Services that manage web apps and services.
- **macOS Server**, like other server operating systems, supports all sizes of networks and servers. One unique feature is that it lets authorized users access servers using their iPhones or other Apple devices.
- **UNIX** is called a multipurpose OS because it can run on a desktop PC or a server. Many **web servers**, which are the computers that deliver webpages to your computer, use UNIX because it is a powerful, flexible OS.

UNIX is similar to Linux, which some servers use as their OS to provide network services such as email and web access.

Identify Mobile Operating Systems

A mobile device such as a tablet or smartphone uses a mobile OS, which has features similar to those of a PC OS, but is focused on the needs of a mobile user and the capabilities of the device. A mobile OS works especially well with mobile device features such as touch screens, voice recognition, and Wi-Fi networks.

Three popular mobile operating systems are iOS, Android, and Windows Phone. Each works with particular brands of handheld computers. See Figure 3-4.

Figure 3-4: Mobile operating systems

iOS is a version of macOS written for Apple mobile devices.

Google developed Android to run on many types of smartphones and tablets.

Windows 10 runs on tablets, while Windows Phone runs on smartphones.

Source: Apple Computer, Source: Samsung

Describe Common OS Tasks

boot process | bootstrap program | ROM (read-only memory) | power-on self-test (POST) | RAM (random access memory) | kernel | resource | input | output | buffer | spooling | device driver | Plug and Play (PnP) | command-line interface | graphical user interface (GUI) | tile | icon | button

An operating system takes care of the technical tasks of running a computer while you work on school or professional projects, watch videos, connect with friends, or play games. To enhance your computer experience, the OS also lets you customize the user interface and set up hardware the way you like it.

Describe the Boot Process

To start an OS, you turn on the computer. Before you can interact with the OS, the computer must complete the **boot process**, which includes the following steps:

1. The computer receives power and distributes it to the computer circuitry.

2. The processor begins to run the **bootstrap program**, a special startup program built into a **ROM (read-only memory)** chip on the computer's motherboard.

The Bottom Line

- The OS controls a computer from soon after you start it up until you shut it down.
- During that time, the OS manages resources including the processor, memory, storage space, and connected devices.
- The OS also provides the user interface so you can perform tasks.

Figure 3-5: Operating system tasks

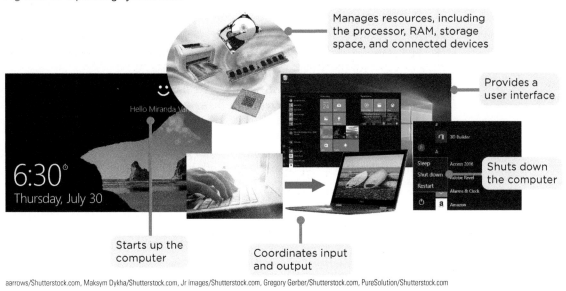

Manages resources, including the processor, RAM, storage space, and connected devices

Provides a user interface

Shuts down the computer

Starts up the computer

Coordinates input and output

aarrows/Shutterstock.com, Maksym Dykha/Shutterstock.com, Jr images/Shutterstock.com, Gregory Gerber/Shutterstock.com, PureSolution/Shutterstock.com

#syssoftware

Windows 10 computers typically take only a few seconds to start up and let you sign in with a picture password, which involves repeating three gestures on a picture.

#syssoftware

The latest MacBook Pro has a fingerprint reader that you can use to verify Apple Pay financial transactions.

3. The computer performs the **power-on self-test (POST)** to check crucial system components.

4. If the POST is successful, the computer identifies connected devices and checks their settings.

5. The computer loads system files into **RAM (random access memory)**, including the **kernel**, or core, of the OS.

6. The OS completes setup tasks, such as identifying you through a camera or fingerprint reader, and then runs startup programs in the background and displays the main user interface.

Track System Resources

An operating system controls your computer by managing its **resources**, which are components the OS requires to perform work, such as the processor, RAM, storage space, and connected devices. To manage RAM resources, an OS keeps track of the apps, processes, and other tasks the system is performing.

Microsoft Windows, for example, displays this information in the Windows Task Manager dialog box. See **Figure 3-6**.

Figure 3-6: Windows Task Manager

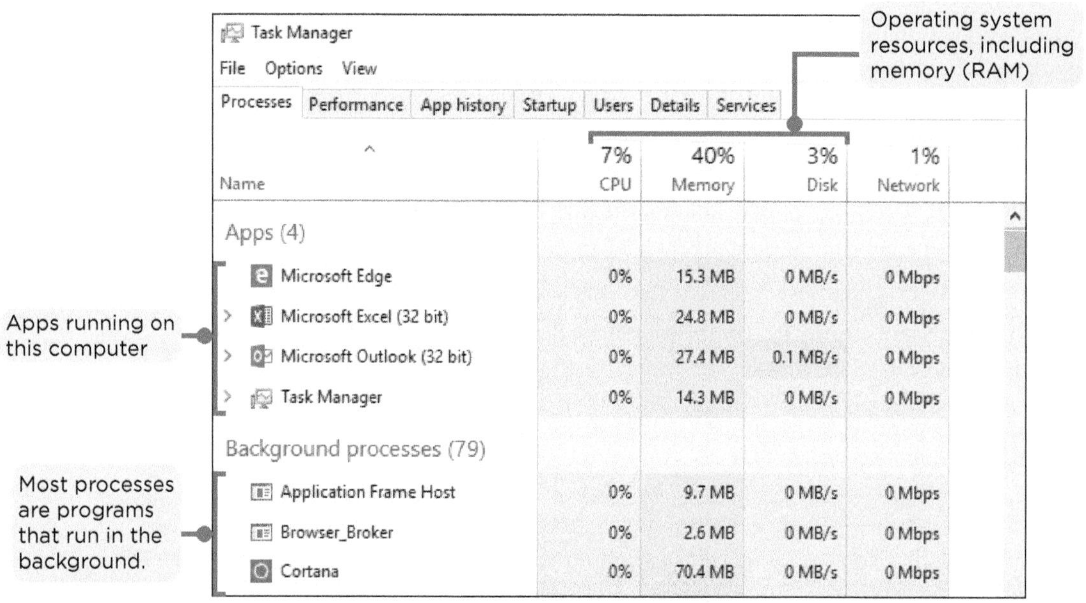

Operating system resources, including memory (RAM)

Task Manager					
File Options View					
Processes Performance App history Startup Users Details Services					
		7%	40%	3%	1%
Name		CPU	Memory	Disk	Network
Apps (4)					
Microsoft Edge		0%	15.3 MB	0 MB/s	0 Mbps
Microsoft Excel (32 bit)		0%	24.8 MB	0 MB/s	0 Mbps
Microsoft Outlook (32 bit)		0%	27.4 MB	0.1 MB/s	0 Mbps
Task Manager		0%	14.3 MB	0 MB/s	0 Mbps
Background processes (79)					
Application Frame Host		0%	9.7 MB	0 MB/s	0 Mbps
Browser_Broker		0%	2.6 MB	0 MB/s	0 Mbps
Cortana		0%	70.4 MB	0 MB/s	0 Mbps

Apps running on this computer

Most processes are programs that run in the background.

For example, the OS tracks the names and locations of your files so you can retrieve them from storage when necessary, and it logs empty areas in storage where you can save new files.

If the OS detects a resource problem, it notifies you and tries to correct the problem. If too many programs are open for the memory to handle, the OS displays a message and does not open additional programs. If a printer is not turned on when you try to print a document, the OS will send you a message to turn it on; if it's out of paper, you will see a message to add paper. If your hard drive has no more space, the OS will let you know that you do not have available space to save another file.

Manage Input and Output

To keep the computer running smoothly, the OS manages input and output. For example, when you type text on the keyboard to provide **input**, the OS accepts and processes that data so the computer can display the text as **output** on the screen.

If a device is slow to provide input or output, the OS uses **buffers**, which are areas of memory that hold data from one device before it is transferred to another device. For example, by using a keyboard buffer, your computer doesn't miss any of your keystrokes, even if you type very quickly.

Placing data in a buffer so it can be retrieved later is called **spooling**. Print spooling allows the OS to send many documents to the printer and then print them in sequence while the computer is performing other tasks.

Manage Hardware

The OS considers every device connected to the computer an input or output resource. For example, a headset microphone is an input resource and a speaker is an output resource, both for audio data.

To control a hardware resource, the OS communicates with a **device driver**, a small program that tells the OS how to interact with that device. Unlike apps, which run in a window on your desktop, device drivers usually run in the background when the OS needs them; you don't need to activate them.

Each device must have a driver. If you install new hardware, the OS usually recognizes the device right away or the next time you start the computer. The OS then tries to install the correct driver so you can use the new hardware immediately. This feature is called **Plug and Play (PnP)**. Most operating systems include drivers for common devices. If the OS can't find the correct driver on your computer, you can download it from the device manufacturer's website.

Define a Graphical User Interface

The main purpose of an OS is to control what happens behind the scenes. It provides a user interface so that you can interact with the OS and other programs.

Some software uses a **command-line interface**, which displays only text. You type commands to interact with a command-line interface. See **Figure 3-7**.

Hot Technology Now

Windows 10 features Plug and Play support for 3-D printers.

Hot Technology Now

On a Windows computer, you can open the command-line interface by searching for *Command Prompt*. On a Mac, you can access the command line using the Terminal application.

Figure 3-7: Command-line user interface

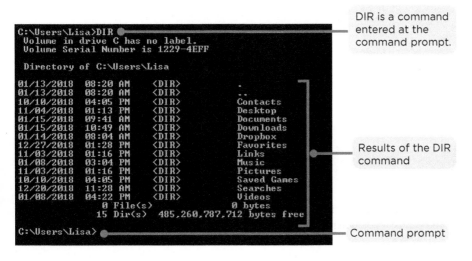

DIR is a command entered at the command prompt.

Results of the DIR command

Command prompt

The software on most devices has a **graphical user interface (GUI)**, which lets you select options and manipulate objects such as buttons and icons using a pointing device or gesture. GUIs are based on graphical objects, where each object represents a computer task, command, or real-world object. See **Figure 3-8** on the next page.

- The Windows Start menu displays **tiles**, colorful rectangles that you use to start apps.
- An **icon** is a small picture that represents a program, file, or hardware device. When you double-click an icon, such as a folder icon, a window opens to display related data.
- A **button** is a graphic that you click to make a selection. Buttons often appear together on a toolbar, taskbar, or ribbon.

Figure 3-8: Graphical user interface

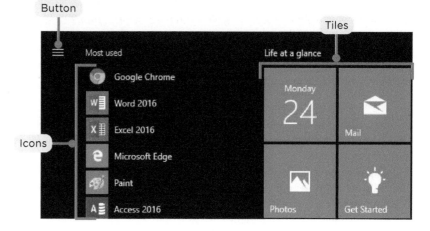

Identify Typical Operating System Tasks

You interact directly with the OS to control parts of your computer and your computer experience:

- **Start programs**: You use GUI objects to start programs. For example, with Windows, you use tiles, buttons, icons, and the taskbar. On a Mac computer, you use icons and the Dock. In a mobile operating system, you select an icon. See **Figure 3-9**.

#syssoftware

You can unpin a Windows 10 Start menu tile by right-clicking the tile and selecting Unpin from Start to hide apps that you do not use often.

Figure 3-9: Starting programs in PC and mobile operating systems

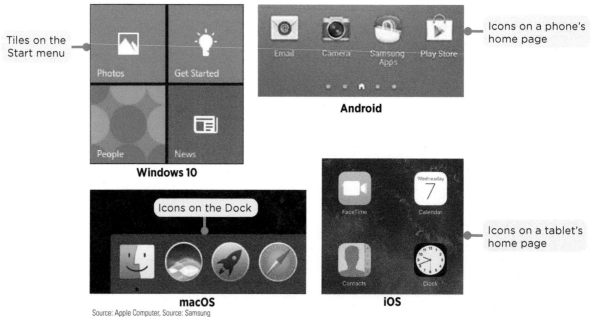

Source: Apple Computer, Source: Samsung

#syssoftware

Windows 10 includes Skype for phone calls, messages, video, and sharing. Skype Translator is part of the Skype for Windows desktop app and translates speech from one language to another as it's spoken.

- **Manage files**: Most operating systems provide programs you use to manage files. For example, you can view a list of folders and files and move, copy, rename, or delete them.
- **Get help**: You also interact directly with the OS to get help. You can learn more about the OS and how to use commands and features.
- **Customize the user interface**: Typically, you can customize the user interface by selecting a theme, which includes a color scheme, a background graphic, sounds, and other elements. If you have special needs, you can customize the interface to accommodate your needs by displaying a larger font or playing narration of on-screen text, for example.
- **Work with hardware**: You use the OS to set up hardware or change hardware settings.

Shut Down Devices

Although you keep a computer running under most circumstances, you should shut it down if the power could be interrupted suddenly, as in the case of an impending thunderstorm or battery outage. To conserve energy, you should also shut down a device if you aren't going to use it for a long time.

Operating systems provide shut down options so you can close programs and processes in an orderly fashion. One option is a complete shut down, which closes all documents and programs and turns off the power to the computer.

Some operating systems have a Sleep option to use low power instead of shutting down. Sleep stores the current state of open programs and documents, saving you time when you resume work.

You can use the OS to set what happens when you press the power button or close the lid on a laptop. You can choose to shut down the computer or put it to sleep.

Manage Your Computer's Windows

window | Minimize button | Maximize button | Close button | Restore Down button | active window | thumbnail | program window | folder window | Snap

Some computer users start desktop apps until their screen is covered with programs and documents. Then they get frustrated when they can't find the information they want.

To avoid frustration and work more effectively, you can manage the windows on your desktop. In any operating system, a **window** is a rectangular area of the screen that displays the contents of a program, file, or folder.

Define a Desktop Window

After you turn on a Windows, Macintosh, Chromebook, or Linux computer, the desktop appears. When you open an app, file, or folder, it appears on the desktop in a rectangular work area called a window.

Most windows share the same elements. **Figure 3-10** shows these elements in Windows 10.

Hot Technology Now

Try this shortcut: Right-click the Start button in Windows 10 to display a menu you can use to access the Command Prompt, File Manager, Task Manager, and more.

The Bottom Line
- Manage windows by switching from one to another, opening and closing them, and arranging them on the desktop.
- Resize windows to make them larger or smaller, revealing less or more of the desktop.

#syssoftware

Using Cortana in Windows 10 and the free Cortana app on your smartphone, you can ask the voice-activated assistant to remind you to pick up items when you leave or arrive at certain GPS locations, including the grocery store. Say "Cortana, remind me to pick up pizza rolls when I am close to Safeway grocery store."

Figure 3-10: Window elements

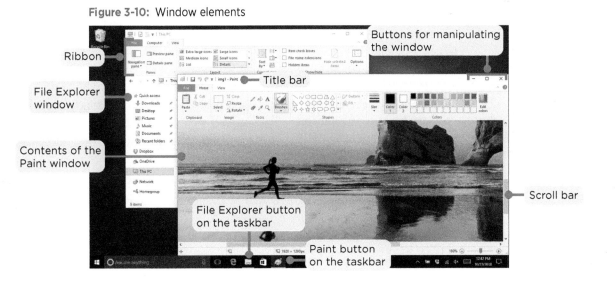

- The center part of a window displays the contents.
- The title bar at the top of a window displays the name of the app, file, or folder shown in the window.
- The title bar also contains buttons for manipulating the window. The **Minimize button** reduces the window to a button on the taskbar. The **Maximize button** enlarges

Figure 3-11: Window-manipulation buttons

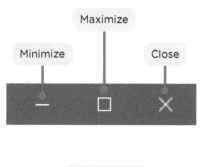

the window to fill the screen. The **Close button** closes the window. The **Restore Down button** returns a maximized window to its previous size. See Figure 3-11.
- Some windows include a ribbon, toolbar, or menu bar, which contains text, icons, or images you select to perform actions and make selections.
- Windows can also include vertical and horizontal scroll bars so you can display contents currently out of view.

Switch Windows

You can have many windows and apps open at one time, each displaying a different document or program. Windows can appear side by side or stacked. The foreground window is the selected or **active window**. Your next pointing device or keyboard action applies to the active window. One way to make a different window active is to select its button on the taskbar or Dock.

You can use many keyboard shortcuts to manipulate windows. In Windows, you can press and hold the ALT key while you press TAB to cycle through thumbnails of the open windows. Release the ALT key to make the selected window active. (A **thumbnail** is a miniature version of a larger image, such as a window.) You can also press and hold the Windows key (the key with the Windows logo) while you press TAB to display thumbnails of all the open windows. Switch to a window by clicking its thumbnail.

Open Windows

You can use two types of windows on a desktop. A **program window** displays a running program. A **folder window** displays the objects in a folder, such as files and other folders.
- To open a program window in Windows 10, for example, you typically click the **Start button**, and then click the **program name**. If a program icon appears on the Windows taskbar, you can select the icon to open a program window.
- To open a folder window, start a file management utility such as File Explorer or Finder, and then navigate to the folder you want.

To close any type of open window, click its Close button. The Close button also appears in the thumbnail when you place the pointer over the button on the taskbar. Another way to close a window is to right-click its button on the taskbar, and then click Close window on the shortcut menu. These techniques work even with minimized windows. Most programs also include a File menu that has a close or exit option.

Arrange Windows

You can arrange windows on the desktop to work effectively and to access other items on the desktop. To move a window, point to its title bar, and then drag the window to its new location.

In Windows 10, you can use the taskbar to display all open windows in one of three arrangements—cascading, vertically, or horizontally:

1. Right-click the **taskbar** (or press and hold the taskbar on a touch screen) to display its shortcut menu.

2. Select **Cascade windows** to arrange the windows so they overlap while displaying each title bar.

3. To stack the windows vertically, select **Show windows stacked**.

4. Select **Show windows side by side** to arrange the windows horizontally across the desktop.

5. Select **Show the desktop** to minimize all open windows and display the desktop.

You can use **Snap** to arrange windows. Drag the title bar of a window to one side of the desktop until the outline of an expanded window appears.

Resize Windows

You can resize windows to display more or less of their contents. The easiest way to make a window larger or smaller when working with any operating system is to point to a border or corner of the window until the resizing pointer appears. See Figure 3-12. Drag the border or corner to resize the window making it larger or smaller as needed.

Figure 3-12: Resizing a macOS window

Resizing pointer

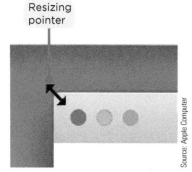

Source: Apple Computer

Manipulate Windows

You can resize a window by maximizing or minimizing it. **Figure 3-13** shows useful buttons for manipulating windows in macOS.

- To make a window fill the desktop, click the Maximize button or double-click the title bar.
- In Windows 10, you can use Snap to maximize the height a window. Drag the top border to the top of the desktop until the window expands to fit the height of the desktop.
- To return a snapped window to its original size, drag the top border of the window until the window snaps to its original size.
- To return a maximized window to its original size, click the Restore Down button or double-click the window's title bar.
- Click the Minimize button to reduce a window to a button on the taskbar. To display a minimized window, click its taskbar button.
- In Windows 10, you can use Shake to minimize all open windows except one. Point to a window's title bar and drag it left and right quickly to shake the window.
- To display the desktop, click the Show desktop button on the far right side of the taskbar.

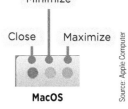

Figure 3-13: macOS window buttons

Minimize

Close   Maximize

MacOS

Source: Apple Computer

Describe Common OS Features

desktop | taskbar | notification area | menu | submenu | dialog box | option button | radio button | check box | list box | multiple-selection list box | icon | Recycle Bin | disk cleanup utility | sector | defragmentation utility | file management utility | file compression utility | decompress

Suppose you've always worked on a Windows computer but now you're visiting a friend who offers to let you use his Macintosh computer. Will you be able to get anything done using a different operating system?

The answer is yes, because PC operating systems share common features. When you become familiar with these features, you can use any personal computer to perform basic tasks and even keep the system in good working order.

> **The Bottom Line**
> - Operating systems with graphical user interfaces have many features in common, including the desktop, menus, icons, and dialog boxes.
> - PC operating systems provide tools that help you maintain computer storage devices and manage files.

Figure 3-14: Common features in PC operating systems

Disk Cleanup is a utility for removing unnecessary files.

Finder is a macOS utility for managing files.

Windows 10 desktop

Use Siri to find files and information.

Recycle Bin icon

Menu bar

Dialog box

Use Cortana to find files, apps, and settings.

Buttons on the taskbar

macOS desktop   App icons

Source: Apple Computer

Use the Desktop

Regardless of the brand of computer, the **desktop** is a main workspace for interacting with your computer. At the bottom of the Windows desktop is the **taskbar**, which contains buttons for running programs, viewing folders, and opening files. On the right of the Windows taskbar is the **notification area**, which displays shortcuts to utilities such as the volume control. Alerts for updating apps also appear in the notification area.

The macOS desktop uses an area called the Dock for starting programs. Linux has bars on the top and bottom of its desktop. Chrome has the shelf; like the Windows taskbar or macOS Dock, the shelf displays icons for starting programs.

Use Menus and Dialog Boxes

How do you make a computer do what you want it to do? One way is to use a **menu**, which displays a list of commands or options. You select the option you want from the list. See **Figure 3-15**.

Figure 3-15: Menus and dialog boxes

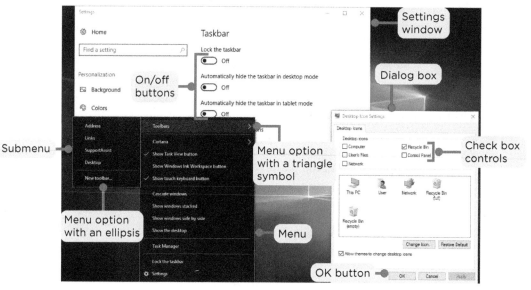

To avoid displaying a very long list of options, many menus organize additional commands on a **submenu**. You can always identify a menu option that leads to a submenu or gallery because it has a triangle symbol. When you select a menu option with an ellipsis (three dots), a dialog box opens. A **dialog box** displays settings associated with a command. Dialog boxes contain controls that you use to select options and enter information to indicate exactly how you want the program to perform the command. For example, click a round **option button** (also called a **radio button**) to select one option from a group of options. Click one or more **check boxes** to identify selections you want from several options. With a **list box** (also called a combo box or drop-down list), you click an arrow and then select an item on a list. In a **multiple-selection list box**, you can make one or more selections. Click or tap the OK button or press ENTER to accept the settings in the dialog box.

Large windows such as the Settings window include touch-friendly buttons that you can tap with a fingertip to turn a setting on or off.

Use Icons and Buttons

Whether you use a Windows, Mac, Chrome, or Linux operating system, you can use icons and buttons to interact with the computer.

- **Icons:** An **icon** is a graphic representing a program, file, or hardware device. Icons can appear on the desktop or in a window. Typically, you double-click an icon to start a program or display the contents of what the icon represents, such as a drive.

#syssoftware

Most Windows apps use a ribbon instead of a menu bar to provide access to commands. In macOS, however, a menu bar is displayed for the active program at the top of the screen.

#syssoftware

Windows 10 is moving toward all touch-friendly controls so that you can use the OS with a pointing device or a touch screen.

- **Buttons**: A button is also a graphic. Buttons are grouped together on a menu bar, toolbar, taskbar, or ribbon interface. You tap or click a button to make a selection. If the button displays an arrow, a menu or gallery appears so you can select an option.

You can create icons for items like files and folders and arrange icons on the desktop or in a window by selecting sort settings. In contrast to icons, buttons are part of a program, so you typically can't create or rearrange them.

Run Disk Utilities

Regardless of the operating system you're using, if your computer starts to slow down, you probably need to use disk utilities to diagnose and repair problems on your hard disk.

To protect you from accidentally deleting a hard disk file, the OS stores the deleted file in a temporary location. In Windows, this location is the **Recycle Bin**. The file still takes up space on the disk, but does not appear in file listings. You then have the option of emptying the Recycle Bin to permanently delete the files. Files deleted from some removable storage devices such as a low-capacity flash drive do not get placed in the Recycle Bin. You can also use a **disk cleanup utility** to find and remove unnecessary files such as those stored in the Recycle Bin.

When you save data on a disk, the OS places it in an available storage area, or **sector**. Although the OS tries to place data in sectors that are next to each other, or contiguous, parts of files can be scattered over the disk. These fragmented files slow a computer's performance.

A **defragmentation utility** reorganizes the files on a hard disk so the OS accesses data more quickly. Although Windows PCs should be defragmented periodically to increase efficiency, Mac and Linux computers might not need to. Follow the recommendations for your computer and operating system.

Run File Utilities

At some point, every computer user wastes time searching for files saved somewhere on the computer. To avoid these frustrating searches, you can use file utilities to manage your computer files. Following are examples of file utilities:

- **File management**: A **file management utility** gives you an overview of the files stored on your computer and lets you rename, delete, move, and copy files and folders. In Windows 10, you use File Explorer.
- **Search for files**: A search tool finds files that meet criteria you specify, such as characters in a filename.
- **File compression**: Use a **file compression utility** to reduce the size of a file so it takes up less storage space on a disk. Compressed files usually have a .zip extension. If you compress a file before attaching it to an email message, for example, the message travels more quickly to its recipient.
- You also use a file compression utility to **decompress**, or unzip, compressed files and restore them to their original size so you can edit the file.

#syssoftware

If the Recycle Bin does not appear on your Windows desktop, use Cortana to search for "Recycle Bin," click "Show or hide common icons on the desktop," and then click the Recycle Bin check box in the Desktop Icon Settings dialog box. Windows tablets hide the Recycle Bin by default and some do not have a Recycle Bin at all to save disk space.

#syssoftware

Windows 10 uses a feature called Automatic Disk Optimization to monitor the hard drive and defragment it (or optimize it) according to a schedule, which is once a week by default.

Compare PC Operating Systems

PC operating system | Windows | window | macOS | Dock | Linux | distribution | General Public License (GPL) | Chrome OS | web app

A **PC operating system** is developed to run on a desktop computer, a laptop, and in some cases, a tablet. Four popular PC operating systems are Windows, macOS, Linux, and Chrome.

Use Microsoft Windows

Windows is a PC operating system developed by Microsoft Corporation. Part of its graphical user interface features **windows**, which are rectangular areas of the screen devoted to a single program and its tools.

Windows 10 is already installed on most new PCs, making it the most popular operating system in the world. According to Microsoft, more than 400 million devices in 192 countries are running Windows 10. Because of its widespread use, you can find plenty of hardware and software designed to run on Windows. The popularity of Windows also makes it a target for security threats.

The Bottom Line
- Because an OS comes installed on new computers, you should know the strengths and weaknesses of the popular PC OSs.
- The OS determines how easy it is to use and upgrade your computer, so consider the user interface and flexibility as two of the most important criteria when comparing PC OSs.

Figure 3-16: PC operating systems

#syssoftware

In Windows 10, you can create multiple desktops for different purposes and projects. For example, you can use one desktop for your work tasks, another desktop for your home environment, and another for your family members to play games on your computer without accidentally deleting your important files.

Windows has a graphical user interface with a Start menu, windows, and a desktop with a taskbar for keeping track of running apps. It accepts touch and voice input. For example, Windows apps let you draw on the screen to create shapes and write notes.

Use macOS

macOS is the PC operating system designed for Apple Macintosh computers. It has a graphical user interface with windows and a desktop. It accepts touch and voice input and includes a menu bar at the top of the screen and the Dock at the bottom. The **Dock** contains icons for accessing files and apps. See **Figure 3-17**.

Figure 3-17: macOS Sierra

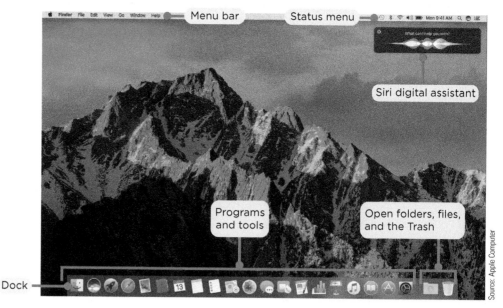

macOS set the original standard for GUI operating systems, and continues to lead the computing industry in user interface design. Siri, the digital assistant, is built into macOS and responds to your voice commands. Other strengths are that it is an easy-to-use, secure, and reliable OS. Weaknesses include a limited selection of hardware and productivity apps other than graphics software.

Use Linux

Linux is a PC operating system related to UNIX, an OS first developed in the 1960s for large, special-purpose computers used by scientists, researchers, and system administrators. Linux is available in versions called **distributions**, including commercial distributions such as RedHat, openSUSE, and Ubuntu. Most distributions of Linux provide graphical user interfaces, though some, such as BSD, are better known for their command-line interfaces.

The main advantage of using Linux is its **General Public License (GPL)**, which makes the OS free to install and use. Linux is the OS of choice for users who want flexibility and control over their computers and don't require commercial software. All distributions of Linux also run on any type of hardware and provide excellent security. The two main disadvantages are that installation and setup can be complicated and little commercial software is developed for Linux. However, plenty of open-source Linux software is available.

Use Chrome OS

Chrome OS is a PC operating system developed by Google to work with Google web apps. A **web app** is software you access and use on the web. The user interface is spare and simple, focusing on accessing the Internet and websites using the Chrome browser. Chrome OS is intended to run on secondary mobile computers such as Chromebooks, not on a user's primary computer. In addition to a browser, Chrome OS includes a file manager for viewing and manipulating files and a media player for viewing images and playing music. See **Figure 3-18**.

#syssoftware

Many operating systems, including macOS and Android, are based on UNIX and Linux kernels.

#syssoftware

Unlike other operating systems, Chrome OS is available only on specific brands of computers, such as Chromebooks, stripped-down, lightweight laptops designed mainly for accessing the web.

Figure 3-18: Chrome OS on a Chromebook

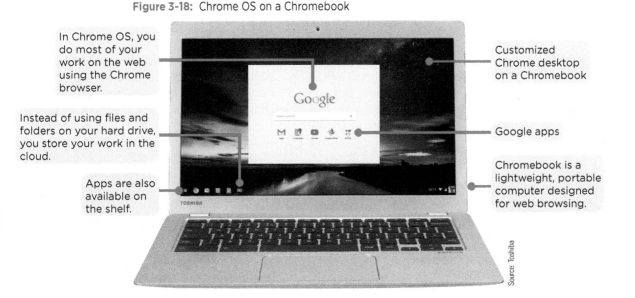

In Chrome OS, you do most of your work on the web using the Chrome browser.

Instead of using files and folders on your hard drive, you store your work in the cloud.

Apps are also available on the shelf.

Customized Chrome desktop on a Chromebook

Google apps

Chromebook is a lightweight, portable computer designed for web browsing.

Source: Toshiba

Select a PC Operating System

When selecting a PC operating system, most users consider ease of use, available programs or apps, and flexibility as the most important criteria. Other criteria include hardware support, software support, security, and availability. The four most popular PC operating systems are Windows, macOS, Linux, and Chrome OS.

To select the right OS for you, determine which of the criteria you consider the most important, and then choose the OS that ranks best in those criteria. Read reviews by users and independent technology experts to find current rankings.

•Compare Mobile Operating Systems

mobile operating system | tablet | touch screen | smartphone | Android | iOS |
Windows Phone | tile | live tile | hub

A **mobile operating system** is developed to run on a tablet, smartphone, or other mobile device. A **tablet** is a handheld mobile computer that includes a **touch screen**, which is a screen you touch to interact with the user interface. Smaller than a tablet, a **smartphone** is a cell phone that includes many features of a computer, allowing it to run general-purpose computing applications. Three popular mobile operating systems are Android, iOS, and Windows Phone.

Figure 3-19: Mobile operating systems

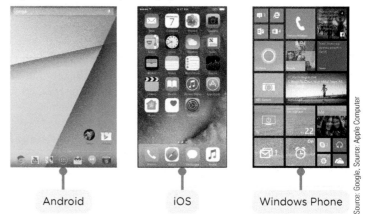

Android   iOS   Windows Phone

#syssoftware

A mobile OS provides the services and features people need and want on a small mobile device, including connecting wirelessly to the Internet, taking and storing photos and videos, and providing mapping directions through GPS. One disadvantage is that a mobile OS cannot run full-featured productivity apps such as the desktop version of Microsoft Office.

Use Android

Developed by Google, **Android** is a mobile OS based on Linux designed to run on many types of smartphones and tablets. Like Linux, Android is open-source software with a permissive license. This means that device manufacturers can modify the operating system to fit the needs of their hardware, and that independent developers can create apps to run on these devices.

Android uses a touch interface that centers on a home screen with rows of app icons. **Figure 3-20** shows the home screen on a Samsung tablet. The home screen is the hub for navigating Android, similar to a desktop on PC operating systems.

Figure 3-20: Android home screen

Search the web

App menu button

Google apps

Android's strengths include its personalization features, ability to run on a range of devices, and its apps. You can download Android apps from the Google Play Store, the primary website that provides games, media players, productivity apps, and other software, often free of charge. Unlike iOS, Android includes a file manager for working with files.

Weaknesses include a slower performance on some devices than that of other mobile operating systems, and frequent updates that device manufacturers control. Some manufacturers offer updates only to a limited selection of smartphones and tablets, leaving other users with outdated software.

Use iOS

Developed by Apple, **iOS** runs only on Apple mobile devices, including the iPhone, iPad, and iPod Touch, and is derived from macOS. Apple Watch runs an operating system called watchOS, which is based on iOS. Like Android, iOS focuses on a touch interface. As shown in **Figure 3-21**, the home screen displays a transparent status bar at the top, icons for apps in the middle, and a dock at the bottom for icons such as email, phone, browser, and music. When you swipe to display another screen of icons for additional apps, the status bar and dock do not change.

Hot Technology Now

According to Strategy Analytics, global shipments of tablets are 64% Android, 22% iOS, and 14% Windows.

Figure 3-21: iOS on Apple devices

Transparent status bar

Apple Watch runs watchOS, based on iOS

Static dock

Source: Apple Computer

Strengths of iOS include its streamlined, fluid user experience, which comes from the ease and consistency of its interface. The quality and number of apps provided with iOS or available for installation are high. You download and install iOS apps exclusively from the Apple App Store, which has strict standards for function and security. Apple also provides annual upgrades to iOS through direct download to all compatible devices.

One drawback of iOS is device selection—iOS is available only on Apple mobile devices, which are usually more expensive than other devices from other manufacturers. Another weakness is that personalization features are limited. For example, the home screen always displays rows of icons, though you can change the home screen background.

Use Windows Phone

Windows Phone is the mobile OS from Microsoft intended to run on certain brands of smartphones, including Nokia Lumina and HTC. Windows Phone provides a touch interface similar to the Windows 10 Start menu. In fact, the home screen in

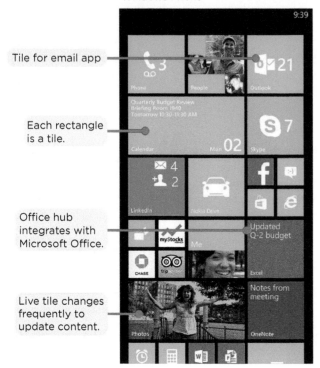

Figure 3-22: Start screen on Windows Phone

Tile for email app

Each rectangle is a tile.

Office hub integrates with Microsoft Office.

Live tile changes frequently to update content.

Windows Phone is called the Start screen. See **Figure 3-22**. It displays **tiles**, which are links to apps, tools, and items such as webpages and contacts. They are called **live tiles** because they change depending on the status or changes to the app. For example, the tile for the email app displays the number of unread messages. A popular feature in Windows Phone is the ability to resize and move the tiles on the Start screen.

Integration among apps is a strength of Windows Phone, which shares content in locations called **hubs**. For example, the Pictures hub shows photos taken with the built-in camera and those posted on social networks including Facebook and Twitter. The Office hub coordinates mobile versions of Microsoft Office apps and their desktop counterparts, which is a big advantage for business users.

Drawbacks to Windows Phone are that it is available on only a handful of devices and currently offers far fewer apps than Android or iOS. However, the number of apps is growing. All are available at the Windows Phone Store.

Select a Mobile Operating System

When selecting a mobile operating system, most users consider five criteria: ease of use, performance, flexibility, range of devices, and number of apps. Performance refers to how reliably the OS performs tasks such as connecting phone calls and running apps. Flexibility refers to how much you can customize the OS.

To select the right mobile OS for you, determine which of the five criteria you consider the most important, and then choose the OS that ranks best in those criteria. Read reviews by users and independent technology experts to find current rankings.

Describe File Basics

The Bottom Line

- To save a file, you must give it a name and choose where you want to store it on your computer.
- To understand how to use a file, you examine its properties and identify its format.
- To protect your files, you back them up.

file | executable file | data file | filenaming convention | extension | directory | path | kilobyte (KB) | megabyte (MB) | gigabyte (GB) | read-only file | file format | native format | Clipboard | source folder | destination folder | compress | extract | archive | backup

You've been working on a screenplay that is sure to make a big splash as a hit movie. You want to know what to do to preserve your creative work and send it to a Hollywood agent. Your most important task is to save the screenplay as a file on a storage device, the cloud, or on your computer.

Define Files

What exactly is a computer file? It's a named collection of data on a storage medium such as a hard disk or USB flash drive. A **file** provides a compact way to store data, whether it's a document, photo, video, email message, computer program, or music.

Files can be divided into two categories. The first category is **executable files**, which are programs containing instructions that tell your computer how to perform, or execute, specific tasks. When you select a program to start, the computer runs the program's executable file.

The second category is **data files**, which contain data such as words, numbers, and pictures that you can manipulate. For example, a document you create or open using Word is a data file.

Figure 3-23: Working with files

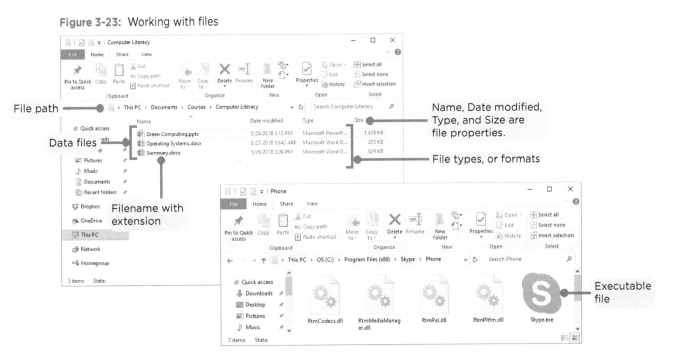

File path

Data files

Filename with extension

Name, Date modified, Type, and Size are file properties.

File types, or formats

Executable file

Name Files

Every file on a computer has a name. When you save a file, you must give it a name that follows rules called **filenaming conventions**. See Figure 3-24.

Each OS has its own filenaming conventions. For example, Windows and macOS filenames can contain up to 255 characters, including spaces and numbers. Windows does not allow filenames to contain some symbols such as the asterisk or slash, while macOS prohibits only the colon.

Most filenames include an **extension**, or a short identifier separated from the main part of the filename by a dot, as in *Screenplay Scene 1.docx*. File extensions provide clues about a file's contents. For example, .docx files are Microsoft Word documents. Windows .exe files and macOS .app files are executable files containing computer programs. Applications automatically add the correct extension when you save a data file.

Figure 3-24: Typical filename

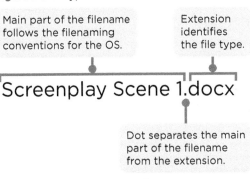

Main part of the filename follows the filenaming conventions for the OS.

Extension identifies the file type.

Screenplay Scene 1.docx

Dot separates the main part of the filename from the extension.

Store Files

To open or save a file, you must know the file's location, which is one of the storage devices on your computer.

- Windows and Linux identify each storage device by a device letter. For example, the main hard drive is usually drive C.
- Instead of using letters, macOS assigns a name to each storage device. For example, the main hard drive is called Macintosh HD.
- For each storage device on your computer, the OS maintains a list of files called a **directory**. The main directory is the root directory, which can be divided into smaller lists. Each list is called a subdirectory, or folder.
- To indicate a file's location, you use a file specification, or **path**. On a PC, a path includes the drive letter, one or more folder names, the filename, and the extension. The parts of the file path are separated by a backslash or an arrow. So, the path to the file might be C > This PC > Documents > Screenplay Scene 1.docx

Review File Properties

Every file has properties such as its name, type, location, and size. File properties also include the dates when the file was created, modified, and last accessed. The modified date is useful if you have several versions of a file and want to identify the most recent version.

#syssoftware

Every file has a set of unique properties, which can vary depending on file type. For example, a song has a Contributing artists property, an image has a Dimensions property indicating the size of the photo, while a text document does not have either.

The OS assigns some properties to files, such as type or format, and keeps other properties up to date, such as date, size, and location. A file manager such as File Explorer displays a selection of file properties, including Name, Size, Type, and Date modified.

File size is a significant property and usually is measured in **kilobytes (KB)** (thousands of bytes), **megabytes (MB)** (millions of bytes), or **gigabytes (GB)** (billions of bytes). The more data a file contains, the larger the file. Large files such as videos fill up storage space faster than do small files such as text documents.

You can find all of a file's properties in its Properties dialog box, including whether it is a **read-only file**, which cannot be modified or deleted.

Define File Formats

File format refers to the organization and layout of data in the file. For example, text files have a file format different from those of graphics files. Graphics data can be stored in many file formats, such as JPEG or PNG. The file extension usually reflects the file format.

If you change a graphics file named Beach.jpg to Beach.docx, however, the file is still stored in the JPEG format, not the Word format. The data elements in the file are arranged in a way unique to JPEG files.

An application can always work with files in its **native format**, which is the format of files created in that application. An application might also work with other formats. For example, Word can work with doc files, docx files, and pdf files. An application typically lists these file formats in its Open dialog box. For example, Figure 3-25 shows native file formats for Word.

Figure 3-25: Microsoft Word file formats

All Word Documents ⌄
All Files
All Word Documents
Word Documents
Word Macro-Enabled Documents
XML Files
Word 97-2003 Documents
All Web Pages
All Word Templates
Word Templates
Word Macro-Enabled Templates
Word 97-2003 Templates
Rich Text Format
Text Files
OpenDocument Text
PDF Files
Recover Text from Any File
WordPerfect 5.x
WordPerfect 6.x

Select, Copy, and Move Files

If you want to copy or move more than one file from one location to another, you must first select the files. Table 3-4 lists methods of selecting files using Windows 10. If you select a group of files but want to remove one from the group, you can deselect, or clear the file's selection. The same methods work with folders.

Table 3-4: Methods of selecting files

To select	Use this method
Files listed sequentially in a folder window	Click the first item, hold down the SHIFT key, click the last item, and then release the SHIFT key.
Files not listed sequentially in a folder window	Press and hold the CTRL key, click each item you want to select, and then release the CTRL key.
All files in a folder window	Click the **Select all** button in the Select group on the Home tab or press the CTRL+A keys.
To clear	Use this method
One file in a group of selected files	Press and hold the CTRL key, click each file you want to remove from the selection, and then release the CTRL key.
All files in a group of selected files	Click a blank area of the folder window.

After you select files, you can copy or move them using one of several methods. Some methods use the **Clipboard**, a temporary holding area for files and information that you copy or move from one place (the **source folder**) and plan to use somewhere else (the **destination folder**). Table 3-5 lists the methods for copying and moving files in Windows 10. The same methods apply to folders.

Table 3-5: Methods of copying and moving files

Method	How to copy	How to move
Shortcut menu	Right-click a file, click Copy on the shortcut menu, right-click the destination folder, and then click Paste.	Right-click a file, click Cut on the shortcut menu, right-click the destination folder, and then click Paste.
Key combination	Click a file, press the CTRL+C keys, click the destination folder, and then press the CTRL+V keys.	Click a file, press the CTRL+X keys, click the destination folder, and then press the CTRL+V keys.
Drag	If the destination folder is on a different drive, drag a file to the destination folder; if on the same drive, press and hold CTRL while dragging.	If the destination folder is on the same drive, drag a file to the destination folder.
Right-drag	Using a mouse or other pointing device, point to a file, hold down the right button, and then drag the file to a new location. Release the button, and then click Copy here on the shortcut menu.	Using a mouse or other pointing device, point to a file, hold down the right button, and then drag the file to a new location. Release the button, and then click Move here on the shortcut menu.

Compress and Uncompress Files

You can **compress** one or more files so they use less space when stored on a disk. You often need to compress files before you share or transfer them, such as when you attach files to an email message before sending it to someone else. Before you can open and edit a compressed file, you must uncompress it, or **extract** it.

PC operating systems include utilities for compressing files. Mobile operating systems often do not include file compression utilities, though you can install file compression apps such as WinZip. A compressed file usually has a .zip extension and is called an **archive**.

To compress files in Windows, do the following:
- Select the files you want to compress.
- Right-click the selected files, point to **Send to** on the shortcut menu, and then click **Compressed (zipped) folder**.

The compressed file has the same name as the file you right-clicked, but uses a .zip extension.

To uncompress files in Windows, do the following:
- Double-click the compressed file (the one with a .zip extension).
- Select the files you want to extract, and then drag them to a folder.

Back Up Files

Have you ever deleted or copied over an important document? Have you lost files after a power failure or virus infection? Everyone has experienced these types of data misadventures. You can't prevent all data disasters, so you need to create **backups**, or copies of files that you store in case the original files are damaged. A backup is a special type of file that allows you to restore data to the original storage location or a replacement device. Backup software can monitor the files on your hard disk, watch for changes, and then make the same changes to files in your backup, which is usually contained on an external hard drive or online server.

To protect your data, frequently back up all the folders containing data files using a backup utility provided by your operating system or a software vendor. To protect your entire system, occasionally create a full system backup.

#syssoftware

In Windows 10, the backup software is called File History. Once an hour by default, it creates backup copies of files you created or modified. The backup software in macOS is called Time Machine, and it works in a similar way.

#syssoftware

To back up files on an iOS device, you can use iCloud or iTunes. To have iCloud back up your device automatically every day, you turn on iCloud Backup in Settings.

#syssoftware

A full system backup is a duplicate of your files at a particular time. Windows also lets you create a restore point, which is a duplicate of your system settings. Use a backup to replace a lost or damaged file. Use a restore point to repair system settings.

Work with Folders

folder | File Explorer | Quick access list

Managing files is an essential skill to master when you work with computers. It allows you to store important data, give files meaningful names, and find files quickly. You store files in folders and subfolders with descriptive names in much the same way you store paper documents in labeled folders in a file cabinet.

Define Folders

Imagine storing a list of your favorite musicians and movies, 250 videos, 1000 songs, and an entire music history book in a file folder. All of these items (or their digital equivalents) can be stored in a single **folder** on your computer's hard drive.

Figure 3-26: Using folders

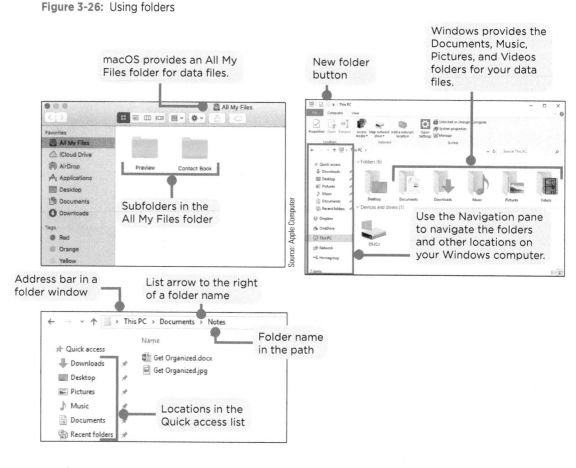

macOS provides an All My Files folder for data files.

New folder button

Windows provides the Documents, Music, Pictures, and Videos folders for your data files.

Subfolders in the All My Files folder

Source: Apple Computer

Use the Navigation pane to navigate the folders and other locations on your Windows computer.

Address bar in a folder window

List arrow to the right of a folder name

Folder name in the path

Locations in the Quick access list

The easiest way to think of a digital folder is to consider the metaphor of a paper folder. You can move documents from one folder to another in a file cabinet, and you can move folders to different drawers. You can also rename folders by changing the name on the label. You can do all of this with digital folders as well.

- By default, Windows includes the Documents, Music, Pictures, and Videos folders for your data files.
- You access all the folders on a Windows computer using **File Explorer**, the Windows file manager. Click the folder name in the navigation pane of a folder window to display its contents in the right pane.
- When you start File Explorer, it opens to show the contents of the **Quick access list**, which are the folders you use frequently. You can pin folders to the Quick access list so they are always easily available to you.

Navigate Folders

Folders let you store your documents in ways that make sense to you. You can customize folder names, folder hierarchy, and folder contents so that the organization of your data is logical and consistent with the way you work.

If you are taking courses at school, for example, you can store your documents for each semester in a folder, then for each course in separate folders within each semester. Each folder can have many subfolders, so for each course you can have folders for notes, papers, or whatever you want. You can navigate among folders using a few different methods:

- Double-click a folder to open it.
- Click a folder name in the path shown in the Address bar to open the folder.
- Click a list arrow to the right of a folder name in the path to display a list of subfolders. You can click a subfolder name to open it.
- Click a folder name and click the **Open** button.
- Type the path to the folder in the Address bar.

Imagine that you recently saw a file that you want to work with, but have forgotten where you stored it. You can use the Recent folders feature to find the file. To do so, click Recent folders in the Quick access list.

Create and Rename Folders

You can create a new folder in a file manager such as File Explorer or Finder. For example, you might want to add a folder to your Pictures folder for photos you took during spring break.

Create a folder: In Windows, you click the **New folder** button to create a new folder. Windows gives the new folder the default name "New folder," but you can replace the default name with one that's more descriptive.

Rename a folder: You can also rename a folder (or file) in three ways:
- Right-click the folder name and then click **Rename** on the shortcut menu.
- Click the folder name to select it and then click it again to make it editable.
- Click the folder, and then click the **Rename** button in the Organize group on the Home tab.
- When the name is selected, type the new name and press ENTER to change it.

Expand and Collapse Folders

To make navigating multiple folders easier, you can expand and collapse folders to display and hide folder contents.

In the navigation pane of a folder window, a folder name with a right-pointing arrow to its left has subfolders. A folder name with no arrow either is empty or contains only documents. See **Figure 3-27**.

You click a right-pointing arrow to display the subfolders. When you do, the arrow points down. To collapse a top level folder, you click the down-pointing arrow.

#syssoftware

Windows and macOS use "folder" as the term for a file container. Many distributions of Linux use the term "directory" instead.

Figure 3-27: Expanding folders

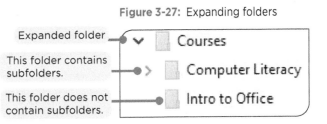

Expanded folder

This folder contains subfolders.

This folder does not contain subfolders.

Move, Copy, and Delete Folders

You can move and copy folders in the folder hierarchy. Moving a folder moves its contents as well. Copying a folder also makes a copy of its contents.

For example, the Personal folder in **Figure 3-28** contains a subfolder called Budget 2018. You want to move that folder to the Budgets folder where it makes more sense.

- **Move a folder**: To move a folder, select it and then drag it over the name of the folder you want to move it to. As you drag, the words "Move to" appear in front of the name of the destination folder. If you move the folder by mistake, you can press CTRL+Z to move it back to its original location.
- **Copy a folder**: If you want to copy a folder and its contents instead of moving it, you can press the CTRL key as you drag. When you do, the words "Copy to" appear in front of the name of the destination folder.

Figure 3-28: Moving folders

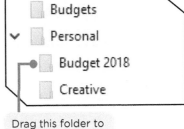

Drag this folder to the Budgets folder to move it there.

To delete a folder and its contents, select the folder and then press the DELETE key. You can also right-click the folder name and click **Delete** on the shortcut menu; or you can click the folder name, and then click the **Delete** button in the Organize group on the Home tab.

No matter which method you use to delete a folder, you will be prompted to confirm the deletion before the operation is complete. If you delete a folder by mistake, you can undo the deletion by pressing CTRL+Z or restore the folder using the Recycle Bin if your computer has one.

Manage Files

Save command | Save As command | USB port | cloud

The Bottom Line

- Save your files on your hard drive, flash drive, or to the cloud so you can easily access them later.
- You should know how to navigate your computer so you can find and open files you've saved.

You often need to save files you receive from others, usually as attachments to email messages, or those you download from websites. If you are creating or editing a file, you should also save it frequently so you don't lose your work. File management rules apply to all types of files, whether they are spreadsheets, photographs, or documents.

Use Save and Save As

The first time you select a command to save a file on a PC, the operating system displays the Save As dialog box or screen, which includes controls that let you specify where to store the file and what filename to use. **Figure 3-29** shows the Save As dialog box for Windows 10.

Figure 3-29: Save As dialog box

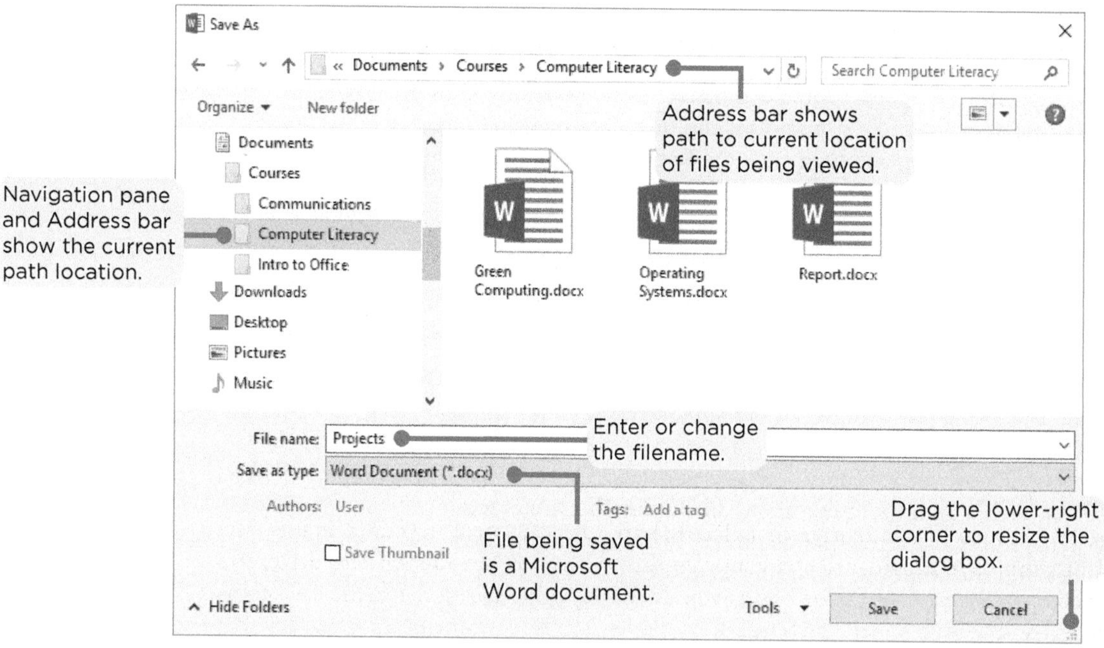

Suppose that after saving the file shown in **Figure 3-29**, which is a Word document, you open it and then make a few changes. Now you have two choices for saving the file:

- **Save command**: Use the Save command to save a document with the same name and in the same location. For example, in Word, you select the Save button on the Quick Access toolbar to save the document without changing its filename or storage location.
- **Save As command**: Use the Save As command to save the document using the Save As dialog box or screen to specify a different name, file type, or storage location. In Word, you click the File tab to display the Save As command.

Save a File to a Location on Your Hard Drive

The Save As dialog box or screen is displayed when you save a file for the first time or when you select the Save As command. The Save As dialog box or screen selects a storage location as follows:

- **New files**: By default, most operating systems save particular types of files in certain locations on your hard drive. For example, when you save a new document in Windows 10 the operating system presents the Documents folder as the storage location.
- **Existing files**: When you save an existing file, the operating system assumes you want to save the file in its current location. For example, if you open a document from the Projects folder in the Documents folder, and then select the Save As command to save the document, Windows displays the Projects folder as the storage location.

In either case, you can navigate to a different location. The following steps explain how to use the Windows 10 Save As dialog box to save a file in a folder on your hard drive.

1. **Open the Save As dialog box.**

   Use the Save command for new files or the Save As command for other files. In Office 365, click the Browse button on the Save As screen to open the Save As dialog box.

2. **Verify the current location.**

   The Address bar in the Save As dialog box shows the current folder. You can widen the dialog box to display the complete location in the Address bar. The Documents, Downloads, Music, Pictures, and Videos folders (and their subfolders) are on your hard drive and are good places to save your files.

3. **Navigate to the folder on your hard drive where you want to save the file.**

   In the navigation pane, click an expand icon next to a location such as the Documents folder to display the folders it contains. Continue clicking expand icons until the folder where you want to save the file is displayed in the navigation pane.

4. **Select the folder where you want to save the file.**

   In the navigation pane, click the folder to select it. You can also double-click a folder in the right pane to select and open the folder.

5. **Save the file.**

   Click the **Save** button in the Save As dialog box to save the file.

Save a File to a Flash Drive

When you save a file to a flash drive, you are saving it in a storage device separate from your hard drive. The advantage of using a flash drive is that you can remove it from a computer and then use it on a different computer.

To save a file to a flash drive, first place the drive in a **USB port** on your computer. The USB port is a rectangular slot on your computer where you can attach a flash drive. You then open the Save As dialog box as you do for any other location: use the Save command to save a file for the first time and use the Save As command to save an existing file to a different location. The following steps explain how to save a file to a flash drive using Windows 10.

1. **Attach the flash drive to your computer, and then open the Save As dialog box.**

   Insert the flash drive into a USB port on your computer, if necessary. Use the Save command for new files or the Save As command for other files. In Office 365, click the Browse button on the Save As screen to open the Save As dialog box.

2. **Verify the current location.**

   The Address bar in the Save As dialog box shows the current folder. Unless you opened the file from the flash drive, the current folder is probably on the hard drive.

#syssoftware

To make your electronic media such as songs and videos easy to find, take advantage of the folders built into Windows for each type of data, such as the Pictures folder for photos, Music folder for songs, and the Videos folder for videos. You can also create folders dedicated to other types of media such as e-books.

3. **Navigate to the flash drive.**

In the navigation pane, click the expand icon next to This PC to display its locations, if necessary. The flash drive usually has a name similar to "Removable Disk" and a drive letter other than C. For example, your flash drive might appear as Removable Disk (E:).

4. **Select the folder where you want to save the file.**

Click the expand icon next to the flash drive name, and then click a folder on the flash drive to select it.

5. **Save the file.**

Type a filename, and then click the **Save** button in the Save As dialog box to save the file in the folder you selected.

Save a File to OneDrive

Hot Technology Now

If you don't have a Microsoft account, you can sign up for one by using your browser to go to outlook.com or to search for "Sign up for Microsoft account."

Besides saving files on your hard drive or a flash drive attached to your computer, you can save them in the **cloud**, which is a storage location on a server. You can access files stored on the cloud from any device connected to the Internet. Microsoft Office apps can use OneDrive, a Microsoft product for saving files in the cloud. When you sign up for a Microsoft account, Microsoft creates a OneDrive for you and reserves space in it for your files. If you are using Windows 10 on your own computer and use your email address as your username, you most likely have a Microsoft account. (You must have a Microsoft account to use OneDrive.) Other cloud storage options include Dropbox and iCloud.

The following steps explain how to save a Microsoft Office 365 file to your OneDrive.

1. **Display the Save As options in Backstage view.**

Click the **File** tab, and then click **Save As** to display the Save As options. See **Figure 3-30**.

Figure 3-30: Saving a file to your OneDrive

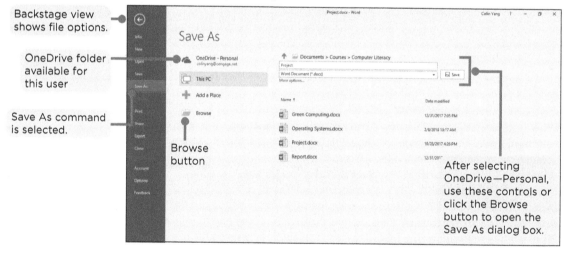

Backstage view shows file options.

OneDrive folder available for this user

Save As command is selected.

Browse button

After selecting OneDrive—Personal, use these controls or click the Browse button to open the Save As dialog box.

2. **Select your OneDrive.**

Your OneDrive appears as OneDrive—Personal in the Save As list.

3. **Navigate to a folder on your OneDrive.**

Use the controls in the right pane or click the **Browse** button to open the Save As dialog box, which displays folders on your OneDrive, including Documents, Favorites, and Public by default.

4. **Open the folder where you want to save the file.**

   Double-click the OneDrive folder where you want to save the file.

5. **Save the file.**

   Type a filename, and then click the **Save** button to save the file.

Open a Saved File

You open a saved file using the same techniques as when saving the file, except you use a different dialog box or window. In most PC operating systems, you can use a file manager such as File Explorer in Windows 10 or the Finder in macOS to open a saved file. If you are working in an application, you use the Open dialog box or screen to open a file.

The following steps explain how to use the File Explorer in Windows 10 to open a file saved on your hard drive or flash drive.

On the Job Now

If you are working in a team and need to share files with other members, compress the files into a single zip archive to make it easy to transfer and manage the files.

1. **Make sure your computer can access the saved file.**

   If you saved the file on a flash drive, attach the flash drive to your computer. If you saved the file on your hard drive, your computer can access it.

2. **Open File Explorer.**

   Display the desktop, and then click the File Explorer icon on the taskbar to open a File Explorer window.

3. **Navigate to the location of the saved file.**

   In the navigation pane, click the expand icon next to This PC to display its locations, including the flash drive. If you saved the file on a hard drive, click to expand icons as necessary to display the folder containing the file.

4. **Open the folder containing the saved file.**

   In the navigation pane, click the folder containing the saved file to display the file in the right pane.

5. **Open the file.**

   Double-click the file to open it in the same application used to create, edit, or save the file. The file extension indicates which application will start when you double-click the file. For example, Word files have a .docx extension, so if you double-click a file with a .docx extension, Word starts and opens the file. If you do not see the file extension, the operating system is hiding it by default. You might see icons that represent the file type.

The following steps explain how to use the Open dialog box in a Microsoft Office 365 application to open a saved file.

1. **Make sure your computer can access the saved file.**

   If you saved the file on a flash drive, attach the flash drive to your computer. If you saved the file on your hard drive or in your cloud account such as OneDrive, your computer can access it.

2. **Display the Open screen.**

   In the Office application where you want to open the file, click the **File** tab, and then click **Open** to display locations containing your files, including OneDrive. From here, you can open a file in three ways:
   - If the file you want to open appears in the list of recent files on the right, click the filename to open the file.
   - If you saved the file in your OneDrive, select your OneDrive, which appears as OneDrive—Personal in the Open list, and then click the **Browse** button to display the Open dialog box.
   - If you saved the file on a flash drive or hard drive, select **This PC**, and then click the **Browse** button to display the Open dialog box.

3. **Open the folder containing the saved file**.

Use the tools in the Open dialog box to open the folder containing the saved file. For example, double-click a OneDrive folder to display its contents or use the navigation pane to display the contents of a folder on a flash drive.

4. **Open the file**.

Double-click the file to open it in the current application.

Customize Microsoft Windows

default setting | shortcut icon | Settings app | Control Panel | property | lock screen | desktop theme | screen resolution | native resolution | screen saver | sound scheme | pinned item | Action Center | user account | Microsoft account | synchronize | local-only user account | administrator account | standard account

When you start working with a new computer, you use its **default settings**—those the operating system sets during installation. The defaults are fine, at first. However, as you learn your way around the computer, you'll probably want to change some settings to make your computer experience more personal, pleasant, and productive.

Figure 3-31: Customizing Windows

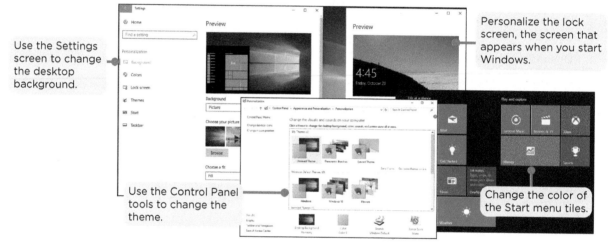

Use the Settings screen to change the desktop background.

Personalize the lock screen, the screen that appears when you start Windows.

Use the Control Panel tools to change the theme.

Change the color of the Start menu tiles.

#syssoftware

Use the Store button on the Windows 10 taskbar to find apps for organizing photos, watching videos, practice typing, playing games, learning a new language, and many more.

Customize Desktop Objects

You're ready to organize photos, watch videos, and play games on your new PC. Where do you start? The desktop. You can use the Desktop Icon Settings dialog box to add icons to the desktop, such as the This PC icon, which you open to display the drives on your computer. See **Figure 3-32**.

Another type of icon you can add to the desktop is a **shortcut icon**, which is indicated by a small arrow next to an icon that illustrates the application or program. You double-click a shortcut icon to run a program or open a file.

One way to customize the desktop is to move the taskbar. You also can make the taskbar larger, add toolbars to it, and hide the taskbar when you're not using it.

Use the Settings and Control Panel Windows

When you're ready to fine-tune Windows so it looks and works the way you want it to, head for the **Settings app** and the **Control Panel**. Both are collections of tools for customizing Windows. The Settings app runs on all types of Windows devices, including tablets and phones, and provides a touch-friendly interface with large icons and controls. For example, you change the desktop background and **lock screen** (the screen that appears when you start Windows) using the Settings app, as shown in **Figure 3-31**.

The Control Panel was designed for earlier versions of Windows and is being phased out of Windows 10. It provides access to traditional dialog boxes that let you select or change the **properties**, or characteristics, of an object. Both the Control Panel and the Settings app organize settings into categories so you can quickly find the tools you need to change the way Windows looks and behaves to better suit the way you work.

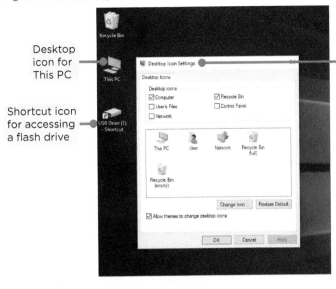

Figure 3-32: Desktop and shortcut icons

Desktop icon for This PC

Shortcut icon for accessing a flash drive

Desktop Icon Settings dialog box

Customize Display Settings

If you want to set your Windows computer apart from other computers, you can start by customizing your desktop.

In the Personalization category, the Settings app provides options for changing the appearance of your desktop, windows, and Start menu. If you select the Themes link, and then click Theme settings, the Control Panel's Personalization window opens, shown in **Figure 3-31**, where you can select a **desktop theme**, which is a predefined set of elements such as background images and colors.

You can use the Settings app or the Control Panel to adjust the screen resolution and color quality for up to two monitors. **Screen resolution** defines the number of pixels on a screen. If you set your screen resolution for more pixels, you can see more content on a screen without scrolling. Your monitor has an ideal setting, which is called its **native resolution**, but you can change it to suit your work style.

Customize Screen Savers and Sounds

Fun and security don't usually go together, but you can have both in one tool: a **screen saver**, which plays animations on your computer screen and hides work in progress while you're away from your computer.

A screen saver is a set of animated images or a slide show that appears after your computer is idle for a certain amount of time. When you move the pointer or press a key, the screen returns to its previous state. To secure a Windows computer, you can set the screen saver to request a password before it stops playing.

Another Windows setting you can personalize is the **sound scheme**, a set of sounds applied to Windows events, such as closing a program. Use the Sound dialog box to select a sound scheme or change individual sounds, such as the one that plays when you exit Windows.

Customize the Taskbar

The Windows taskbar contains the Start button, Cortana search box, pinned items, program buttons, and the notification area. See **Figure 3-33** on the next page.
- **Pinned items**: A **pinned item** is an icon that always appears on the taskbar, such as the Microsoft Edge and File Explorer icons.
- **Window buttons**: Other taskbar buttons are for open windows. If you open two or more windows in a single program, the windows are grouped on one taskbar button. You can change this setting to display each window as a separate button. You can drag taskbar buttons, including pinned items, to rearrange them in the order you prefer.

#syssoftware

All operating systems let you customize global settings such as passwords, power management, and the appearance of the desktop or home screen.

On the Job Now

Many businesses and schools use screen savers that promote new products or class offerings.

On the Job Now

Both macOS and Windows provide assistive technologies that help people with disabilities work productively with their computers. macOS includes features such as VoiceOver, Zoom, and Dictation, while Microsoft includes the Ease of Access Center.

Figure 3-33: Windows taskbar

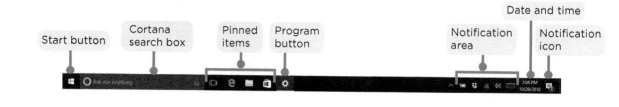

Figure 3-33: Windows taskbar

On the Job Now

The overuse of any keyboard may cause serious injury to your hands, wrists, arms, neck, or back. This injury is called carpal tunnel syndrome. Take breaks often and use proper ergonomics when typing to avoid carpal tunnel syndrome.

- **Notification area**: To keep the notification area free from clutter, you can select the icons you want to display all the time. To display the other icons, click the Show hidden icons button.
- **Action Center icon**: This icon displays a number to indicate how many messages are waiting for you in the **Action Center**, a panel that keeps track of your notifications. You can customize the taskbar to show or hide the Action Center icon.

Customize the Keyboard and Pointing Device

If you want to change how your keyboard responds to your keystrokes when working in Windows, use Cortana to search for "keyboard," and then click Keyboard in the search results to open the Keyboard Properties dialog box, where you can change settings that affect the keyboard speed.

Search for "keyboard" in the Settings app to select touch keyboard settings, such as whether to play key sounds as you type.

You also use the Settings app to customize your touchpad and mouse, if your computer has them. For example, you can select the primary mouse button and specify the sensitivity of your touchpad. Manufacturers of pointing devices often include options for their device in the Mouse Properties dialog box, which you open from the Settings app. See **Figure 3-34**.

Figure 3-34: Pointing device settings

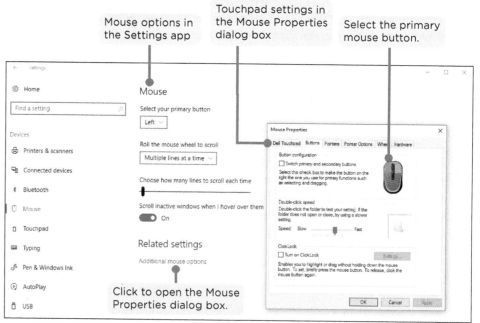

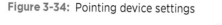

Set Up User Accounts

User accounts protect your computer against unauthorized access. A user account includes information such as a user name, or user ID, and a password. A user account also includes permissions that indicate which files and folders you can access and what changes you can make to the computer. Finally, a user account keeps track of your personal preferences, such as your desktop theme or screen saver.

You can create two types of accounts in Windows 10:

- **Microsoft account**—This type of account provides access to Microsoft cloud computing services, such as Outlook.com for email and OneDrive for file storage. With this type of user account, you can use Windows 10 and some Windows apps to access files and other data stored in your online Microsoft account. If you run Windows 10 on more than one PC, you can also **synchronize**, or sync, (that is, to make sure data on the two devices matches) your settings, preferences, and some apps so that all your PCs are set up the same way. The advantage of a Microsoft account is that you provide one user name and one password to connect to the cloud and to sync settings.

- **Local-only user account**—This type of account accesses only resources on your computer. If you want to allow family members or other people to use your computer occasionally, you can set up a local-only user account for those users.

In addition, the Microsoft or local-only user account can be an administrator or standard account, which determines how much control the user has over the computer. See **Figure 3-35**.

#syssoftware

Go to twitter.com, then search for @SAMTechNow, the book's Twitter account, and follow @SAMTechNow to get tweets on your home page.

#syssoftware

You can customize your user account by changing your picture or displayed name, for example. The administrator account can customize other settings such as permission to access a folder containing system software.

Figure 3-35: Windows user account

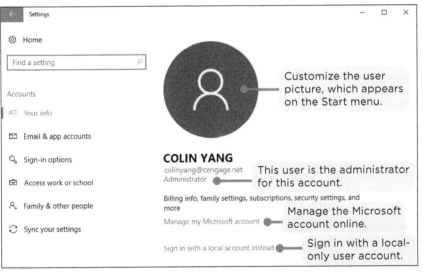

The first account you set up on a new Windows computer is an **administrator account**, which has full access to the computer to add other user accounts and install software. **Standard accounts** are designed for everyday computing. You can access the files and folders in your account, but not the files and folders of other users.

Chapter Review

Identify System Software

1. What is system software and what types of programs does it include?
2. What is the difference between system software and application software?

Define Operating Systems

3. What is the purpose of an operating system?
4. Name four types of operating systems and briefly describe them.

Describe Common OS Tasks

5. What are the four resources that an operating system manages?
6. What types of computer tasks does an operating system typically handle?

Manage Your Computer's Windows

7. Name three window elements that all operating systems have in common.
8. Explain how to switch windows in various operating systems.

Describe Common OS Features

9. Name five features that operating systems with graphical user interfaces share.
10. What is the purpose of a disk utility? What is the purpose of a file utility?

Compare PC Operating Systems

11. What are four popular PC operating systems in use today?
12. Compare Windows with macOS.

Compare Mobile Operating Systems

13. What is a mobile operating system? What are the three popular mobile operating systems in use today?

Describe File Basics

14. What is a file? What are the two main categories of files you use on a computer?
15. What is significant about file formats?

Work with Folders

16. Describe two ways to open a folder in Windows.

Manage Files

17. What is the main difference between the Save command and the Save As command?
18. Describe one way to open a saved file using an Office application.

Customize Microsoft Windows

19. What tools do you use to customize the Windows desktop?
20. What is a desktop theme?

Test Your Knowledge Now

1. _____ software is the software that runs a computer.
   a. System
   b. Desktop
   c. Command
   d. GUI

2. File management programs such as File Explorer are examples of _____.
   a. mobile operating systems
   b. utility software
   c. data files
   d. user interface software

3. The _____ is the set of programs that manages and coordinates all the activities on your computer.
   a. boot manager
   b. multiprocessing software
   c. disk cleanup software
   d. operating system

4. As you work with a computer, many activities, or _____, compete for your operating system's attention.
   a. processes
   b. parallels
   c. cores
   d. multithreads

5. During startup, the computer performs the _____ to check crucial system components.
   a. processing pass
   b. read-only memory (ROM) test
   c. buffer check
   d. power-on self-test (POST)

6. To keep the computer running smoothly, the OS manages _____, such as text you type on a keyboard, and _____, such as data displayed on the screen.
   a. spooling / buffers
   b. device drivers / hardware
   c. input / output
   d. income / outcome

7. A(n) _____ is an object typical of a graphical user interface.
   a. icon
   b. command line
   c. General Public License (GPL)
   d. kernel

8. A(n) _____ displays an app running on the desktop.
   a. folder window
   b. program window
   c. icon
   d. button

9. A(n) _____ utility reduces the size of a file so it takes up less storage space on a disk.
   a. disk cleanup
   b. search
   c. file compression
   d. active window

10. Four popular PC operating systems are Windows, macOS, Chrome, and _____.
    a. watchOS
    b. iOS
    c. Linux
    d. Android

11. Developed by Google, _____ is a mobile OS based on Linux and is designed to run on many types of smartphones and tablets.
    a. Embedded OS
    b. Windows Phone
    c. iOS
    d. Android

12. Developed by Apple, _____ runs only on Apple mobile devices, including the iPhone, iPad, and iPod Touch.
    a. iOS
    b. macOS
    c. watchOS
    d. Android

13. A(n) _____ file is a program containing instructions.
    a. data
    b. extension
    c. executable
    d. path

14. _____ refers to the organization and layout of data in the file.
    a. File sector
    b. File format
    c. Fragmentation
    d. File property

15. Some methods of copying and moving files use the _____, a temporary holding area for files and data.
    a. native format
    b. Temporary folder
    c. taskbar
    d. Clipboard

16. In the navigation pane of a folder window, you click a right-pointing arrow next to a folder name to _____ the folder.
    a. expand
    b. rename
    c. delete
    d. collapse

17. Use the _____ command to save the document with the same name and in the same location.
    a. Open
    b. Save As
    c. OneDrive
    d. Save

18. Settings the operating system sets during installation are called the _____ settings.
    a. shortcut
    b. desktop
    c. theme
    d. default

19. The _____ is the screen that first appears when you turn on a Windows computer.
    a. lock screen
    b. Settings app
    c. screen saver
    d. pinned items screen

20. If you have more than one PC with a Microsoft account, you can _____ your settings and preferences so that they match on all devices.
    a. optimize
    b. synchronize
    c. synthesize
    d. export

21. In the space next to each term below, write the letter of the phrase that defines it:
    a. path
    b. compress
    c. data file
    d. boot process
    e. taskbar

    _____ A specification that includes a drive letter, one or more folder names, a filename, and an extension

    _____ What you can do to one or more files so they use less space on a disk

    _____ A series of events that begin when you turn on the computer

    _____ Where the Start button, pinned items, and notification area appear

    _____ Contains words, numbers, or pictures that you can manipulate

Try This Now

1: Get Started with Windows

Note: This assignment requires the use of Windows 10.

Technology continues to change, but knowing what has changed as the operating system updates is important. Using the Cortana search tool in Windows, type **Get Started** to find and then watch videos on using the new features in Windows.

    a. Watch a video about Windows Hello and then read the Windows Hello documentation. Write a paragraph of at least 100 of your own words about Windows Hello.

    b. Watch a video about the Maps app and then read the Maps documentation. Write a paragraph of at least 100 of your own words about Maps.

    c. Read about Microsoft Edge. Create a list of four features of Microsoft Edge and then explain each feature in your own words.

2: macOS Support

Being versatile and switching from a Windows PC to a Mac is helpful in the business world. Using a Mac computer or the site apple.com, find the macOS support webpages, and then answer the following questions by searching the help topics. If you are using a Mac, be sure to identify your version of the operating system.

    a. What does the F11 function key on a keyboard do?

    b. What steps do you follow to take a screenshot (a picture of the entire screen)?

    c. macOS includes VoiceOver, a built-in screen reader that describes aloud what appears on your screen and speaks the text in documents, webpages, and windows. How do you turn on VoiceOver?

Mobile OS

3: Mobile Operating Systems

The latest versions of Android, iOS, and Windows Phone offer exciting new features for mobile devices.

    a. Select one of the three major smartphone platforms. If money were no object, which new phone model would you select today? What is the price of this phone?

    b. List five features of the mobile OS on your selected phone, and then explain each feature in your own words.

    c. Write a paragraph describing the three smartphone apps you use the most.

Critical Thinking Now

1: What's New in Windows?

A new generation of updated features is available in the latest operating system produced by Microsoft. Research the most recent version of Windows and create a table listing six features that were not in the previous release in the first column and an explanation of each feature in the second column. Be prepared to explain which feature is the most interesting to you and why.

Magnifier

RESEARCH

2: What's New for Mac?

Cutting-edge technology is showcased within the latest version of macOS. Research the most recent version of macOS and create a table listing six features that were not in the previous release in the first column and an explanation of each feature in the second column. Be prepared to explain which feature is the most interesting to you and why.

3: Advantages and Disadvantages of Upgrading to Windows 10

Companies all over the world are weighing the advantages and disadvantages of moving to a new operating system. Research the advantages and disadvantages of upgrading to Windows 10 and write a paper of 200 words or more summarizing what you learned.

Ethical Issues Now

Accessibility options are built into Windows to help people who may have trouble using their computers due to sight limitations or other special needs. Your boss has requested that you create a chart of the Ease of Access features in Windows 10 with the name of the feature in the first column and the explanation of that feature in the right column. Name at least five accessibility features.

Team Up Now—Wolfram Alpha Data Analysis

Wolfram Alpha is a data knowledge engine developed by Wolfram ResearchShare. Wolfram Alpha connects to online databases worldwide to answer your questions. Each team member should perform the following searches at the Wolfram Alpha website (wolframalpha.com). Copy the information you find and then paste it into a Word document.

    a. Compare Microsoft and Apple stock prices.
    b. Search for your school's name.
    c. What is the current price range of your favorite laptop, such as a MacBook or Surface Pro?
    d. What is the current price range of your favorite smartphone? How much does the smartphone cost in euros?
    e. What are the dimensions of your favorite tablet?
    f. When was Steve Jobs (founder of Apple Computer) born? What was the weather like in your city on that date?
    g. How many visits a day for the website facebook.com?
    h. List the population, location, climate, and any other significant data about one of your favorite major cities in North America.

As a team, compare your responses. For each question, locate the sources at the bottom of each results page. List one of the sources for each response. Submit the responses and sources of each team member to your instructor.

Key Terms

Action Center
active window
administrator account
Android
archive
backup
boot process
bootstrap program
buffer
button
check box
Chrome OS
Clipboard
Close button
cloud
command-line interface
compress
Control Panel
data file
decompress
default setting
defragmentation utility
desktop
desktop theme
destination folder
device driver
dialog box
directory
disk cleanup utility
distribution
Dock
embedded OS
executable file
extension
extract
file
file compression utility
File Explorer
file format
file management utility
filenaming convention
folder
folder window

General Public License (GPL)
gigabyte (GB)
graphical user interface (GUI)
hub
icon
input
iOS
kernel
kilobyte
Linux
list box
live tile
local-only user account
lock screen
macOS
Maximize button
megabyte (MB)
menu
Microsoft account
Minimize button
mobile operating system (OS)
multiple-selection list box
multiprocessing
multitasking
multithreading
native format
native resolution
network OS
notification area
OneDrive
operating system (OS)
option button
output
parallel processing
path
personal computer (PC) operating
  system
pinned item
platform
Plug and Play (PnP)
power-on self-test (POST)
process
program window

property
Quick access list
radio button
random access memory (RAM)
read-only file
Recycle Bin
resource
Restore Down button
ROM (read-only memory)
Save As command
Save command
screen resolution
screen saver
search utility
sector
server OS
Settings app
shortcut icon
smartphone
Snap
Software as a Service (SaaS)
sound scheme
source folder
spooling
standard account
submenu
synchronize
system software
tablet
taskbar
thumbnail
tile
touch screen
update
USB port
user account
user interface
utility software
web app
web server
window
Windows
Windows Phone

Application Software

Using Excel spreadsheets, Tyrell records his findings and analyzes them using formulas, converting them to the appropriate units. Part of his research requires him to graph trends using a 3-D clustered column chart.

Using a Word document, Tyrell summarizes his findings in a report and a Sway presentation to share them with others.

iStockphoto.com/fotoedu

Tyrell Williams is majoring in economics. He uses application software including Microsoft Office to record, catalog, analyze, store, and report economic trends. He uses Excel spreadsheets to create sophisticated formulas and graphs. PowerPoint and Sway help him create and share interactive reports, presentations, stories, and research findings, and present his conclusions on the web.

Define Application Software

application software program | software application | app | productivity software | local application | portable application | web-based application | mobile application | mobile app | PDF (Portable Document Format) | word processing | spreadsheet | presentation | database | graphics | communications | social networking | personal information management | note-taking | webpage authoring | groupware | convergence

Whether you're listening to music, writing a paper, searching the web, or checking your email on your mobile phone, chances are you are using application software. **Application software programs** (also called **software applications** or just **apps**) help you perform a task when you are using a computer or smartphone. While system software gives you tools to interact with your computer, application software lets you perform specific tasks, such as writing a document, analyzing a set of numbers, or preparing a presentation.

Productivity software is application software that makes people more productive by automating repetitive tasks. It helps them create documents, store and analyze data, and create persuasive presentations using text and images. Programs sold in productivity suites, or collections, include word processing, spreadsheet, database, presentation, and graphics programs.

The Bottom Line

- Application software can enhance, manage, and simplify your personal and professional life.
- Application software programs can be installed locally on your computer's hard drive, on a network, on a portable storage device, online on the web, or on a mobile device.

Figure 4-1: Applications cover a wide range of features and functions

Applications exist for businesses, multimedia professionals, students, and home users.

Use application software to prepare a presentation for a new business proposal, write a lab report, prepare your taxes, send email, or create a newsletter for your club.

pizuttipics/Fotolia LLC, Milles Studio/Shutterstock.com, Scanrail/Fotolia LLC, Phovoir/Shutterstock.com

Hot Technology Now

One-third of students use school-issued mobile devices for increased learning opportunities.

#appsoftware

Google Drive provides 15GB of free online storage. You can store files that you create with your hardware devices or files that you create with your web-based applications.

Access Apps

Software applications can be categorized by how you access them or by the device on which you use them. **Local applications** are installed on your computer's hard drive. They tend to be programs with lots of features and functionality. Microsoft Office is a popular suite of applications for word processing, spreadsheets, databases, email, and presentations. It can be installed locally on a computer.

Portable applications are stored on and run from portable removable storage devices such as flash drives or from the web. You connect the flash drive to a computer to run the application. Portable applications save valuable space on your computer. OpenOffice.org Portable is a portable application suite offering programs similar to Microsoft Office products.

Web-based applications are programs that you access over the Internet in a browser on your computer or as an app on your mobile device. Because these programs run off the Internet, web-based apps often offer collaboration features that installed apps can't handle. The files you create are typically stored online along with the program. Google Docs, as well as Microsoft Office 365, are web-based applications used for creating documents, spreadsheets, databases, and presentations. Microsoft Office 365 is a renewable subscription service with pricing options for different users. **Mobile applications**, commonly called **mobile apps**, work on your smartphone or tablet. Though they can be limited in functionality, mobile apps give you on-the-go computing capabilities. See **Figure 4-2**.

Figure 4-2: Web-based applications

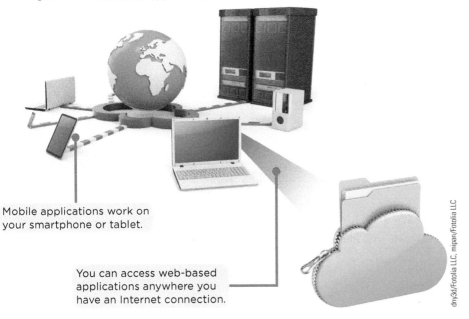

Mobile applications work on your smartphone or tablet.

You can access web-based applications anywhere you have an Internet connection.

dny3d/Fotolia LLC, mipan/Fotolia LLC

Identify Common Features of Apps

Application software programs have many common features; they
- are usually represented on the desktop by an icon.
- can be started by double-clicking or by tapping the tile or icon.
- open in a window on your desktop.
- are identified by a title bar at the top of the program window.
- have menu commands that you use to work in the program.
- have buttons you click or tap to issue commands or perform other actions.

To save your work, you create a file that stores the information and data from the program. You give each file a unique filename. The program might automatically add a dot (.) and a file extension to the name, which identifies the file type, such as .docx for a Word file or .xlsx for an Excel file or .jpeg for an image file. You might have already used PDF files; **PDF** stands for Portable Document Format; these files are readable in Adobe Reader, a free program you can download from the web.

Describe Types of Apps

Some of the most popular application software programs include word processing, spreadsheet, database, graphics, and presentation software. There are also apps for communication and a variety of other tasks for daily life and business. See **Table 4-1** on the next page. In addition, mobile apps on mobile devices such as smartphones and tablets can help you get directions, play games, browse the web, create lists, manage calendars, send email, and communicate with others.

Several of these applications (word processing, spreadsheet, presentation, and database) are also classified as **productivity software**, which helps people be more productive by automating common or repetitive tasks. Other, more specialized productivity software types include those listed in **Table 4-2** on the next page.

#appsoftware

You can use Microsoft Office programs to edit and then save your files in the .pdf (Portable Document Format) so you can share your files with others who might not have the Office programs.

On the Job Now

As an app developer, you may be called upon to work in several different genres such as Reference, Games, or Health. Be aware that your app must match an app store's list of categories and subcategories, which reflect the app type and genre.

Table 4-1: Application types

Application type	Use to
Word processing	Create, edit, format, view, print, and publish documents.
Spreadsheet	Perform numerical analysis and enhance the appearance of data for lists, forms, budgets, schedules. Spreadsheet files can include numbers, charts, graphics, text blocks, and data tables.
Presentation	Create electronic slides for presentations. Presentation files can include text, images, charts, audio, video, and animation.
Database	Create and manage large or small databases with items such as customer or inventory data, employee information, or personal or professional collections.
Graphics	Create, view, manipulate, and print digital images such as photographs, flowcharts, logos, drawings, clip art, and diagrams.
Communications	Have voice conversations or send text and video to one or more people.
Social networking	Create and post graphics and text for sharing ideas with groups of people.

Table 4-2: Specialized productivity software

Personal information management	Organize calendars, schedules, and address books.
Note-taking	Convert, organize and store handwritten notes, webpage clips, and other files.
Webpage authoring	Create and manage webpages.
Groupware	Collaborate with multiple users on documents, participate in online web conferences.

Hot Technology Now

A program in Office 365 called Power BI (Business Intelligence) includes a suite of business analytics tools to analyze data and share insights to make business decisions.

Identify Trends in App Development

Convergence and mobility are continuing trends in application software. **Convergence** means that the distinction between "categories" of application software is becoming more blurred (see **Figure 4-3**). For example, word processers can be used to seamlessly create and post entries to social media.

Figure 4-3: Software convergence and mobility

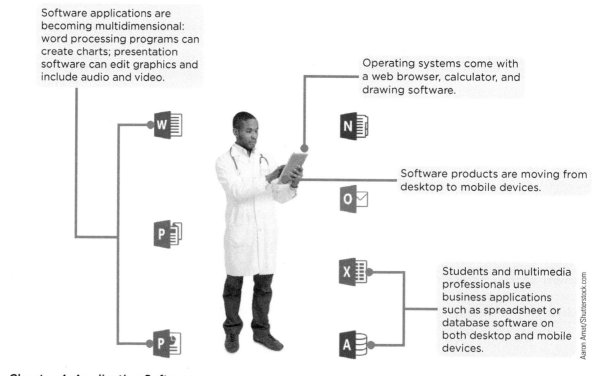

Software applications are becoming multidimensional: word processing programs can create charts; presentation software can edit graphics and include audio and video.

Operating systems come with a web browser, calculator, and drawing software.

Software products are moving from desktop to mobile devices.

Students and multimedia professionals use business applications such as spreadsheet or database software on both desktop and mobile devices.

Aaron Amat/Shutterstock.com

Computing is also becoming increasingly mobile. Application software is moving from the hard drive on your desk in an office to more portable devices and networks such as portable drives, smartphones, and the web.

Update Apps

Many applications are connected to the Internet. Because of this connectivity, updating the applications to include the most recent features, or fix any bugs, often occurs automatically. Mobile apps are always connected to their source provider as long as a user in on Wi-Fi or within range of cellular service. Applications provided as a subscription, such as Office 365 and Adobe Creative Suite are automatically updated. Typically, a user will get a notice that the update is available and they can schedule its installation at a convenient time.

Define Word Processing Software

word processing software | document | insertion point | document management tools | format | font type | font size | point | font style | font color | indent | tab | alignment | line spacing | paragraph spacing | margin | bullet | page break | page orientation | template | desktop publishing (DTP) software | web development software | note-taking software | speech recognition software

Have you written a research paper lately? How about a letter? If yes, then chances are you used **word processing software**, one of the most widely used types of application software.

Identify the Key Features of Word Processing Software

Although the user interface and functionality of word processing programs may differ, all programs share some common key features. The files you create are called **documents**, which are organized into pages. When you start a word processing program, a blank document opens on the screen. The screen displays an **insertion point** to mark your place and a scrolling mechanism to navigate the screen. You have access to variety of commands and options you can use to create the document.

You use the keyboard to type letters and numbers, and the corresponding characters appear on the screen. Some programs also make it possible for you to speak into a microphone; the program translates your words into text to create a document. As you type, or enter text, the word processing software automatically "wraps" words onto a new line. When the text fills a page, new text automatically flows onto the next page.

Formatting features modify the appearance of a document. Editing, review, reference, and graphics capabilities enhance document content. **Document management tools** protect and organize files and let you collaborate with others.

The Bottom Line
- Creating documents electronically allows you to create, edit, format, and manage your work easily.
- Word processors have text and document formatting options as well as document management tools.

On the Job Now

Some of the most popular word processing programs used on the job today include Microsoft Word, Apple iWork Pages, Corel Word-Perfect, and Apache OpenOffice.

Figure 4-4: Word processors create documents

Use word processors to create, edit, format, view, print, and publish a wide variety of documents such as letters, invitations, flyers, reports, and research papers.

Businesses use word processing programs to create memos, contracts, invoices, and marketing brochures.

Courtesy: Friends of the Shade Tree

Format Text Using Word Processing Software

You can highlight important information, make text easier to read, and add flair to your document using text formatting. You **format** text by changing the font type, size, style, color, and effects. Most programs provide a wide range of font types, styles, colors, and effects. See Table 4-3.

Table 4-3: Text formatting options

Format option	Description and use	Examples
Font type	Defines what characters look like. Some fonts have rounded letters; others are more angular. Some are formal; others are more casual.	Times New Roman Comic Sans MS **Arial Black**
Font size	Determines the size of the character, measured in **points**; each point is 1/72 of an inch; change the title font to be bigger than the rest of your text or use smaller fonts for footnotes or endnotes.	This text is 12 points This text is 18 points
Font style	Adds visual effects features to text; bolding text makes it stand out on the page, shadow gives it depth, underlining, italicizing, and highlighting text provide emphasis.	**bold** shadow underline *italics* highlighting
Font color	Determines the color of each character and adds interest; be sure to use font colors that show up well against the document background.	Red text Blue text Green text

#appsoftware

You can add further interest with text effects such as reflection, strikethrough, edges, and outlining.

On the Job Now

You can create a professional document using built-in Microsoft Office templates such as a resume, purchase order, press release, memo, bill of sale, sample proposal, cover letter, meeting minutes recap, or invoice.

Format Documents Using Word Processing Software

To give a document a cohesive appearance, you can apply styles and features to a whole document, or to paragraphs or sections of a document. Good formatting improves a document's appearance and readability by creating visual balance, controlling white space, and enhancing layouts. See Table 4-4.

You can determine how the text is placed on the page. When creating a document, you can also insert manual **page breaks** to specify a specific location for a new page to begin. A manual page break will start a new page no matter how much text is on that page. **Page orientation** can be portrait or landscape. You can also insert borders around paragraphs and pages to create a specific style, for example for a document that is a menu or invitation.

You can forgo all formatting decisions by creating documents from pre-formatted templates. **Templates** are documents that contain document formatting such as margins, fonts, and page layouts that you use to create new documents. They are available for common types of documents such as letters, flyers, invitations, and legal contracts. Most word processing programs provide a collection of built-in templates; you can find even more on the Internet.

Use Advanced Word Processing Features

Word processing programs provide tools to improve document content and appearance, making it easier for you to create documents. Some of these features are listed below:

- **Spelling and grammar-checking tools** find and fix errors.
- **Research tools** help you find just the right word, search online to check facts, and provide topic-related information.
- **Language tools** translate passages and help create multi-lingual documents.

- **Tables** and **columns** organize data.
- **Graphics** such as photographs, pictures, logos, charts, and screenshots illustrate ideas and add visual appeal.
- **Headers** and **footers** display document information such as title, page number, date, and author on every page.
- **Reference features** follow standard style guidelines and add professionalism to reports with tables of contents, bibliographies, footnotes, citations, and index.
- **Hyperlinks** direct readers to related documents, email addresses, or websites.

Table 4-4: Document formatting options

Format option	Determines	Example/Description
Indent and **tab**	Where text begins on a line in relation to the left margin	This paragraph uses a hanging indent of 0.5" from left margin for lines after the first line.
Alignment	How a line or paragraph is placed between the two margins on the page: right, center, or along both edges	Align paragraphs at the left, right, center, or along both edges: center aligned left aligned right aligned
Line spacing	How much "white space" between each line of text; can set before and after spacing; can be measured in points	This text has line spacing set to 2.0.
Paragraph spacing	How much "white space" between each paragraph; can set before and after spacing; measured in points; affects document length	These paragraphs have 6 points of line spacing after each one. These paragraphs have 6 points of line spacing after each one.
Margins	Where text begins from the left side of a page and where it begins to wrap on the right side of the page; you also set top and bottom margins	Narrow margins make a wider line, or more text on the page.
Bullets	The placement of a character before each line of text	This is a bulleted list: • New York • Chicago • Miami

Manage Word Processing Documents

Word processing software offers document management tools that you use to edit, share, protect, and save your documents. Tools that make it easy to edit, delete, and rearrange text within a document are essential parts of any word processor. Even more useful are the tools that you can use to copy text and graphics from one document to another. See **Figure 4-5** on the next page.

When working collaboratively on documents, multiple users can read and edit a document simultaneously. Changes and edits can be tracked by the individual, compared between users, and merged into a final document. You can prevent unwanted changes by marking a document as "read-only" to disable editing. You can also restrict access by setting a password. When you are done working, save your file as a Word document, a text document, or in other formats such as Portable Document Format (PDF), a webpage, or in an earlier version of your word processing software if you need to share it with others.

#appsoftware

You can send documents as email attachments or share files using a cloud computing service. When you share a document in the cloud, the recipients can make changes to the document at the same time. If they are unsure of the edits, they can have a discussion using comments and tracked changes to compare versions, without creating multiple copies of the file.

Figure 4-5: Creating a document with text and graphics

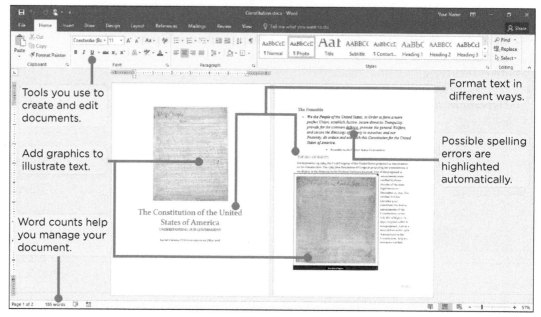

Tools you use to create and edit documents.

Add graphics to illustrate text.

Word counts help you manage your document.

Format text in different ways.

Possible spelling errors are highlighted automatically.

Who uses word processors? Table 4-5 summarizes how word processing software is used to create a vast variety of documents.

Table 4-5: How word processors are used

Who uses word processing	To create
Businesses executives, office workers, medical professionals, and politicians	Agendas, memos, contracts, proposals, letters, reports, email, newsletters, and personalized bulk mailings and labels
Personal users	Letters, greeting cards, notes, event flyers, and checklists
Students	Essays, reports, stories, and resumes
Conference promoters, personal event planners	Business cards, postcards, invitations, conference tent cards, name and gift tags, and stickers
Web designers	Documents that are converted to HTML to be published as webpages

Identify Apps Related to Word Processing Software

Some key features of word processing software are incorporated into related types of application software, such as desktop publishing, web development software, note taking software, and speech to text programs. See Table 4-6.

Table 4-6: Programs related to word processors

Related program	Function	Use to create	Examples of programs
Desktop publishing (DTP) software	Combines word processing with advanced graphics capabilities	Flyers, newsletters	QuarkXPress, Adobe InDesign, and Microsoft Publisher
Web development software	Allows non-technical users to create webpages by automatically coding text with HTML tags	Webpages	iWeb, Adobe Dreamweaver, and Amaya
Note taking	Allows you to store and access thoughts, ideas, lists, and web content from different sources all in one place	Notes	OneNote, EverNote
Speech recognition software	Has many features of word processing software, but you enter text by talking into a microphone rather than typing	Documents	Dragon Naturally Speaking and Windows Speech Recognition

Define Spreadsheet Software

spreadsheet | worksheet | workbook | cell range | value | label | formula | cell | cell address | cell reference | argument | operator | function | absolute reference | relative reference | filter | What-If analysis | pivot table | macro | chart | line chart | column chart

When you want to manipulate numbers or display numerical data, a spreadsheet is the tool you want for the job. **Spreadsheet** files can include numbers, charts, graphics, text blocks, and data tables. Because it performs calculations electronically, spreadsheet software (see **Figure 4-6**) reduces data errors. It is especially useful for tasks involving repetitive or complex calculations.

Spreadsheet software originated as an electronic alternative to paper spreadsheets used by bookkeepers and accountants to track sales and expenses. Use of the software expanded to other business departments, such as sales, marketing, and human resources. Spreadsheet software is also widely used outside of the business world, in fields such as science, mathematics, and economics, and by home users, students, and teachers.

Figure 4-6: Spreadsheet software

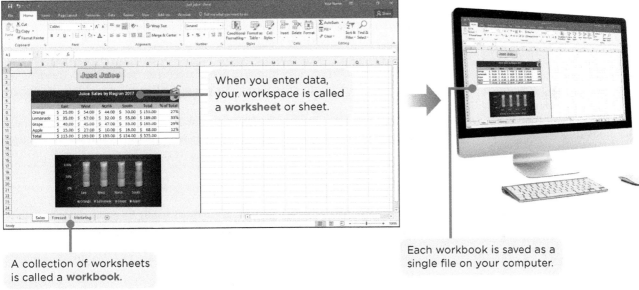

When you enter data, your workspace is called a **worksheet** or sheet.

Each workbook is saved as a single file on your computer.

A collection of worksheets is called a **workbook**.

Igor Klimov/Shutterstock.com

Define Worksheets and Workbooks

Spreadsheet software has many common features. See **Figure 4-7** on the next page.

A **cell range** is a group of cells. Cell ranges can be adjacent, with all cells touching, or nonadjacent, where not all cells are touching. To enter data in a worksheet, you click a cell to make it active and type the desired characters. You can also copy or import data into a cell. You navigate a worksheet using scroll bars and arrows, move to other worksheets by clicking sheet tabs, and find formatting and data analysis commands on menus.

Identify the Key Features of Spreadsheets

You use spreadsheet software to create, edit, and format worksheets. To create a worksheet, you enter values, labels, and formulas into cells. A **value** is a number, a **label** is descriptive text, and a **formula** performs a calculation that generates a value. Editing tools let you modify worksheet data. A workbook includes several worksheets in a single file. You can change a cell value, modify a formula, move and copy cells, or delete cells. When you change a cell value or formula, spreadsheet software recalculates the workbook automatically. You can also insert or delete entire rows and columns.

Hot Technology Now

Popular spreadsheet programs include Microsoft Excel, Corel Quattro Pro, Apple iWork Numbers, and OpenOffice Calc.

Figure 4-7: Basic features of spreadsheet software

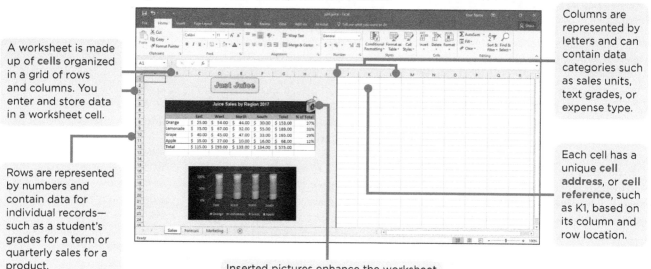

A worksheet is made up of **cells** organized in a grid of rows and columns. You enter and store data in a worksheet cell.

Columns are represented by letters and can contain data categories such as sales units, text grades, or expense type.

Rows are represented by numbers and contain data for individual records—such as a student's grades for a term or quarterly sales for a product.

Each cell has a unique **cell address**, or **cell reference**, such as K1, based on its column and row location.

Inserted pictures enhance the worksheet.

On the Job Now

Almost every job or vocation that needs numerical analysis uses spreadsheets, including jobs as accountants, project managers, payroll managers, supervisors, business analysts, inventory specialists, and sales.

#appsoftware

Among the most common uses of absolute reference is dealing with a percentage. The percentage may relate to tax, interest rate, discount, or bonus.

Hot Technology Now

The Bureau of Labor Statistics (bls.gov) website collects, processes, and analyzes essential statistical data about career outlooks, productivity, and jobs.

Spreadsheet software often includes many additional features such as:
- formatting tools to change a worksheet's appearance.
- page layout and view features to change the zoom level, divide a worksheet into panes, or freeze rows and columns to make large worksheets easier to read.
- file management features to control how you save files and let multiple users share a workbook.
- printing features to control whether you print entire worksheets or parts of one.
- web capabilities to share workbooks online, insert hyperlinks, and save worksheets as webpages.

Define Formulas and Functions

Spreadsheet software performs numerical analysis using formulas and functions. A formula contains a calculation, which specifies the operation to be performed, and **arguments**, which are the values involved in the calculation. To enter a calculation, you use mathematical **operators**, such as "+" or "–," or functions. Formulas can contain multiple mathematical operators and functions.

A **function** is a predefined calculation such as SUM or AVERAGE. Spreadsheet programs provide a wide variety of functions. For example, logical functions such as AND, OR, and IF test data conditions. Financial functions such as RATE and PMT calculate interest rates and loan payments.

Formula arguments can be values or cell references. An **absolute reference** refers to a fixed cell location that never changes. A **relative reference** identifies a cell by its location relative to other cells and changes when a formula is moved or copied.

Formulas and functions begin with an equal sign (=); arguments are enclosed in parentheses. You can type a formula directly into a cell or an area above the worksheet called the formula bar, or you can use menu commands. Cells containing formulas display the value generated by the formula.

Analyze Spreadsheet Data

Once you enter data in a worksheet, you can manipulate it with a variety of tools to make the data more meaningful.
- Rearrange your data by sorting it on one or more categories; you might sort clients by revenues to identify your most valuable customers.

- **Filter** worksheet data to display only the values you want to see, such as filtering students who got a B or better on a test.
- **Search** to locate specific data without having to scroll through an entire worksheet.
- Use **What-If analysis** tools to test multiple scenarios by temporarily changing one or more variables to see the effect on related calculations.
- Use **pivot tables** to create meaningful data summaries to analyze worksheets containing large volumes of data.
- Automate your worksheets with **macros**, small programs you can create to perform a predefined action that you have to repeat frequently by just clicking a button.

On the Job Now

If your job is related to investing in the stock market, you can use the Excel Stock charts for stock price data, including high and low closing values and volume.

Create Charts Using Spreadsheet Software

Another important feature of spreadsheet software is the ability to create charts. **Charts** are graphical representations of data that visually illustrate relationships and patterns.

The most popular types of charts are line charts, column charts, and pie charts. A **line chart** tracks trends over time. A **column chart** compares categories of data to one another, and a pie chart compares parts (or slices) to the whole. Other chart types include scatter, radar, doughnut, stock, surface, area, and bubble. Each type of chart has multiple layout options. You can choose the chart type and layout that best suit your data. See **Figure 4-8**.

Figure 4-8: Charts in a spreadsheet

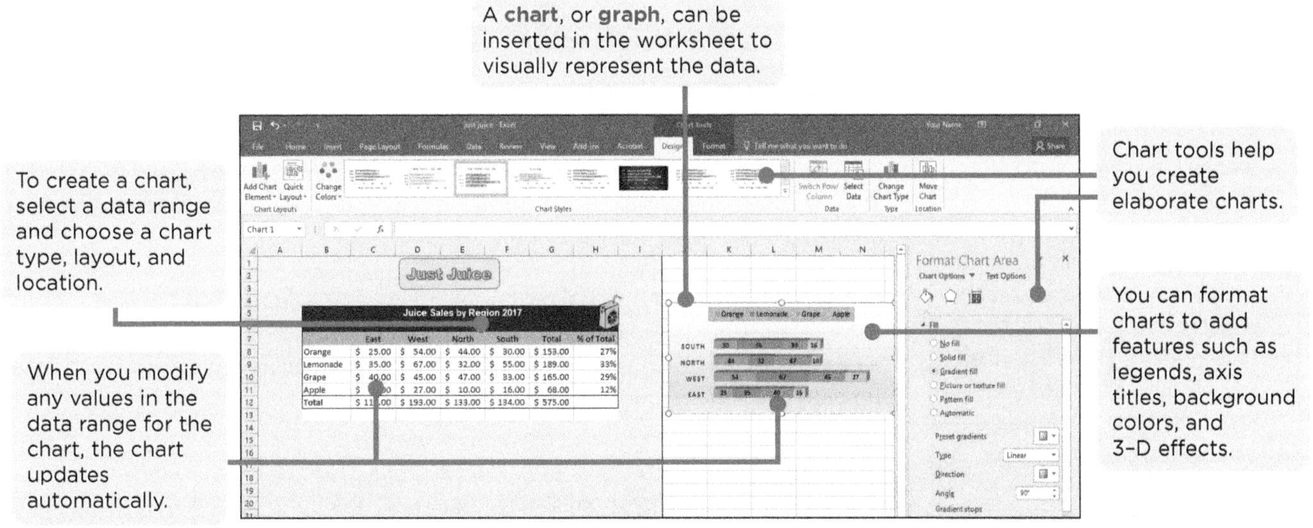

A **chart**, or **graph**, can be inserted in the worksheet to visually represent the data.

To create a chart, select a data range and choose a chart type, layout, and location.

When you modify any values in the data range for the chart, the chart updates automatically.

Chart tools help you create elaborate charts.

You can format charts to add features such as legends, axis titles, background colors, and 3-D effects.

Format Spreadsheets

You can change how a worksheet looks using formatting features as well as by inserting elements, such as graphics. Formatting highlights important data and makes worksheets easier to read; elements enhance a worksheet. When you format a number, the underlying value remains the same even if its outward appearance changes. See **Table 4-7** on the next page.

Spreadsheet software has helpful features. You can create rules to automatically format cells based on their values. For example, you can specify that all cells with a value greater than 10 percent have a yellow fill color and bold text. Tables are specially formatted data ranges with built-in sorting and filtering capabilities. Most spreadsheet programs provide templates for common applications such as calendars, invoices, and budgets.

On the Job Now

One of the country's top jobs is the position of a Data Scientist, according to Glassdoor.com, with a salary of approximately $117,000.

Table 4-7: Formatting a spreadsheet

Formatting option	Use to	Example
Currency	Identify currency value such as euros, pounds, or dollars	$4.50 or £4.50 or €4.50
Decimal places	Display additional level of accuracy	4.50 4.500, 4.5003
Font types, colors, styles, and effects	Emphasize text and numbers	4.50 4.500, ***4.5003***
Alignment	Align text across cells for a title heading; center, or left- or right-align labels or values	Student Scores 75 / 80 / 95
Borders and shading	Enhance the worksheet	Student Scores 75 / 80 / 95
Cell height and width	Emphasize certain cells	Student Scores 75 / 80 / 95 / 88
Photographs, clip art, shapes, and other graphics	Illustrate a point; can format, reposition, and resize	☺ Student Scores 75 / 80 / 95 / 88
Headers and footers	Create professional reports	Bergen Data Analysis: Fall Report — Page 3 of 5

•Define Presentation Software

The Bottom Line
- Slides in presentations contain graphics, text, video, and other media; slides are enhanced with transitions and animations.
- Presentation software is used to supplement lectures, classroom projects, and public meetings.
- Presentations are an essential tool for businesses and educators, and can create award certificates, calendars, cards, and invitations.

Presentation software (see **Figure 4-9**) lets you create electronic slides for slide shows that can be viewed on a single computer, on a projection device, or over the Internet. You can share your ideas in person or on paper, or create a presentation that runs unattended in a kiosk, such as a booth at a trade show or airport.

Identify the Key Features of Presentation Software

You use presentation software to create a series of slides to visually display your messages or ideas. Each slide has a specific layout based on its content, and each layout contains placeholders for text and graphics.

Figure 4-9: A presentation presents ideas

You can present your ideas in a concise multimedia format with pictures, charts, audio, video, animation, and even recorded narration.

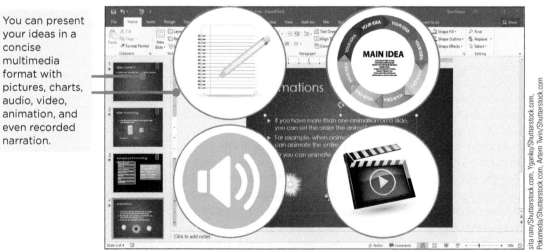

sita ram/Shutterstock.com, Yganko/Shutterstock.com, Pokomeda/Shutterstock.com, Artem Twin/Shutterstock.com

As you work, you can display presentations in different views. Some views divide the program window into multiple panes, or sections, such as slide, outline, or notes panes. You can insert, copy, and move slides, which contain content placeholders for various objects on each inserted slide. You click slide objects to select them.

You navigate between slides using scroll bars or arrows. In some views, you can drag **thumbnails**, small versions of each slide, to change the order of slides in the presentation. Each presentation program has a unique set of tools to format, edit, animate, and enhance slides in the presentation.

Hot Technology Now

Popular presentation software programs include Microsoft PowerPoint, Apache OpenOffice Impress, Apple iWork Keynote, and Google Docs Slides.

Insert Content on Slides

Slides can contain text, graphics, and audio and video clips. See Table 4-8.

Table 4-8: Slide content

Slide content	How to enter	Provides
Text in a paragraph or bulleted list	Click a placeholder and type, or copy and paste text from another file, or insert text from a document file.	Content; most programs offer a variety of bullet styles, including number and picture bullets
Graphics such as line art, photographs, clip art, drawn objects, diagrams, data tables, and screenshots	Click a content placeholder, draw directly on the slide, or copy and paste a graphic from another file.	Illustrations to convey meaning and information for the slide content
Media clips, such as video and audio, including recorded narrations	Click a content placeholder and choose a file, or insert the file directly onto a slide by recording it.	Media content to enhance a slide show
Links	Click content placeholder, copy and paste links from a website or type the link directly.	Links to another slide, another document, or a webpage
Embedded objects	Click menu commands or a content placeholder.	External files in a slide
Charts	Link or embed a worksheet or chart from Excel or create a chart directly within PowerPoint.	Graphic display of data to support your presentation

Format Presentation Content

In addition to content, slides include formatting, which is applied to text, objects, individual slides, or entire presentations.

- Format text using tools similar to those in word processing software; choose font types, sizes, colors, and styles such as italics or bold.
- Change text direction, align text on a slide or within a text box, and add text effects such as shadows or reflections.
- Format objects by modifying fill colors and by adding styles, outlines, and effects.
- Resize graphics to make them larger or smaller, rotate a graphic, or change its shape.
- Add SmartArt graphics that combine predesigned text, shapes, and images to convey ideas.
- Format charts and worksheets when presenting numerical data to emphasize a point, show trends, or explain budgets.
- Move objects to different locations on a slide and change their placement relative to other objects; modify alignment and join objects to form a group.

Hot Technology Now

A cloud-based program at prezi.com adds a canvas that you can zoom in and out of to create unique slides for an online presentation.

Design Effective Presentations

When you create a slide presentation, there are several guidelines that you can follow to help you succeed at your task and create an effective presentation.

- **Be mindful of your target venue and audience**: Is your presentation going to be viewed in a large lecture hall? Over the web by hundreds of people, in a kiosk? Answers to these questions can help you create slides to meet the needs of your audience. Web presentations should use graphics best designed for websites.
- **Limit your words**: Slides should supplement a presenter's lecture or speech and should have limited text. You want the audience to use the slides as a guideline and

listen to the speaker. Many use the 6×6 rule as a guide; no more than six lines of text with no more than six words per line.

- **Use graphics wisely**: Be tasteful and careful in your selection of graphics. You don't want to overwhelm your audience with a barrage of meaningless pictures. Also consider the copyright and verify that you have permission to use any graphic that you didn't create yourself.
- **Don't overuse transitions and animations**: PowerPoint has a vast collection of visual motion effects called transitions and animations that you can use in a presentation. But you want the audience focusing on the content, not the elaborate effects on the screen. Pick one or two transitions and apply them to the entire presentation. Use animations sparingly—only when they add to the content on the slides.
- **Consider accessibility factors**: Color blindness affects a portion of our population, so do not use red and green to distinguish content. Also, use large fonts to help readers with the text; fonts on slides should be no smaller that 20pt.
- **Use the Spelling and Grammar Feature**: No matter how much effort you put into a presentation, if your slides have spelling and grammar errors, your content will lose credibility. PowerPoint comes with a built-in grammar and spelling checker—use it before releasing your slides.
- **Use Mix**: PowerPoint includes a powerful presentation tool, Mix that enables a user to create interactive presentations that include video and audio.

Use Presentation Templates and Masters

You can format an individual slide or an entire presentation. Adding headers and footers lets you display the presentation title, slide number, date, logos, or other information on a single slide or all slides automatically. Choose your own formatting options with slide masters. A **slide master** automatically applies any new formatting to all slides in your presentation that use that master. You can change slide orientation or modify slide dimensions. See **Figure 4-10**. Use built-in templates for common slide designs such as diagrams, calendars, business and academic presentations, awards, and more.

Figure 4-10: Advanced formatting in PowerPoint

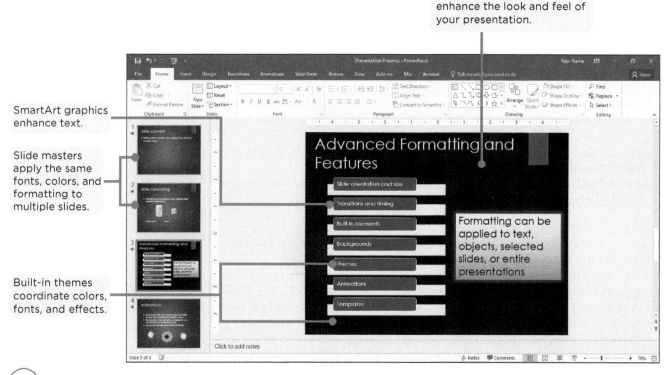

Slide background designs enhance the look and feel of your presentation.

SmartArt graphics enhance text.

Slide masters apply the same fonts, colors, and formatting to multiple slides.

Built-in themes coordinate colors, fonts, and effects.

Include Animations in Presentations

To liven up your presentation, you might try adding **animation**, or movement, to an object or text. PowerPoint offers a variety of animations, such as entrance, exit, and emphasis, each with a number of visually interesting options. A photograph can "fade in" as you display a slide, or an object can "fly in" from the side.

You can set animations to start manually when you click or tap, or to start automatically when you advance a slide. You can also set the duration of an animation effect. Animations can move horizontally, vertically, or diagonally across the slide. You can set the order for multiple animations. For example, you can animate a bulleted list to appear one item at a time, appearing to fade in and then change color, followed by a graphic floating in from the bottom of the slide.

Include Transitions in Presentations

Transitions are the visual animations that occur as you move from slide to slide in a presentation. For example, you can make a new slide appear with a "ripple" effect, or "push" the existing slide off the screen with the next one as it comes into view.

Transitions have several options you can control. You can change the direction, set the duration, and add sound effects; you can apply a transition to all slides or just selected slides in the presentation. As with animations, you can set transitions to start with a mouse click or begin automatically after a set amount of time.

#appsoftware

Most software lets users change basic settings to match their preferences, such as print options or how frequently a document is saved. In Microsoft Office, view settings by choosing File > Options.

Share and Display Presentations

The purpose of a presentation is to show it to other people. You can share and display your presentation on a computer screen or project it onto a larger screen for an audience. You can run slide shows manually, with the presenter controlling slide order and advancement. Or you can set up a self-running slide show that runs automatically in a kiosk at a trade show or convention. You can print paper copies of your slides, such as handouts that show multiple slides per page, and include notes or comments.

You can also share and display presentations online. Colleagues or classmates can view a presentation from a remote location using a web browser, either at a specified time or whenever a viewer chooses. Most presentation programs let you work collaboratively to create the presentation, with colleagues, who edit the presentation for content or format.

Define Database Software

database | record | view | field | field name | data type | property | table | relational database | sort | filter | form | control | query | report | server

A **database** is a collection of data, organized and stored electronically. Database software lets you create and manage databases. Databases are used by businesses for inventories, employers for employee data, governments for information, medical professionals for patient records, and so much more.

Identify the Key Features of Database Software

Data, organized into **records** (rows of data), is stored in tables in a database. When you use database software, you create objects, which can be tables, forms, queries, or reports that you use to store, enter, view, or share the data. You can enter data manually, a record at a time, or by importing larger amounts of data from external files.

You input data and navigate records by using forms. You retrieve data using queries and print reports to view results. After opening an object, you choose a view, depending on what you need to do. Each **view** is designed to perform specific tasks. Depending on the view, the software displays different command options and work areas. You enter and edit data in some views. You design, modify, and format layouts of reports, forms, tables, and queries in others.

> ### The Bottom Line
> - Personal computer database software is designed for small businesses and individuals, and some database software programs are designed for large, commercial databases, such as online retail sites or airline reservation systems.
> - Database software stores data in tables as records.
> - Forms, queries, and reports, as well as filtering and sorting features in database software, are used to organize, analyze, access, and view data.

Figure 4-11: Databases

If you shop online, you search databases of products to find what you want.

When you make a purchase, a database stores your transaction information.

Large databases store billions of pieces of data and handle hundreds or thousands of users at a time.

Odua Images/Shutterstock.com

Hot Technology Now

Some of the most popular databases include Microsoft Access, Microsoft SQL Server, Oracle, and SAP databases.

Define Fields and Records

To understand databases, you need to understand how data is stored and organized. Each piece of data in a database is entered and stored in an area called a **field**, which is assigned a **field name**. Fields are defined by their **data type**, such as text, date, or number. The text data type stores data as characters that cannot be used in mathematical calculations. Logical data types store yes/no or true/false values. Hyperlinks store data as URL addresses. See **Figure 4-12**.

Figure 4-12: Fields and records

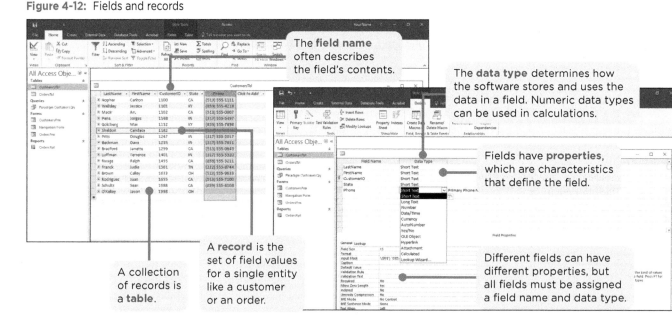

The **field name** often describes the field's contents.

A collection of records is a **table**.

A **record** is the set of field values for a single entity like a customer or an order.

The **data type** determines how the software stores and uses the data in a field. Numeric data types can be used in calculations.

Fields have **properties**, which are characteristics that define the field.

Different fields can have different properties, but all fields must be assigned a field name and data type.

Use Database Tables

Tables are organized in grids of rows and columns, much like worksheets. Tables store data for the database. Columns contain fields; rows contain records. A database can contain a single table or a collection of tables. Most database programs create **relational databases**, where two or more tables are related (connected). Relational databases link tables with common fields so that data doesn't have to be repeated, making it less prone to error.

You can **sort** table data by one or more fields to create meaningful lists. For example, you might sort by customer order amount to view high-value customers first. **Filters** lets you see only the records that contain criteria you specify.

Use Database Forms

A **form** is a database screen primarily used for data entry. Like paper forms, database forms guide users to fill in information in specified formats. A form is made up of **controls** or placeholders that specify where content is placed and how it is labeled. Forms can also contain buttons and graphics.

You can use controls to reduce data entry errors by limiting user choices. List boxes prompt users to choose items from a list, preventing them from entering any other data. Forms also help users navigate database records and find specific information.

Define a Database Query

A **query** extracts data from a database based on criteria that the query creator specifies. Criteria are conditions for a field. For example, you can use a query to find all customers in California who placed an order of more than $1000.

Query elements include the tables and fields you want to search and the parameters, or pieces of information, you want to find. You can use text criteria or logical operators to specify parameters. The query displays results in a datasheet, which you can view onscreen or print. You can save queries to run later; query results are updated using the current data in the tables each time you run the query.

Use Database Reports

A **report** is a user-designed layout of database content. Like forms, reports have label controls to describe data and other controls that contain values. You might prepare a monthly sales report listing top deals and agents or an inventory report to identify low-stock items. Most database programs provide tools to create reports. Report elements include the data along with design elements such as headers, footers, titles, and sections. You design the report with formatting and layout options, select the data you want to include based on the data set, or based on queries using specified criteria, and then run the report to populate it with data.

You can group data into categories and display totals and subtotals on fields that have numeric data. You can sort and filter data by one or more fields and add graphics such as charts, diagrams, or logos.

Manage Databases

Databases are complex files. Databases with multiple users usually need a database administrator to oversee the database. The administrator has several important responsibilities, including:

- controlling access to the database by regulating who can use it and what parts of the database they can see; for example, you don't want all employees to be able to view salary information.
- ensuring data integrity and minimizing data entry errors by controlling how data is entered, formatted, and stored.
- preventing users from inadvertently changing or deleting important data.
- controlling version issues, which arise when multiple users access the same data simultaneously, so that changes aren't lost or overwritten.
- managing database back-up plans regularly to avoid or recover damaged or lost files.
- establishing and maintaining strict database security to protect susceptible data from attacks from hackers.

Use Databases

Databases play significant roles in our world.

- Individuals might use database software on a personal computer to keep track of contacts, schedules, possessions, or collections.
- Small businesses might use database software to process orders, track inventory, maintain customer lists, or manage employee records.

By the Numbers Now

When an Access database reaches 2 gigabytes in size, a business should consider using a larger database such as Microsoft SQL Server or Oracle.

On the Job Now

Employment of database administrators is projected to grow substantially through 2022. Database administrators work in many different industries, including computer systems design and related services firms, insurance companies, banks, and hospitals.

#appsoftware

"Big data" refers to data collections so large and complex that it is difficult to process using traditional data applications. An example is how Amazon determines products that you might like based on your shopping patterns.

Databases frequently acquire and share data from other sources. Because multiple users need access to the database, and databases can be quite large, the software generally runs on a shared computer called a **server**. Data can be exported from a database into other programs, such as spreadsheets or word processors. You can convert database data to other formats, including HTML, to publish it to the web. In fact, web-based databases are increasingly popular; even Facebook uses database software.

Although you may never need to create a database as large as the ones YouTube, Facebook, or iTunes use, database software is helpful for performing personal and professional data-related tasks.

Define Graphics Software

bitmap | vector | pixel | clip art | red eye | filter | cropping

When you edit digital photos or create an image with a paint program, you're using graphics software. You can create, view, manipulate, and print many types of digital images using graphics software programs.

Figure 4-13: Using graphics software with bitmap or vector graphics

Andrija Markovic/Fotolia LLC, dhipadas/Fotolia LLC, Source: 2016 Adobe Systems, Inc.; Photo courtesy of Rachel Bunin

Identify Image File Formats

There are two kinds of digital images: **bitmap** and **vector**. Bitmap images are based on **pixels**—short for "picture elements." A bitmap assigns a color value to each pixel in a graphic. Together, the colored pixels give the illusion of continuity and result in a realistic-looking image. See **Figure 4-14**. A high-resolution photo can contain thousands of pixels, so bitmap files can be large and difficult to modify. Resizing a bitmap image can distort the image and decrease its resolution by decreasing the number of pixels per inch.

Vector graphics tend to be simple images such as shapes, lines, and diagrams. Clip art images are typically stored as vector graphics. Vector graphics use mathematical formulas instead of pixels to define their appearance.

Clip art refers to small graphic image files available on the web that can be used in documents, presentations, or worksheets. Clip art libraries include images that are available, sometimes for free or a small fee. Clip art is a quick way to add simple graphics to your work.

Figure 4-14: Comparing bitmap to vector images

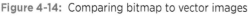

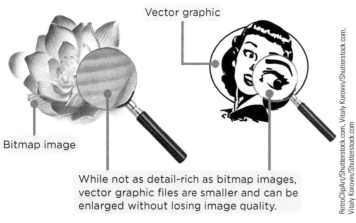

While not as detail-rich as bitmap images, vector graphic files are smaller and can be enlarged without losing image quality.

RetroClipArt/Shutterstock.com, Vitaly Korovin/Shutterstock.com, Vitaly Korovin/Shutterstock.com

Identify the Key Features of Graphics Software

Graphics software programs use a variety of drawing and editing tools to create, modify, and enhance images. Image files include many formats. Common image formats are JPG, GIF, and PNG. You can use tools to change the size, color, shape, and rotation angle of a graphic. See Table 4-9 for a summary of common graphics program features.

Describe Paint Apps

You use paint software to create graphics by drawing or "painting" images on the screen. Most paint programs have limited capabilities and produce fairly simple bitmap images. Some programs also provide templates for adding graphics to popular documents such as greeting cards, labels, and business cards. See Figure 4-15 on the next page.

#appsoftware

Some image-editing programs let you combine bitmap graphics and vector graphics in a single composition. A file containing both bitmap and vector graphics is called a metafile.

Table 4-9: Key features of graphics software programs

Feature	Description	Example
Freehand drawing	Use your mouse or a stylus to draw pictures on the screen; for example, choose a crayon, calligraphy pen, or airbrush style.	
Shape tools	Create straight lines and shapes.	
Color graphics	Use color palettes to fill shapes with color or create color brushstrokes, lines, and borders.	
Filters and effects	Add visual interest to graphics; add shadows, glowing edges, reflections, and textures.	Photo courtesy of Rachel Bunin
Text tools	Add explanatory or creative text to graphics; use interesting font types, colors, sizes, and styles.	Tools

Describe Drawing Apps

Drawing apps let you create simple images. Graphics created with drawing programs tend to look flat and almost cartoon-like. In contrast to paint software, drawing programs generally create vector graphics. One major advantage is that you can modify and resize them without changing image quality. Some drawing programs can layer graphics one on top of the other to create more complex graphics, or collages of images.

By the Numbers Now

Mobile apps typically use .png graphic files, because of the small file size and fast loading speed.

Figure 4-15: Paint program tools

Paint programs feature freehand drawing tools such as pens, pencils, brushes, paints, and colors, as well as tools to draw or insert shapes and lines.

Editing tools add effects such as shadows and glows, modify the color palette, create animations, and change borders, backgrounds, and fill colors. You can even change and create color palettes.

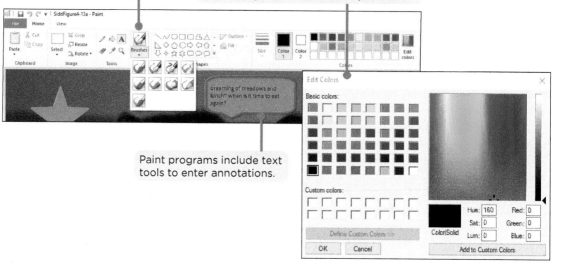

Paint programs include text tools to enter annotations.

Drawing programs feature freehand drawing tools such as pens and brushes, as well as simple tools such as lines, shapes, and colors. You can use drawing programs to create original art, logos, diagrams, schematics, blueprints, business cards, and flyers.

Describe Photo-Editing Apps

Photo-editing software lets you edit, enhance, and customize digital photographs. Professional photographers, engineers, scientists, and just about any professional that works with photographs use photo-editing software. Photo-editing software brings out creativity in people and can be used for personal projects. In addition to sharing many of the features of other graphics software programs, photo-editing software contains tools specially designed for manipulating photographs.

You can fix poor-quality photos by modifying individual pixels to correct discoloration, "erase" creases, or delete spots. You can retouch skin tones by erasing blemishes. See **Figure 4-16**. You can use tools to remove **red eye**, an effect that can happen when the flash from a camera is used on light-eyed people and makes them appear to have red eyes. You can adjust picture contrast, brightness, and sharpness to improve a photo's appearance. You can even turn color photos into black and white images or create a sepia-toned effect.

Photo-editing software usually includes a wide range of unique **filters** and effects, such as the ability to make a picture look blurred, texturized, or distorted. **Cropping** lets you remove parts of the image deleting unwanted objects or people from your photo. You can also insert objects into your photo or rearrange a picture's composition.

Figure 4-16: Photo editing enhances photographs

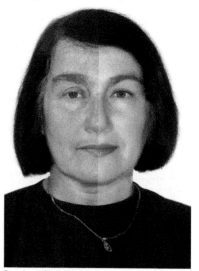

Dreamframer/Shutterstock.com

Define Mobile Apps

mobile application (mobile app) | native application (native app) | web application
(web app) | app store

The growth of mobile computing has spawned a whole new category of application software—**mobile applications**, commonly referred to as mobile apps. **Mobile apps are software programs that run on mobile devices such as smartphones and tablets.**

Mobile apps were originally developed as productivity tools based on desktop PC tools such as email, contact databases, and calendars. Mobile devices typically come with these apps pre-installed, as well as web browsers, media players, and mapping apps. Table 4-10 lists some common mobile apps.

The Bottom Line

- Mobile apps let you use your mobile device as an extension of your desktop computer—without being tied to your desk.
- Mobile apps can be native or web based; each type has its features and drawbacks.

Figure 4-17: Using mobile apps

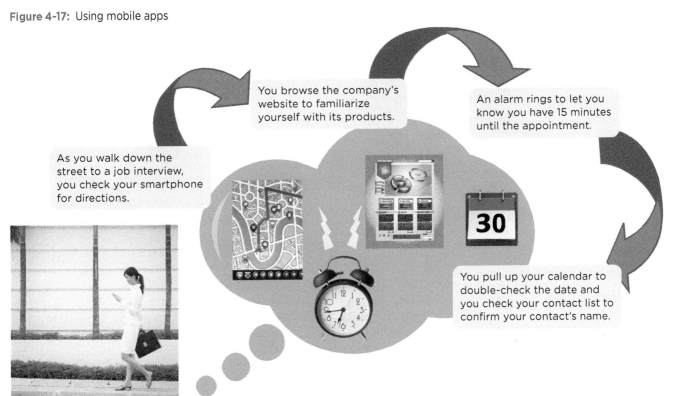

You browse the company's website to familiarize yourself with its products.

An alarm rings to let you know you have 15 minutes until the appointment.

As you walk down the street to a job interview, you check your smartphone for directions.

You pull up your calendar to double-check the date and you check your contact list to confirm your contact's name.

Blend Images/Shutterstock.com, lineartestpilot/Shutterstock.com, blinkblink/Shutterstock.com, lendy16/Shutterstock.com, eltoro69/Shutterstock.com, Mmaxer/Shutterstock.com

Table 4-10: Common applications for mobile devices

Type of app	What it can do for you
Email	Send and receive emails from your mobile device
Contact management	Organize your address book
Calendar or scheduling	Track daily appointments and set reminders; sync your mobile calendar with your desktop calendar or share your calendar with colleagues or family members
Web browsing	Find articles, research products or companies, or find any information on the webapps
News	Stay up to date on current affairs
Video or media player	Watch the latest YouTube video or listen to songs
GPS and mapping apps	Find directions, locate the nearest coffee shop, or even avoid traffic jams
Location-sharing	Share your whereabouts with friends and family

#appsoftware

If you try to open a document on your smartphone that has content that is not supported in Word Mobile, you can still open the document. The unsupported content will not be displayed though, and you might not be able to edit the document on your phone.

Describe the Pros and Cons of Mobile Apps

While mobile apps are popular and useful, they do have significant limitations. The small-scale operating systems of mobile devices cannot support full-scale software programs such as Microsoft Word or Excel or Adobe Acrobat. Consequently, mobile apps tend to be limited in functionality and scope; each app usually focuses on a single task such as mapping, note taking, or scheduling. See **Figure 4-18**.

Keyboard and touch screen space is another limiting factor; mobile apps can't require heavy data or text input from users. When input is required, apps include on-screen keyboards, autocorrect features, handwriting recognition capabilities, and built-in word and phrase lists.

Figure 4-18: Using mobile apps with small screens

Mobile apps must be compact and efficient in design to work within limited screen space.

When you download the app the installation program places an icon on your screen.

Twin Design/Shutterstock.com

RoSonic/Shutterstock.com

Hot Technology Now

The Yelp app on your smartphone and Yelp.com are crowd-sourced listings of reviews for many city's restaurants and services, often listing their hours of operation, contact information, and menus. You can even make reservations right from the app.

Identify the Key Features of Mobile Apps

Limitations aside, mobile apps are tremendously useful. The ability to access the Internet is a key feature shared by most mobile apps. Connectivity is crucial to today's mobile user; people want to stay connected to their office, home, and friends at any given time, no matter where they are.

Although mobile devices cannot run full-scale versions of desktop software programs, some mobile apps are compatible with these programs so you can transfer files between your desktop and mobile devices.

Most mobile apps are platform-specific; an app designed for an Apple iPhone will not work on an Android phone, and vice versa.

Hot Technology Now

One of the fastest growth areas in app development is chatbots. A chatbot performs as a real person might, by performing text-based or spoken conversations with humans, typically for customer service.

Compare Native Apps and Web Apps

A **native application (native app)** is a program that has been designed to run on a specific operating system such as Android, iOS, or Windows. Tablets, for example, each use a specific operating system based on the manufacturer. Native apps that have been designed for an Apple iPad running iOS, for example, will be optimized for that device and must be installed from the Apple store in order to run on that device. A **web application (web app)** is not installed on a user's device; instead, it resides on a server on the Internet, and it is run by a user through a web browser. Web apps are not device specific.

There are benefits and disadvantages to both systems, and some companies, such as Facebook and Google, provide both a native app and a web app to reach the broadest group of users possible. Native apps and web apps differ in functionality and user interface. Often, a native app can take advantage of the features of a specific device, such as the camera, whereas the web app, working through the browser, cannot.

Explore More Apps

In addition to standard apps, you can choose from thousands of others. Some apps are practical; others are fun; see Table 4-11 for some examples.

Table 4-11: Fun and useful applications for mobile devices

Type of app	Helps you to
Social media	Stay connected with family and friends; for example, post a Facebook status update from your smartphone or "tweet" your thoughts via Twitter
Organizational	Take notes, set reminders, and make checklists; you can transfer files between devices using cloud (Internet) storage; jot down notes from a client meeting and forward the file to your office computer
Voice recognition	Search the Internet with Cortana or Siri using your voice or make hands-free calls while driving
Travel	Book airline, hotel, and restaurant reservations, and read and post reviews
Language and translation	Facilitate foreign travel; interpret content in languages you don't speak or understand
Fitness	Set weight-loss goals, track your workouts, find a gym, and count calories
File sharing and storage	Collaborate with co-workers, organize your documents, and share photos and other files online
Banking	Manage your money and pay bills; deposit checks, file your taxes
Home maintenance	Monitor temperature control, door locks, lighting, and pets

Use App Stores

While some apps come pre-installed on mobile devices, the majority are downloaded by users from manufacturer or third-party websites, sometimes called **app stores**. Some apps are free; those that are not free usually cost less than $5.

Mobile apps are written by the mobile device or operating system manufacturer, or more commonly, by third-party programmers. In recent years, the number of third-party app developers has expanded exponentially, fueling the tremendous growth in the number and variety of mobile apps. Most app stores specialize in apps for a particular type of smartphone or platform.

Chapter Review

Define Application Software

1. Define local, portable, and web-based applications. Include the main distinguishing feature and give an example of each one.

2. List three common features and three uses of application software programs.

3. Explain the two ways in which you might access web-based applications.

Define Word Processing Software

4. List and describe three common key features of word processing programs.

5. Explain how you might use three document formatting options, then list and explain how you might use three features of a word processor to improve the content in a document.

6. List and describe five text formatting features and explain how you might use them in a document.

Define Spreadsheet Software

7. Describe the basic structure of a workbook using the following terms: column, row, cell, cell range, worksheet, and tab.

8. Define and give an example of each of the following spreadsheet terms: label, value, formula, function, and cell range.

9. Give three examples of how you can analyze data using spreadsheet software.

Define Presentation Software

10. List and then describe three different elements you can place on a slide.

11. Explain how animations and transitions enhance a slide show.

12. How does the slide master affect the appearance of a presentation?

Define Database Software

13. Briefly describe each of the following database objects: table, form, query, and report.

14. Explain how basic data is stored in a database; use the terms field, data type, and record in your explanation.

15. Describe what type of information you might store in a database, then give an example of one record that might be in that database.

Define Graphics Software

16. List and explain three common key features often part graphics software programs.

17. Explain the difference between bitmap digital images and vector digital images.

Define Mobile Apps

18. List and describe the uses of three common applications for mobile devices.

19. Explain two ways to enter text data in most mobile apps.

20. What are the common ways you get mobile applications on your digital device?

Test Your Knowledge Now

1. Programs that you access over the Internet using your computer's browser, or as an app on your mobile device, are _____ applications.
   a. local
   b. web-based
   c. portable
   d. browser

2. Which of the following is NOT a reason for using web-based application software?
   a. collaborative working
   b. saving storage space
   c. enhanced features of the software
   d. accessibility from any location

3. Which of the following is NOT a feature of a software application program?
   a. fixed features that never change
   b. upgrades automatically
   c. double-click or tap the icon or tile to start
   d. has menu commands and buttons you click or tap to issue commands

4. Which of the following is a text formatting feature of word processing?
   a. spell check
   b. italics
   c. adjustable margins
   d. hanging indents

5. If you wanted the same text to appear at the top and bottom of every page of your document, you would use the word processor _____ to complete the task.
   a. formatting tools
   b. headers and footers
   c. language tools
   d. tables and columns

6. _____ determine where text begins on a line from the left margin.
   a. Line spacing tools
   b. Indents and tabs
   c. Headers and footers
   d. Text formatting tools

7. A _____ is a number, a _____ is descriptive text, and a _____ performs a calculation in a spreadsheet.
   a. label, value, formula
   b. formula, label, value
   c. value, label, formula
   d. value, formula, label

8. Formulas in a spreadsheet_____.
   a. create labels
   b. define cell ranges
   c. perform calculations to generate values
   d. always include absolute references

9. An absolute reference refers to _____.
   a. a group of cells that share common formulas
   b. a fixed cell location that never changes even when a formula is moved or copied
   c. a cell identified by its location relative to other cells and changes when a formula is moved or copied
   d. a group of cells that are contiguous

10. A slide _____ automatically determines the underlying formatting for slides that use it in your presentation.
   a. master
   b. transition
   c. animation
   d. layout

11. How the presentation appears as a viewer moves from one slide to the next slide in a presentation are called a(n)_____.
   a. video
   b. transition
   c. animation
   d. master

12. The motion of an object or text on a slide is called a(n) _____.
   a. transition
   b. animation
   c. video
   d. master

13. You enter data in a database manually by entering one _____ at a time.
   a. table
   b. form
   c. record
   d. query

14. Most database programs create relational databases, where two or more tables are linked tables with common _____ so that data doesn't have to be repeated, making it more prone to error.
   a. absolute
   b. fields
   c. integrated
   d. query

15. A _____ is a database object primarily used for data entry.
   a. query
   b. record
   c. table
   d. form

16. A _____ extracts data from a database based on specific criteria.
   a. table
   b. query
   c. form
   d. record

17. Bitmap images are based on _____, short for picture elements.
   a. vectors
   b. filters
   c. pixels
   d. PNGs

18. There are two kinds of digital images: bitmap and _____.
   a. vector
   b. pixel
   c. graphic
   d. web

19. A _____ application is a program that has been designed to run on a specific operating system, rather than residing on a server in the Internet.
   a. web-based
   b. native
   c. mobile
   d. local

20. If you are traveling and need directions and maps, your mobile device should have _____ apps.
   a. BMP
   b. GPS
   c. JPG
   d. GIF

21. Identify each of the following terms by writing the matching letter on the line in the figure below with the spreadsheet feature used:
   a. cell
   b. formula
   c. value
   d. label
   e. worksheet

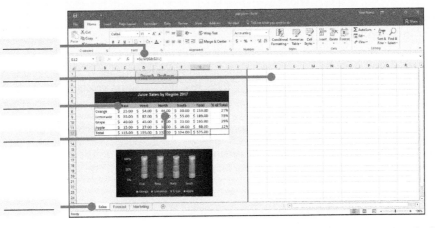

Try This Now

1: Artistic Effects for Graphics in Microsoft Word

Note: This assignment requires the use of Microsoft Word 2013 or Word 2016.

Microsoft Word lets you apply artistic effects to a picture to make it look more like a sketch, drawing, or painting.

    a. Open a blank document in Microsoft Word and click the Insert tab. In the Illustrations group, select Pictures.

    b. Insert a picture of yourself into the Word document, adjusting its size if necessary so it's about three inches wide.

    c. Copy and paste the original picture five times (each one on a separate line) in the Word document. Click to select each copy, click the Picture Tools Format tab, then in the Adjust group, click Artistic Effects and select an artistic effect. Select a different effect for each picture. Label each picture with the name of the artistic effect the appears in its ScreenTip.

    d. Copy and paste the original picture five more times on separate lines in the Word document. Click to select each copy, then on the Picture Tools Format tab, in the Adjust group, select Color and select a different color for each one.

    e. Save the document and submit it to your instructor.

2: PowerPoint Animation

Note: This assignment requires the use of Microsoft PowerPoint 2013 or PowerPoint 2016.

Using PowerPoint, you can animate an object on your PowerPoint slide to do something special such as move a logo from the bottom to the top of a slide for more visibility.

    a. Open Microsoft PowerPoint. Create a blank presentation. Select the Insert tab. In the Images group, select Online Pictures. Insert an image of a hot air balloon on the first slide. If necessary, resize the hot air balloon image to a size of about one inch by one-inch.

    b. Select the hot air balloon image. On the Animations tab, use the Add Animation button in the Advanced Animation group to apply an entrance effect to the object that you clicked. Select Add Animation to add any three Emphasis animations. Lastly add any Exit animation.

    c. To view the animations, select the Preview button in the Preview group.

    d. Save the presentation and submit the file to your instructor.

3: Creating a Technology Presentation with Sway

Note: This assignment requires a Microsoft account. You can create one for free at outlook.com.

Open the website Sway.com. Watch the video tutorials to learn how to create a Sway. Sign in with a Microsoft account. Note that to place a Sway presentation in the hands of any audience you can share it using a webpage link.

    a. Create a new presentation in Sway about a cutting-edge technology topic that interests you. Provide a title for the Sway Storyline and select a background image.

    b. Create three separate sections about your topic, and include text, an image, a video, and a paragraph in each section.

    c. Share the link to your Sway with your instructor and class in the format specified by your instructor.

Microsoft Sway

Critical Thinking Now

1: PowerPoint Usage in Your Career

PowerPoint presentations are used in a variety of careers. Research detailed uses of presentations used in business activities in varied industries. Create a list of 10 specific presentation titles and add what kind of job would use that type of presentation using PowerPoint in business today.

2: Office 365 Personal

Your family is considering purchasing a subscription to Office 365, the Personal version. Research the Office 365 Personal subscription and write at least 150 words about the features and benefits of this subscription for your situation.

3: Comparing Google Drive to Office Online

Both Google and Microsoft offer free, lightweight online versions that include word processing, spreadsheet, and presentation programs. Write at least 150 words comparing the features of Google G Suite and Microsoft Office Online. In your opinion, which one comes out on top for your purposes?

Ethical Issues Now

Intellectual property is the protection of ideas, which includes the name, designs, inventions, images, and symbols that a company uses. These are all part of a company's assets, which can influence its success. However, information technology has enabled other businesses or companies to imitate or copy ideas from others and use it as their own.

iStockphoto.com/Warchi

a. At a travel agency, your boss has asked you to create a trip flyer, using a word processor, that will be emailed to customers. You need travel destination images for the sales flyer and your boss has told you to "just copy them off our competitor's website." Write a paragraph about the ethical situation that you are facing.

b. Research the legal penalties you and your company may face for using another company's intellectual property without permission. Write a paragraph about these penalties.

Team Up Now—Wolfram Alpha Data Analysis

Wolfram Alpha is a data knowledge engine developed by Wolfram Research Share. Wolfram Alpha connects to online databases worldwide to answer your questions. Each of the team members should perform each of these searches at Wolfram Alpha. For each of the questions, locate the sources at the bottom of each of the results page.

a. What is the population of your birth city?
b. How common is your first name?
c. What is the median salary of a career field of interest?
d. Where was the strongest earthquake in the world in the last 24 hours? What was its magnitude?
e. Determine the number of calories from your most recent meal.
f. What was the weather on the day you were born in your birth city?
g. Locate the price of gas from a neighboring state/province and compare it to your state/province.

As a team compare your responses. List one of the sources for each of the responses. Submit the responses and sources of each of the team members to your instructor.

Key Terms

absolute reference
alignment
animation
app
app store
application software program
argument
bitmap
bullet
cell
cell address
cell range
cell reference
chart
clip art
column chart
communications
control
convergence
cropping
data type
database
desktop publishing (DTP) software
document
document management tools
field
field name
filter
font color
font size
font style
font type

form
format
formula
function
graphics
groupware
indent
insertion point
label
line chart
line spacing
local application
macro
margin
mobile app
mobile application
native application
notetaking software
operator
page break
page orientation
paragraph spacing
PDF (Portable Document Format)
personal information management
pivot table
pixel
point
portable application
presentation
presentation software
productivity software
property

query
record
red eye
relational database
relative reference
report
server
slide master
social networking
software application
sort
speech recognition software
spreadsheet
tab
table
template
thumbnail
transition
value
vector
view
web application (web app)
web-based application
web development software
webpage authoring
What-if analysis
word processing
word processing software
workbook
worksheet

The Web

This semester Hudson is taking Introduction to Business Law online. His entire course uses MindTap (a personalized online learning platform) for his readings, multimedia, activities, and assessments.

Hudson uses the web throughout the day on his tablet to work on his classes, add updates to his blog, engage with educational websites, read sports and news articles, and check his social networks such as Facebook and Twitter.

iStockphoto.com/Eva Katalin Kondoros

Hudson commutes to school each day and uses the time to complete his assignments. Connecting to the cloud to store and retrieve files with his tablet, Hudson leverages the web as a power user. Hudson uses his favorite browser, Microsoft Edge, with multiple tabs open to simultaneously check his grades in his online classes, read an op-ed article for his political science class, and watch a required video class lecture on YouTube.

Define the Web

World Wide Web | Internet | webpage | Hypertext Markup Language (HTML) | HTML tag | website | World Wide Web Consortium (W3C) | podcast | RSS feed | streaming video | online game | social networking

Since the early days of its development, the **World Wide Web**, now commonly referred to as "the web," has changed the way we get information, are entertained, conduct business transactions, and communicate. The web is part of the Internet. The **Internet** is the physical network that transmits data and helps us access the wealth of information on the web. The Internet is the largest computer network in the world and is composed of millions of interconnected computer networks, devices, and cables around the globe. Today, more than 2.5 billion people use the Internet and the web.

Define a Webpage

What exactly is the web? What is a webpage? Even though you probably have already used a computer or your smartphone to access the web, it is helpful to understand that "the web" is made up of webpages stored on computers around the world. See **Figure 5-1**.

Figure 5-1: A webpage

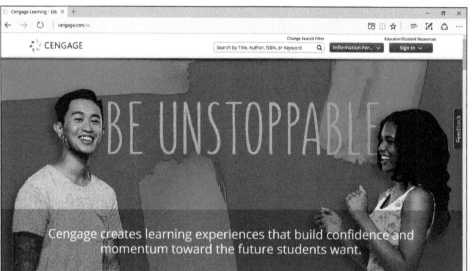

A **webpage** is a **Hypertext Markup Language (HTML)** document. This means that each webpage is a text document containing embedded HTML tags. **HTML tags** are codes that define the webpage. These tags determine how text and graphics will appear on pages. See **Figure 5-2**.

HTML code identifies each item in the document with specific information on where and how the image, video, paragraph, or any element should appear on the webpage.

A collection of webpages makes up a website. A **website** is usually created and maintained by a company, organization, institution, group, or even individuals. Websites generally focus on a specific topic, business, or purpose. Billions of websites around the world make up the web.

Manage the Web

Have you ever wondered who is in charge of the web? Who maintains the webpages? Who coordinates the individual networks around the world? Fortunately, there is no one person or group responsible for the web. That would be impossible. The majority of websites are maintained by the person, group, company, government, or organization that establishes the site. For example, a university is responsible for maintaining its

By the Numbers Now

In North America, 89% of the population are regular Internet users.

On the Job Now

The top five languages for webpages on the Internet include English, Chinese, Spanish, Arabic, and Portuguese. Consider creating your workplace website in multiple languages to reach a larger audience.

Figure 5-2: HTML pages make up the Web

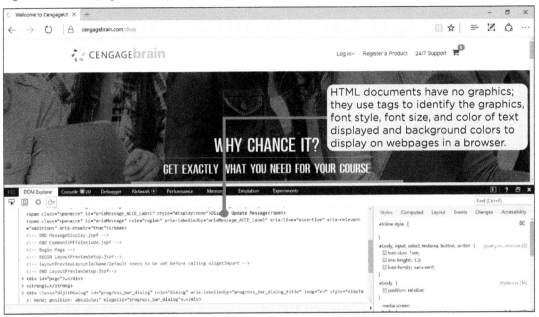

website and making sure the information is current for students and faculty. A travel agency makes sure that the airline and hotel links on its website are accurate. Each company or organization is also responsible for maintaining its hardware and the part of its network that connects to the Internet.

One of the leading organizations that set guidelines for the web is the **World Wide Web Consortium (W3C)**, which consists of hundreds of organizations and experts that work together to write web standards. See **Figure 5-3**. The W3C publishes standards on topics ranging from building webpages, to technologies for enabling web access from any device, to browser and search engine design—and much more.

Hot Technology Now

The site validator.w3.org can validate a website against the W3C web standards. This site checks links within the site, site efficiency, and site rule errors.

Figure 5-3: The World Wide Web consortium webpage

Source: 2016 W3C

Use the Web

The web has redefined how business is conducted around the world. Businesses can store data and buy and sell their products on the web; web apps and cloud computing make it possible for people in different locations to work on the same files simultaneously. Using social networking sites such as Facebook, Twitter, or Pinterest, businesses can share events and significant product or service announcements. LinkedIn is a standard used to expand professional networks, find jobs, and find potential employees.

People routinely use the web to buy tangible products such as clothes, as well as digital products such as music and movies. Online reservation systems let us book travel reservations, concert and event tickets, and doctor's appointments. Tangible products are shipped to physical destinations; digital products are delivered through a computer or even a smartphone or tablet.

News websites constantly update with the latest local or global events. You can subscribe to news services and specify areas of interest so alerts arrive in your inbox or on your smartphone. You can listen to **podcasts**, which are prerecorded audio files, to keep up with your favorite topics such as news, health, or politics. Though an older technology, **RSS feeds** let you subscribe to receive text, video, or graphics content you specify to your phone or desktop.

You don't need to be an established business to buy or sell products through the Internet. The Internet can function like a global garage or tag sale. You can buy and sell from other individuals through online auction sites such as eBay and uBid, or online classified ads on sites such as Craigslist or Freecycle. The web has also changed the way other traditional businesses now operate. You can rent vacation homes for short or longer term stays through AirBnB, HomeAway, or VRBO. You can call for a ride from Uber or Lyft.

The web is used to trade stocks and conduct online investment activities and services as well as engage in financial transactions. Online banking is offered by most banks, so you can check account balances and pay bills directly from any digital device with an Internet connection.

The web is essential in the employment market. Employers post job openings, job-seekers post resumes, and search sites try to match them. The web delivers information; you can use the web to take courses online to advance your career, and even get a college degree. See **Figure 5-4**.

Figure 5-4: Taking classes online

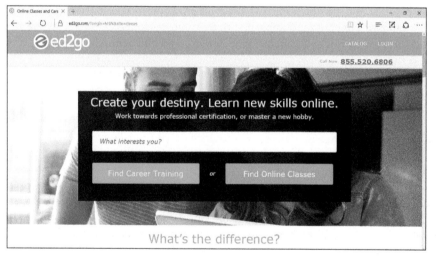

Entertainment and Social Networking

- The web is a primary source of delivery for video entertainment. You can order and watch a new or older movie or television show right from your computer or smartphone. You watch these movies or programs using **streaming video**, a technology that transfers a segment of a video file from the web to your computer, which plays while the next segment is sent.
- Use websites to play multiplayer **online games** with others around the world. In augmented reality games such as Pokemon Go, players use smartphones for global positioning to find and collect virtual tokens based on players' physical locations.

- Websites are available for socializing and communicating. Regardless of the device you use or whether you access the web from your home or on the go, the web provides valuable tools for interactions. Participate in **social networking** using sites such as Facebook, Instagram, Pinterest, Snapchat, and Twitter to communicate and share your ideas, announcements, videos, photos, music, and links to websites. Multiplayer gaming is another form of social networking.
- To communicate with others around the world, or even just next door, you can send and receive real-time messages using instant or text messaging (IM) programs. Messaging is available on computers as well as on most cellular phones. You can add video, pictures, graphics, and sound to messages. Messaging is available through various websites such as Google, Facebook, Skype, WhatsApp, and others. Messaging is often part of a cellular or mobile phone package.

Use a Browser

browser | home page | start page | hyperlink | mouse over | uniform resource locator (URL) | Address bar | navigation bar | cache | breadcrumb | navigation bar | favorite | bookmark | tabbed browsing | history list | pop-up blocking | private browsing | phishing | pharming | hacked | App Tab | sync feature | VoiceOver | Privacy pane | mobile browser | virtual keyboard | pinch-to-zoom | gesture

To access the World Wide Web, or "the web," you open a browser. A **browser** is an application that helps you communicate, access, and share information on the web. The first graphical web browser, Mosaic, used hyperlinked text and graphics to navigate between webpages and was instrumental in the development of the web as we know it today.

Navigate a Website

Browsers have tools to make navigating the web, or moving from one page to another, easy and fun. The page that appears when you open a browser is called the **home page**, or **start page**. These are also terms used to define the first page of a website. Browsers come with many buttons and menus to help with navigation. If you add a Home button to your menu bar, you can click or tap it to return to the Home page. Webpage navigation is possible because of **hyperlinks**, which are clickable or tappable words or graphics that you can use to move from one webpage to another or from one part of a webpage to another. With a mouse, you can point to, or **mouse over**, page elements to learn more, or right-click for further options.

Each webpage has a **uniform resource locator (URL)**, which is a webpage address that identifies that page on the web. Each time you click a hyperlink, you go to another webpage and the URL in the Address bar changes. All browsers have an **address bar** to let you know where you are on the web. You can also type the URL of the webpage you want to go to. Most address bars let you type either a phrase or a web address to display a page or list of pages matching the criteria. Regardless of your navigation method, the webpage loads, or appears, in the browser window. The **navigation bar** on a browser typically has Back, Forward, Refresh, and Home buttons.

As you navigate websites, your browser keeps a copy of each page you view in a **cache**, so that the next time you go to it, it will load more quickly. The browser also keeps track of pages you have viewed in sequence by tracking **breadcrumbs**—the path you followed to get to a page. Each browser lets you delete the information that your browser tracks.

Although there are many browsers to choose from with various unique features, the most commonly used browsers include Microsoft Edge, Google Chrome, Mozilla Firefox, and Apple Safari. Internet Explorer is still widely used, but is gradually being replaced by Microsoft Edge.

The Bottom Line
- Browsers let you view, or browse, webpages and navigate websites using controls and menus.
- Browsers, such as Microsoft Edge, Chrome, Firefox, and Safari, have many common features including tabs, search bars, and other tools to help you find information on the web.
- Mobile browsers optimize the display of a webpage most effectively for small screens on mobile devices such as smartphones.

Identify Common Browser Features

Most web browsers include common features, so if you have used one browser, you won't have trouble learning another. Some of these features are:

- **Favorites**, or **bookmarks**, which are saved shortcuts to webpages.
- **Tabbed browsing** to access several webpages in the same browser window.
- A **history list** of the webpages you visit for a day, a week, a month, and so on.
- **Pop-up blocking** in your browser to prevent pop-up ads, or advertisements that appear in separate windows, distracting you from the page you are viewing, when you connect to a webpage.
- **Private browsing** mode, which lets you surf the web without leaving history, temporary Internet files, or small text files called "cookies" that webpages store on your computer's hard drive to identify you when you visit their site.

Focus on Security and Privacy

Many web browsers have built-in security features that let you block spyware and pop-up ads, as well as protect you from other hazards on the web. For example, **phishing** is the use of emails that look legitimate—but aren't—to get sensitive data. Such emails usually contain links that take you to fake websites. Once you are at the website, any personal information you add can be used to steal your identity.

You should never click links to a website that come in an email. If your bank needs to contact you and sends you a message, open a new browser window and type in the bank's URL to begin contacting the bank. **Pharming** is a scam in which a server is hacked and used to re-route traffic to a fake website to obtain personal information. **Hacked** means a computer has been taken over by an unauthorized user.

Although you must always be vigilant for fraud and other hazards when you visit websites, your browser can help protect you from some pitfalls. Some browsers warn you of unsafe websites. However, when you conduct financial transactions on the Internet, such as banking, shopping, or investing, you should use a secure connection. Browsers have different methods of showing you that a website is secure. Most browsers place some type of lock icon or identifying color in the browser bar.

A lock button next to a website's address in Microsoft Edge means that data you send and receive from the website is encrypted, making it difficult for anyone else to access to this info. It identifies the website as verified, which means the company running the site has a certificate proving they own it. You can click a lock button to see who owns the site and who verified it. A gray lock means that the website is encrypted and verified, and a green lock means that the site has an Extended Validation (EV) certificate, and has passed a rigorous identity verification process. See **Figure 5-5**.

Figure 5-5: A secure page

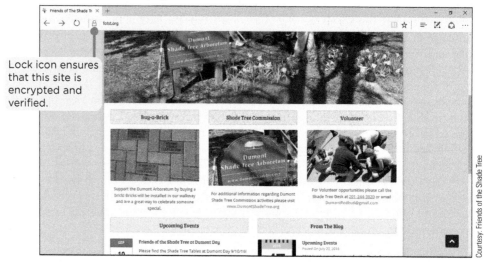

Lock icon ensures that this site is encrypted and verified.

Courtesy: Friends of the Shade Tree

Use Microsoft Edge, Google Chrome, and Firefox

Popular browsers include Microsoft Edge, Google Chrome, and Firefox. Although there are feature differences among these browsers, most enable you to do the following:

- Receive warnings of suspected phishing or malware while you browse.
- Remove unnecessary security warnings for downloads from verified sites.
- Connect to your cloud storage using the browser.
- Use a combined search and Address bar, where you can type in searches as well as web addresses.
- Translate a webpage to a different language in the browser.
- Use enhanced tab features, such as the ability to pin websites to the tab gallery, taskbar, or Start screen for one-click navigation.
- View multiple websites simultaneously.
- Use an **App Tab** to pin any website icon so the website is easily available. The App Tab displays a blue highlight when the corresponding site changes. App Tabs have no Close button, so you cannot accidentally close them. App Tabs open automatically for convenience. In Edge you can also pin a website tab so it opens each time the browser opens.
- A **sync feature** connects your desktop and mobile devices so you can access your browsing history, passwords, and bookmarks on all your devices.
- Screen features that provide additional help for URLs you can't remember. As you type a site name, the feature locates possible matches from your history, bookmarks, and open tabs.
- The ability to restore a session if your computer shuts down; all your pages reopen without your having to remember what you were looking at before the shutdown.
- Privacy features to protect your work and your identity as you browse webpages.

Use Safari on Apple Computers

Safari, the default browser for Mac and iOS, is the browser used most by people with Macs and Apple computers. Safari features include the following:

- Built-in support for Apple's **VoiceOver** screen reader. VoiceOver describes aloud what appears on the screen and reads the text and links of websites, making the web accessible to people with visual impairments.
- Enhanced keyboard navigation for navigating the web without a mouse, as well as multi-touch gestures—such as double-tapping the trackpad with two fingers to magnify part of a webpage.
- A **Privacy pane**, which displays information such as tracking data left by websites you visit so you can remove the data and protect your privacy.

Use Mobile Browsers

You can access webpages on your mobile device using a **mobile browser**, which is specially designed for small screens. Popular mobile browsers include Opera, Google Chrome, Windows Mobile, Firefox Mobile, Dolphin for Android, and Safari Mobile. See **Figure 5-6**.

Mobile browsers must display content on small screens. Some browsers, such as Opera and Safari Mobile for iPhone, render webpages as they would appear on your desktop or laptop computer, making navigation difficult or cutting off content. Mobile browsers also need to accommodate the low memory capacity and low bandwidth of wireless handheld devices.

To help you view webpages on the go, most mobile browsers also do the following:

- Provide **virtual keyboards**, which can be operated with a mouse or keyboard, in addition to touchscreen keyboards, and let you enter text without leaving the page you are viewing.
- Offer a **pinch-to-zoom** feature that capitalizes on mobile device touch screens: they let you use two fingers to adjust the screen size by pinching your fingers together or apart to shrink or enlarge a page.
- Let you draw shapes, called **gestures**, to issue instructions that your mobile device can execute. See **Figure 5-7** on the next page.
- Let you sync your mobile device with your desktop computer to transfer history, passwords, and bookmarks.

Figure 5-6: Google mobile browser on a mobile device

Figure 5-7: Gestures for mobile devices

Hot Technology Now

Gestures are possible because of sensor hardware and touch-screen technologies, which continue to develop and improve. The HoloLens Augmented Reality device displays the Microsoft Edge browser as a hologram that you can "air" tap.

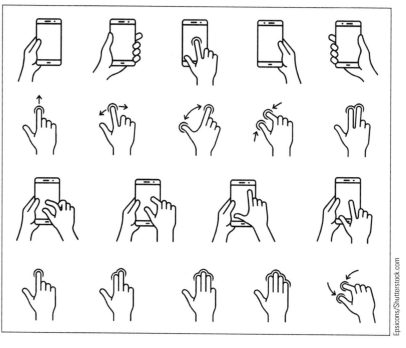

Epsicons/Shutterstock.com

The Bottom Line

- Cascading style sheets (CSS), XML (eXtensible Markup Language), and HTML5 create the code that works to create the webpages you see and use.
- Uniform resource locators (URLs) create a unique address for each webpage so it can be found by any browser on the Internet.
- Scripts make webpages interactive.

Examine Webpages

Hypertext Markup Language (HTML) | HTML tag | Cascading style sheet (CSS) | Responsive Design | Responsive Web Design (RWD) | XML (eXtensible Markup Language) | database | static web publishing | dynamic web publishing | script | HTML script | server-side script | dynamic webpage | client-side script

Have you thought about creating a webpage, but don't know where to start? Believe it or not, there are just three basic technologies involved in creating even the most dynamic multimedia webpages: HTML, CSS, and XML.

Use HTML to Create Webpages

A webpage is a document that contains HTML (Hypertext Markup Language) tags. See **Figure 5-8**. HTML has had several versions; the current version is HTML5. **HTML tags**

Figure 5-8: Creating HTML tags

Hypertext Markup Language (HTML) provides a structure for creating and formatting Web pages.

PixDeluxe/Shutterstock.com

are pieces of code that control how the document is displayed on the webpage—the text size, where a graphic is placed, and so on. There are several options for creating HTML tags. You can manually add HTML tags to a text document using a simple text editor such as Notepad, a program that comes with the Windows operating system, although this is tedious and not recommended. You could also use an HTML conversion utility to generate tags from existing documents.

Web authoring software, such as Adobe Dreamweaver, and several free open source programs such as Bluefish, provide tools for creating webpages. You can create navigation bars, drop-down lists, and other features by using premade templates available online. Some ISPs (Internet Service Providers) and web hosting companies offer online web authoring tools, similar to templates, where you can drag and drop elements onto a webpage. See **Figure 5-9**.

Figure 5-9: Tools for creating websites

garagestock/Shutterstock.com

Use CSS to Format Webpages

Cascading Style Sheets (CSS) is a way to use simple code to describe how webpage elements are to be displayed and presented on a screen in a browser. The advantage of CSS is that you define elements in a section of code and then you can reuse it throughout the webpage to create a consistent look. Webpage developers use CSS to specify colors, layout, and fonts. By using CSS as part of the webpage code, it allows the page to appear similarly on different types of devices, such as desktop computer screens, small screens such as smartphones or tablets, or even printers. This approach to webpage development is called **Responsive Design** or **Responsive Web design (RWD)** so that anyone coming to a webpage has an optimal viewing experience, regardless of the device they are using. See **Figure 5-10**. This includes the ability to read the text on the page, see the graphics, and navigate through the page without having to resize or scroll. CSS is independent of HTML and can be used with any XML-based markup language.

Figure 5-10: Responsive web design

iStockphoto.com/RidoFranz

Use XML to Structure Data

While HTML provides a way to format a webpage, **XML (eXtensible Markup Language)** provides a way to classify the contents of the webpage, making it easier to organize.

XML lets a webpage developer customize HTML tags to organize components of the page into different files. XML files give the pages a uniform look by defining how each element looks. For example, one file could define elements for name, address, contact information, etc. Another file might contain the actual content, such as product information; and a third file might identify the format, such as an HTML document.

Organizations such as news companies use this kind of structured system to identify and change the content of their webpages, without having to work with the layout or format. So, when you visit the page, you recognize the colors, graphics, and the way the text is placed on the page, but each day, new content is shown to you.

XML can also help you conduct more efficient online searches. When you visit sites that sell items such as music recordings, for example, XML enables cataloging by title, artist, genre, and many other ways to help you find just what you're looking for.

Use Web Databases

When you use websites to make travel arrangements, post to social media sites, or shop, the content you see is data. The data for websites is stored in **databases**, which are organized collections of data. Accessing a database on the web requires a browser.

One way to display data from a web database is to use the database's report utility to convert a database report into an HTML document that a browser can display. This is

Hot Technology Now

Free website development sites, such as wix.com, weebly.com, and wordpress.com, offer hundreds of templates that allow you to create a professional-looking webpage even if you are not an experienced developer.

On the Job Now

Many companies have a web development team that combines graphic artists, database administrators, and HTML/web script code developers.

called **static web publishing** because the HTML document is a snapshot of the data—it's fixed and cannot be changed. Another way to display data from a Web database is to create webpages on demand, retrieving the most current data at the moment you request it. This is called **dynamic web publishing**. When you shop at a home goods store, for example, the webpage will show you only the inventory in stock, or available to order. There could be hundreds of people shopping at once, so the database must be continuously updated to offer customers the best information for available products.

Use Client and Server Scripts

Have you ever wondered how a webpage fills in your delivery address after you've typed your billing address? Scripts make this possible. A **script**, often called an **HTML script**, is a set of program instructions that make webpages interactive. For instance, scripts help your browser fill in your username and password on some websites, allow e-commerce sites to verify credit card data, and let you complete online forms for ordering products.

A script can be embedded directly into the HTML code for a webpage or in a file referenced in the HTML code. Depending on the type of script, the server or the browser runs the script when you visit the webpage. A disadvantage to scripts is that they can pose a security risk, and some browsers do not allow them to run. You can generally run scripts safely if you are using a secure connection.

The data you enter is stored in your computer's memory. When you click the Submit button, your browser collects the data and sends it to a specified script on an HTTP server to be processed. If a website is using a secure connection, however, it is usually safe to run scripts on that site.

There are two types of scripts. One is a **server-side script** because it runs on a server rather than on your computer. A server-side script accepts data from fill-in forms, and then processes the data and generates a custom HTML document for the browser to display as a webpage. These webpages are called **dynamic webpages**. Webpage developers write server-side scripts using languages such as Perl, PHP, C, C++, C#, and Java.

The other type of script is a **client-side script**, which runs on your local computer. Your browser executes the script, which means the browser must be able to use the programming language in which the script is written. VBScript and JavaScript are two popular languages for writing client-side scripts.

Use the Web to Find Information

search engine technology | search engine | web crawler | spider | indexing utility | query processor | keyword | search phrase | hit | wildcard character | Boolean operator | web master | search engine optimization (SEO) | meta keyword | keyword stuffing

You can find virtually any information you want on the Internet; all you need to do is to search for it. **Search engine technology** makes finding the information you want easier by letting you enter search criteria and then doing the legwork for you.

Use Search Sites to Find Information

Search sites are websites designed specifically to help you find information on the web. Popular search sites include www.google.com, www.bing.com, and www.yahoo.com. Search sites use software programs called **search engines** to locate relevant webpages. A search engine creates a simple query based on your search criteria and stores the collected data in a search database.

Some search sites such as Google, shown in **Figure 5-11**, use their own search engine, while others use third-party technology. For example, Bing (from Microsoft) powers Yahoo! search. Regardless of whether you use a search site or enter your criteria in a search box on a webpage, you'll be using a search engine to find information.

Use Search Engines to Find Information

Search engine technology has four components: a web crawler, an indexer, a database, and a query processor. See **Table 5-1**.

Figure 5-11: Google home page

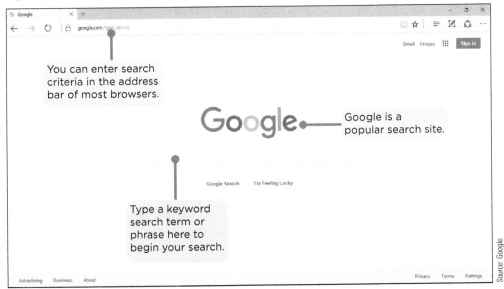

You can enter search criteria in the address bar of most browsers.

Google is a popular search site.

Type a keyword search term or phrase here to begin your search.

Source: Google

Table 5-1: Search engine components

Component	Description
Web crawler or **spider** program	An automated program that uses hyperlinks to jump between webpages, collecting data about each page as it goes; web crawlers can reach millions of webpages each day.
Indexing utility	Receives data from a web crawler and then compiles the collected data into an organized list of key words and URLs
Query processor	Looks for your search criteria in the indexed database and then displays the list of results as URLs with corresponding descriptive information

To conduct a web search, you can type keywords into a search site or into the search box found on most webpages. **Keywords** are one or more words that describe what you're looking for. Multiple keywords are called a **search phrase**.

The search engine uses your keywords to return a list of **hits**, or links to webpages that match your criteria. See Table 5-2 for some examples of search phrases and keywords to search for information on buying used Android smartphones.

Table 5-2: Examples of search phrases

Keyword or phrase	Possible results	Suggested change
Looking for a used smartphone	A list of all used phones; returns too many hits	Add the word "Android."
Looking for a used Android smartphone	Still too many hits	Remove or omit common words such as "the" and "an"; remove verb.
Used Android smartphone	Too many hits; results still includes other smartphones	Search for an exact phrase by entering it in quotation marks.
Used "Android smartphone"	List of used Android smartphones	

If your search returns too many hits, continue adding words to narrow your search. You can also use a **wildcard character** such as the asterisk to search for derivations of a word. For example, if you want to search for all forms of words related to chlorine, you can search for *chlori* to get websites about chlorine, sodium chloride, chlorination, and so forth.

Use Boolean Searches

You can create better search criteria by using a search operator, also called a **Boolean operator**. A Boolean operator is a word or symbol that identifies the relationship between keywords. See **Table 5-3**.

Table 5-3: Examples of Boolean searches

Boolean operator	Example	Results	Explanation
AND	Android smartphones AND tablets	Devices that are Android smartphones and tablets	The AND operator indicates that both (or all) terms in the criteria must appear on a webpage for it to be included in the results. Some engines use the plus symbol instead of the word AND. AND Results are inclusive of all possibilities using the key terms or phrase.
OR	Smartphones new OR used	All smartphones whether they are new or used	Either (or any one) of the search terms must appear on a webpage for it to be included as a search result.
NOT	Android smartphones NOT apps	Only smartphones, not Android apps	The search term must not appear on a webpage for it to be included as a search result. Some engines use the minus sign instead of NOT.

Use Advanced Search Forms

You may be unable to narrow the list of results for your search by simply entering keywords or Boolean operators. Some search engines provide forms to help simplify your search. Such forms are available via the advanced search link on the main page of a search engine's website. **Figure 5-12** shows an advanced search form. With a little practice, you can create efficient web searches whether you use additional keywords, wildcard characters, Boolean operators, or an advanced search form.

Figure 5-12: Advanced search form

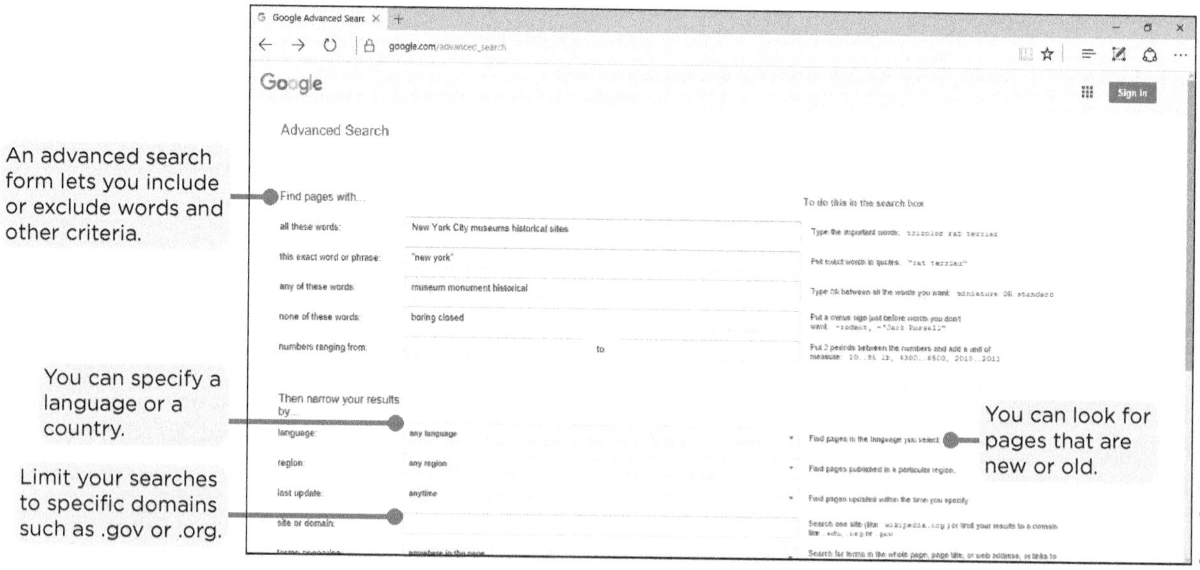

An advanced search form lets you include or exclude words and other criteria.

You can specify a language or a country.

Limit your searches to specific domains such as .gov or .org.

You can look for pages that are new or old.

Source: Google

Improve Page Rankings

Although web crawlers discover millions of websites each day, a **web master**, the person who maintains a website, can manually submit URLs to a search engine. A web master can submit URLs for paid placement on the page or as banner or pop-up ads, for which merchants are charged only if the ad is clicked.

The order in which search results appear depends on the relevance of keyword matches and link popularity. Legitimate **search engine optimization (SEO)** techniques are often used to improve page ranking. Link popularity means that pages with links to popular websites get higher ratings. Some website operators attempt to push their sites to the top of result lists by manipulating **meta keywords**, or words entered into the header section of the webpage when it's created. This is an unethical practice called **keyword stuffing**. For this reason, many sites no longer use meta keywords to determine page ranking. Socially responsible search sites have procedures to override attempts at keyword stuffing and post their policies on paid placements.

Review Webpage Content

While anyone with a computer and Internet access can create a webpage containing any content, governments and organizations can block or limit access to sites or content they deem inappropriate for any reason. Internet censorship is the control or suppression of what can be accessed, published, or viewed on the Internet for moral, social, or political reasons.

Government regulators, businesses, universities, and schools may block websites or filter search results that promote political or social agendas. Reasons include the need to protect minors from inappropriate or illegal content or governments' desires to control their citizens' access to information. For example, some countries don't allow citizens access to Facebook, YouTube, or Twitter.

Businesses and educational institutions may block or filter content to protect workers or students from explicit or offensive content in the workplace or in schools. Even in countries where there is a free and open Internet, companies and institutions may legally block employees from using social networking sites for people using their computers to help ensure productivity.

#worldwideweb

Organizations have rules for filtering explicit content. Government censorship is a sensitive issue; practiced in some countries and shunned in others.

Describe Website Structure

uniform resource locator (URL) | encryption | Hypertext Transfer Protocol Secure | digital certificate | link | bitmap graphic | vector graphic | streaming | banner ad | pop-up ad | click-through rate | cookie | targeted marketing

Suppose you want to find a book published by Cengage Learning. You go to the Cengage website. Like any website, it has many components and features to help deliver its content to you.

Define URLs

A **uniform resource locator (URL)** is a series of letters and numbers that identifies a webpage. Generally, the owner of the URL determines the URL. Since every page has a unique URL, owners may have to compromise on the name if it's already taken. The URL identifies the webpage as a unique page on the Internet and provides information about the page's location, type, and security. See **Figure 5-13**.

The Bottom Line

- Website designers use various tools to create secure sites.
- Components such as graphics, video, audio, and text come in various file formats.
- Hyperlinks, whether text or graphic, are essential to navigating webpages and can provide instant access to related information.
- Websites are often funded through advertising in the forms of banners and pop-up ads.

Figure 5-13: Cengage website URL

URLs use forward slashes—not backward slashes—and cannot contain spaces; use a hyphen or underscore character.

A URL indicates the communications protocol used to transport the web page over the Internet, the web server hosting the page, names of folders where the page is stored, the file name, and any file extension.

The beginning of a URL is the protocol, or set of rules, the page uses. **Hypertext Transfer Protocol (HTTP)** is a communications protocol that transports data over the web. The most common protocols are http for regular webpages, https for secure pages, and File Transfer Protocol (FTP) for transferring files. Some URLs will display file extensions, such as .html or .htm, to help identify the type of webpage. HTML tags specify how components of the page should appear in the browser.

Secure Websites

Secure websites are essential to protecting sensitive data. A secure website is one that uses encryption to safeguard transmitted information. A website can be secured using several methods. **Encryption** is the process of temporarily scrambling data so it is not readable until it is decrypted. The "https" prefix stands for **Hypertext Transfer Protocol Secure**. Websites such as banks and retail stores use the https protocol to make a secure connection to your computer. See **Figure 5-14**. Secure websites often use a **digital certificate** to verify the identity of a person or an organization.

Figure 5-14: A secure connection

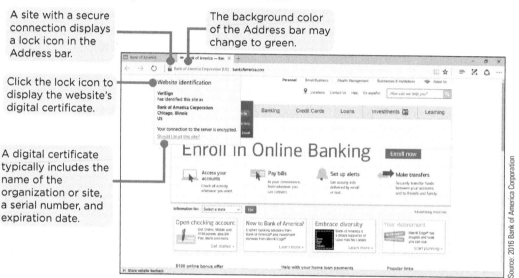

A site with a secure connection displays a lock icon in the Address bar.

The background color of the Address bar may change to green.

Click the lock icon to display the website's digital certificate.

A digital certificate typically includes the name of the organization or site, a serial number, and expiration date.

Source: 2016 Bank of America Corporation

Identify Webpage Components

Buttons and text boxes let you make choices and enter information. And without components such as links and graphics, webpages would be incredibly dull and not very useful. Web graphics are either bitmap or scalable vector.

- **Links** let you jump from page to page by clicking, following your interests. A link contains the URL of a webpage and can be text, such as an underlined word or phrase, or a graphic.
- **Bitmap graphics** consist of pixels, meaning that they lose quality when enlarged. JPG files compress bitmap graphics to save space and download time.
- Scalable **vector graphics** use mathematical formulas instead of pixels and are widely used on webpages because they maintain the same quality on all screens and have small file sizes.

Include Video and Audio on Webpages

Many websites use video, which consists of images displayed in motion and usually accompanied by audio. Although a server can transmit an entire video file before it begins to play on your computer, videos are typically transmitted using **streaming**, where a small segment of the file is transmitted and begins to play while the server sends the next segment. There may be times when you want to store the video on your computer; if a video is available for download, you can click a link on the webpage to download it. The video will be downloaded from a web server, where it is stored, to your computer.

Webpages can also contain audio—speech, music, or other sounds—which can be part of a video or played as background music. Often a webpage will offer a mute icon that you can click if you don't want to hear the sound.

Earn Revenue from Websites

Websites, especially e-commerce sites, seek to monetize their sites, which means to generate revenue by renting advertising space. When users tap or click a pop-up or a banner ad, the browser connects directly to the advertiser's site. A **banner ad** is an advertisement that appears in a webpage, typically near the top or at the side or bottom margins. A **pop-up ad** is an advertisement that appears in a separate window when you access a webpage. See **Figure 5-15**.

Figure 5-15: Pop-up and banner ads

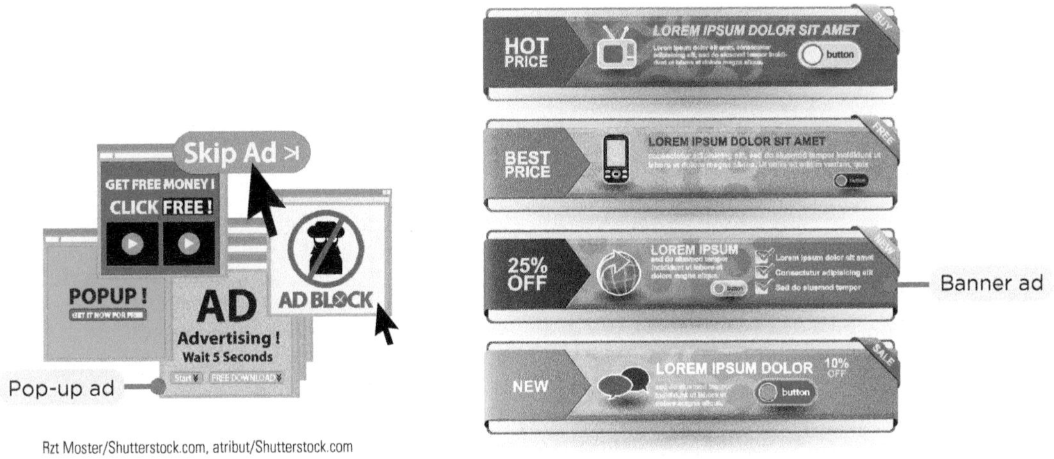

Banner ad

Pop-up ad

Rzt Moster/Shutterstock.com, atribut/Shutterstock.com

A website that hosts an ad earns a small fee based on the **click-through rate**, which is the number of times that visitors click the ad to connect to the advertiser's site. The ad revenue helps support the sites and reduces costs to consumers.

However, pop-up and banner ads often install a **cookie** (a small data file) on the user's computer to track spending and browsing patterns, which can be a privacy concern. Browsers contain settings allowing users to block them, but this may cause other ecommerce features to be less effective. A further disadvantage is that popups can be overly intrusive on mobile devices with small screens, so some search engines, such as Google, are discouraging advertisers from using popups that disrupt the user experience.

When e-commerce first became popular, people were learning how to buy and sell on the Internet and often would click ads. Over time, however, click-through rates have declined because consumers often ignore ads or install software, or set their browsers, to block them. Advertisers now try to find newer ways to reach users. One important way is **targeted marketing**, which attempts to match browsing behavior, user profiles, and buying habits with products. For example, if a person searches for 'snow boots' using a search engine, this information is then used to place an advertisement for the snow boot company on the pages they visit, even if unrelated to shopping or snow, or boots, to help promote the snow boot company page. Location and demographics can also help sellers choose targeted ads. However, privacy remains an ongoing concern for many users and consumer advocates.

Define Types of Websites

domain name | IP address | top-level domain (TLD) | Domain Name System (DNS) | domain name server | web portal | content aggregator | distributed content | wiki | blog | social networking | file-sharing site

With millions of sites on the web, how can you efficiently find the information or product you want? Websites have different content, structures and purposes, including news, information, or business, and may be a platform for blogs, wikis, social

#worldwideweb

Contextual ad targeting online is based on your age/gender/income demographic, your social media presence, and cookies from your past website history.

The Bottom Line

- Every website has a unique IP address and a corresponding unique domain name. The domain name helps identify the type of website.
- Top-level domains (TLDs) help identify the type of website.
- Websites with user-supplied content comprise a large part of the web.

networking, education, entertainment, advocacy, web applications (web apps), content aggregators, and personal information. Websites can be identified by their domains.

Define Domain Names and IP Addresses

Domain names can help you understand the various areas of the internet. A **domain name** is a string of text characters that describes a particular area of the Internet, such as whitehouse.gov or cengage.com. A domain name is related to a website's Internet Protocol (IP) address, a series of numbers allocated to each network on the Internet to ensure that every web location is unique. While you can type an IP address into your browser's Address bar, it can be hard to remember if you're not a computer, so it's easier to use the text-based domain names. See **Figure 5-16**.

Figure 5-16: IP address and domain name for the White House

104.109.178.94 is the **IP address** for the domain whitehouse.gov.

Every domain name ends with an extension that indicates its **top-level domain**, or **TLD**. In the domain name www.whitehouse.gov, ".gov" is the TLD.

Source: Whitehouse.gov

Manage Domain Names

Although it's hard to imagine, every domain name and its corresponding IP address have been entered into the **Domain Name System (DNS)**, which is a world-wide database. Rather than storing it in a single location, many Internet servers host part of the DNS to keep it secure. These servers are called **domain name servers**, or DNS servers, and typically are associated with Internet Service Providers (ISPs). When you're using a browser and request a website by its common domain name, such as cengage.com, a DNS server looks up the IP address so your browser can display the correct page.

Who issues domain names? The Internet Corporation for Assigned Names and Numbers (ICANN) coordinates Internet addresses around the world. ICANN supervises several for-profit accredited domain registrars, such as DreamHost and GoDaddy, and these organizations handle domain name requests.

Identify Top-Level Domains (TLDs)

In a web address, the three-letter extension after the period indicates a top-level domain (TLD), such as the "com" in "cengage.com". All domain names have a top-level domain. As you visit websites, you might notice some that have top-level domains other than .com. Originally, the United States had the seven TLDs, listed in **Table 5-4**.

Table 5-4: Traditional original TLDs and sites they represent

TLD	Generally used for
.com	Most commercial sites that sell products and services
.edu	Academic and research sites such as schools and universities
.gov	U. S. government organizations
.int	International treaty organizations
.mil	Military organizations
.net	Network providers, ISPs, and other Internet administrative organizations
.org	Organizations such as political or not for profit. Any website can have the .org TLD but, traditionally, only professional and nonprofit organizations such as churches and humanitarian groups use it.

As Internet activity increases, ICANN continues to add new domains to the original seven TLDs, along with two-letter codes for countries such as .au (Australia), .ca (Canada), .de (Germany), and .jp (Japan). See Table 5-5.

Table 5-5: Additional TLDs and sites they represent

TLD	Generally used for
.aero	The aviation industry
.biz	Unrestricted use, but usually identifies businesses, along with the .co and .com TLD
.info	Resource sites; allows unrestricted use
.jobs	Employment sites
.mobi	Sites optimized for mobile devices
.pro	Licensed professionals
.coop	Cooperatives, wholly owned subsidiaries, and other organizations that exist to promote or support cooperatives
.museum	Museum associations, and individual members of the museum profession

Identify Types of Sites

What do you want to do on the web today? Chances are, a certain type of website provides just what you're looking for. The web not only displays information but also lets you interact with it. You can contribute thoughts and images to the ongoing "conversation" through public forum sites, blogs, and chat rooms.

Using search sites and portals such as Google and Yahoo!, you need to remember only one URL to access a variety of services such as maps, shopping, and news. A **web portal**, or **portal** is a website that combines pages from many sources and provides access to those pages. On entertainment websites, you can view or discuss activities ranging from sports to videos. For example, you can cast a vote on a topic for a television show.

A **content aggregator** site such as News360 and Flipboard gathers, organizes, and then distributes web content. Subscribers choose the type of content they want, and receive updates automatically. News is an example of **distributed content**, content created by a news organization and published directly to platforms they don't control. For example, news organizations often create content for direct publishing to social media platforms.

As the web becomes more interactive, an increasing amount of content is supplied by users. You can contribute comments and opinions to informational sites such as news sites, blogs, and wikis. A **wiki** is a collaborative website where you and your colleagues can modify content on a webpage, and then publish it just by clicking a button. Wikis are great for group projects. A **blog**, short for "web log," is a webpage listing journal entries in chronological order. One person usually creates a blog to reflect his or her point of view. **Social networking** sites such as Facebook, Twitter, and Instagram let participants share personal information, upload photos and other media, and make new friends. **File-sharing sites** such as YouTube and Flickr let you post and share photos, music, and other media.

Work with Web Apps

web application (web app) | application service provider (ASP) |
Software as a Service (SaaS) | cloud storage | online storage

Do you ever need to check your email or consult a map from home, work, and school? You can do that, and perform many other tasks, using a **web application**, or web app. **Web apps** are applications that reside on a server on the Internet, rather than a user's device, and are run by a user through a web browser.

On the Job Now

For a career in the United States Army, view more information on the site www.army.mil. Notice the .mil file extension.

By the Numbers Now

Of the $540 billion spent on worldwide advertising, 42% is spent on television ads and 25% is spent on digital media web-based ads.

Hot Technology Now

Websites such as join.me (screen sharing site) and bit.ly (shortens long URLs) have purchased TLDs to make their domain names easier to remember.

The Bottom Line

- Web apps run in a browser, so they are accessible from most any device with Internet access.
- Web apps are not typically stored on your computer or other device, though some host websites such as Google Earth or Skype for Business may require you to download additional software.
- Web app advantages include being able to access files and features while on the go and sharing information seamlessly with others; disadvantages include needing Internet access to get at your files and programs.

Define Web Apps

A web app runs in any browser that supports basic web technologies such as HTML and JavaScript. Web apps are popular because most devices have a browser as basic software and therefore can access and run the web app. Some web apps are free, others charge only for enhanced features or services, and some require ongoing usage fees.

Application service providers, or **ASPs**, provide software-based services over the Internet. Running software directly from the Internet is called **Software as a Service**, or **SaaS**. Office 365 and Google Drive is an example of SaaS. Web apps often incorporate other reusable web apps, such as an interactive calendar, calculator, or currency converter for online shopping or auctions.

Web app sites include online tax preparation, such as TurboTax and document storage such as Carbonite. You can also use web apps such as Office 365 and Google Drive or OneDrive to create and manage documents and presentations. Sway is a webpage- and presentation-building Office 365 product that appears only in a browser and stores the "sways" on a cloud server.

Use Webmail

Email is used worldwide for personal and business correspondence because of its convenience and speed, as well as its ability to track, store, and organize information and send to many people at once. Although there are drawbacks, including privacy concerns, email has become the primary written communications tool for most people.

Instead of using an email program installed on your computer, such as Outlook, you can use a webmail service such as Gmail or Outlook.com to send and receive email. A webmail service provides a webpage for your email, which you access using a browser. You get an email address with the domain of the provider, such as yourname@gmail.com or yourname@outlook.com. You can access your account from any computer or device with an Internet connection, even computers at a public location such as a library.

Use Online Storage Sites

As more applications are becoming web based and consumers want to access their files from anywhere using multiple devices, online or cloud storage is increasingly important. Some websites provide storage, some provide web apps, and some do both. See **Figure 5-17**.

Figure 5-17: Web apps in the cloud

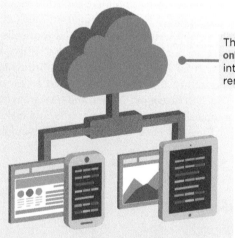

The terms **cloud storage** and **online storage** are often used interchangeably to describe remote storage on the Internet.

Microsoft OneDrive is a host site that provides cloud storage for files as well as Microsoft Office web apps, allowing you to both create and store data on Microsoft servers. Cloud storage sites that provide web apps provide privacy and security using password protection. Google Drive performs similar services. Some sites, such as DropBox and iCloud, provide file storage but do not provide apps to edit or create the files.

Cloud storage services vary among providers and may be restricted to specific types of files. For example, you can store only photos on Flickr. The primary goal of some cloud storage sites, such as Box, Amazon CloudDrive, DropBox and iCloud, is to provide online storage, but they don't let you change or work with files. Online and cloud storage sites are usually password-protected, and you can specify whether your files are private or shared. You can share some or all of your files with others by granting access.

Use Productivity Applications

Productivity apps help you accomplish specific tasks such as creating a document or presentation. Google Drive offers productivity apps such as word processing, spreadsheet, presentation, and database software along with cloud storage. You can use online presentation sites such as Prezi to create and share presentations.

Microsoft Office web apps and Google Drive offer simplified versions of productivity apps and are ideal for individual users who want to collaborate with others. Microsoft Office 365 is the online version of Microsoft Office, designed primarily for businesses or large groups of users. It also includes Microsoft server products and Office web apps—the browser-based versions of Excel, Word, PowerPoint, OneNote, Sway, Power BI, Yammer, Delve, and Planner.

Identify Popular Web Apps

There are many popular web apps that provide you with the tools you can use for daily activities as well as help you manage your finances and business needs. See Table 5-6.

Hot Technology Now

Google Hangouts supports video calls with up to 25 friends.

#worldwideweb

The most popular social media sharing sites include Facebook, YouTube, Twitter, Pinterest, and Tumblr.

Table 5-6: Some other web apps

Web app	Function category	Notes and description
www.britannica.com http://www.dictionary.com/ IMDB.com	Online reference software	Look up information and facts on specific topics such as synonyms, definitions, and movie and TV trivia
YouTube Pinterest Tumblr Instagram	Media sharing	Share graphics and video
Kayak TripAdvisor Expedia Yelp	Travel and Leisure	Make travel arrangements, find local hotels and restaurants, read and contribute traveler reviews
Adobe Express Flickr AmazonPhotos	Online photo editing and sharing	Extra storage and features cost money
Gmail Outlook.com Yahoo! Mail	Email programs	Create, send, and manage email messages
Turbo Tax Online TaxACT Online	Tax preparation	Some tax preparation programs let you prepare your return for free, but may charge for printing or electronic filing
Google Earth Google Maps BingMaps	Mapping applications	Require software download; Google and MapQuest offer part of web app free, but charge for advanced features.

Compare the Pros and Cons of Web Apps

You should weigh the advantages and disadvantages of using web apps and decide what best suits your needs. The advantages of using web apps are as follows:

- You can collaborate on projects with coworkers in multiple locations, even if you have different work schedules.
- You can access your work from any location because data is stored on the app's website.
- You save storage space on your computer.
- You don't have to install updates, since the newest version is always available on the app's website.
- You can access web apps from any device with a browser and Internet connection, including computers, smartphones, or tablets.

The disadvantages of using web apps are as follows:

- If a cloud computing provider has technical problems, web apps and related data could become unavailable.
- If a provider goes out of business, you can lose functionality and files.
- Some web apps offer fewer features and may run more slowly than installed applications.

Define Electronic Commerce

e-commerce | business-to-consumer (B2C) | cookie | consumer-to-consumer (C2C) | business-to-business (B2B) | 3-D Secure | biometrics | Transport Layer Security (TLS) | Hypertext Transfer Protocol Secure (HTTPS) | electronic wallet | digital wallet | online investing | aggregator site | digital gift certificate | digital gift card | digital coupon

E-commerce refers to the purchase of products such as clothing and electronics, intangible products such as music, and services such as education, airline and concert tickets, hotel reservations, and gift certificates, over the Internet. Some businesses offer shopping both in the store and online. Both businesses and consumers use e-commerce to enhance their organizations and lives. E-commerce is divided into business models, shown in **Figure 5-18**, based on the type of buyer and seller.

Use Business-to-Consumer E-commerce

In the **business-to-consumer (B2C)** e-commerce model, businesses provide goods and services to consumers. The most widespread example of this is online shopping. To shop online, you can visit the website of a store, browse pictures and descriptions of items you want to purchase, and then follow directions for payment.

Single merchants typically operate B2C sites. A B2C store keeps its inventory information in a database. As you browse through the merchandise, the merchant's web server and database work together to create a webpage for the item that you select. Businesses typically ship physical goods to your front door via the postal service or a commercial delivery service.

The site tracks your selected items using cookies. A **cookie** is a small file generated by a web server that acts like a storage bin for the items you place in your shopping cart. Cookies store shopping cart item numbers, credit card numbers, and other information.

Recipe and food delivery services such as Home Chef, Blue Apron, and Hello Fresh deliver fresh ingredients with instructions on how to create meals in your own kitchen as part of a subscription service. Advances in packaging, including insulated boxes and chemical ice packs, make it possible for the food to arrive fresh, not frozen, and even on hot days in warm climates!

Use Consumer to Consumer E-commerce

One common example of C2C transactions are online classified ads such as those found on Recycler, Freecycle, and Craigslist. Online auctions are another example of the **consumer-to-consumer (C2C)** business model. An online auction works much like a real-life auction or yard sale.

Hot Technology Now

Amazon, the world's largest e-commerce company, is developing a delivery system called Amazon Prime Air to get packages into customers' hands in 30 minutes using unmanned aerial vehicle drones.

On the Job Now

Many B2Bs use RFID (Radio Frequency Identification) to identify products. Its advantage is that it requires no human intervention; tags can usually be read even when they are not facing a reader antenna for inventory and location.

C2C sites have multiple sellers, with different sellers for different items, rather than a single merchant hosting a B2C site. To sell a collection rare prints or your homemade knits or pottery, for example, you could post an ad on an Internet auction site such as eBay or ebid Auctions, and potential buyers could bid on the collection. The auction site coordinates the bidding process and the transactions between buyer and seller, but does not handle the actual merchandise. Many C2C sites use email forwarding, which hides real email identities, to connect buyer with seller and still protect everybody's privacy. You pay a small fee to the auction site if you sell the item.

Most real estate transactions now begin with clients and agents meeting on a website. Real estate agencies can post listings and buyers can do research ahead of time on the homes, condos, or apartments through the websites. People can also list their homes for sale on many for sale by owner sites. Sites such as Zillow, StreetEasy, and the MLS (Multiple Listing Services) aggregate properties from several other sites.

Use Business-to-Business E-Commerce

The **business-to-business (B2B)** e-commerce model involves the transfer of goods, services, or information between businesses. In fact, most e-commerce is actually between businesses. Services that businesses provide to each other include advertising, credit, recruiting, sales and marketing, technical support, and training. Businesses also use B2B e-commerce to purchase raw materials, tools and machinery, office furnishings and equipment, and transportation services in a global market.

Make E-Commerce Payments

When you shop or bank online, be sure the website uses a secure connection. The prefix "https" and a locked padlock icon should appear in the Address bar, and the background should turn green. **3-D Secure** is a standard protocol for securing credit card transactions over the Internet. 3-D Secure uses both encryption and digital certificates. Sites that use Verified by Visa, MasterCard SecureCode, and American Express SafeKey use the added 3-D Secure protocol.

It is now possible to use smartwatches and smartphones to make ecommerce payments. ApplePay and Google Wallet are two of several mobile payment and digital wallet services available on smartphones. Simply by presenting the watch or phone to a scanner or reader, often available in stores, you can make an electronic payment. See **Figure 5-19**.

Figure 5-18: Common e-commerce business models

Business-to-consumer (B2C)

Consumer-to-consumer (C2C)

Business-to-business (B2B)

Scott Maxwell LuMaxArt/Shutterstock.com

E-commerce is divided into business models based on the type of buyer and seller.

Figure 5-19: Paying with a smartphone

Xavier Arnau/Getty Images

Visa is one of several companies exploring **biometrics**, the use of unique physical characteristics to pay for products electronically and through the web. A fingerprint scan or retina scan would identify the payee and perform the commercial transaction.

E-commerce sites also use **Transport Layer Security (TLS)** and **Hypertext Transfer Protocol Secure (HTTPS)** technologies to encrypt data. This helps protect consumers and businesses from fraud and identity theft when conducting commerce on the Internet.

When paying, you may be asked to submit your credit card number directly on a form at a merchant's website when you check out. Some sites offer to store this information for you. You can also make a person-to-person online payment, especially on auction sites. Peer-to-peer payment services, such as Square Cash, PayPal.me, and Venmo, are such services in which you open an account and deposit money from your bank or provide your credit card number. You make direct payments through a smartphone or website.

Another payment option is an **electronic wallet**, also called a **digital wallet**, such as Google Wallet and Apple Passbook, which stores the payment information you enter when you finalize an online purchase. You also can pay using a one-time-use or virtual account number, which lets you make a single online payment without revealing your actual account number. These numbers are good only at the time of the transaction; so, if they are stolen, they are worthless to thieves.

Use Online Banking and Investing

The number of consumers who bank online is growing rapidly. You can check account balances, transfer funds among accounts, pay bills electronically, and perform other transactions without leaving your home. Online banking is not only convenient for the consumer but also useful in reducing costs for the bank.

You can also manage your stocks and other securities online. These activities are called **online investing**. You typically can view stock quotes on search and news websites, but you need an online broker for investment activities. Online investing services let you buy and sell stocks, view performance histories, and set up an online portfolio to display the status of your investments.

Use Comparison Shopping Sites

Websites such as BizRate, NexTag, and PriceGrabber are called **aggregator sites** because they specialize in collecting and organizing data from other consumer websites. They save you time and money by letting you compare prices from multiple vendors.

Digital technology has changed the way the travel industry does business. You can make reservations and purchase your own tickets and accommodations online. You can even write reviews about your experiences for other consumers to read. Some e-commerce sites such as Orbitz, Trivago, TripAdvisor, Expedia, Travelocity, and Kayak consolidate travel information on flights, hotel reservations, and rental cars. You can use this collected information to find the best deals and discounts and research destinations.

Use Digital Deals and Discounts

Although using an online payment service is the most common way of exchanging digital cash, e-commerce also uses **digital gift certificates**, **digital gift cards**, and **digital coupons**. Digital coupons consist of codes that you enter when you check out and pay for online purchases. You can print and use digital gift certificates and digital gift cards at restaurants or other businesses. TumbleDeal, Google Offers, and Groupon are examples of deal-of-the-day websites. Rules and restrictions vary among the sites. Ebates and similar sites such as Discover and MrRebates will give you cash back on purchases at certain sites if you activate their app or start shopping by clicking through their website before you shop. Essentially you are getting a small fee for sharing your shopping habits and following their suggestions for shopping at certain sites. They pay you a portion of the commission they earn. See **Figure 5-20**.

Hot Technology Now

Yelp.com operates an "online urban guide" and business review site that is helpful to find highly rated restaurants and other local services.

Hot Technology Now

Sites such as CouponCabin.com and CouponMom.com provide coupon codes, printable coupons, and local coupons for discounts.

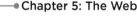

Figure 5-20: Digital coupons and gift cards promote shopping

Some websites specialize in collecting and offering deals or coupons, often daily, and often via email or mobile phone.

Redemption rates are high with mobile phones because consumers typically have their phones with them when they shop.

Rawpixel.com/Shutterstock.com

Describe the Internet of Things

Internet of Things (IoT) | barcode | QR code | Radio Frequency Identification (RFID) | Near Field Communication (NFC)

The Internet is not only people using keyboards and screens to access and share information and commerce. Objects also use the Internet. Several technologies exist that transmit data to and from computers through the Internet automatically, without any human intervention. The **Internet of Things (IoT)** refers to a network of "smart" objects that use embedded sensors, software, and wireless connectivity to enhance daily living. Examples might include a warehoused inventory item you need to find, a shipped package you need to track, and a refrigerator that can communicate its energy use or even send you a shopping list.

Tag and Track Objects

The Internet of Things is possible because all digital devices in an office or home are connected and can share data. The Internet of Things (IoT) has the basic premise that all objects can be tagged, tracked, and monitored through a local network, or across the Internet. In this way, we can tag and therefore know where people, products, and other objects are, and their relationship to each other, at any given time. Several technologies make IoT possible.

Use Barcodes and QR Codes

Barcodes, printed codes that look like a series of stacked bars, have been used in stores and supermarkets to code items for pricing and inventory for many years. Each bar has a number value. Barcode readers are used to scan the code to tie into a database that contains the specific product. Barcodes are not unique: a code in one store might identify a bar of soap, but can identify a chair or other product in another.

QR codes look like squares with square pattern blocks inside the main square object. QR codes can be found in magazines, on billboards, in packaging, on tags for products, and in digital form on websites. There are several websites that you can use to generate a QR code free of charge that you can then print on your own printer or save or send as a digital file. See **Figure 5-21** on the next page.

Each QR code is unique and may be used to open a browser to view a URL, save a contact to the address book, or compose text messages. Both QR code and barcode readers are available on mobile devices such as tablets and smartphones. Use a smartphone to scan a QR code in a magazine, bulletin board, or on a sign in a public place.

The Bottom Line
- Barcodes and QR codes can be scanned or clicked to access databases or websites on the Internet.
- RFID and NFC technologies make it possible to scan and transmit data just by having a transponder nearby an object that has a chip.
- Businesses can use RFID and NFC technologies to manage and analyze sales, control and track inventory, and optimize the flow of goods.

Figure 5-21: Creating and printing QR codes

Barcode readers scan the code and send the information to a database on the remote computer, often on the Internet.

Barcodes and QR codes can be used to scan and track packages.

Sergiy Zavgorodny/Shutterstock.com

Figure 5-22: QR codes

RedKoala/Shutterstock.com

QR codes can be used to connect to a website to get more information about a product or service. See **Figure 5-22**. Scanners are generally free apps, so you can access the information for a product directly from your mobile device as long as you are on the Internet.

Use RFID and NFC

IoT is based on RFID and NFC technologies, which allow tagging, tracking, and communication between objects, and facilitate mobile payments for products and services. Companies such as Google invested heavily into devices with NFC technology to be able to cash in on the markets for and benefits of IoT.

We live in a world where wireless transmissions are commonplace. Two wireless technologies used for tagging and tracking are **RFID** or **Radio Frequency Identification** and **NFC** or **Near Field Communication**. Both use radio signals for tagging and tracking, sometimes replacing barcodes.

RFID tags

- contain an antenna for transmitting data and a memory chip that stores data;
- are a one-way system and work at distances of many feet and even at high speeds;
- have been in used by businesses for product tracking and loss prevention as well as in employee ID badges;
- provide security access to secure areas for selected people; and
- are used by pet owners who chip their pets to identify them in case they are lost; by transportation departments on car tags to collect tolls; by airlines, to track and control commercial shipping baggage; in "smart passports" and credit cards; and in identification badges that let employees access secure areas.

NFC chips

- are similar to RFID but go beyond RFID capabilities;
- work with NFC readers installed on smartphones to provide two-way communication at very short ranges (about 10 centimeters) or by touching two devices;
- can be used by organizations, medical professionals, and businesses to collect and transmit information, so that users with readers installed on smartphones can get data about events or products and share back information; and
- support applications such as digital wallet and contactless payment systems that can be used from a smartphone.
- ApplePay and Android Pay use NFC to allow people to use their smartphones to pay for products simply by placing the phone up to a scanner or terminal to transmit the necessary payment data and complete the transaction. See **Figure 5-23**.

Hot Technology Now

Smartphones using Apply Pay can make digital payments in over a dozen countries at the point of sale.

Figure 5-23: Mobile payment using NFC (near field communication)

scyther5/Shutterstock.com

Use IoT in Inventory and Tracking

As a business owner, you want to have a supply of products when customers arrive in your store or order online. However, how can you know the right amount of product to buy, stock, and warehouse? The Internet of Things can help you manage and plan for warehousing and shipping.

Through RFID and NFC tracking, products can indicate where they are. Why ship a bicycle from California to New York, when there is one located much closer in New Jersey? By creating smart communities and smart products, we can reduce shipping time, reduce costs, and make business more efficient.

Looking Ahead

The Internet of Things has enhanced daily lives in many ways and will continue to do so in ways we cannot even begin to imagine. Some possible uses for tagging things to the Internet include the following:

- Payment systems for transportation systems such as urban buses and subways and for toll roads
- Traffic monitoring and management
- Medical management for patients in remote locations to reduce office visits
- Crowd management at large events
- Home monitoring systems for heat, water, and light to save energy
- Household management for home products such as food in the refrigerator, medicine in the cabinet, and personal care products in the closet

Advances in wireless communications and the Internet have been joining forces to further enhance our daily lives.

 #worldwideweb

Go to twitter.com, search for @SAMTechNow, the book's Twitter account, and then follow @SAMTechNow to get tweets on your home page.

Chapter Review

Define the Web

1. Explain the difference between the Internet and the web.
2. Define and distinguish between these terms: web, website, webpage.

Use a Browser

3. List four common features of all browsers.
4. Name three current browsers and explain two security features that work to keep you safe while you view webpages in a browser.
5. List and explain two of the challenges of mobile browsers and explain how responsive design works in this environment.

Examine Webpages

6. Explain what a URL is and how it is used on the web.
7. Give an example of how you can identify a secure website and what types of sites might be secured.

Use the Web to Find Information

8. What is the difference between a search engine and a search site?
9. Describe the functions of a web crawler, an indexing utility, and a query processor. Explain how they work together to provide search results.
10. Create two different search criteria for finding information about your hometown using Boolean operators. Explain the type of results you can expect from each search.

Describe Website Structure

11. What is a link and what is its function in a webpage?
12. What is the difference between scalable vector graphics and bitmap graphics?

Define Types of Websites

13. Define the terms "domain name" and "Internet Protocol (IP) address." Explain how they are related and how you use either one to display a website.
14. List three TLDs, explain what they mean, and give an example of each.

Work with Web Apps

15. Define and explain the term "web app."
16. What are three advantages and three disadvantages of working in the cloud?

Define Electronic Commerce

17. Define the term "e-commerce" and explain how it is used in our daily lives.
18. Name three ways you can pay for a service or product you purchase online.

Describe the Internet of Things

19. Define "RFID" and "NFC."
20. Explain two ways in which RFID technology is used today and two ways in which NFC technology is used today.

Test Your Knowledge Now

1. The _____ is the physical network that transmits data and helps us access the wealth of information on the _____.
   a. web, Internet
   b. Internet, web
   c. webpages, online
   d. World Wide Web, applications

2. You can listen to _____, which are prerecorded audio files, to keep up with your favorite topics such as news, health, or politics.
   a. wikis
   b. blogs
   c. podcasts
   d. YouTube

3. A webpage is a text document with _____ tags.
   a. HTTP
   b. graphic
   c. Hypertext Markup Language (HTML)
   d. RFID

4. Webpages include _____ that direct you to other webpages.
   a. graphics
   b. hyperlinks
   c. tags
   d. address bars

5. Pop-up and banner ads can install a _____ on a user's computer to track spending and browsing habits.
   a. hyperlink
   b. graphic
   c. QR code
   d. cookie

6. The use of emails that look legitimate but are designed to capture the recipient's private information is called _____.
   a. pharming
   b. snooping
   c. phishing
   d. spam

7. Which of the following is not a web browser?
   a. iCloud
   b. Edge
   c. Chrome
   d. Safari

8. _____ is the name of the communications protocol that transports data over the web.
   a. Uniform resource locator (URL)
   b. Hypertext Transfer Protocol (HTTP)
   c. Hypertext Markup Language (HTML)
   d. WWW Consortium (W3C)

9. The common way to view video from a website is to use _____.
   a. streaming
   b. downloading
   c. dynamic viewing
   d. style sheets

10. _____ is a way to use simple code to describe how webpage elements appear in a website.
    a. Dynamic scripting (DSS)
    b. Cascading Style Sheets (CSS)
    c. Xtensible markup Language (XML)
    d. Hypertext Protocol (HTTP)

11. Google, Bing, and Yahoo! are examples of popular _____ sites.
    a. query
    b. email
    c. search
    d. e-commerce

12. Search engine technology has four components: a web crawler, an indexer, a(n) _____, and a query processor.
    a. site
    b. database
    c. engine
    d. utility

13. Which of the following is an example of a Boolean search query?
    a. "What street is the farm on?"
    b. "Find all farms that are not in Dumont"
    c. "When does the farm open?"
    d. "Where can I buy a smartphone?"

14. Mobile browsers optimize the display of a webpage most effectively for small screens on mobile devices using _____ design.
    a. mobile indexing
    b. responsive design
    c. HTML code matching
    d. Web crawling

15. _____ is the process of temporarily scrambling data so it is not readable until it is decoded.
    a. Coding
    b. Certification
    c. Encryption
    d. Securing

16. Webpages use scalable _____ graphics, which use mathematical formulas instead of pixels, to maintain the same quality on all screens and have small file sizes.
    a. bitmap
    b. vector
    c. video
    d. portable

17. A _____ is a series of program instructions that can be embedded directly into the HTML code for a webpage or in a file referenced in the HTML code.
    a. vector
    b. bitmap
    c. script
    d. GIF

18. _____ addresses are allocated to each network on the Internet to ensure that no two computers have the same address.
    a. HTML
    b. HTTP
    c. URL
    d. IP

19. The three letters that follow a "dot," as in .edu, .org, or .mil, are called _____.
    a. IoTs
    b. top-level domains
    c. domain name systems
    d. IP Addresses

20. A _____ is a webpage listing journal entries, in chronological order, that usually reflect an author's point of view.
    a. wiki
    b. blog
    c. page
    d. social network

21. In the space next to each image below, write the letter of the technology it represents.
    a. URL
    b. scanner
    c. QR code
    d. Gestures
    e. HTML code

RedKoala/Shutterstock.com, Epsicons/Shutterstock.com, Sergiy Zavgorodny/Shutterstock.com

Try This Now

1: Advanced Google Search and Google Scholar

When searching for information on the Internet, finding up-to-date, precise information is vital. The Google advanced search feature provides options for exact words, Boolean operators, numeric ranges, specific language, reading level, and last update date.

    a. Open a browser and go to the site www.google.com/advanced_search to view the Google Advanced Search form.

    b. In the exact word or phrase text box, type "fitness tracker." The quotes are necessary to search for the exact phrase with the words in that specific order.

    c. In the language text box of the advanced Google Search, select English.

    d. In the last update text box of the advanced Google Search, select past week to locate current information.

    e. Select the Advanced Search button. Open the first non-ad result site on the results page.

    f. Read the site and write at least 100 words about the fitness tracker subject mentioned on this site.

    g. Go to the site scholar.google.com. Search for "gender and Internet usage." How do these references differ when you perform the same search using google.com?

2: Researching Career Salaries

Researching position availability and range of salary in your career field is an important step in finding your dream job. Whether you are looking for a summer job or a full-time position, online career search sites are the first place to begin a successful job search. Open a browser and go to the site www.glassdoor.com.

    a. Select the Salaries options and search the job title Data Scientist. In your own words write a paragraph of your findings and be sure to mention salary and companies that are hiring this position.

    b. Using Glassdoor, search for three other job titles that you are considering in your career path. Research both the salaries and job openings close to your home. In your own words, write 150 words of your findings and be sure to mention the salaries you find and the companies that are hiring these positions.

3: Consumer Web Reviews Using TripAdvisor

TripAdvisor.com has given a voice to the consumer to share reviews of their experiences at local eateries, hotels, and things to do. Open a browser and open tripadvisor.com. Search for a large city that you would like to visit anywhere in the world.

    a. Search for the top five rated restaurants in the selected city using Trip Advisor. List the five restaurants with the highest rating, and for each one, list the type of food and address. Copy and paste a review from each of the restaurants into a Word document.

    b. Search for the top five things to do in the selected city using TripAdvisor. List the things to do with the highest rating, and for each one, list the type of activity. Copy and paste a review from each of the things to do into the Word document.

    c. Research and write at least 100 words about how some businesses try to manipulate their reviews on a site such as TripAdvisor.

    d. Save the document and submit it to your instructor.

Critical Thinking Now

1: The Best Web Browser

Everyone wants a browser that is fast, secure, and easy to use. Select three current browsers (desktop or mobile) and research the features of each one. Write at least 200 words that compare the three browsers and recommend the browser that is best in your opinion. Be sure to mention speed, security, features, and your own opinion.

2: Digital Storytelling with the Sway Web App

Note: This assignment requires a Microsoft account. You can create one for free at outlook.com

    Open the website Sway.com. Your school's International Club is planning a Spring Break trip to Edinburgh, Scotland and your role is to create an overview of the city of Edinburgh in a digital story using the Sway web app. Watch the tutorial videos to learn to create a Sway. Sign in with a Microsoft. To place a Sway presentation in the hands of any audience you can share a webpage link and share it with your class and instructor.

    a. Create a new presentation in Sway about Edinburgh, Scotland. Provide a title for the Sway Storyline and select a background image.

    b. Research the major tourist venues in Edinburgh using tripadvisor.com. Create three separate sections about what to see in Edinburgh, and include text, an image, a video, and a paragraph in each section.

    c. Share the link to your Sway with your instructor in the format specified by your instructor.

3: Personalized Remarketing

Remarketing is the way sellers, in trying to market products, repeatedly show you products you have researched. By reminding you of products you have searched for online, by placing them in personalized ads on other websites you visit, you are reminded and perhaps persuaded to buy a previously viewed product from a retailer's website. For example, if you have been researching a new smartphone online, that same model of smartphone may reappear in ads over the next few weeks on other unrelated websites that you frequent.

Research how effective remarketing is with online shoppers. Write at least 150 words about your impressions of personalized remarketing and its effectiveness.

Pay Per Click

Ethical Issues Now

A virtual wallet such as Android Pay and Apple Pay can offer many services that include payment functionality and organizational capability.

a. Research the safety of using credit cards in face-to-face transactions compared to using mobile wallet payments. Be sure to include additional advances to store coupons, boarding passes, and event tickets. Write at least 150 words on the advantages and disadvantages of using each.

b. If you could save money by using discounts that have been applied to your personal mobile wallet payment account, would you consider using Google Wallet or Apple Passbook? Why?

c. How could you use mobile wallets to organize store loyalty cards?

Team Up Now—Messaging, Voice, and Video Calls with Google Hangouts

Collaborate

Note: This assignment requires the use of a webcam.

Company employees and student teams connect daily using remote web conferencing and web applications. Discuss a date and time that you can meet online with your classmate team using Google Hangouts. One person on the team must be designated to initiate the hangout and invite the other team members. Each of the team members must first create a free Google account. Read about setting up a Google Hangout at hangouts.google.com.

a. When everyone on the team has arrived in the Google Hangout, take a screen shot with all the team members' names listed.

b. Collaborate with your team members to determine how Google Hangouts and similar tools could be used for business teams. Create a short 150+ word document with your ideas.

c. Submit the combined screen shot and paragraph to your instructor.

Key Terms

3-D Secure
Address bar
aggregator site
App Tab
application service provider (ASP)
banner ad
barcode
biometrics
bitmap graphic
blog
bookmark
Boolean operator
breadcrumbs
browser
business-to-business (B2B)
business-to-consumer (B2C)
cache
Cascading Style Sheets (CSS)
click-through rate
client-side script
cloud storage
consumer-to-consumer (C2C)
content aggregator
cookie
database
digital certificate
digital coupon
digital gift card
digital gift certificate
digital wallet
distributed content
domain name
domain name server
Domain Name System (DNS)
dynamic webpage
dynamic web publishing
e-commerce
electronic wallet
encryption

favorite
file-sharing sites
gesture
hacked
history list
hit
home page
HTML script
HTML tag
hyperlink
Hypertext Markup
  Language (HTML)
Hypertext Transfer Protocol (HTTP)
Hypertext Transfer Protocol
  Secure (HTTPS)
indexing utility
Internet
Internet of Things (IoT)
IP Address
keyword
keyword stuffing
link
meta keyword
mobile browser
mouse over
navigation bar
Near Field Communication (NFC)
online game
online investing
online storage
pharming
phishing
pinch-to-zoom
podcast
pop-up ad
pop-up blocking
Privacy pane
private browsing
QR code

query processor
Radio Frequency Identification (RFID)
Responsive Design
Responsive Web Design (RWD)
RSS feed
script
search engine
search engine optimization (SEO)
search engine technology
search phrase
server-side script
social networking
Software as a Service (SaaS)
spider
start page
static web publishing
streaming
streaming video
sync feature
tabbed browsing
targeted marketing
top-level domain (TLD)
Transport Layer Security (TLS)
uniform resource locator (URL)
vector graphic
virtual keyboard
VoiceOver
web
web application (web app)
web crawler
web master
webpage
web portal
website
wiki
wildcard character
World Wide Web
World Wide Web Consortium (W3C)
XML (eXtensible Markup Language)

Purchasing and Maintaining a Computer

...pping for a new computer. With so ...ces including tablets, laptops, and ...computers with brand names such as ...Apple, Asus, Dell, and more, she needs ...n to make the right decision.

Understanding computer specifications can be confusing unless you understand what all those numbers represent.

iStockphoto.com/97

Bre Pauley's faithful old laptop has finally reached the end of its life and it's time to buy a new one. She plans to bring her laptop to class, so battery life, weight, and a keyboard are important factors. Bre knows that getting the most features while staying within her budget is the key goal in her computer search.

In this Chapter

Buy a Computer

peripheral device | form factor | desktop | all-in-one computer | laptop | 2-in-1 computer | hybrid laptop | hybrid tablet | tablet | mobile device | operating system | platform | processor | central processing unit (CPU) | random access memory (RAM) | gigabyte (GB) | storage device | byte | terabyte (TB) | internal hard drive | external hard drive | solid state drive (SSD) | service plan | extended warranty

Computers are part of your daily life. If you don't already own a computer, you've probably used one in a computer lab or a library, or perhaps you've borrowed one from a family member or friend. At some point, you'll probably need to buy a computer. Computers can be expensive, so you want to make an informed purchasing decision. The more you know before you buy a computer, the better your chances of getting the best computer for your needs.

Figure 6-1: Weighing purchasing options

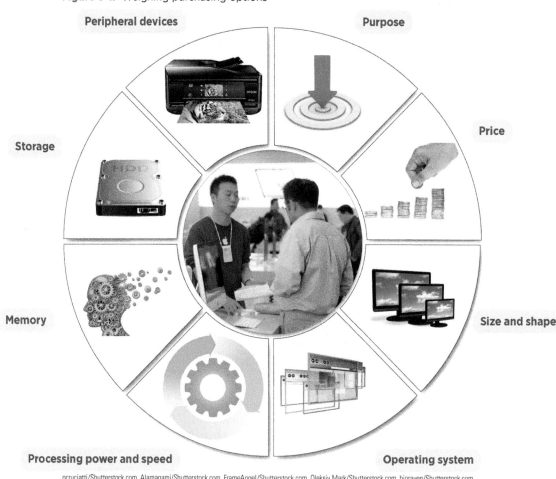

pcruciatti/Shutterstock.com, Alamagami/Shutterstock.com, FrameAngel/Shutterstock.com, Oleksiy Mark/Shutterstock.com, bioraven/Shutterstock.com, AlexAranda/Shutterstock.com, Lightspring/Shutterstock.com, All Vectors/Shutterstock.com, Courtesy of Epson America Inc

Consider Budget and Intended Uses

How much money do you have to spend on a computer? Once you determine your budget, you can narrow your search to look for the best computer that fits your budget.

Can you afford to buy everything you want all at once? Maybe you can buy the basic computer now and add peripheral devices such as a scanner, camera, or printer later. A **peripheral device** is hardware you add to your computer system for additional functionality. If you have a restricted budget, buy a computer with a more powerful processor and less memory—you can add more memory to it later.

Before you buy a computer, think about why you need it and how you intend to use it. Consider the following questions:

- Are you going to use the computer for school or work, to create presentations, write reports and other documents? Do you need to research information on the web?
- Do you plan to use the computer primarily to post to social media such as Facebook, Twitter, and Instagram?
- Do you want to download and read e-books?
- Will you communicate with friends and relatives through chat, email, and text messaging?
- Do you plan to create and track the budget for a small business? Track your personal finances?
- Will you create soundtracks, videos, or presentations? Do you plan on storing hundreds or even thousands of music, videos, and photographs? Will you store files locally or in the cloud?
- Will you be viewing, creating, and posting video on the Internet, perhaps to your own YouTube channel?
- Are you majoring in a field that requires a powerful computer such as engineering or app development?
- Are you an artist or engineer working with complex graphic files?
- Do you use a computer to play high-end computer games?
- Does the computer need to be durable? Will you be working in the field or in an environment that is at risk for drops, spills, or weather exposure?
- Are you going to use the computer while traveling? Do you work in remote areas or harsh environments?

The answers to these questions will help you decide the size and shape, operating system, hardware specs, and peripherals to look for in a computer.

Select a Computer Form Factor

Once you've determined the tasks you want to perform and your budget, you can decide the **form factor**, or size and shape of the computer, that will work best for you. See Figure 6-2.

#buyacomputer

If you need Microsoft Office or other installed programs, keep in mind that some tablets and Chromebooks cannot run all programs.

Hot Technology Now

PC Magazine at pcmag.com has computer reviews and comparisons based on price range, manufacturer, computer type, and other criteria.

By the Numbers Now

According to LaptopMag, the longest battery life of a tablet on a single charge is over 17 hours with continuous surfing over a wireless connection.

Figure 6-2: Some form factor options

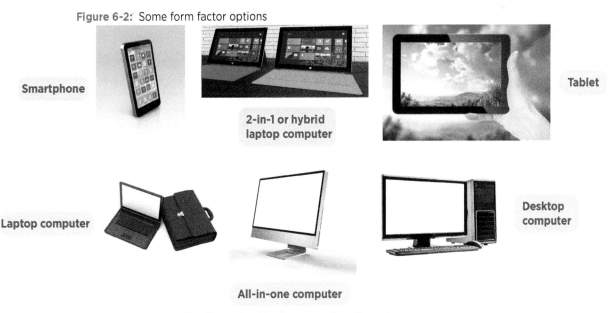

Smartphone

2-in-1 or hybrid laptop computer

Tablet

Laptop computer

All-in-one computer

Desktop computer

Denis Rozhnovsky/Shutterstock.com, Chesky/Shutterstock.com, digieye/Shutterstock.com, Daboost/Shutterstock.com, Pieter Beens/Shutterstock.com, Julia Ivantsova/Shutterstock.com

The basic computer types can be further organized into a number of form factors to help with your purchasing decision. Your choices include desktop, all-in-one, laptop, 2-in-1 computer, hybrid laptop, or hybrid tablet, tablet, and mobile device such as a smartphone. Each form factor has advantages and disadvantages. You want to be sure to get the most processing speed and memory for your money in the form that best meets your needs. Table 6-1 explains some of the available options.

Table 6-1: Comparing form factors

Form factor	Advantages	Disadvantages
Desktop	Less expensive than a comparable laptop; can be powerful; often used by businesses	Box is larger; takes up a significant amount of space and is difficult to move
All-in-one	Internal system components and electronics are integrated into the back of the monitor, so the computer is one unit; powerful alternative to desktop unit	Can be expensive; not very portable; have limited upgrade options
Laptop	Light and portable; most can run using battery power for hours; can feature standard to high-end performance; uses built-in webcam and solid state drives; weighs from 2 to 8 pounds	Prices vary, but can be expensive
2-in-1 laptop, hybrid laptop, or hybrid tablet	Provides an attachable/detachable, flip-back, or swivel keyboard base that may also include extra ports or drives; converts to a tablet for mobility when keyboard is not wanted and can use a virtual keyboard instead	Added cost; some have less than optimal battery life
Tablet	Smaller and cheaper than laptop computers; can be laid flat, and most fit easily into a purse or backpack; useful for online applications	Less powerful; fewer features; offers less functionality than other types of computers; not suitable for performing application-intensive tasks; may require extra cost for cellular connection in addition to Wi-Fi
Mobile device	Small and portable; includes phone and text capabilities often through cellular service and Wi-Fi connections	Less powerful; fewer features; small screen

Select a Computer Platform

Once you determine the form factor for your computer, the next decision you need to make is what operating system you will use. The **operating system**, or **platform**, coordinates the functions of your computer's hardware components and determines the types and brands of application software you can use.

The main operating systems for computers are Windows, macOS, and Chrome OS. Tablet computers and mobile devices have various operating systems depending on the manufacturer, such as Android, Windows Mobile, Chrome OS, and Apple iOS.

Some people choose a platform based on its user interface, or "look and feel," which controls how information appears on the screen and how you interact with the computer. Others may choose a platform based on the software they anticipate running on their machine. Make sure the software you want to run will operate with your chosen platform. For example, form factors that run Windows 10 come equipped with touch screens, front-facing webcams, and a minimum of 1 GB of RAM.

Evaluate Hardware Requirements

It is important to evaluate your hardware requirements. The **processor**, or **central processing unit (CPU)**, controls the computer's operations. Faster, more powerful processors provide more computing power. It is advisable to purchase the fastest processor, most memory, and largest amount of storage you can afford.

Hot Technology Now

To read unbiased reviews and comparisons on tech products, check out CNET (cnet.com).

You should take the time to review the specifications and recommendations for the following 64-bit processors: Intel Core i7, i5, and i3 processors, Intel Pentium, Celeron, Xeon, Intel Mac, and AMD Zen. Computers with the Intel i7 processors are best for complex technical uses, while i5 computers are designed for programmers, web designers, and other users. The i3 processors are best for light use such as Microsoft Office, web research, and email, and are common on student computers. Most widely available computers offer sufficient processing power for the average home or student user.

Random access memory (RAM) is temporary storage used to store data and operate programs while the computer is running. The amount of RAM you need depends on what programs you intend to run. RAM is measured in **gigabytes (GB)**. In general, 4 to 16 GB is recommended for most users.

Storage devices store files permanently so you can retrieve them later. For example, you can write a paper, save it to a storage device, and then open it later to print it. Storage capacity is measured in **bytes**; some built-in hard drives now boast over a **terabyte (TB)**, which is 1 trillion bytes, of storage. Most computer storage devices can store between 500 GB and 1 TB of data, although tablets and mobile devices store considerably less. Most computers have an **internal hard drive** that can be supplemented with an **external hard drive** or portable hard drive that connects through a USB port. A **solid state drive (SSD)** is a hard drive with no moving parts and is therefore more durable and suitable for portable computers. SSDs tend to be more expensive than magnetic hard drives with the same storage capacity. However, SSDs generate less heat and also access data three to four times faster than typical mechanical hard drives.

Buy Peripheral Devices

Depending on your budget and needs, you may decide to purchase computer accessories, such as peripheral devices, to enhance your computer. Many peripheral devices can connect wirelessly using Bluetooth technology, giving you a wider range of use and added convenience. Peripheral devices can include a printer, a headset, external speakers, a scanner, a keyboard and mouse (for laptops or tablets), a webcam (for a desktop), or an external hard drive.

Desktop and laptop computers provide flexibility by letting you add devices that plug into USB ports. For example, flash drives and external hard drives are external USB devices that provide extra storage. You might also want to attach a mouse and a camera. Consider a computer with several USB ports to accommodate several peripheral devices.

Make the Purchase

Once you've determined the kind of computer you need, research your purchasing options to narrow your choices; then you're ready to go shopping. Where do you begin? Here are some tips:

- Consult knowledgeable salespeople at electronics retailers, get expert opinions by reading computer and consumer magazines, and look online for reviews and comparisons of different computer types, brands, and models.
- Organize your findings in a spreadsheet, table, or chart.
- Look for the options that best fit your needs and budget while offering the most power and functionality.
- You might prefer to buy your computer at a local retailer, or you could purchase it online directly from the vendor or an online retailer. Many people buy a computer online for the best price and have the computer delivered to their doorstep.
- Another decision you will have to make is whether to purchase an extended warranty or service plan. Most computers come with a 1-year warranty on parts. **Service plans** and **extended warranties** are useful if you are not familiar with computers, or if you feel your computer might need replacement parts due to wear and tear after the manufacturer's warranty expires. Before purchasing a plan or extended warranty, read through it from start to finish to see if it is right for you.

No matter where you purchase your computer, thoughtful research will help you get the best computer for your needs and your budget.

#buyacomputer

Professional users often choose i5 processors and serious gamers often require the more powerful i7 processors.

On the Job Now

Many business people use scanning apps such as Office Lens to turn their smartphones into portable scanners to photograph receipts for expense reports or checks to make bank deposits.

Hot Technology Now

Not all universal serial bus cables and ports are the same; there are several versions including USB type A, B, and C. Be sure you use the right USB cable for the port and peripheral device.

Install Hardware

driver | device driver | radio frequency (RF) | Bluetooth | wireless printer | pair

Consider what your first steps will be when the computer arrives. Most devices come with startup instructions in the box. Read the instructions and set aside some time, if possible without interruptions, to familiarize yourself with your purchase. If you bought a laptop computer, take it out of the box, plug one end of the power supply into the wall and the other into the unit to charge the battery, then turn it on. If you bought a desktop computer, you may have to connect the mouse, keyboard, and monitor to the system unit. However, if you bought a tablet or other mobile device and need to connect it to a peripheral device, such as a printer or mouse, you have to get the devices working together.

Install Necessary Device Drivers

Purchasing a computer usually involves setting up the computer to work with peripheral devices such as a printer or a camera. A **driver** or **device driver** is a software program that works to connect and control devices attached to your computer so they can communicate and work together. Device drivers are necessary for printers, monitors, external hard drives, headsets, and other peripherals to work with laptops, desktops, as well as devices such as an iPad or smartphone.

When you buy a computer, the operating system typically includes essential device drivers for displays and keyboards. When you install a new peripheral device, it typically installs the device drivers necessary to operate the device. However, if you have an older or uncommon peripheral device, you may have to go to the product manufacturer's website and download and install the latest driver to your computer before you can use the device.

To make sure the driver is installed and working properly, try to connect to the device. If there is a problem, typically, the operating system will send you an alert and direct you to find, download, and install the proper driver. If the drivers become out of date and stop working, your operating system may display a message to this effect or update the driver automatically. To update drivers manually, you can usually download the latest versions from the manufacturer's website.

Pair Bluetooth Devices and Install Wireless Devices

There are two main methods you can use to connect peripheral devices to your computer: by attaching them to the computer with wires or cables, or wirelessly. Wireless devices connect by using radio frequency (RF) or Bluetooth, two methods of wireless communication. **RF** uses simple radio waves to communicate, and **Bluetooth** is a widely used, short-range communication technology that uses low energy, high speed signals. Common wireless devices that you might need to install are a **wireless printer** and a wireless mouse. RF devices require a transmitter, which is built into the mouse, and a receiver, a small nib which is plugged into the computer's USB port. A Bluetooth mouse transmits directly to the Bluetooth technology in your computer, so it doesn't occupy a USB port.

Figure 6-3: Use Bluetooth to print from a smartphone

baloon/Shutterstock.com

#buyacomputer

Bluetooth is a short-range network, typically less than 300 feet. The devices have to be within that range when pairing in order to use a smartphone in a car, play music, or print documents.

For any wireless devices with Bluetooth technology, such as headphones, speakers, mouse, or a printer, you need to **pair** them, or establish a connection with, your computer or other device so they can communicate. For example, you can pair a smartphone or tablet with a printer to print a document directly from that device. You can pair a tablet with speakers to play music, or pair a wearable device such as an Apple Watch, to your tablet to share information. See **Figure 6-3**.

Pairing involves selecting options on both devices. Turn on your computer's Bluetooth feature, then turn on your printer's or speaker's Bluetooth, which makes it "discoverable." Open your phone or tablet's Settings menu. Bluetooth-enabled devices will have a settings category often called "Wireless & network." In that category, select the Bluetooth option, make sure Bluetooth is set to visible. If necessary, click Scan. Your device will scan for and display all available Bluetooth devices in range under "Available devices." Select the device and complete the pairing.

Protect Computer Hardware

uninterruptible power supply (UPS) | power fluctuation | power spike | power surge | surge suppressor

We protect and maintain equipment and devices that we value, such as our car. Computers are made of sensitive electronic components that are easily damaged, but we often fail to take even simple steps to protect and maintain them.

Protect Devices from Extreme Temperatures and Physical Impact

Computers are made of both electronic and mechanical parts that are designed to function in regulated environments, with controlled temperature and humidity levels. Heat is bad for electronics, so computers have built-in cooling systems to keep components from overheating. Keep your computer in a well-ventilated area; never place it near a radiator or leave it in the sun, where it could be damaged beyond repair.

Figure 6-4: Use common sense

Avoid physical impact.

Be careful using a computer in extreme hot or cold climates.

Chepko Danil Vitalevich/Shutterstock.com, Dariush M/Shutterstock.com, zentilia/Fotolia LLC

#buyacomputer

Do not leave your phone in a hot car because condensation can gather under the screen and ruin the display. The mobile battery can overheat and possibly explode or never hold a charge again.

Figure 6-5: Use a special tote to carry your computer when traveling

photomark/Shutterstock.com

Freezing conditions can also seriously damage your computer's mechanical and electronic components, so never leave your laptop in your car on a cold day, or outside overnight. As a rule of thumb, if you feel comfortable, your computer will be comfortable as well.

Computers, components, and peripheral devices are not made to withstand significant physical impact. Be aware of the objects in use near your computer equipment, and take care when moving objects nearby.

Portable computers are designed for mobility and need to be protected during transport. See Figure 6-5. Pack your device in a specially designed, padded case during transport to cushion it from any impact or other jarring motions. If your work requires a lot of physical movement, or if you work outside in extreme weather conditions, consider using a weatherized or ruggedized laptop or mobile computer.

Protect Devices from Liquids and Dust Particles

Computers run on electricity or battery power; neither should come into contact with liquids. Always keep beverages and other liquids at a safe distance from your computer to prevent short-circuiting its components in the case of a spill. When using your

smartphone or other computer equipment outside, keep it out of the rain. If you must take your computer near a beach or lake, put it in a waterproof carrier for protection against water and other hazards.

Keep dust, dirt, and sand away from your computer. If dirt or sand particles get into the keyboard or system unit, they'll damage the computer components. If dirt gets in the fan of the power supply, it can cause the fan to stop working and your computer will overheat. Keep a can of compressed air near your work area and use it regularly to remove dust particles from vents, ports, keyboards, and fan components.

Protect Devices from Power Fluctuations

Computers and other digital devices need power to work. Power is supplied by either AC current from a wall outlet or from a battery. If the power goes off, or your battery runs out of power, the device will shut down. Loss of power won't damage your equipment, but it may cause you to lose unsaved files. You can avoid data loss by installing an **uninterruptible power supply (UPS)**, a short-term battery backup that comes on automatically in case of power loss.

More damaging than power outages are **power fluctuations**. **Power spikes**, or **power surges**, can occur before and after outages. Small surges can damage your computer over time, but the large power surges from lightning can wipe out your computer. To prevent power fluctuations from damaging electronic components, you should always use a **surge suppressor** with your computer. See **Figure 6-6**.

Figure 6-6: Devices to help with power problems

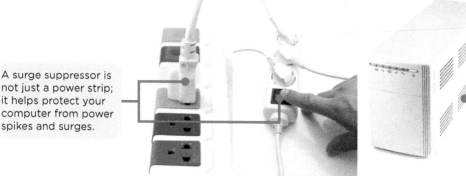

A surge suppressor is not just a power strip; it helps protect your computer from power spikes and surges.

An uninterruptible power supply provides power in the event of a power failure or loss of power to the computer.

mbongo/Fotolia LLC, improvize/Fotolia LLC, by-studio/Fotolia LLC

Use common sense to save battery life when using a laptop, smartphone, or other portable device. Some apps use more power than others; be sure to close them when they are not needed. You can dim the display to use less power. You should turn Wi-Fi Auto-Search to Off if you don't need to find a signal, you can also disable Locator services if not needed at the time. Most devices have power settings that include ways to reduce power usage such as putting the device in a sleep mode temporarily when not in use or shutting down when you don't need the device for a longer time. For example, in Windows 10, click the Start button, then select System > Power & sleep to locate the power settings; in iOS click Settings to view power setting options. For macOS, click the Apple icon, select System Preferences, then click the Energy Saver icon.

Safeguard Your Computer

global positioning system (GPS) | real-time location system | radio-frequency identification (RFID) tag | cloud backup | password | personal identification number (PIN) | username | two-factor authentication| firewall | data encryption | full disk encryption (FDE) | Encrypting File System (EFS)

Your computer is valuable, not just for its resale value, but for its contents. Often, the data on a computer is worth more than the computer itself, because the time you spend in creating or acquiring data has value. If you spent weeks writing a research paper and your laptop is then stolen or destroyed, you would have to invest considerable time and effort to recreate the paper. In addition, your computer contains a wealth of data about you, your friends and colleagues, and perhaps your company. You wouldn't want your Social Security or credit card numbers falling into the hands of a thief.

Secure Devices

Because computers are valuable, they are often targeted by thieves. If you use your computer in a public space, such as a coffee shop or library, do not leave it unattended. When you are not using your computer, you should store it in a secure place away from public view.

But you cannot stand guard over your computer all the time. If you leave your computer in an unsecured location from time to time, such as a dorm or open office, you need to protect it from theft. Use a cable lock to secure the computer to a table or desk. If possible, lock up your peripherals as well. See **Figure 6-7**.

Recover Stolen Devices

If your computer does get lost or stolen, you can use innovative tracking technology to get it back. Using **global positioning system (GPS)** technology and **real-time location systems** such as **radio-frequency identification (RFID) tags**, you can install computer-tracking software and equipment on your laptop or smartphone. See **Figure 6-8**.

Figure 6-7: Lock your portable computer

igor kisselev/Shutterstock.com

Cable lock

Hot Technology Now

Store your documents, pictures, videos, and music using cloud computing technologies such as OneDrive, iCloud, DropBox, or Google Drive.

Figure 6-8: Tracking devices through RFID and GPS technology

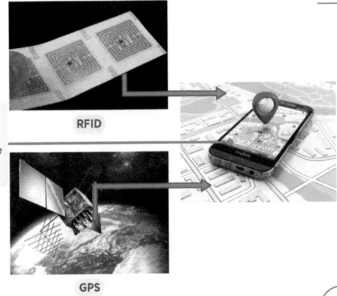

The tracking system sends out a signal when activated. An online service that you must subscribe to traces the signal and pinpoints the location of the device.

RFID

GPS

edobric/Shutterstock.com, Albert Lozano/Shutterstock.com, Maxx-Studio/Shutterstock.com

Other technologies, such as LoJack for Laptops, Lookout, Samsung Find My Mobile, Google Android Device Manager, and Find My iPhone, go one step further by letting you remotely lock and/or delete sensitive data from your computer, or any device, before thieves can access it.

Back Up Data

The files on your computer contain valuable information and represent hours of work. Some files, such as photos or videos, may be irreplaceable, so you need to make sure you never lose them. Your best protection is to back up your files to an external storage location and then store these backups in a safe place. Consider off-site locations to prevent loss from fire or flooding.

You can use personal storage devices such as external hard drives, flash drives, or even DVDs to back up your files. See **Figure 6-9** on the next page.

You can also back up your files to remote servers over the Internet using **cloud backup** or cloud storage. With cloud backup (see **Figure 6-10** on the next page),

#buyacomputer

Many phone makers are adding a smartphone "kill switch" that prohibits a stolen device from unauthorized use.

Hot Technology Now

The Windows 10 feature called On-Demand Sync displays the stored files on your OneDrive in the Windows File Explorer.

Figure 6-9: Back up your data

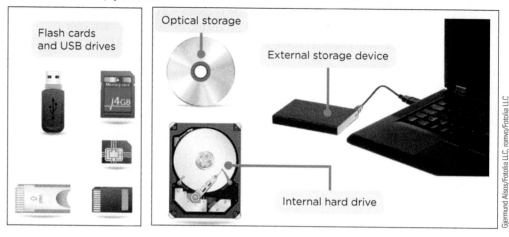

Flash cards and USB drives

Optical storage

External storage device

Internal hard drive

Gjermund Alsos/Fotolia LLC, ramvo/Fotolia LLC

Figure 6-10: Cloud storage

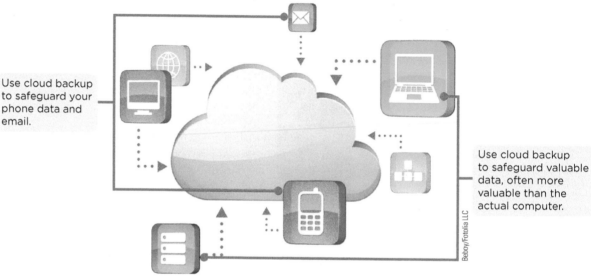

Use cloud backup to safeguard your phone data and email.

Use cloud backup to safeguard valuable data, often more valuable than the actual computer.

Beboy/Fotolia LLC

you can retrieve your data anytime from anywhere in the world as long as you have an Internet connection. You can also configure your system to run backups automatically on a regular basis.

Some disadvantages of cloud backup and storage are:

- The unpredictability associated with relying on an outside vendor—for example, if the servers go down periodically, you may have to wait to access your data.
- If your cloud provider suddenly goes out of business, you may not have access to your data.
- If your Internet connection fails, you may have to manage for a length of time without access to your files.
- There is always the potential for a security breach.

Make sure you have contingency plans in case any of these events occur.

Use Passwords

Passwords, personal identification numbers (PINs), and usernames are the keys to your digital world. You need these keys to access your personal accounts with online retailers, banks, and social websites. **Passwords** are short words or phrases kept secret by a person and used to gain access to a website or data. Passwords often combine letters, numbers, and characters to prevent unauthorized users from getting them and using them for illicit activities. **Personal identification numbers**, often called **PINs**,

Hot Technology Now

File History is the backup and restore feature on a Windows 10 computer. File History regularly backs up versions of your files in the Documents, Music, Pictures, Videos, and Desktop folders on your PC.

are short number sequences, also kept secret and frequently used by banks, used to access accounts. **Usernames** are words determined by users to identify themselves in the digital world, such as on websites or blogs. Your computer should be password protected as well. If it is ever lost or stolen, no one can access your files without first entering the correct password.

Other safeguards include **two-factor authentication**. When you try to access your computer or sign on to a backup server or website such as your bank or Facebook, you can have a unique code sent to your mobile device. Once you type in your password, you also enter the temporary code, which expires after a short time, to gain access. This helps to protect unauthorized users from getting into your data, because they not only need the password but the code. Windows Hello and other biometric methods will scan your face or read a fingerprint to ensure that it's really you trying to gain access to your data or device.

Follow these rules for creating good, also called strong, passwords:

- Use passwords that are at least eight characters with a combination of upper- and lowercase letters, numbers, and symbols.
- Never use dictionary words, birthdays, names, or information specific to your family.

Use a different password for sensitive activities such as banking. In addition, you can use password management software, which creates complex passwords for each of the websites you visit and stores them under one master password that only you know.

Build a Firewall

A thief does not have to physically steal your computer to gain access to its files and data. If your computer is connected to the Internet, a hacker can gain access to your files without your knowledge or permission. Protect your computer from remote intrusion by installing a firewall. A **firewall** inspects data being transmitted by your computer to external recipients to prevent unsolicited data exchanges. It also inspects incoming data for harmful content and blocks it from entering your computer. See **Figure 6-11**. A firewall can be made up of both hardware and software components. Many routers provided by ISPs include firewall software, and firewall software is part of most operating systems.

As an added precaution, you should shut down your computer or disconnect it from the Internet if you are not using it for extended periods of time.

Encrypt Data

If your computer contains sensitive data, you can add an additional layer of protection beyond passwords and firewalls by using data encryption. **Data encryption** "scrambles" or encodes data so that even if unauthorized users somehow gain access to your files, they will not be able to read or understand what is in them. **Full disk encryption (FDE)** automatically protects all of the data on your computer. You can also choose to encrypt specific files and folders using the **Encrypting File System (EFS)** in Windows or FileVault for macOS.

As with most hazards, prevention is the best medicine. Keep your computer safe by keeping it in sight, locking it up when unattended, installing tracking software, setting passwords, using a firewall, and encrypting sensitive data. And always back up your data to an off-site location.

Troubleshoot Common Hardware Problems

head crash | random access memory (RAM) | virtual memory | video card

You press the power switch. The computer does not respond, no lights come on—nothing happens. Did the power supply fail? Did your hard drive crash? Is your display broken? Perhaps the computer starts but it's not working properly. Computers are notoriously prone to problems. You first must determine if the problem is a software or hardware failure. If hardware, you should be able to troubleshoot some common hardware problems without incurring the time and expense of professional repairs.

Figure 6-11: An illustration of a firewall

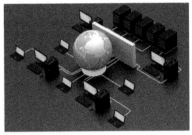

Tonis Pan/Shutterstock.com

The Bottom Line

- You rely on your computer every day, so when it doesn't work, it's important to be able to fix it as quickly and reliably as possible without any data loss and without spending a lot of money.
- Common hardware problems include a drive crash, general disk problems, display or monitor failures, input device problems, failures of peripheral devices, and power problems.

Figure 6-12: Common problems

Storage hard drive failure

Other electronic parts failure

Power problems

Display problems because of broken screen or video card problems

Troubleshoot Storage Device Problems

You store documents, photographs, software, and other files on your computer's hard drive. Magnetic hard drives, mostly found in older desktop computers, are fragile and susceptible to damage from motion and outside elements like dirt and dust. They are usually built inside airtight enclosures.

If you boot up your computer and it doesn't get past the startup screen, the problem might be with the hard drive. Magnetic hard drives operate with a read/write head hovering about two-millionths of an inch over the disk platter. See **Figure 6-13.**

Figure 6-13: Hard disk drive read/ write head on platter

If the head touches the platter, or if dirt gets on the disk, you can have a hard drive crash or **head crash.** You won't be able to access files or run programs. A head crash most likely means you need to replace the drive. Solid state storage devices, which are much less susceptible to damage and failure, do not have any moving parts, so if you have problems with a solid state drive, it's probably due to some other electronic problem. You might not be able to prevent a head crash, but you can make sure your files and programs aren't lost by regularly backing them up to an external drive or cloud storage.

Manage Disk Space

Your hard drive has limited storage space. If you don't have enough free space, you won't be able to save any more files and you'll also have trouble running your programs. When a program needs more **random access memory (RAM)**, the temporary storage used while the computer is running, than is currently available on the computer, it calls on the hard drive to create **virtual memory**, which is temporary space on the disk. If your hard drive is too full, the program won't run.

You should always have at least 200 MB of free space on your hard drive. To find out how much disk space you have if you use Windows, from the desktop, locate and select your hard drive on the computer and then select the Properties command. For Mac users, you can determine the amount of free space by selecting About This Mac from the Apple menu; in the window that opens, select More Info, select Storage, and then you can review the storage used and available in the window that appears.

What can you do if your hard drive is too full? Here are some helpful tips:

- Free up space by uninstalling unused programs and deleting old files; be sure you back up any old but needed files before deleting them.
- In addition to the utilities that run automatically through your operating system, run a disk cleanup utility to identify and remove other extraneous files you no longer need.
- Optimize the way your remaining files are stored by verifying that your disk defragmentation utility is set to run at regular intervals such as weekly or monthly. Defragmenting reorganizes your hard drive to maximize free space.

#buyacomputer

Windows 10 computers are set by default to optimize drives weekly.

Solve Display Problems

If your system unit works properly, but the monitor doesn't, you won't be able to operate the computer. A damaged screen on a laptop or tablet is not easy to remedy, so if you determine you need to repair your laptop or tablet screen, take the entire computer to an authorized repair shop.

However, if a desktop computer's screen remains blank after you turn on the computer, and the indicator lights on the monitor don't illuminate, your monitor may be the problem. You can follow these simple steps to troubleshoot the problem:

1. First, for a standalone monitor, check to see that it is plugged into the power source.

2. If you have power, but still don't see any images, verify that the monitor is connected to the computer.

3. If that checks out, you may have a hardware failure. Plug a different monitor into your computer. If it works, the problem is with your first monitor and not your computer.

4. If the second monitor is blank, you may have a damaged **video card**. This is a circuit board that processes image signals. In either case, you'll need to take the monitor or computer to a technician for repair.

Solve Keyboard Problems

What if your keyboard isn't working? If your computer uses an external keyboard, check to make sure the keyboard is plugged into the correct port. If your keyboard is wireless, be sure the batteries are not out of power, and make sure there is nothing blocking the signal to the computer.

Prevent other keyboard problems by taking some simple precautions. Don't eat or drink while typing. Food particles can make keys sticky, and liquids can short out electrical connections. Keep dust and dirt away with regular cleaning using a can of compressed air or a vacuum cleaner designed for electronic devices.

Hot Technology Now

Most tablets communicate with their keyboards using Bluetooth for a wireless connection. Bluetooth keyboards are available in standard, portable, mini, and foldable form factors.

Solve Pointing Device Problems

If you turn on your computer, and you don't see a pointer on the screen, you might have problems with your pointing device. If you are using an attached mouse, make sure the cable that attaches your device to your computer is plugged in. A wireless pointing device has a number of parts that need to work together. See **Figure 6-14**.

First, check the batteries; install fresh batteries on a regular basis. If your wireless pointing device uses Radio Frequency and uses a USB transmitter/receiver, check that the transmitter is inserted correctly in the USB port and make sure that it properly connects the device to the computer. If it uses Bluetooth, make sure the device is properly paired. As with any electronic device, make sure it's not dirty and ensure that the table or mouse pad is clean. If dirt gets inside the electronics, a mouse may not work properly.

If your touchpad isn't responding, it may be disabled. Detach all USB devices, turn the computer off, and then restart the computer and see if that fixes the problem. If your computer is running Windows, check the Devices settings or the Device Manager in the Control Panel for any signs of trouble. If all these don't yield positive results, you may have to take the computer to an authorized repair shop.

Figure 6-14: Wireless mice have many parts

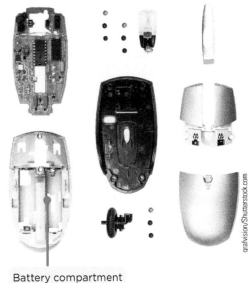

grafvision/Shutterstock.com

Battery compartment

Solve Printer Problems

If you click Print and nothing happens, you can follow these simple steps to troubleshoot printer problems:

1. **Power**: First, check to see that the printer is plugged in.

2. **Connectivity**: Is the printer properly attached to the computer? For wireless printers, this will not be an issue unless there's a problem with the device drive or Bluetooth pairing. Check that all those elements are working.

3. **Toner or ink**: Look to see if the computer's operating system is sending you any messages—the printer might have low toner or ink. Most systems will guide you through the replacement process.

4. **Paper**: Maybe the printer is out of paper, or maybe there's a paper jam. Most printers will send a message identifying this problem and allow for easy access to the paper feeding mechanisms. You can open the panel and gently dislodge the jammed paper.

Checking connections and replacing paper, toner, and ink are fairly simple tasks. But if there is a broken part, such as a belt or power supply, you'll have to contact a computer technician or buy a new printer.

Troubleshoot Power Problems

If you press the computer's power button and you don't get any response, you may have a power problem. You can follow these simple steps to troubleshoot power problems:

1. If the computer is using wall current, check to see that it's plugged in, that power is going to the outlet or power strip, and that you have all cables connected.

2. If the computer or device is portable uses a battery, check to see that the battery is charged.

3. If all that is working properly, the power supply may have failed, and you'll need to take the computer to a computer technician for repair.

4. Portable computers and external peripherals may have an AC adapter as an external power supply. Check to see that the power supply on the cable is not damaged. You can purchase a new adapter at most computer stores or online.

What if you can't connect to the Internet or other network? Make sure your router and modem have power and are connected properly to your computer. Are all the lights on and flashing? Try resetting either device by turning it off, then on again, with the power switch.

Troubleshoot External Storage Problems

Are you having trouble getting your computer to recognize a storage device when you try to retrieve or open files? Learning how to troubleshoot and fix common problems can save you a lot of time, frustration, and money.

If your storage device is not working, perhaps there's dirt inside it, or perhaps it was damaged by liquid or extreme temperatures. Damage or dirt on solid state storage devices, such as cards and drives, is less obvious. You can try cleaning the connection points with a vacuum cleaner with special attachments and filters or a can of compressed air, using safety precautions.

Keep Your Computer in Working Condition

magnetic hard drive | head crash | solid state drive (SSD) | flash drive | solid state storage | memory card

Buying a computer is a significant investment for many people. Just as you should care for your car with regular oil changes and checkups, you should care for your computer with regular maintenance routines. You can take advantage of some well-known tips on how to care for your computer and peripheral devices. If your digital devices are kept in good working condition, they will work properly and last longer, giving you better value for your money.

#buyacomputer

Universal chargers fit many devices, but be careful that the voltage, input, and output are identical to your specifications.

Hot Technology Now

If you have no other options except to start over, you can do a full system restore on your Windows 10 computer using the Reset this PC commands. It will reset Windows 10, giving you the options of removing your apps and settings while keeping your files, or removing everything, including all files, apps, and settings.

The Bottom Line
- Taking care of your hard drive, removable media, and computer hardware is often a matter of common sense and will go a long way in protecting your computer investment in time and money.
- Maintaining peripherals is as important as maintaining the main computer.

Figure 6-15: Proper maintenance will protect your investment

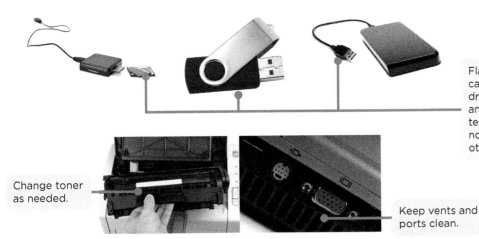

Flash cards, flash drives, card readers, and external drives should be kept clean and away from extreme temperatures, and should not be subject to drops or other blunt force.

Change toner as needed.

Keep vents and ports clean.

Natalia Siverina/Shutterstock.com, Serg64/Shutterstock.com, kavring/Shutterstock.com, Roman Gorielov/Fotolia, Norman Pogson/Shutterstock.com

Maintain the Hard Drive

A **magnetic hard drive** is a sensitive device. Potential hazards abound that could cause a **head crash**, rendering the drive useless. If your data is not backed up, you will most likely lose of all your files. How can you avoid such a disaster?

First, back up your data on a regular basis so you will be protected in the event your hard drive does crash. To help prevent the hard drive from crashing, you should keep the computer in a dust- and dirt-free environment. Never bump into a computer while it is accessing the drive. Don't place the computer in extreme temperatures, and don't drive with it on the seat of your car, where a sudden stop can send it flying. **Solid state drives (SSDs)**, which have no moving parts, are less susceptible to dirt and impact but should still be treated with care.

Maintain Removable Media

Like hard drives, portable media devices can be fragile. A **flash drive**, for example, is a small portable solid state storage device that plugs into a USB port. **Solid state storage** is a computer storage technology that stores data electronically. It is widely used because of its durability and portability. Therefore, a flash drive can be thrown into a purse or pocket, or attached to a key ring as an accessory. It is better to keep all media away from dust, dirt, and other hazards. Some helpful hints for caring for your removable storage media include the following:

- If your flash drive has a protective case or cover, use it to keep dust and dirt away from the USB plug.
- Store the **memory cards** from your digital camera in their cases when not in the camera.
- Use a felt-tip marker to clearly label all portable media; and then store everything in a temperature-controlled, clean, safe place.

Care for Display Screens

A display device is not like a window that you can just spray and wash. The membrane covering many screens is delicate and can be easily damaged. Touch screens in particular get dirty from being touched so often. Some helpful hints for caring for your computer or tablet display include the following:

- Before cleaning, always turn off your display device.
- Use cleaning products specifically meant for computer screens. You can also use a 50/50 solution of water and alcohol, but do not use ammonia-based products.
- Spray the cleaner on a lint-free, soft cloth, rather than directly on the screen. Wipe the cloth gently over the screen area. See **Figure 6-16**.
- Apply a screen protector to most tablets and smartphones to add fingerprint resistance and reduce glare.

On the Job Now

Many companies require screen filters to ensure privacy. For example, if you are seated next to someone on a train, the plastic privacy filter helps to mask confidential information.

Figure 6-16: Cleaning a screen

cunaplus/Shutterstock.com

If you clean your screen regularly, you will see more clearly and reduce eye strain when you use the computer.

Maintain Keyboards

When you work on your computer, your fingers are constantly touching the keyboard. Even if you wash your hands before using your computer, a practice that is not always possible, your keyboard is going to get dirty. Grime, hair, dust, and food will also likely coat the keys and fill in the spaces between the keys of a well-used keyboard. Some helpful hints for caring for your removable storage media include the following:

- Clean your keyboard regularly to keep keys from sticking or becoming unresponsive.
- Gently turn the keyboard upside down to release large particles.
- Use a special keyboard vacuum, not a regular household vacuum cleaner, to get rid of smaller particles. See **Figure 6-17**. Strong suction can dislodge the keys.
- Wipe the keys periodically with a soft cloth. Do not spray cleaners directly onto the keys.
- Keep a can of compressed air handy to spray over the keyboard now and then to remove dust and dirt.

Maintain Pointing Devices

Like keyboards, pointing devices are subject to heavy physical contact. As your hands rest on the mouse or other type of pointing device, residue from your hands can transfer to the device. If you use a mouse pad on a well-used surface, dust from the pad will get on the mouse. Some helpful hints for caring for your pointing device include the following:

- Gently wipe the bottom optical surface with a soft cloth.
- To keep the buttons in working order, use a vacuum designed for electronic devices. You can also gently shake and then blow on the mouse to remove dust. See **Figure 6-18**.
- Replace batteries regularly on wireless mice.
- If you use a laptop with a touch pad, keep your hands and fingers clean to keep residue off the pad.

Maintain Printers

Maintain your printer not only by caring for the device itself but also by being mindful of the key consumables you use with it: ink or toner, and paper. Some helpful hints for caring for your printer include the following:

- Be sure to use the specific ink or toner recommended by the printer manufacturer.
- Toner can leave residue in the printer. To prolong the useful life of your printer, use your printer's cleaning cycles on a regular basis to reduce or eliminate this residue. To run a cleaning cycle, locate and press the proper button on your printer or computer, and then follow the given instructions.
- Store your paper in a dry area—humidity can cause the paper to stick and then jam during printing. If the paper jams, follow the instructions on your printer for gently removing the paper.
- To clean the inside of your printer, open the printer and use a can of compressed air to blow out any paper residue or dust. Use cloths or swabs to wipe surfaces with special cleaning fluids.

Clean an Electronic Device

As with any appliance or machine, a clean computer or electronic device works better than a dirty one. Sometimes, lack of care and maintenance can cause a computer to stop working altogether, so treat your computer kindly. Here are some helpful hints and tips:

- Clean the exterior regularly. Wipe down the exterior with lint-free antistatic wipes. Blow compressed air around openings, such as ports and vents, to clear dust.
- If you have a computer that requires a case to be opened, you can have a professional technician perform a cleaning service if you are not comfortable opening it yourself.

Figure 6-17: Cleaning a keyboard

Venus Angel/Shutterstock.com

Figure 6-18: Cleaning a mouse

anaken2012/Shutterstock.com

Hot Technology Now

To print to a remote wireless printer, try the AirPrint app for iPads or PrinterShare app for Android devices.

- If your computer can be opened and you choose to clean the interior yourself, first check with the computer manufacturer to make sure you don't void the warranty by opening the case. Some require that only professionals open them. Then be sure the computer is unplugged before starting. Wear an antistatic wristband to protect the components from static electricity. Use a special vacuum to clear away as much dust as possible, and then blow the interior with compressed air to get rid of particles the vacuum couldn't get.
- Clean any computer on a flat, stable surface such as a table to avoid dropping any part of it.

Proper maintenance of your computer and peripherals will keep them running smoothly and trouble-free.

Use Software to Maintain Your Computer

disk cleanup utility | disk defragmentation utility | disk optimization utility | computer virus | spyware | adware

You turn on your computer. It takes a while to boot up, even more time for the hour glass or spinning disk to stop whirling, and even longer for all the icons on your desktop to load. Perhaps you can't print from your printer, run your scanner, or save the photos from your camera. What's going on? Chances are you need to do some software computer maintenance.

Use Disk Cleanup Tools

A **disk cleanup utility**, available on many operating systems, removes unused files from your hard drive so the computer doesn't search through unneeded files. Unnecessary files can be anywhere on your hard drive. For example, when you place items in the Recycle Bin and don't empty it, those files remain on your computer, taking up space. When you browse the Internet, your computer stores multiple temporary Internet files.

The Windows Disk Cleanup utility, which runs automatically can identify files such as these and others that can be safely removed. You can change the frequency in which it runs through the operating system utility. The utility also indicates how much space you will gain by removing the unnecessary files. See **Figure 6-19**.

<aside>
The Bottom Line
- Utility programs can help return your computer to better working condition by scanning for viruses and spyware.
- Be sure that your computer updates drivers, and frequently run the programs that clean up and optimize your hard drive.
</aside>

Figure 6-19: Disk Cleanup for Windows

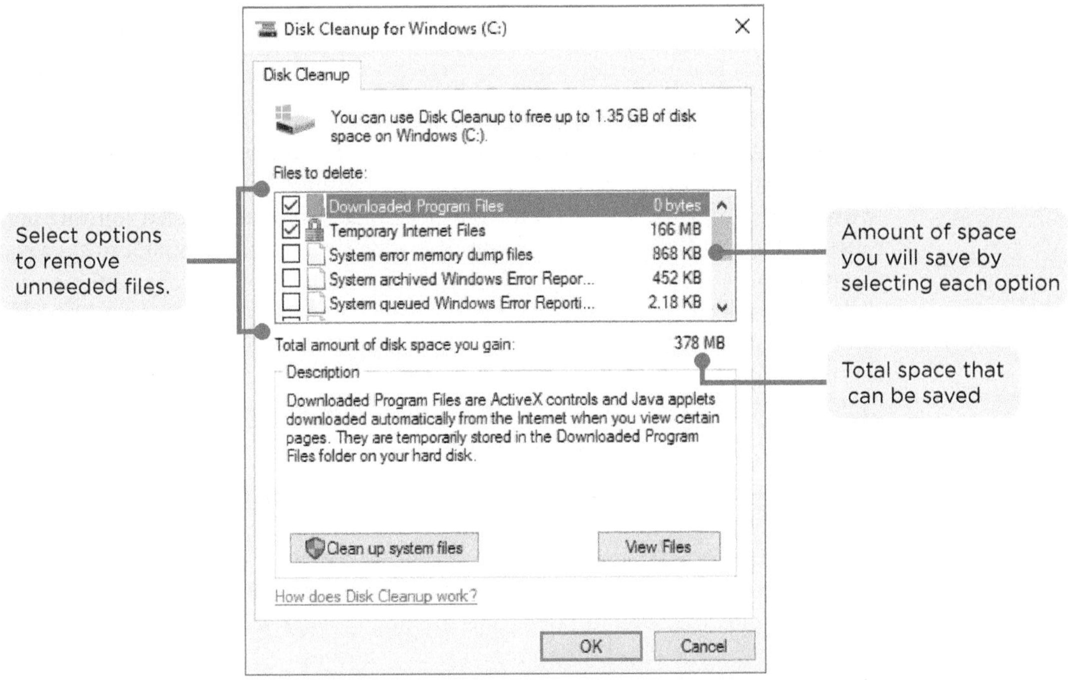

Select options to remove unneeded files.

Amount of space you will save by selecting each option

Total space that can be saved

To start the Disk Cleanup utility in Windows, enter the keywords "Disk Cleanup" in the Search box, then in the search results, click Disk Cleanup. (Different versions of Windows may use a different sequence.) Select the drive you want to clean up and click OK. Disk Cleanup scans your computer to find files to delete. You can see a brief description of each type of file before completing the cleanup. If you have any concerns, you can choose to keep any file.

Optimize Magnetic Drives

A **disk defragmentation utility** or **disk optimization utility**, available on many operating systems, reorganizes the data on a magnetic hard drive so that you can access files more quickly. In Windows, search for the Optimize Drives utility from the Search bar by searching on the keyword "optimize." This utility runs at regular intervals in the background by default, or you can set the utility so that it runs at your preferred scheduled intervals to keep your computer working well.

The Disk Defragmentation utility or Optimize Drives window displays the Disk Defragmenter or optimization schedule, noting the last time it ran and when it's scheduled to run next. See Figure 6-20.

Figure 6-20: Optimize Drives utility

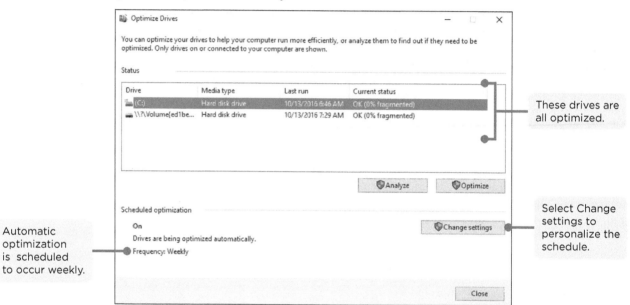

Automatic optimization is scheduled to occur weekly.

These drives are all optimized.

Select Change settings to personalize the schedule.

System and Security Maintenance

The software on your computer is often updated automatically for a variety of reasons including fixing known bugs and adding security features. You should update software when prompted. Because updates to your operating system or installed software may cause conflicts with existing drivers, the operating system has the ability to alert you to any conflicts. If you are running Windows 10, click the Notifications button on the right side of the taskbar to open the Action Center and view any messages, such as if a restart is required. Be sure to check the Action Center periodically to see if any action is needed. You can view and edit your security and maintenance settings by choosing Control Panel > System and Security > Security and Maintenance. See Figure 6-21.

Schedule Virus and Malware Protection

A **computer virus** is malicious software that infects your computer without your knowledge or permission. A virus can wreak havoc on your computer by stealing data, wiping out files or entire hard drives, and slowing down performance. Viruses infect computers via email, web downloads, and visits to Internet websites. Protect your computer from viruses by installing and running virus protection software as part of your maintenance routine. Many programs are available.

Figure 6-21: Security and Maintenance settings

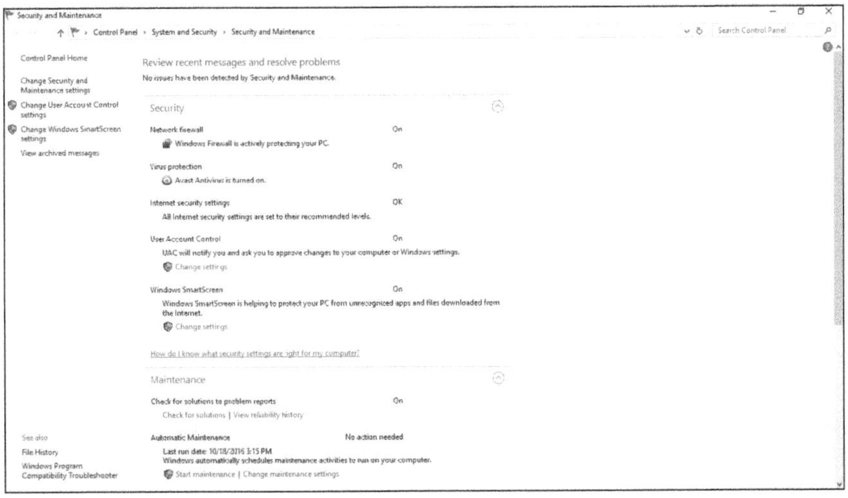

Once you've installed a virus protection program, set it to scan any incoming messages and programs to protect your computer, and be sure to keep it up to date. Many programs include options to automatically update the software on a regular basis.

Like viruses, spyware and adware are among other types of malware and install themselves on your computer without your knowledge or permission. **Spyware** poses a security risk because it can track and steal your personal information. It can also change the settings on your browser without your permission. **Adware** programs show you unsolicited advertisements in banners or pop-up windows.

The best way to avoid spyware and adware is to install and run prevention software. Spyware and adware removal software can detect and remove these unwanted programs from your computer. Be sure to keep your removal programs up-to-date, because new spyware and adware are constantly being created.

With proper maintenance and care you should be able to have many years of productive trouble-free use of your computing device.

#buyacomputer

Go to twitter.com, and then search for @SAMTechNow, the book's Twitter account, and follow @SAMTechNow to get tweets on your home page.

Chapter Review

Buy a Computer

1. What is the definition of "form factor"? List two form factors. How does form factor affect your buying decisions?

2. Explain the different ways you can connect with wireless devices and give two examples of how you might use wireless peripheral devices.

3. Name two of the main options you have for operating systems.

4. List five questions you should ask yourself before you prepare a budget for your computer purchase.

Install Hardware

5. Explain the first steps you should take when a new desktop computer arrives and compare it to the first steps when a new laptop computer arrives.

6. List different methods you can use to connect peripheral devices to a computer.

7. Describe the purpose of device drivers and describe two different ways you might obtain them.

Protect Computer Hardware

8. With the goal of keeping your hardware safe, name three physical hazards you should avoid.

9. What is the danger of dust and liquid to a computer system?

10. Explain the difference between a UPS and a surge suppressor.

Safeguard Your Computer

11. Name two ways you can prevent your computer from being stolen.

12. Name two ways you can prevent your data from being stolen. Define two-factor authentication.

13. List four good habits to practice when creating a password, and give an example of a strong password.

Troubleshoot Common Hardware Problems

14. Explain two possible causes for a hard drive crash and describe the symptoms of a hard drive crash.

15. Describe what can go wrong with your display. What steps can you take to isolate the problem?

16. List three steps you can you follow to troubleshoot printer problems.

Keep Your Computer in Working Condition

17. Describe how you can work to keep your hard drive working properly.

18. Explain the best way to clean a display screen and keyboard.

19. What are two steps you can take to make sure your wireless mouse and keyboard function properly?

Use Software to Maintain Your Computer

20. Explain and compare what the disk cleanup and the disk optimization utilities do to help you maintain your computer.

21. Explain the differences between a computer virus, spyware, and adware and how they each can affect your computer.

Test Your Knowledge Now

1. _____ is a form factor that is not a portable computer.
   a. Tablet
   b. Laptop
   c. Desktop
   d. Smartphone

2. Before buying a computer, you should first determine your _____.
   a. budget
   b. hardware
   c. form factor
   d. software

3. A _____ is a portable computer with a removable keyboard.
   a. tablet
   b. desktop
   c. laptop
   d. 2-in-1 computer

4. A(n) _____ determines the software that can run on the device.
   a. form factor
   b. operating system
   c. Bluetooth
   d. RAM

5. When you are buying a computer, you should consider getting the best _____ you can afford at the time because it is the most important component in a computer.
   a. peripherals
   b. CPU
   c. RAM
   d. monitor

6. _____ is the measurement used to describe the amount of random access memory in a computer.
   a. Megabytes
   b. Terabytes
   c. Gigabytes
   d. Kilobytes

7. What measurement would not be used to describe the amount of built-in computer storage?
   a. Terabytes
   b. Megabytes
   c. Kilobytes
   d. Gigabytes

8. The major advantage of a tablet is _____.
   a. portability
   b. storage capacity
   c. expandability
   d. long battery life

9. If you want to protect yourself from a power failure if the power goes out, you should buy a _____ so you can still use your computer.
   a. battery
   b. GPS
   c. UPS
   d. surge suppressor

10. Buy a _____ to protect your computer from power fluctuations.
    a. GPS
    b. battery
    c. UPS
    d. surge suppressor

11. If your computer doesn't have enough RAM, it can use _____ to help with the shortfall.
    a. Bluetooth
    b. power supply
    c. virtual memory
    d. USB ports

12. Which of the following is most likely to help you locate a stolen computer?
    a. UPS
    b. RFID
    c. RAM
    d. CPU

13. To best protect your data and have access to it from anywhere in the world, you can use _____ storage technology.
    a. cloud
    b. HDD
    c. SSD
    d. random

14. Getting a code sent to your smartphone after you enter a password to access your computer is an example of _____.
    a. biometrics
    b. two-factor authentication
    c. cloud technology
    d. anti-virus software

15. The main disadvantage of cloud storage is that _____; therefore, you might not be able to get your files.
    a. the devices are fragile and have poor connectivity
    b. access is available only from tablets
    c. the servers may be unreliable
    d. providers frequently go out of business

16. The app used to free up space on your drive by removing unnecessary files is the _____ utility.
    a. Disk Defragmenter
    b. Spyware
    c. Disk Optimizer
    d. Disk Cleanup

17. Short number sequences used to access your bank accounts are called _____.
    a. PINs
    b. passwords
    c. spyware
    d. utilities

18. _____ are necessary for peripherals to work with laptops, desktops, as well as tablets or smartphones.
    a. Ports
    b. Batteries
    c. Device drivers
    d. Firewalls

19. Which of the following does *not* belong in your toolkit to keep your computer clean?
    a. Can of compressed air
    b. Soft cloth
    c. Small electronics vacuum
    d. Ammonia and bleach wipes

20. _____ is a form factor that looks like a laptop but has a removable keyboard.
    a. Tablet
    b. All-in-on computer
    c. Hybrid desktop
    d. 2-in-1 computer

21. In the space next to each image below, write the letter of the term that describes each form factor.
    a. smartphone
    b. tablet
    c. desktop
    d. laptop

Daboost/Shutterstock.com

Try This Now

1: Shop for a College Laptop

Investigate the purchase of a laptop for school that is powerful, versatile, and affordable.

a. Open the website amazon.com and search for a Lenovo laptop. Select a laptop that is reasonably priced, current, and powerful using the criteria that you read about in the chapter. Take a screenshot of your selection that shows an image of the computer as well as its price and specifications.

b. Open the website newegg.com and search for a Samsung laptop. Select a laptop that is reasonably priced, current, and powerful using the criteria that you read about in the chapter. Take a screenshot of your selection that shows an image of the computer as well as its price and specifications.

c. Open the website bestbuy.com and search for a Microsoft laptop or 2-in-1 computer. Select a laptop or 2-in-1 computer that is reasonably priced, current, and powerful using the criteria that you read about in the chapter. Take a screenshot of your selection that shows an image of the computer as well as its price and specifications.

d. Place the three screenshots in a single Word document, and add your answers to the following: Which of the three websites was easiest to search? Which one of the three laptops would you prefer? Why?

2: Shop for a Tablet to Use as a General Purpose Device

Investigate the purchase of a tablet that serves as a general purpose device for activities such as reading, a universal remote control, notetaking, recipes, and a productive second screen. Search for an affordable full-size tablet with a diagonal screen measurement that is more than 9 inches.

a. Open the website bestbuy.com and search for the latest iPad. Select an iPad that is reasonably priced, current, and powerful using the criteria that you read about in the chapter. Take a screenshot of your selection that shows an image of the computer as well as its price and specifications.

b. Open the website dell.com and search for a Dell tablet. Select a tablet that is reasonably priced, current, and powerful using the criteria that you read about in the chapter. Take a screenshot of your selection that shows an image of the computer as well as its price and specifications.

c. Open the website frys.com and search for a Lenovo tablet. Select a tablet that is reasonably priced, current, and powerful using the criteria that you read about in the chapter. Take a screenshot of your selection that shows an image of the computer as well as its price and specifications.

d. Place the three screenshots in a single Word document, and add your answers to the following: Which of the three websites was easiest to search? Which one of the three tablets would you prefer? Why? Which of the tablets included a keyboard?

3: Shop for an All-in-One Computer

Investigate the purchase of an all-in-one computer for your home that is powerful, versatile, and current. Search for a large all-in-one computer with a diagonal screen measurement that is more than 26 inches.

All-in-One Computers

Glovatskiy/Shutterstock.com

a. Open the website hp.com and search for an HP all-in-one computer. Select an all-in-one computer that is current and powerful using the criteria that you read about in the chapter. Take a screenshot of your selection that shows an image of the computer as well as its price and specifications.

b. Open the website staples.com and search for any all-in-one computer. Select an all-in-one computer that is current and powerful using the criteria that you read about in the chapter. Take a screenshot of your selection that shows an image of the computer as well as its price and specifications.

c. Open the website costco.com and search for any all-in-one computer. Select an all-in-one computer that is current and powerful using the criteria that you read about in the chapter. Take a screenshot of your selection that shows an image of the computer as well as its price and specifications.

d. Place the three screenshots in a single Word document, and add your answers to the following: Which of the three websites was easiest to search? Which one of the three all-in-one computers would you prefer? Why? What were the screen sizes of each one? Were the keyboards wireless?

Critical Thinking Now

1: CNET Unbiased Reviews

When you research buying a computer online, finding unbiased information on a retail site can be challenging. The website cnet.com publishes objective reviews and news on the latest technology products. Using CNET, search the reviews for the best tablets. Read through the five top choices and watch the videos, if available. Write at least 100 words on which tablet you would select based on CNET's recommendations. Provide details such as name, price, and the bottom line from the review.

2: Capturing Images with Your Smartphone Camera Using Office Lens

Note: This assignment requires the use of a smartphone and a Microsoft account.

Download the free app Office Lens from any app store to your smartphone.

Voice Activation

a. Using the Whiteboard option, use Office Lens to take a picture of a Whiteboard or a paper document. Save the image to OneDrive in Office Lens.
b. Using the Business Card option, use Office Lens to take a picture of a business card. Save the image to OneDrive in Office Lens.
c. Research two more features of Office Lens and write 100 words about these features in a Word document. Paste the shared link to the two images files stored in your OneDrive in the Word document and submit to your instructor.

3: Headset for Cortana or Siri

Cortana and Siri are voice activated assistants available in Windows 10 and macOS. At your job, a Bluetooth headset would provide a hands-free solution to interact with Cortana or Siri on your computer in an office setting. Research an ideal headset and write 100 words in a Word document detailing your choice, the cost, and features.

Ethical Issues Now

As an employee of a major smartphone company, you have been issued a prototype smartphone for testing purposes that has not been released to the public. You are under strict orders not to let the phone out of your sight. Today you had lunch at a local restaurant and left the phone behind on the table. After realizing the loss, you returned to the restaurant an hour later, but the prototype phone was gone.

a. Knowing that you will be fired if the press is shown your prototype phone, should you tell your boss? Why or why not?
b. Research a similar news story and write a synopsis of at least 100 words of what actually happened in the real-life story.

Team Up Now—School Lab Maintenance

Based on the computer's operating system in your school's computer lab, work together as a team to create a computer maintenance checklist that contains text and video tutorial links.

a. Research preventative maintenance tasks to keep your school's computer lab running smoothly.
b. Create a checklist of five tasks that your team determines as critical to maintaining the computer.
c. Search for a correlating video that provides a tutorial for each of the five tasks on the checklist and add the links to the checklist.
d. Submit the checklist and video links to your instructor.

Key Terms

2-in-1 computer
adware
all-in-one computer
Bluetooth
byte
central processing unit (CPU)
cloud backup
computer virus
data encryption
desktop
device driver
disk cleanup utility
disk defragmentation utility
disk optimization utility
driver
Encrypting File System (EFS)
extended warranty
external hard drive
firewall
flash drive

form factor
full disk encryption (FDE)
gigabyte (GB)
global positioning system (GPS)
head crash
hybrid laptop
hybrid tablet
internal hard drive
laptop
magnetic hard drive
memory card
mobile device
operating system
pair
password
peripheral device
personal identification number (PIN)
platform
power fluctuation
power spike

power surge
processor
radio frequency (RF)
radio-frequency identification (RFID) tag
random access memory (RAM)
real-time location system
service plan
solid state drive (SSD)
solid state storage
spyware
storage device
surge suppressor
tablet
terabyte (TB)
two-factor authentication
uninterruptible power supply (UPS)
username
video card
virtual memory
wireless printer

The Connected Computer

Lochlan works with confidence, knowing that his school's network security software is keeping his data safe from intruders.

...chlan and his study group ... using cloud computing to ... a draft of their project ...gether, even though they ... in different locations.

Lochlan's laptop is connected to his school's wireless LAN, so he can access the Internet to do research right outdoors.

iStockphoto.com/UberImages

Lochlan Fix is working on a project for his online philosophy class. Thanks to wireless technologies, Lochlan can connect to the Internet to do research, conduct Skype video meetings with his study group, and use email to send questions to his professor, all while enjoying the great outdoors.

Define a Network

The Bottom Line

- Networks can be simple or complex, and network components can interact in different ways.
- Networks can span limited areas the size of your home office or school, or they can be as large as a town or a country.
- The Internet, a collection of personal, local, regional, national, and international computer networks, is the largest network in the world.

Networks let people share resources, devices, information, software, and data. A **network** is a system of two or more computers and communications devices linked by wires, cables, or a telecommunications system. Networks can connect devices over large or small areas.

Identify Network Hardware and Software

How do networks make connections? They use both hardware and software.

- Simple networks, such as those you find in a home, often use the networking features of the home PC's operating system.
- Larger and more complex networks require more sophisticated network software. Networks that connect to other networks use special types of communications devices.

For hardware, networked computers need the components shown in Table 7-1.

Figure 7-1: Networks connect people

Networks connect people who are near each other or halfway around the world.

Wired networks are connected by wires or cables...

...while wireless networks use airwave signals instead of wires.

Szasz-Fabian Jozsef/Shutterstock.com

Table 7-1: Network components

Component	Looks like this	Purpose
Network interface card (NIC)	 moritzrus/Shutterstock.com	A circuit board with special electronic circuits that connects a computer to a network
Hub or switch	 Rob Hyrons/Shutterstock.com  Darryl Brooks/Shutterstock.com	A device that provides a central point for cables in a network; hubs are less common as they transfer all data to all devices; most networks now use switches, which transfer data only to the intended recipient
Router	 Sashkin/Shutterstock.com	A device that connects two or more networks and directs, or routes, the flow of information along the networks; a **wireless router** communicates using radio signals instead of cables

Identify Network Architecture

Network architecture determines how networked computers interact with one another. Networks commonly use one of two architectural models: peer-to-peer or client/server.

A **peer-to-peer (P2P) network** is best suited for networks of 10 or fewer computers, like those found in homes or small offices. Each computer maintains its own files and software. All computers have the same capabilities and responsibilities, but share resources and peripherals such as printers.

In a **client/server network**, one central computer, called the **server**, controls access to network resources. The other computers or devices are called **clients**. The clients request services from the server. For example, a client computer might ask the server for access to a software program, a customer database, the Internet, or a printer.

Identify Local Area Networks

A **local area network (LAN)** connects computers and devices in a limited area, such as a home, a school, or an office complex. Each computer or device on the network is called a **node**. Many LANs are designed as client/server networks. The network server is a centralized location for common files and software.

Organizations use LANs so people can share files and software, send and receive email, use high-speed printers, access the Internet, video-conference with satellite offices, and more.

Networks can save organizations money by allowing users to share resources. For example, most software developers sell special versions of their software for use on networks. Organizations pay a license fee per user rather than installing a program on each machine. The per-user license fee is generally less than the cost of each installation.

Set Up a Home Network

If you have a computer at home, you probably use it with peripheral devices such as a printer, scanner, or external hard drive. If you have more than one computer, it makes sense for all computers to share the same devices. You probably also want your computers to connect to the Internet.

To connect your home computers to peripheral devices and to the Internet or other networks, you can create a local area network (LAN), which connects computers within a small geographic area, such as a home or a small office building. Your home LAN can be wired, wireless, or a combination of both.

For hardware, you may need to install a number of devices, such as those shown in Table 7-2.

Table 7-2: Network devices

Network device	Purpose
Wireless access point	Connects wireless devices to a wired network
Router	Sends data between networked computers
Broadband modem	Connects a computer to the Internet

If you are connecting your network to one outside your home, you only need a modem. Routers and modems are relatively inexpensive and easy to install. See Figure 7-2 on the next page for a typical home network setup.

For software, most current operating systems, such as Windows and macOS, have controls that let you set up and run home LANs.

Identify Personal Area Networks

A **personal area network (PAN)** or a **wireless personal area network (WPAN)** connects personal digital devices within a range of about 30 feet (9 meters). For example, a PAN can connect a portable device such as a smartphone with a computer to sync data files using a Wi-Fi signal, or a headset to a smartphone using **Bluetooth**, a short-range wireless technology. Wireless personal area networks work without using wires or cables.

#ConnectingNow

If you are hanging out on campus, you must be within 300 feet of a network router to connect to the rest of the world.

On the Job Now

As hospitals and other healthcare organizations increase their use of information technology, they will need more computer network architects to manage the growing systems and networks. Employment of network and computer systems administrators in general is expected to grow faster than the average and with a median salary of $100,240.

Hot Technology Now

To view your local network connection on a Windows computer, select Settings on the Start menu, and then select Network and Internet to view the basic network information and to set up connections.

#ConnectingNow

Change the preset password on your home router to a strong password, which is long and uses numbers, letters, and symbols.

Figure 7-2: Typical home network setup

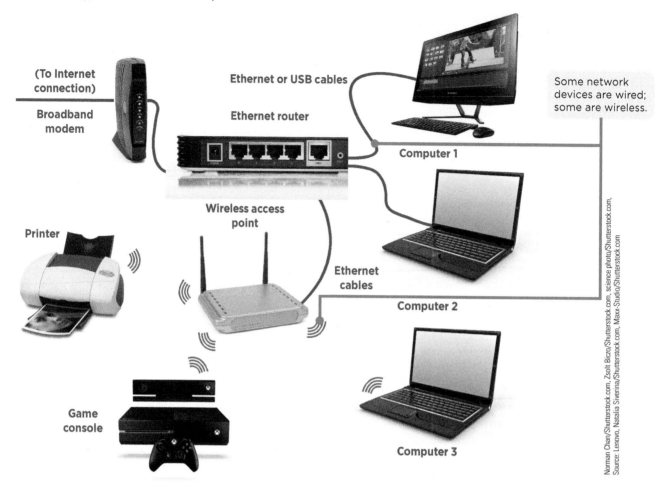

Bluetooth is a type of PAN technology that you can use in the following ways:
- Connect a printer or mouse to your computer.
- Connect your cell phone to a headset or car speakers so you can use the phone hands-free while in the car.
- Transmit data wirelessly from a media player to your computer speakers.

Another form of personal area network is a **body area network (BAN)**, consisting of small, lightweight biosensors implanted in the body. The sensors monitor and collect information and can wirelessly transmit significant health changes immediately to a medical professional, who can inform the patient of the correct treatment. While still in development stages, BANs hold potential in diabetes and cardiac monitoring, sports and fitness, and many other areas.

Identify Wide Area Networks

A **wide area network (WAN)** is a network that connects devices in two or more LANs located in a large geographic region. A WAN is appropriate for a state, country, or other large area where data needs to be transmitted over long distances. The Internet is classified as a WAN. See **Figure 7-3**.

A WAN can be one large network, or a series of interconnected LANs:
- **A multinational company** would use a WAN to connect all their offices around the world.
- **Governments** might use WANs to facilitate communications between different departments. A **metropolitan area network (MAN)** is a public, high-speed network owned and operated by a city or county.
- **A national retail chain** could use a WAN to connect store locations to headquarters, so every store can access centralized systems for inventory, personnel, and marketing.

On the Job Now

The U.S. military has replaced many of its wired connections with the Wireless Network Defense program, which maintains a wireless network even if one connection is damaged.

#ConnectingNow

A **neighborhood area network (NAN)** connects devices within a limited geographical area, usually including several buildings, covering a wider area than public wireless networks found in coffee shops or book stores that offer free Wi-Fi.

Figure 7-3: WAN using multiple networking technologies

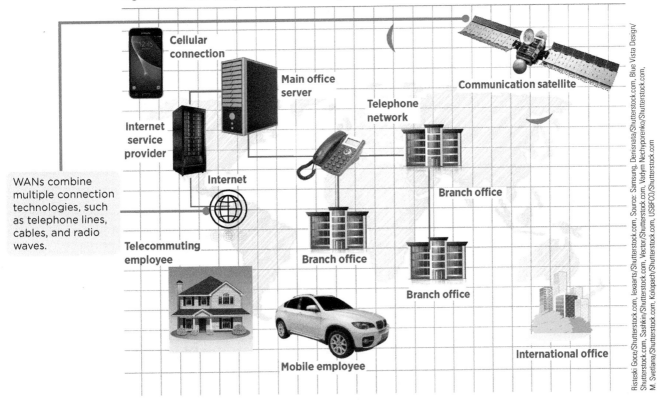

WANs combine multiple connection technologies, such as telephone lines, cables, and radio waves.

Connect to a Network

network standard | Ethernet | Power over Ethernet (PoE) | Phoneline/HomePNA | Powerline | Wi-Fi (wireless fidelity) | Bluetooth | 3G | 4G | Ethernet standard | network interface card (NIC) | digital modem | router | LTE (Long Term Evolution)

Computers need specific network hardware, services, and standards to connect to a LAN or a WAN. In addition, connecting to the Internet often requires services from an Internet service provider. All communication technologies need global standards so they can understand one another. See Figure 7-4.

The Bottom Line

- To communicate, networks must conform to network standards.
- To connect to a network, computers need hardware devices and connection options.

Figure 7-4: Network connections

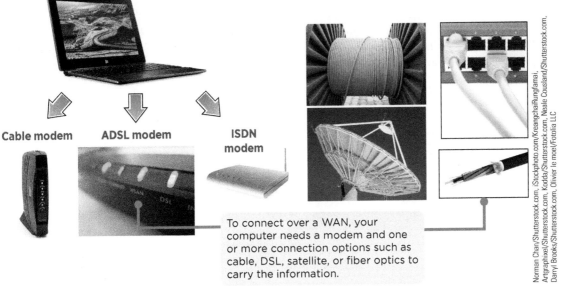

Cable modem   ADSL modem   ISDN modem

To connect over a WAN, your computer needs a modem and one or more connection options such as cable, DSL, satellite, or fiber optics to carry the information.

Define Network Standards

Computers need a common language to communicate over networks. Network hardware and software must work together, regardless of who made them or where they are located. To ensure that any computer in any part of the world can connect to any network, organizations such as ANSI and IEEE propose, develop, and approve network standards.

Network standards specify the way computers access a network, the type(s) of hardware used, data transmission speeds, and the types of cable and wireless technology used. See Table 7-3 for a summary of some important network standards.

Table 7-3: Network standards and how they are used

Standard	Example devices that use standard	Used for
Ethernet	Alexander Kalina/Shutterstock.com	Establishing wired networks
Power over Ethernet (PoE)	Kodda/Shutterstock.com	Transferring both power and data via an Ethernet network
Phoneline/HomePNA and **Powerline**	Sergey Andrianov/Shutterstock.com, gyn9037/Shutterstock.com	Connecting computers through ordinary telephone wires and coaxial cables
Wi-Fi (wireless fidelity)	Scanrail1/Shutterstock.com	Creating wireless home and small business networks
Bluetooth	arosoft/Shutterstock.com	Allowing a wide assortment of devices to communicate wirelessly over short distances
3G, 4G	Kristina Postnikova/Shutterstock.com, Zern Liew/Shutterstock.com	Establishing cellular networks

Use Ethernet Technology

Ethernet is the most widely used standard for wired networks. The **Ethernet standard** controls how adapter cards, routers, and modems share access to cables and phone lines. The standard also dictates how devices transmit data.

Several versions of Ethernet have been released; each upgrade has increased the speed of data transmission. The transfer rate for the original Ethernet standard was 10 Mbps (million bits per second), which is extremely slow by today's standards. The latest evolution is a 100-Gigabit Ethernet with a data transfer rate of up to 100 Gbps (billion bits per second). Faster data transfer rates allow for smoother transmission of video files.

Identify Communications Hardware

Computers need appropriate communications hardware to connect to networks, such as network cards, adapters, modems, routers, hubs, and switches. To connect to a network, your computer might need a **network interface card (NIC)**, which can be wired or wireless. See **Figure 7-5**.

#ConnectingNow

If you need to connect to the Internet and wireless connections are unavailable, you can connect using an Ethernet cable.

By the Numbers Now

Over 43% of international phone calls are made using Skype.

Figure 7-5: Wired and wireless network interface cards (NICs)

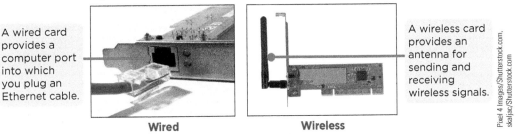

A wired card provides a computer port into which you plug an Ethernet cable.

A wireless card provides an antenna for sending and receiving wireless signals.

Wired   **Wireless**

Pixel 4 Images/Shutterstock.com, skaljac/Shutterstock.com

Most modems today are digital. A **digital modem** sends and receives data and information to and from a digital line. Three types of digital modems are ISDN (for ISDN lines), DSL (for DSL lines), and cable (for cable TV lines), shown in **Figure 7-6**. All these modems typically include built-in Wi-Fi connectivity.

Figure 7-6: Types of modems

Cable

DSL

ISDN

Artgraphixel/Shutterstock.com, iStockphoto.com/KreangchaiRungfamai, Norman Chan/Shutterstock.com

Hubs and switches provide a central point for network cables. Hubs transfer all data to all devices and switches transfer data only to specified recipients. Recall that most modern networks use switches rather than hubs. A **router** manages network traffic by evaluating network messages and routing them on the best path to their destination. The same is true of a wireless access point, which you'll learn more about in the section "Use Mobile Hotspots" later in this chapter.

Use Internet Service Providers

Once you have connected to your local network, you need a way to connect to the Internet, which you do through an Internet service provider (ISP). ISPs use specialized equipment to connect you, for a fee, to the Internet. These connections are made using satellites, cable, phone, or fiber-optic lines. (An ISP is different from a cellular provider, which only provides calling and Internet service for your cellphone, not for your laptop or tablet.)

Most ISPs today offer broadband connectivity capable of transmitting large amounts of data at high speeds. Service areas vary; some ISPs offer service nationwide, while others service a smaller area. In the past, you had to dial up to reconnect to the Internet after every session. Most connections today are always-on connections, meaning your computer remains connected to the Internet at all times.

Define Cellular Standards

Mobile phone standards have evolved to meet the ever-increasing demands of consumers, who want data as well as voice communication on their phones. Cellular companies constantly upgrade their networks and standards for faster, better data transmission. While 3G cellular networks offer Internet services virtually anywhere cellular phone service is used, 4G networks offer high-speed Internet service. It is less widely available, but is expanding rapidly, and should be the dominant cellular standard by 2017. A new, faster 5G standard is expected by 2020.

Many 4G Internet connections can be as fast, or faster, than cable modem or DSL connections. **LTE (Long Term Evolution)** and WiMAX are competing 4G standards offered by different cellular providers.

Describe How Networks Work

resource | data | network hardware | cable | port | RJ-11 port | modem | cable modem | DSL modem | wireless modem | hub | switch | node | protocol | TCP/IP | IPv4 | IPv6 | bandwidth | broadband | narrowband

Networks connect computers and digital devices to share **resources** (such as storage devices, printers, servers, and communications hardware) and **data** (programs and information).

Figure 7-7: Sharing resources and data

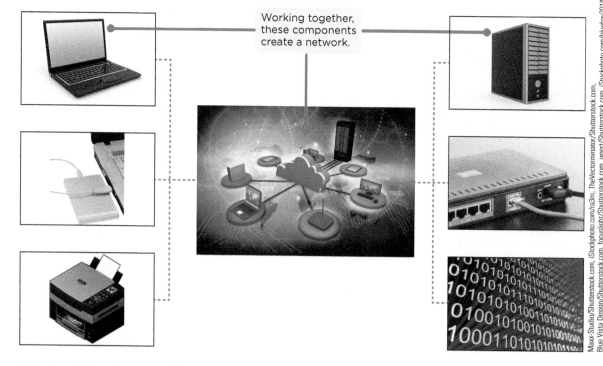

Working together, these components create a network.

Network hardware includes clients, servers, modems, network interface cards, hubs, switches, cables, and routers. In order for these components to communicate, they must adhere to common network rules.

Identify Network Cables, Connectors, and Ports

Wired networks have **cables** that connect network devices through **ports** (outlets), using connectors that match each type of port opening. See **Figure 7-8**. Some networks use telephone cables, which connect through telephone **(RJ-11) ports**.

Figure 7-8: Connectors and ports

Wired network cables, or Ethernet cables, connect through Ethernet ports using RJ-45 connectors.

Ethernet port and connector

USB ports and connector

USB (Universal Serial Bus) ports connect devices that are wired for USB using USB connectors.

Serial port and connector

Pixel 4 images/Shutterstock.com, TheVectorminator/Shutterstock.com, iStockphoto.com/AdrianHanco

Depending on data transfer requirements, networks use one of the following types of cables: a) Twisted pair, which has the slowest rate of data transfer; b) Coaxial; and c) Fiber optic, which has the fastest rate of data transfer.

Describe Network Modems

A **modem** is a communications device that connects a communications channel such as the Internet to a sending or receiving device such as a computer. Dial-up modems convert digital data into analog data and back, so networks can transmit and receive data via analog telephone lines.

- **Cable modems** send and receive digital data over a cable TV connection. In some cases, the cable modem can be part of a set-top cable box.
- **DSL modems** are external devices that use existing standard copper telephone wiring to send and receive digital data.
- **Wireless modems** are often built into laptop and tablet computers, or they attach via a USB port. A cell phone can work as a modem, too.

Define Hubs, Switches, and Routers

A **hub** or **switch** is a central point of connection for network cables. A **node** is any device connected to a network. Hubs and switches allow nodes to communicate with each other. Switches are more efficient than hubs because hubs transfer data to all devices, while switches send data only to the intended recipient.

By the Numbers Now

A small business or home wireless network can be set up for under $50. Often ISPs provide a free wireless router with a service contract.

By the Numbers Now

The normal range of a residential wireless modem (a modem with a built-in wireless router) is 150 feet.

Routers allow networks to communicate with each other. Routers can also connect networked computers to the Internet, so multiple users can share a connection. Most routers are also switches that contain ports for connecting computers.

Define Network Protocols

For network devices to communicate with each other, they must follow a common set of rules, or **protocols**. All computers on the Internet follow **TCP/IP** (Transmission Control Protocol/Internet Protocol), a network protocol that defines how messages (data) are routed through a network. Part of TCP/IP is IP, or Internet Protocol. Each computer on a network has a unique IP address.

There are two versions of IP addresses: **IPv4** (Internet Protocol Version 4) and **IPv6** (Internet Protocol Version 6). IPv4 was the standard protocol until recently, but the growing number of Internet-connected devices requires more IP addresses than IPv4 can provide. The newer IPv6 addresses use 128 bits, in contrast to IPv4's 32 bits, vastly expanding the possible number of IP addresses, which should be sufficient for the foreseeable future.

Describe Bandwidth Factors

Networks transmit data using information "roads" and "highways." Smaller roads carry less information than the larger highways. A common term used to describe information-carrying capacity is **bandwidth**; the higher the bandwidth, the more information the channel can transmit. **Broadband** refers to high-capacity channels, while **narrowband** refers to slower channels with less capacity.

Internet connections vary in bandwidth. Dial-up is a slow narrowband service, while DSL, satellite, cable, and FTTP are considered broadband. If you want to watch movies or use the Internet for video, you need a high bandwidth option, such as one of the following:

- **DSL (digital subscriber line)** uses a regular telephone line connection, while cable uses a cable TV connection.
- **FTTP (Fiber to the Premises)** uses fiber-optic cable.
- **Fixed wireless** uses a dish-shaped antenna on a building to communicate with a tower via radio signals.
- **Wireless Internet Service Providers (WISPs)** are rapidly becoming a popular broadband option for rural areas.

Identify Types of Networks

topology | network architecture | network topology | star network | bus network | ring network | mesh network | tree topology | full mesh topology | partial mesh topology | domain-based network | client/server network | domain controller | server | client | peer-to-peer (P2P) network | Internet peer-to-peer (Internet P2P) networking | file sharing | BitTorrent | network server | file server | print server | database server | web server | wired network | wireless network | mobile computing | Wi-Fi network | WiMAX | LTE | hot zone | hotspot | Wi-Fi hotspot | tether | wireless access point | personal mobile hotspot | personal hotspot | data encryption | intranet | extranet | virtual private network (VPN)

A network can be defined by its **topology**—or how computers and devices are physically arranged within it. **Network architecture**, like building architecture, determines the logical design of computers, devices, and media within a network. See **Figure 7-9**. The two main types of network architectures are client/server and peer-to-peer (P2P).

Define Network Topologies

Network topology defines the physical layout of, and relationship between, network devices. **Table 7-4** describes several types of basic network topologies.

#ConnectingNow

To find your computer's IP address, type "IP address" in your browser's search box. Your IP address will be displayed at the top of the search results.

Hot Technology Now

You can test the speed of your network connections at speed-test.net. The site tells you how fast you can download and upload data, and can recommend tools for improving your speed.

The Bottom Line

- Network topologies include star, bus, ring, and mesh networks, as well as combination topologies.
- Network architecture includes client/server and peer-to-peer (P2P).
- Networks can connect resources using wired or wireless connections.

Figure 7-9: Network topology and architecture

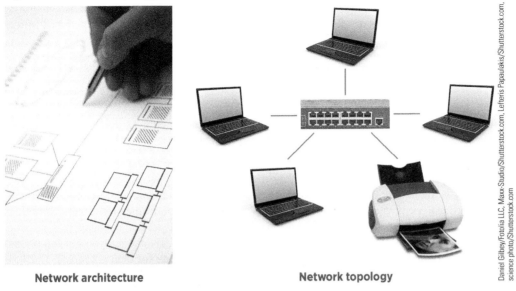

Daniel Gilbey/Fotolia LLC, Maxx-Studio/Shutterstock.com, Lefteris Papaulakis/Shutterstock.com, science photo/Shutterstock.com

Network architecture   **Network topology**

Table 7-4: Network topologies

Topology	How the network is arranged	Details
Star network		Each device is attached to the central device such as a server or switch. If the central device fails, none of the attached devices can work.
Bus network		All devices attach in a line to the central cable or bus, which carries the data. If the cable fails, all devices on the cable fail.
Ring network		Data travels from one device to another around the ring. If one device fails, the entire network could stop working. Ring networks are no longer common.
Mesh network		All devices interconnect with each other. Used most often with wireless networks. No single device keeps the network working. If one device fails, the network will keep working if the data can use an alternate path.

Martina Vaculikova/Shutterstock.com

Figure 7-10: Example of a tree topology

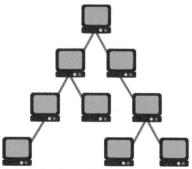

Martina Vaculikova/Shutterstock.com

Figure 7-11: Network server

dotshock/Shutterstock.com

Some networks combine topologies to connect smaller networks and form one larger network. For example:

- Two star networks may be joined together using a bus to form a network with a **tree topology**. Trees are easily expanded. School and business networks are often based on tree topologies. See **Figure 7-10**.
- In a **full mesh topology**, each device on the network is connected to every other device on the network.
- With a **partial mesh topology**, some devices are connected to all other devices, while others are connected only to those devices with which they exchange the most data.

Identify Client/Server and Peer Networks

Networks can be client/server (also called **domain-based**) or peer-to-peer (also called client-to-client). **Client/server networks** have a domain controller that acts as a gateway to the network and its resources. A **domain controller** is a **server**, a computer on the network that controls access to hardware, software, and other resources. The other computers on the network request services from the server. Some servers provide centralized storage for programs, data, and information. The **clients** are other computers and mobile devices on the network that rely on the server for their resources.

In a client/server network, computers are not "equal," because they don't all have the same access to network resources. To log onto a typical client/server network, you need a username and password; the network is controlled by a network administrator.

Peer-to-peer (P2P) networks are networks of equals (peers), and typically have up to 10 computers. They are less expensive and easier to set up than client/server networks because they have no dedicated servers (servers that only serve the network, and are not shared). A peer-to-peer network does not require a controller or a network administrator, because each computer or device is equal on the network and controls access to its operating system, application software, data files and devices. Peers can share files and peripheral devices such as printers with peers. Most home networks are peer-to-peer networks.

Internet peer-to-peer (Internet P2P) networking is a specific type of P2P networking where files are shared over the Internet directly between individual users. Also called **file sharing**, Internet P2P is commonly used to exchange music and video. File sharing networks such as Bitcoin, Spotify, and Tradepal also use Internet P2P networking. However, copyright law and ethics are an issue with Internet P2P. File sharing is illegal if the content is copyright-protected and the exchange is unauthorized.

BitTorrent is a P2P file-sharing protocol that speeds up the download process by dividing files into smaller units, spreading them across multiple networked computers, and downloading from multiple sources at once. BitTorrent is used for distributing music and movies over the Internet.

Identify Types of Network Servers

Networks can have many types of servers, each performing different tasks. Servers are typically powerful computers with lots of memory and very large hard drives for storage. A **network server** works to manage network traffic. It provides access to software, files, and other resources that are being shared via the network. For example, cloud computing requires network servers. See **Figure 7-11**.

Table 7-5 describes common servers and their purposes.

Table 7-5: Types of servers and their purposes

Server type	Purpose
File server	Stores and manages files
Print server	Manages printers and documents being printed on a network
Database server	Stores and provides access to a database
Web server	Delivers webpages to computers that request pages through a browser

Figure 7-12: Internet connection speeds

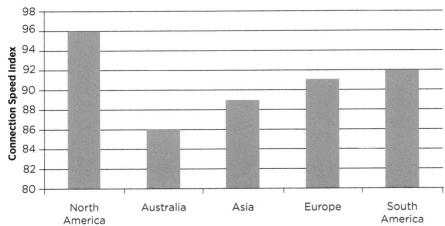

By the Numbers Now

The Internet Traffic Report monitors the speed and reliability of Internet traffic around the world. **Figure 7-12** compares Internet connection speeds in North America, Australia, Asia, Europe, and South America. The higher the index value, the faster and more reliable the Internet connection.

Describe Wired and Wireless Networks

Devices on a network can connect to each other in one of two ways: with or without wires.

- **Wired networks** send signals and data through cables, which may have to travel through floors and walls to connect to other network devices. Wired networks tend to be more secure and transmit data faster than wireless networks.
- **Wireless networks** send signals through the airwaves. Usually, they do not require cables. Wireless networks tend to be more convenient and easier to set up than wired networks, but can be less secure. Wireless networks make it possible to connect devices in locations where physical wiring is not possible or is difficult.

Most networks use a combination of wired and wireless connections.

Connect to a Wi-Fi Network

In contrast to wired networks, wireless networks communicate via signals through the air, connecting devices without the use of cables. Smartphones, laptops, tablets, and other handheld devices can connect wirelessly to networks to share data and services, which is known as **mobile computing**.

Wireless LANs use the Wi-Fi standard to connect to the Internet, which is why they are called **Wi-Fi networks**. **Wi-Fi**, short for wireless fidelity, uses the 802.11 wireless protocol. Wi-Fi adapters are often built into portable computers. You can also connect to Wi-Fi networks using a wireless modem. With a range of about 150 feet, Wi-Fi networks can expand the reach of a wired network, though only by the same distance. Because wired networks are difficult or impossible to move, they are limited in the amount of area they can cover.

WiMAX and **LTE** are standards for longer-range wireless network connections, up to 30 miles. Cities and cellular networks use these standards to provide high-speed Internet and network access from fixed locations called **hot zones** or **hotspots**. The global telecommunications industry has invested heavily in LTE, leaving the future viability of WiMAX in question.

Smartphones use Wi-Fi in addition to 3G (3rd generation) and 4G (4th generation) cellular networks. Fifth generation (5G) networks are not expected until 2020. Bluetooth can connect mobile devices at short distances, such as to broadcast your smartphone calls over the GPS receiver in your car.

A recent survey found that more than 80% of the adult population owns a smartphone with data capabilities. More than half of Americans now use mobile phones instead of landlines.

#ConnectingNow

Place the access point or router in a central location in your home away from physical obstructions such as plaster or brick walls that weaken the signal.

Use Wi-Fi Hotspots

Wi-Fi hotspots let you connect your Wi-Fi-enabled laptop, tablet, or smartphone to the Internet in a public space such as a coffee shop or library.

To connect to a Wi-Fi hotspot:

1. Click the network icon on your Wi-Fi enabled device. (On a Windows computer, the icon is typically located on the right side of the taskbar.) A window opens showing available networks. See **Figure 7-13** on the next page.

Figure 7-13: Connecting to a Wi-Fi hotspot

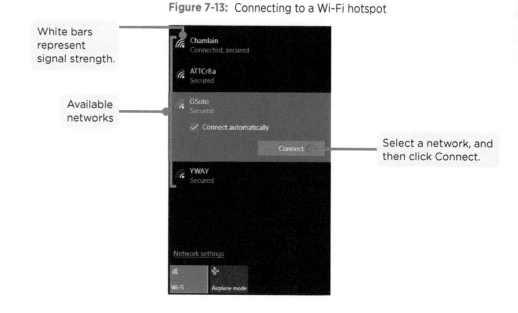

White bars represent signal strength.

Available networks

Select a network, and then click Connect.

2. Some networks display a browser window to ask you to agree to their terms.

3. If you are connecting to a private network, it asks you for a username and password.

Hot Technology Now

To locate free Wi-Fi hotspots in your town or city, search for your location at openwifispots.com.

Figure 7-14: Using a phone as a mobile hotspot

Solomonkein/Shutterstock.com, Maxx-Studio/Shutterstock.com

Use Mobile Hotspots

If you are using your tablet, desktop, or laptop computer in an area with no available Wi-Fi networks, you can still connect it to the Internet if you have a mobile phone. You **tether** (connect) your mobile phone to your computer, using a USB cable or Bluetooth, and then turn on your mobile phone's tethering feature. Your computer can then connect to the Internet using the mobile phone's Internet connection.

To connect more than one computer to the Internet using your mobile phone, you can use the phone as a **wireless access point** (see **Figure 7-14**), called a **personal mobile hotspot**. Turn on your phone's mobile hotspot feature (also called a **personal hotspot** in Apple iOS). The devices connect to the Internet using Wi-Fi. Some mobile phones limit the number of devices you can connect to the mobile hotspot.

Mobile phone carriers might charge extra for tethering and mobile hotspot service, and you might need to add this feature to your data service package. Check with your mobile carrier to make sure your phone supports tethering and mobile hotspots.

Mobile networks need protection from unethical users who might try to capture your data as it's transmitted through the airwaves. To guard against data theft, most cell networks use **data encryption**, which scrambles and unscrambles data so that it is not usable en route. If you use tethering or mobile hotspots, verify that your carrier encrypts data.

Compare Intranets, Extranets, and VPNs

An **intranet** is a private corporate network for use by authorized employees. Organizations use intranets to coordinate internal email and communications. An intranet typically works like the Internet by allowing employees to use a web browser to access data posted on webpages. A company may also set up an **extranet** that allows outsiders, such as customers or suppliers, to access part of its intranet.

A **virtual private network (VPN)** is a private, secure path across a public network (usually the Internet) that allows authorized users secure access to the company network. A VPN can allow an employee located at a satellite office or public wireless hotspot to connect securely to the company network via the Internet. VPNs use encryption and other technologies to secure data transmitted along the path.

Define the Internet

Internet | Internet backbone | network service provider (NSP) | Internet service provider (ISP) | cloud computing | World Wide Web | web | webpage | link | website | home page | web browser | Internet2 | net neutrality

The **Internet** is the largest network in the world, consisting of millions of computers connected through millions of networks spanning the globe. See **Figure 7-15**. These interconnected personal, local, regional, national, and international computer networks share data and tasks, carrying voice, data, video, and graphics.

The **Internet backbone**, the essential infrastructure of the Internet, is owned by several telephone and communications companies around the world; no single entity controls or owns the Internet. Backbone links and routers are maintained by **network service providers (NSPs)**. An **Internet service provider (ISP)** is a company that offers Internet access to individuals, businesses, and smaller ISPs.

The Bottom Line
- People use the Internet every day for tasks such as visiting websites to listen to music, do their banking, and stay in touch with family and friends.
- Although many people think the web is the same thing as the Internet, in fact, the web is only part of the Internet.

Figure 7-15: Connecting to the Internet

The Internet is a vast source of information and data available as text, audio, video, and graphics.

The Internet provides a way for people around the world to communicate using text, voice, video, and images.

You can connect to the Internet through desktop and laptop computers, tablets, and smartphones.

nmedia/Shutterstock.com

Large, powerful computers use the Internet to exchange the information and data needed for shared processing tasks and services. For both personal and business reasons, many people store files and access applications over the Internet, a practice referred to as **cloud computing**.

Describe Internet Growth

The U.S. Department of Defense (DOD) took the first step in developing the Internet when it created a network called ARPANET in 1969. For the most part, only scientists and researchers used the Internet until 1989, when Tim Berners-Lee proposed organizing the Internet into "pages" of related information. He wanted to link the pages using clickable text and images. He called this design the **World Wide Web**. Webpage addresses that start with "www" indicate that they are part of the World Wide Web.

After computer manufacturers began to sell affordable personal computers to the general public, the University of Illinois developed the first easy-to-use software for viewing webpages, a web browser called Mosaic. Since then, the web has grown from about 100,000 users to about 37 billion in late 2016.

Define the Web

The World Wide Web, or **web**, is one part of the Internet. The web consists of a huge collection of interconnected **webpages**, documents connected through **links** that include text, graphics, sound, and video. You click the links to go from one webpage to another. Webpages are organized into **websites** according to their function, business, organization, or interest. The first page that a website displays is called its **home page**,

On the Job Now

A web graphics designer creates visual concepts by hand or using computer software to communicate ideas that inspire, inform, or captivate consumers.

By the Numbers Now

According to Google, 2.3 million searches are conducted using their search engine every minute worldwide.

which contains links to other webpages that can be within or outside of the website. **Web browsers** such as Internet Explorer, Microsoft Edge, Safari, and Google Chrome make it possible for you to view and link to webpages. See **Figure 7-16**.

Figure 7-16: Library of Congress home page

The Internet address identifies this webpage.

You access websites with a web browser, which is an app you use to search for and navigate to webpages.

Click text or graphic links to open other webpages in this Library of Congress website.

www.loc.gov

By the Numbers Now

The Internet2 connects more than 60,000 U.S. educational, research, government, and community institutions.

Describe Internet2

As the Internet continues to grow, new technologies develop. **Internet2** is a not-for-profit project founded in 1996 to develop and test advanced network technologies for use in the near future.

Originally, the Internet was used mainly to transmit text, which requires little bandwidth. Millions of people now access the Internet each day, increasing demands for bandwidth. Because they often use the Internet for data-intensive applications such as high-definition television and video communications, the potential for Internet traffic jams is growing. The Internet2 initiative is working to ensure that Internet technology keeps pace with growing demand.

Describe Net Neutrality

When you use the Internet to research information, buy a product, or use social media, ideally all websites have an equal chance of providing services to you. This concept is **net neutrality**—one website has the same value or priority as other websites. Net neutrality supports the Internet's core principle that its networks should be neutral.

However, companies that provide Internet services want to distribute or charge for bandwidth depending on location, content, or provider of the website. For example, they might want to charge more for high-bandwidth services, such as online movies, or provide certain services at different speeds, such as slow download speeds for sites that allow illegal media sharing. Currently, ISPs in the United States are legally prohibited from providing better service or changing bandwidth for any content, even their own.

Companies that oppose net neutrality do not want the government to control or influence the flow of data on the Internet. Those in favor of net neutrality believe it is the government's role to ensure that all traffic on the Internet is treated equally.

Net neutrality is a complex issue because the Internet is a global entity. If it can be regulated, who will do the regulating? Should mobile broadband access be included in legislation involving net neutrality? In the United States, the Federal Communications Commission will continue to release rules and the courts will continue to decide cases that affect Internet access for years to come.

Identify the Value of Networks

infrared technology | groupware | network attached storage (NAS) | remote storage | cloud computing | synchronize (sync) | email | text communication | one-to-one instant messaging | chat | text messaging | video chat | webcast

Networks connect you to friends, neighbors, and other people all over the world. Email, text messaging, and web browsing are all possible because of networks.

Figure 7-17: Networked world

You can use networks to share hardware and software resources and to centralize file storage.

Mobile devices using wireless technologies have expanded network access so you can communicate and share resources from remote locations virtually anywhere in the world.

Using a network, you can participate in multiplayer computer games or online conferences from a satellite office.

bannosuke/Shutterstock.com, Dragon Images/Shutterstock.com, Andrey_Popov/Shutterstock.com

Share Hardware Resources on a Network

Computer networks make it possible to share hardware devices among users. See Figure 7-18. Colleagues in a small office can use the same printer, fax machine, scanner, or other device. Sharing hardware saves money.

Figure 7-18: Sharing hardware in a network

Shared network devices use either wired or wireless technology. You can wirelessly sync your smartphone to your laptop computer.

Bluetooth and Wi-Fi devices use radio waves to transmit signals. For example, you could transfer information from your smartphone to your computer if both were Bluetooth-enabled.

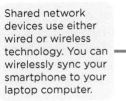

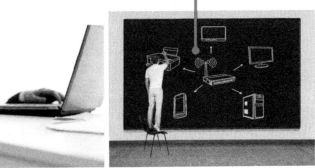

Devices with **infrared technology**, such as this mouse, communicate with direct light beams between infrared (IrDA) ports on the devices.

Christos Georghiou/Shutterstock.com, vetkit/Shutterstock.com, Dean Drobot/Shutterstock.com

Share Software Resources on a Network

Licensed software agreements allow businesses to share software resources while saving a significant amount of money. Coworkers can share software and hardware if the network uses a central server.

When companies install software on a central server only, troubleshooting problems and running software updates are greatly simplified because the work is limited to a single installation.

With **groupware**, several colleagues can work together on a single document at the same time. Group members can communicate to manage projects, create documents, schedule meetings, and make group decisions. Sharing software and hardware resources through network technology lets organizations and people work together more effectively and more efficiently than ever before.

Store Data on a Network

Organizations use network storage in their corporate networks and individuals use them in home networks. Some storage devices, called **network attached storage (NAS)**, connect directly to a network. NAS servers provide a centralized location for storing programs and data on large and small networks. Depending on its size and processor configuration, an NAS server can support from two to several thousand connected computers. Servers accessed via the Internet provide remote, or online, storage. Online storage is used in cloud computing, which is the delivery of computing services via the Internet.

Several commercial providers offer **remote storage** as a service. These sites include Google Drive (for email, Google apps, and files), Flickr (for photos), OneDrive (for Microsoft Office applications and files), Apple iCloud, and Dropbox. **Table 7-6** compares the three major online storage providers for personal files.

Table 7-6: Personal online storage providers

Feature	Apple iCloud	Google Drive	Microsoft OneDrive
Web address	icloud.com	google.com/drive	OneDrive.com
Storage capacity	5 GB free storage	15 GB free storage	5 GB free storage
Extras	Store iTunes purchases such as music and TV shows without affecting your storage quota.	Share and collaborate on files including documents, music, images, and videos.	Save Office files directly to OneDrive.

Share Files Using Cloud Computing

Cloud computing is Internet-based delivery of computing services, including data storage and application software. See **Figure 7-19**.

One advantage of storing your files and folders "in the cloud" is that you can easily share them with others. For example, if you want to share a file and folder you've stored on OneDrive, the Microsoft cloud storage location, open the file or folder you want to share, click Share, and choose to send an email link directly from OneDrive. You can also copy a link, specify whether the person can edit the file or folder, and then paste the link in any email or document. To share the file or folder with a larger audience or the general public, you can paste the link into a social media site such as Facebook, Twitter, and LinkedIn.

Sharing files in the cloud also lets you collaborate with others. People with whom you share files can add comments, suggestions, and revisions, making file collaboration an easy way to work with a team.

You can use accounts to control who has access to your cloud-based information. Each cloud storage provider, such as Microsoft or Google, lets you create one or more accounts, each with a password, that let you control visibility and access to online files and folders.

Finally, cloud computing makes it possible for you to synchronize your information stored online. For example, Microsoft OneDrive lets you **synchronize (sync)**

Figure 7-19: Cloud computing

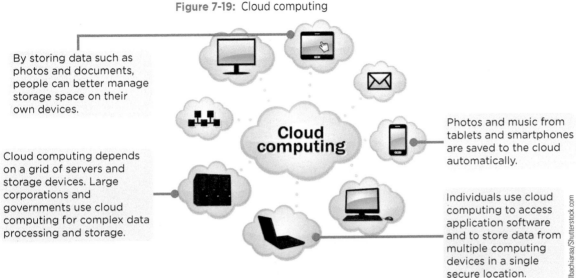

By storing data such as photos and documents, people can better manage storage space on their own devices.

Cloud computing depends on a grid of servers and storage devices. Large corporations and governments use cloud computing for complex data processing and storage.

Photos and music from tablets and smartphones are saved to the cloud automatically.

Individuals use cloud computing to access application software and to store data from multiple computing devices in a single secure location.

Albachiaraa/Shutterstock.com

device settings (such as your desktop or lock screen background), apps, folders, and files, including photos, so they are available using multiple devices, such as Mac and Windows PCs and Android phones. When you copy files and folders into a OneDrive folder on your PC, that folder's contents appear on OneDrive in the cloud, which you can access from any computer. You can also set up your smartphone to copy each picture into your Camera Roll folder in OneDrive, so you can back up and view all your photos on OneDrive using a web browser. Apple iCloud works the same way.

Along with its benefits, cloud computing has some drawbacks. Internet-based computing poses security and privacy risks. If you lose your Internet connection, you lose your ability to access the cloud, and everything you store on it, until your connection is restored.

Communicate on a Network

Local area networks and the Internet let people communicate in several different ways. **Email** offers a multitude of academic, business, and personal communication uses. Networks also make **text communication** possible, including **one-to-one instant messaging** in real time, **chat** (messaging) in online chat rooms, and **text messaging** from mobile devices such as smartphones.

Finally, with the expansion of broadband capabilities, networks let you communicate using **video chat** for personal and business uses. To use video chat on a computer, your device needs to be connected to a speaker and microphone (or a headset), a web cam, and a display device. You can use smartphones for video chatting as well as desktop, laptop, and tablet computers. See **Figure 7-20**. **Webcasts** (video broadcasts of events transmitted across the Internet) help people stay in touch and conduct meetings.

 #ConnectingNow

Office 365 allows you to access OneDrive, the Microsoft cloud storage service, seamlessly while using the Office suite. The One-Drive folder appears as a storage location in the Open and Save as dialog boxes.

Figure 7-20: Video chatting on a smartphone

LDprod/Shutterstock.com

Identify Network Risks

online security risk | hacker | cracker | malware | computer crime | cybercrime | identity theft | theft by computer | evil twin | war driver | cookie | spyware | adware | phishing | virus | worm | Trojan horse | ransomware | rootkit | zombie | bot | botnet denial of service (DoS) attack | distributed denial of service attack | cyberterrorism | social engineering

Networks connect you to other people and resources, but they also expose you to **online security risks**, which are actions that can damage or misuse your computer and data when you are connected to a network. Online security risks include unauthorized use of your computer and access to your data, exposure to malware, and network attacks.

> **The Bottom Line**
> - Recovering from a network attack or data theft can take a lot of time and money.
> - You need to know about common online security risks so you can safeguard your data, software, and hardware.

Figure 7-21: Network risks

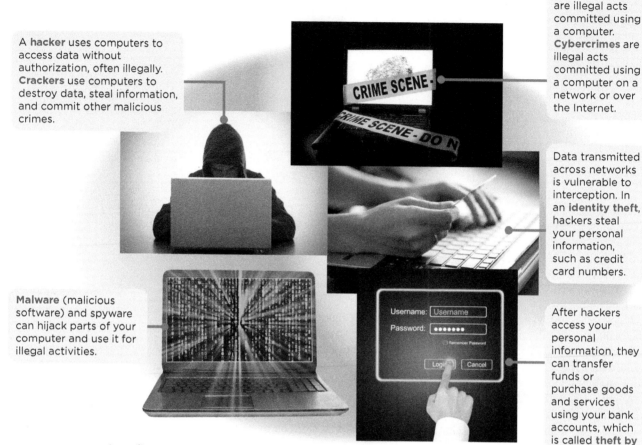

A **hacker** uses computers to access data without authorization, often illegally. **Crackers** use computers to destroy data, steal information, and commit other malicious crimes.

Computer crimes are illegal acts committed using a computer. **Cybercrimes** are illegal acts committed using a computer on a network or over the Internet.

Data transmitted across networks is vulnerable to interception. In an **identity theft**, hackers steal your personal information, such as credit card numbers.

Malware (malicious software) and spyware can hijack parts of your computer and use it for illegal activities.

After hackers access your personal information, they can transfer funds or purchase goods and services using your bank accounts, which is called **theft by computer**.

zimmytws/Shutterstock.com, tommaso79/Shutterstock.com, Juergen Faelchle/Shutterstock.com, sixninepixels/Shutterstock.com, Dusit/Shutterstock.com

---

Figure 7-22: War driver

Vladimir Mucibabic/Fotolia

Describe Unauthorized Network Use

Hackers use computers and networks without authorization so they can access valuable data and services without being detected. To bypass basic security measures on computers and networks, hackers detect, guess, or steal passwords and usernames. They also take advantage of wireless networks in public places, which have little or no security, and home computers that have always-on Internet connections. For example, an **evil twin** is a normal-looking yet fraudulent Wi-Fi network that allows hackers to capture personal information users transmit using it. Protect your personal information by never using public networks to access bank accounts or other sensitive information.

Besides hackers, unauthorized users can be **war drivers**, people who drive around and connect to wireless networks to gain free Internet access. See **Figure 7-22**.

Identify Privacy Risks on a Network

While networks make information sharing easy, they can also introduce risks. Much of your personal information is readily available to the general public. When you purchase an item over the Internet, your purchase information is available to others. If you register on a website, post a photo, or log a comment, this information can also be available to the general public. Monitoring software allows businesses to track its employees' remote connections and check for unauthorized data use. Video cameras in public places can track your activities and publicize them without your permission.

Information about you on private networks can also be viewed without authorization. For example, large hospital networks have been known to leak sensitive medical information about patients when their network security was breached.

Define Cookies, Spyware, and Adware

Commercial website vendors employ cookies to identify users and customize webpages. **Cookies** are ordinary text files that contain personal data such as your username, viewing preferences, and browsing history. Some websites provide cookies to other websites without your consent to display ads based on your browsing history, for example. Security experts warn that these types of cookies violate user privacy.

Spyware is a form of malware secretly installed on networked computers. Spyware tracks and transmits personal data, such as financial information or browsing habits, without your knowledge or permission. Surreptitiously tracking and transmitting data uses a lot of computer resources. If you notice slowdowns such as a lag between typing text on the keyboard and viewing it on the screen, spyware might be installed on your computer.

Adware displays unwanted advertisements in banners or windows on your computer, even when you are not visiting a website. While most adware itself is more annoying than dangerous, some adware comes with spyware attached.

Describe Theft by Computer

Theft by computer is a growing problem in the networked world. To steal using networked computers, a thief can be seated thousands of miles away. Computer thieves can transfer funds among accounts, steal money, and purchase goods using stolen credit card numbers.

Thieves can even steal your identity by accessing personal information such as your name, Social Security number, or bank account numbers, which is called identity theft. They can use it to assume your identity to open lines of credit in your name, order goods and services online, and then pay for them using your funds. Besides stealing your money, identity thieves damage your credit score and integrity.

Phishing scams use email to try to trick you into revealing personal information on the pretense of being your bank or other legitimate institution. See Figure 7-23.

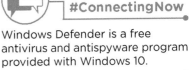

#ConnectingNow

Windows Defender is a free antivirus and antispyware program provided with Windows 10.

#ConnectingNow

A virtual currency called Bitcoin has been used to launder profits of both online and offline criminal activity.

Figure 7-23: Phishing examples and characteristics

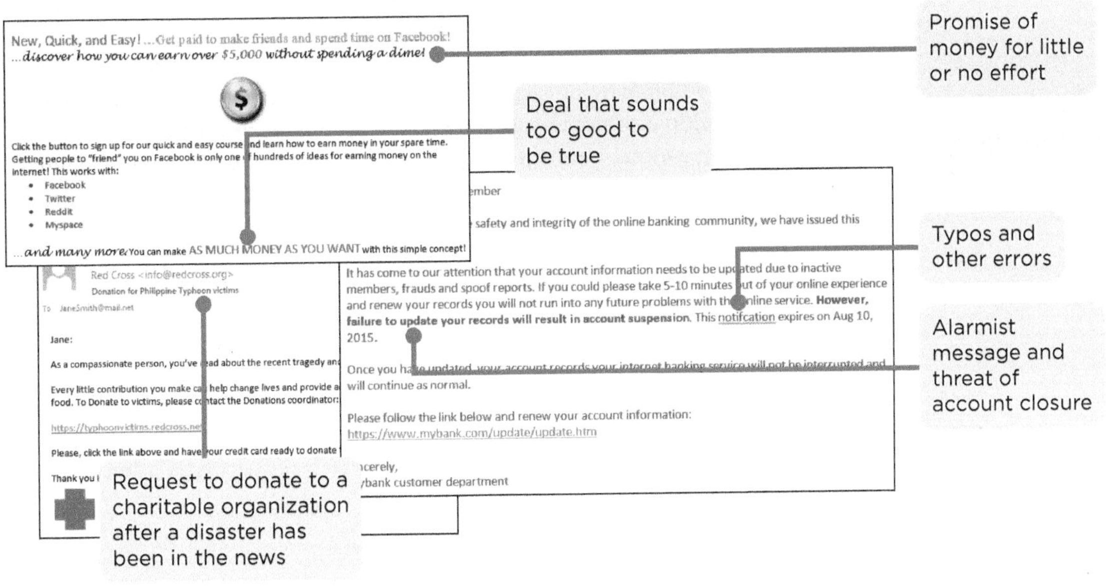

Promise of money for little or no effort

Deal that sounds too good to be true

Typos and other errors

Alarmist message and threat of account closure

Request to donate to a charitable organization after a disaster has been in the news

Define Malware

Malware is software written with malicious intent that installs itself without permission and can damage data and programs. Table 7-7 describes common forms of malware.

Table 7-7: Common forms of malware

Type	Description
Virus	Damages data or changes computer settings without your knowledge
Worm	Copies itself repeatedly, using up computer and network resources
Trojan horse	Hides in or disguises itself as a legitimate program until it is installed on a computer, and then damages files
Spyware	Tracks and transmits personal data without your knowledge or permission
Ransomware	Prevents access to your computer or files until you pay a fee, known as a ransom
Rootkit	Makes normally hidden files accessible and therefore vulnerable to attack

#ConnectingNow

All platforms can be infected with malware. Almost 700,000 new malware threats for the Android platform were detected in the past year.

On the Job Now

Companies hire forensic scientists who specialize in network traffic to analyze networks and search for botnets.

By the Numbers Now

DoS attacks increased 75% from 2015 to 2016.

Malware installs itself on your computer when you download an infected file from a website or open one attached to an email message. To spread, viruses and worms might send copies of themselves to contacts in your computer's address book. Each message appears as though it came from you, when it was actually generated by malware in your network.

Define Bots and Zombies

If hackers gain unauthorized access to networked computers, they can take over the computers and turn them into **zombies**, which are computers controlled by outsiders without the owners' knowledge. After creating a zombie, a hacker can install a **bot**, a program that performs a repetitive task such as sending phishing email messages. The hacker can also group these zombies together to form a **botnet**, which would send out massive amounts of phishing messages, for example. Botnet attacks often go unnoticed by the victim. The only symptom is a slowing down of your computer as the processor is hijacked for illegal activities.

Describe Denial of Service Attacks

Hackers often use a botnet to launch a **denial of service (DoS) attack**, a bombardment of network traffic or messages designed to overload a server. The purpose of a DoS attack is to disrupt network services, such as Internet access.

By overwhelming the server, a DoS attack can also stop all communications and services for a company or website. In a **distributed denial of service attack**, an attacker users multiple computers to launch such an attack. While recovering from a DoS attack, organizations can forfeit significant revenue from customers and advertisers. **Cyberterrorism**, or the intentional attacks that disrupt computers, networks, and public and financial services on a large scale, is another risk that results from networked computers.

Describe Social Engineering

Another risk of working in a networked world is known as **social engineering**, where attackers attempt to exploit human weaknesses by building relationships with victims for the purpose of stealing confidential information. For example, a phone caller might pose as a computer repair person in order to steal account passwords. By pretending to know information about the users, the scammer builds trust relationships that eventually convince victims to divulge information.

Secure a Network

encryption | firewall | authentication | biometric device | wireless network key | network security key | SSID (Service Set Identifier) | WPA (Wi-Fi Protected Access) | WPA2

Although you want to access your home network quickly and easily, you don't want uninvited guests to do the same. Likewise, businesses need to provide easy access to their networks for their employees, while keeping out others who access networks with malicious intent. The goal of network security is to allow only authorized users to access a network.

Use Common Sense to Secure Data

To access a wired network, an intruder needs physical access to the router via a cable. To access many wireless networks, however, an intruder just needs to use a wireless-enabled device within range of your wireless router.

Figure 7-24: Network security methods

Encryption scrambles or codes data as it is transmitted over a network.

Authentication identifies you to the network. The most common type of authentication is providing a username and password.

Firewalls create a blockade between corporate or personal networks and the Internet.

Biometric devices authenticate identity by scanning your physical characteristics, such as a fingerprint.

chaoss/Shutterstock.com, bofotolux/Shutterstock.com, beboy/Shutterstock.com, Nelia Sapronova/Shutterstock.com, ymgerman/Shutterstock.com

If your network carries sensitive data, use common sense to make sure it's secure.
- **Create strong passwords** for your home network. Include at least eight characters, numbers, letters, or symbols that are not easy to figure out.
- **Set permissions** to determine who can access which resources. Limit access as much as you can.
- **Do not write usernames and passwords** in places where they can be found by others.
- **Enable the highest level of encryption**, such as WPA2 or WPA-TKIP, for a wireless router, and change the router's default administrator password.

#ConnectingNow

On your home wireless router, change the Service Set Identifier (SSID) from its default to a unique name that is difficult for others to guess.

While you are online, you can protect your privacy in the following ways:
- Give out as little information as possible.
- Manage and monitor your privacy settings on social networking sites.
- Be thoughtful when sending email and text messages. You can never be sure who is reading or sharing your message, so private information should be sent with discretion.

Define Authentication Methods

Identification and authentication methods can be used to verify identity on a computer or network. See Table 7-8.

Table 7-8: Authentication methods

Method	Description
Username	A unique name you create to identify yourself to a computer system
Password	Combination of characters; often used with passwords to create a unique passcode
CAPTCHA	A system requiring you to type characters that match a series of distorted characters on the screen; used to verify that your entry is not computer-generated
Physical object	An object such as a room key or ID card that verifies your identity when trying to enter a building, office, or other restricted space

Figure 7-25: Iris scanning

tlorna/Shutterstock.com

Biometric devices add a layer of protection by restricting access on the basis of who you are. For example, if intruders steal a network password, you can still block them from accessing your network using biometric technology.

Biometric devices authenticate identity by scanning a person's physical characteristics, such as fingerprints, face, eyes, handprint, voice, or even signature. Fingerprint readers are the most common biometric device in use today. You might see one at a bank, on an ATM, or attached to a PC. Windows 10 includes Windows Hello, a feature that lets any authorized users sign into their accounts using a fingerprint reader or a camera that identifies your face or your eye's iris. Iris scanners are increasingly used. See Figure 7-25.

Encrypt Network Data

As shown in Figure 7-24, encryption scrambles or codes data as it is transmitted over a network. If intruders intercept a file in transit, they cannot make sense of the data they find.

You use a **wireless network key** (also called a **network security key**) to scramble and unscramble the data being transmitted between wireless devices.

You can activate encryption for your network through the router. Open the router software using a browser, and then use the router configuration software to set up an encryption protocol and create a wireless network key.

Many wireless networks in coffee shops, hotels, and airports are not encrypted, so they are open to the public. Do not transmit private information on public networks.

Use a Firewall on a Network

Firewalls are designed to block intruders from accessing corporate or personal networks. If you have an always-on connection to the Internet, you can be vulnerable to intrusions. Personal firewalls constantly monitor all network traffic to keep your network secure.

Firewalls are often built into operating systems, such as Windows Firewall for Windows computers. See Figure 7-26. Firewalls are also built into the router software of many routers.

You can also install third-party personal firewall programs on your computer to detect and protect your computer from unauthorized intrusions.

Figure 7-26: Windows Firewall

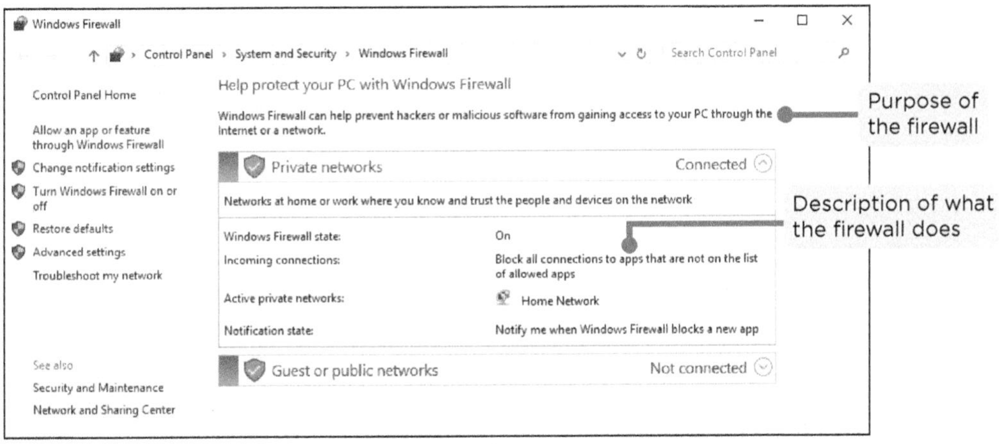

Purpose of the firewall

Description of what the firewall does

Secure a Wireless Router

Wireless routers can make your network and your data vulnerable, but you can secure it by taking some precautions: 1) Change the factory-supplied name (**Service Set Identifier or SSID**) to one that is different from the manufacturer or model number; 2) Change the default password from the one found on the router label; 3) Verify that the router is encrypted, preferably with **WPA (Wi-Fi Protected Access)** or **WPA2** encryption; 4) Disable the remote management feature, so that hackers cannot access the router without being physically connected to the computer.

#ConnectingNow

Go to twitter.com, search for @SAMTechNow, the book's Twitter account, and then follow @SAMTechNow to get tweets on your home page.

Chapter Review

Define a Network

1. What are the two main types of network architecture? Briefly describe each one.
2. What do you call a network that spans long distances? Give two examples of areas where such a network would be appropriate.
3. What type of network connects digital devices within about 30 feet of each other? Give one example.

Connect to a Network

4. Give three examples of network standards, and state how each one might be used.
5. What piece of hardware lets your computer connect to networks?
6. What do you call a company that connects you to the Internet?

Describe How Networks Work

7. What is a modem? Name three types of modems.
8. Explain why bandwidth is a consideration in network connections.
9. Describe the purpose of a network protocol and give an example.

Identify Types of Networks

10. What lets your laptop, tablet, or smartphone connect to the Internet in a coffee shop?
11. Name three types of network topologies and briefly describe the layout of each one.
12. How does a client/server network differ from a peer-to-peer network?

Define the Internet

13. Name three services available over the Internet. How might you use each service in your daily life? Which of the services do you use most often and why?
14. Describe three Internet services you can use to communicate with colleagues or friends. What are the key benefits of each service? How are the three services different from each other?

Identify the Value of Networks

15. Name three personal online storage providers, and compare their features and free storage limits. Check the website of each one to determine up-to-date storage information.
16. What is cloud computing and what are its advantages and disadvantages?

Identify Network Risks

17. What is the difference between hackers and crackers? How do hackers and crackers gain unauthorized access to a computer?
18. What are the common forms of malware and how does it infect a computer?

Secure a Network

19. What are three common-sense strategies for securing a home network?
20. How do encryption and firewalls protect network data?

Test Your Knowledge Now

1. A circuit board with special electronic circuits that connects a computer to a network is called a:
   a. network interface card (NIC).
   b. router.
   c. hub.
   d. switch.

2. A network architecture in which all computers are equal in capability and responsibility is called a:
   a. client/server network.
   b. wireless access point.
   c. peer-to-peer network.
   d. wide area network.

3. A company that offers Internet access to individuals and businesses is a(n):
   a. network service provider.
   b. Internet service
   c. Internet backbone.
   d. wide area network.

4. The most common networking standard for wired networks is:
   a. Ethernet.
   b. Wi-Fi.
   c. Bluetooth.
   d. 4G.

5. The hardware that sends and receives data and information to and from a digital line is a(n):
   a. network interface card.
   b. digital modem.
   c. Internet service provider.
   d. Wi-Fi hotspot.

6. Which network standard lets devices communicate wirelessly over short distances?
   a. Ethernet
   b. Phoneline
   c. Bluetooth
   d. 4G

7. Which of the following network types uses radio signals to connect computers and devices?
   a. Ethernet
   b. modem
   c. Wi-Fi
   d. DSL modem

8. RJ-11 and USB are examples of:
   a. ports.
   b. networks.
   c. cables.
   d. domain controllers.

9. What type of network has all devices attached in a line to a central cable?
   a. ring
   b. bus
   c. star
   d. mesh

10. A networked computer that controls access to hardware, software, and other network resources is called a:
    a. client.
    b. router.
    c. server.
    d. modem.

11. You click a(n) _____ to go from one webpage to another.
    a. URL
    b. link
    c. window
    d. app

12. A _____ connects devices within a limited geographical area, such as several buildings.
    a. mesh network
    b. wide area network
    c. neighborhood area network
    d. bus network

13. With _____ computing, you can access files and applications over the Internet.
    a. cellular
    b. Bluetooth
    c. Wi-Fi
    d. cloud

14. Which of the following is not a way of sharing an online file with others?
    a. Send an email link
    b. Copy a link and paste it in an email
    c. Paste a link to a social media site
    d. Copy your telephone numbers to OneDrive

15. Which of the following provides calling and Internet service for your cellphone, but not your laptop or tablet?
    a. URL
    b. Cellular provider
    c. Network service provider
    d. Internet service provider

16. A(n) _____ is a type of cybercrime in which hackers steal your personal information, such as bank account numbers.
    a. botnet
    b. Trojan horse
    c. identity theft
    d. denial of service attack

17. The type of malware that copies itself repeatedly, using up computer and network resources, is called a _____.
    a. worm
    b. virus
    c. cookie
    d. Trojan horse

18. Which one of the following is not a network authentication method?
    a. password
    b. CAPTCHA system
    c. firewall
    d. fingerprint reader

19. You use a(n) _____ to scramble and unscramble the data being transmitted between wireless devices.
    a. wireless network key
    b. data encryption
    c. ID card
    d. wireless router

20. _____ constantly monitor all network traffic to keep your network secure.
    a. Firewalls
    b. Modems
    c. Biometric scanners
    d. Spyware programs

21. In the space next to each image below, write the letter of the phrase that describes it:
    a. Directs the flow of information along a network
    b. Device that sends and receives data to and from a digital line
    c. Central point for cables in a network
    d. Connects a device to an Ethernet network
    e. Card that connects a computer to a network

____ ____ ____

____ ____

Try This Now

1: Test Your Home or Local Coffee Shop Network's Performance

Your local Internet service provider offers different connection options. You should test your network connection to confirm it uses the speed you purchased. Test the speed of your wireless or wired network at your home, workplace, or local coffee shop and compare it to the speed of your school's network.

Open your browser on any computer and then visit the speedtest.net website. Click the Begin Test button to test the performance of each network. The test may take up to a minute to complete.

    a. How did the speed of your home, workplace, or local coffee shop compare with the speed of your school's network? Share the download and upload speeds of each location.

    b. Describe four Internet activities that would be best on the fastest network speed.

    c. How does the speed of your home network affect your ability to have a home office or take a class online? Explain.

2: Tether Your Smartphone

The cost of using the 4G signal from your smartphone to provide web access to your laptop can depend on your phone's service provider.

    a. Research the cost of tethering a smartphone with three major carriers. Write a paragraph in your own words detailing the cost of tethering your device. Be sure to mention the amount of data included.

    b. Does the cost vary for Android and iOS phone?

3: Connect with a Classmate with a Free Video Call Using Skype

Note: This assignment requires a mobile device with a camera or a computer with a webcam.

Skype

Connecting through a video call adds a personal and professional touch within the business environment. Skype Video is an easy way to communicate to another Skype user for free from your computer (PC or Mac) or mobile device, such as an Apple iPhone or Android smartphone. Download and install the free Skype app on your smartphone or open Skype.com. Create a free Skype account or use an existing Microsoft account. Arrange with a classmate to have a three-minute Skype Video call and discuss the interesting facts you learned about the connected computer. Take at least three screenshots of your active video call and place them in a Word document to submit to your instructor.

Critical Thinking Now

1: Securing an Internet Service Provider

After moving to a new apartment complex, you are faced with signing up for a local ISP. Your local neighborhood has DSL, cable modem, and satellite service available. Write a paragraph on the advantages and disadvantages of each of these service providers. Consider typical cost, bandwidth speed, service contracts, and data limits.

2: Protecting Your Wireless Apartment Network

After reading this chapter, you realize that the wireless network in your apartment is not secure. Unauthorized users could sit outside your apartment and perform illegal activities on your home network in your name. In addition, they may be able to view your personal files and slow down your network speed considerably. Write a paragraph including at least four steps that will secure your home wireless network.

3: Super Bowl Biometric Security

The Super Bowl is investigating ways to confirm the identity of the ticket holders. The Super Bowl Commission is warning fans to beware of fraudulent online ticket sales for the next Super Bowl as the commission works with national agencies to use biometric security to address the problem. Write a three-paragraph proposal, with each paragraph describing one of three biometric security technologies that could be used to determine ticket holder authentication. Research the pros and cons of each of these biometric technologies.

Ethical Issues Now

Today you are flying to a spring break destination in Florida. As soon as you arrive at the airport, you notice signs indicating that the Internet airport wireless service is $5.99 an hour. Out of curiosity, you check to see if any free wireless networks are available because you really need to transfer money from your online savings account to your checking account for the trip. The strongest wireless network is named FreeAirportWIFI and it is not secure.

Free Wi-Fi

a. What might happen if you use the unsecured network? Explain.
b. Why would someone name their wireless connection FreeAirportWIFI if it is not part of the airport services?
c. Where should you conduct your online banking? Why?

Team Up Now—Scam or Protect Yourself

No one ever plans to have their identity stolen, but ignorance can unfortunately lead to years of credit score recovery and legal red tape. One of your college roommates realized that their online bank balance was much lower than expected. In addition, that roommate received three separate email messages from different credit card companies saying that they had been approved and the new credit cards had been mailed to an unknown address.

a. Each member of the team should develop a hypothesis of how it was possible for someone to steal your roommate's identity. Create a combined document of the individual hypotheses.
b. Research what your roommate should do now. Name at least four steps that they should take to investigate this crime.
c. Should your roommate consider using a paid service to monitor their identity, such as LifeLock? Are services like this necessary?
d. Identify a YouTube video that would be best to share in your dorm for others so they do not fall victim to the same risk.

Key Terms

3G
4G
adware
authentication
bandwidth
biometric device
BitTorrent
Bluetooth
body area network (BAN)
bot
botnet
broadband
broadband modem
bus network
cable
cable modem
chat
client
client/server network
cloud computing
computer crime
cookie
cracker
cybercrime
cyberterrorism
data
data encryption
database server
denial of service (DoS) attack
digital modem
distributed denial of service attack
domain controller
domain-based network
DSL modem
email
encryption
Ethernet
Ethernet standard
evil twin
extranet
file server
file sharing
firewall
full mesh topology
groupware
hacker
home page
hot zone
hotspot

hub
identity theft
infrared technology
Internet
Internet backbone
Internet peer-to-peer (Internet P2P)
    networking
Internet service provider (ISP)
Internet2
intranet
IPv4 protocol
IPv6 protocol
link
local area network (LAN)
LTE (Long Term Evolution)
malware
mesh network
metropolitan area network (MAN)
mobile computing
modem
narrowband
neighborhood area network (NAN)
net neutrality
network
network architecture
network attached storage (NAS)
network hardware
network interface card (NIC)
network security key
network server
network service provider (NSP)
network standard
network topology
node
one-to-one instant messaging
online security risk
partial mesh topology
peer-to-peer (P2P) network
personal area network (PAN)
personal hotspot
personal mobile hotspot
phishing
Phoneline/HomePNA
port
Power over Ethernet (PoE)
Powerline
print server
protocol
ransomware

remote storage
resource
ring network
RJ-11 port
rootkit
router
server
Service Set Identifier (SSID)
social engineering
spyware
star network
switch
synchronize
TCP/IP (Transmission Control Protocol/
    Internet Protocol)
tether
text communication
text messaging
theft by computer
topology
tree topology
Trojan horse
video chat
virtual private network (VPN)
virus
war driver
web
web browser
web server
webcast
webpage
website
wide area network (WAN)
Wi-Fi (wireless fidelity)
Wi-Fi hotspot
Wi-Fi network
Wi-Fi Protected Access (WPA)
WiMAX
wired network
wireless access point
wireless modem
wireless network
wireless network key
wireless personal area network (WPAN)
wireless router
World Wide Web
worm
WPA2
zombie

Safety and Security

Shondra is aware of the digital footprint that she leaves when she posts to her social media profile.

...u don't need a ...bility ball like ...ndra's for proper ...onomics, but ...ding the best ...ing position ...eves aches and ...ns in her neck, ...ulders, and back. ...lso makes her ...re productive.

Higher-resolution screens provide clarity, but the smaller fonts force your eyes to work harder.

Andrey_Popov/Shutterstock.com, Denys Prykhodov/Shutterstock.com

Shondra Andrews is applying to a job internship program. To prepare, she is creating a LinkedIn profile using her all-in-one computer. She can use a flat surface for angled viewing. Placing the computer on a table allows for a more relaxed and natural posture, alleviating the strain caused by tablet lap viewing. In addition to caring for her physical well-being, Shondra is careful to create a positive online persona, realizing that future employers will have access to every social media posting.

Avoid Personal Health Risks

repetitive strain injury (RSI) | carpal tunnel syndrome | computer vision syndrome | Internet addiction | ergonomics

As we work, study, communicate, and play, we spend long hours looking at a screen or using a keyboard. While we enjoy the benefits of electronic devices, we also have to consider their effects, including stress on both our bodies and minds. Learning about and addressing the negative effects of constant electronic device use can help us remain productive and healthy. A proper environment can help you stay healthy and work productively.

Identify Repetitive Strain Injuries

As we use computers, one personal health risk that we may face is a **repetitive strain injury**, or **RSIs**, which is caused by performing the same movement over and over again. The use of computers, tablets, smartphones, and other electronic devices is a leading cause of RSIs. **Carpal tunnel syndrome** is an RSI that affects the wrist, hand, and arm, and is aggravated by prolonged keyboarding or gesturing on tablets. Symptoms of RSIs include pain, tingling, and numbness as well as difficulty in performing simple movements. RSIs are also caused by performing an action while in an awkward or stressful position. For example, cradling a cell phone or tablet that's too wide or heavy to hold comfortably while you tap, swipe, rotate, or pinch can lead to RSIs.

Figure 8-1: Be aware of personal health risks while using computers

Robert kneschke/Shutterstock.com, Rido/Fotolia LLC

Reduce Neck and Eye Strain

Any prolonged digital viewing can cause eye and neck strain. Your eyes can become dry and strained when you look at computer monitors and screens because you blink less. Looking at characters on a screen also makes it harder for our eye muscles to maintain focus. Some people develop **computer vision syndrome**, which can result in eyestrain, headaches, dry eyes, blurry vision, or even double vision. Its effects are not limited to discomfort—you may be less productive at work or school. For some, "I have a pain-in-the-neck at work" is not just a saying. Craning your neck to get in the right position to see clearly, reading through glare, or finding a comfortable place to hold a device can give you a stiff neck that can quickly develop into a distracting headache.

Identify Behavioral Health Risks

Most of us enjoy connecting with friends and family on the Internet, browsing the web, and shopping or playing games online. However, for some people, spending too much time online can lead to a feeling of disconnectedness in other areas of their lives and to feeling out of control due to technology overload and compulsion.

Internet addiction is the excessive use of the Internet for gaming, video, web surfing, texting, blogging, social networking, or shopping. Some people can't stop using the Internet without feeling ill at ease or anxious, which interferes with other aspects of their lives. Internet addictions can cause neglect of face-to-face interactions and isolation from the real world. Or worse, Internet encounters can prompt face-to-face meetings that lead to dangerous situations. Online predators are skilled in assuming an alluring online persona.

If you suspect your computer and Internet use are obsessive and beyond normal, therapists and support groups can help. Balance your technology use with healthy activities, and stay connected to the offline world.

Follow Ergonomic Guidelines

The best ways to prevent RSIs and eye and neck strain from using digital devices are to maintain proper posture and to configure your work area ergonomically. **Ergonomics** is the study of safe and efficient working environments. Some helpful tips for working safely and avoiding injury include the following:

- When sitting at a desktop computer, adjust the height of your chair so that your arms and knees form right angles and your eyes are even with the top third of the monitor.
- Position the keyboard so that your wrists are straight while typing.
- When using laptops and tablets, use a stand or a hard binder to raise the device so that you work with the keyboard or tablet screen at an angle. See **Figure 8-2**.

Most important, whenever possible, break up your workflow—blink often, take breaks to refocus your eyes, get up and move around, and download apps to schedule break reminders. Consider using a speech-to-text system to reduce repetitive typing.

On the Job Now

The number-one job skill necessary in the top 60 growth job fields, according to an IDC study, is oral and written communication.

On the Job Now

Some companies offer their employees standing desks. Using a standing desk can benefit your health. When sitting for long hours, you can suffer from metabolic problems and circulatory issues.

Figure 8-2: Set up workspaces with ergonomics in mind

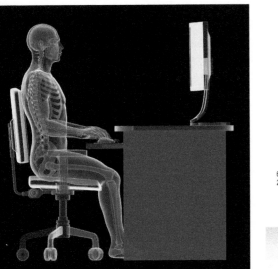
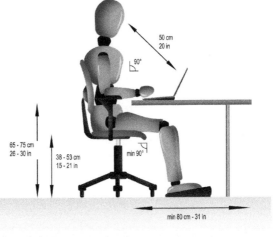

Sebastian Kaulitzki/Shutterstock.com, Maluson/Shutterstock.com

Avoid Data Risks

solid state hard drive | magnetic hard drive | Blue Screen of Death (BSoD) | hacker | cybercrime | hacktivist | white hat | black hat | strong password | cloud storage system | cyberterrorism | cyberterrorist | cyberattack | wireless sniffing | packet | uninterruptible power supply (UPS)

If you use technology, you're sure to create and acquire a great deal of data stored in files. If you are unable to access files, whether they are lost or corrupted, you can lose hours of work and valuable information, causing a crisis. You can lose documents, photos, journals, projects, personal histories, and even your identity. There are several smart strategies you can follow to protect your data.

Identify Hardware Failure

If the screen or pointing device on your computer or mobile device fails, or some other peripheral device breaks, your data is still intact. However, the storage devices where you store your data—music, photos, video, documents, and messages—can fail or be damaged, leading to data loss.

The Bottom Line
- Possible causes of data loss include the following: a hard drive crash, natural disasters destroying devices, physical damage to devices as a result of water or exposure to extreme climates, theft or loss of devices, and unsecured cloud storage.
- If hackers steal your data, identity theft or monetary loss can result.
- Protect data by backing up regularly and following security protocols.

#security

Although declining in popularity, optical storage media used for backup, such as CDs and DVDs, can also fail if they become dirty or scratched.

Figure 8-3: Sign of a hard drive crash

AlexLMX/Shutterstock.com

On the Job Now

When an employee connects a personal smartphone to his or her company's wireless network, that person's email and website activity can be tracked and subsequently logged while on company property.

Hot Technology Now

With the Internet of Things, consumers may invite a new wave of cyber-attack risks into their home thermostats, TVs, and refrigerators. Manufacturers are facing increased pressure to improve security on such connected devices, to avoid the danger of hackers taking control of entire home systems.

Solid state hard drives that have no moving parts are relatively stable; however, magnetic hard drives are much more prone to damage. A failing hard drive might show symptoms such as frequent slowdowns or freezes and a screeching, grinding, or repetitive clicking sound.

Almost any storage device, such as your mobile phone, will fail if it gets wet or damaged. When a hard drive fails, Windows users see what is commonly called the Blue Screen of Death (BSoD). See Figure 8-3. Mac users see the "Marble of Doom," also called "Spinning Beach Ball of Death," or simply the spinning wait cursor that remains on the screen for a long time. These symptoms indicate a serious problem.

Avoid Attacks and Hacks

Besides hardware failure, your data is at risk from hackers—people who break into computers and computer networks, often by exploiting weaknesses and preventable flaws. The crime of hacking into and attacking networks is known as cybercrime.

Some hackers just want to show off their skills and don't intend to do any serious damage. Others have political motivations and may attempt to suppress free speech. Many hackers call themselves hacktivists and have a social goal or impact. The hacker community includes white hat (nondestructive) and black hat (extremely destructive) hackers. Black hat hackers can do real harm through espionage, theft, or disruption of the network. Hackers can target individual computer users, but they are more likely to target major corporations and divisions of government.

Avoid Loss and Theft

You only need to experience one serious data loss to understand its consequences. For both companies and individuals, hardware failure and human error are the most common causes of data loss. Some simple practices and common-sense behaviors can help prevent loss or theft:

- Portable devices and portable media, such as flash drives, DVDs, or CDs, can easily be misplaced or stolen, so it is good practice to have organized storage cabinets in accessible places. Keep devices and media safely stored in locked boxes or rooms, if possible.
- Account numbers and passwords are vulnerable and are prime targets for theft. It is important that you create strong passwords that cannot be easily figured out by someone trying to break into your account. It also is important that you do not share sensitive data with unauthorized users. If you have to write passwords down so you don't forget them, do not keep the paper with that sensitive information anywhere that is easily accessible or near a device.

Loss and theft can be expensive. Businesses must calculate the expense of rebuilding a secure environment that was compromised, fund crisis and media management, and pay legal fees. Companies may also face state and federal fines and customers that sue for damages. Furthermore, the harm to a company's reputation may be irreparable and result in a smaller customer base, which means lost revenue. Many companies and organizations, in an effort to help secure their data, do not allow offsite storage on portable devices.

Anticipate Natural Disasters

Every year, natural disasters remind us of the vulnerability of our business, academic, or personal records to catastrophic data loss. Hurricanes and storms account for almost half of total losses. Fires, floods, hurricanes, lightning, tornadoes, and earthquakes can strike electronics unexpectedly and destroy all your data. Floodwaters are particularly damaging because of debris, sediment, and contamination.

Make sure you have a data recovery plan before a disaster strikes, such as storing backups in a different location or online. Cloud storage systems have backups at various online locations that provide additional protection. By storing data in the cloud, you provide additional protection for your data.

Be Aware of Cyberterrorism

Cyberterrorism is the premeditated disruption of computers and networks. A cyberattack centers on areas that will affect the most people: telecommunications, utility storage and delivery, water supply, transportation systems, emergency services, and banking and financial services. Cyberterrorism is a low-cost action with a high-cost impact.

Cyberterrorists use automated attack tools that travel through networks to harm computer programs to wreak their havoc. Cyberterrorists can be politically motivated, taking time to plan elaborate international attacks and ensuring they get publicity. A cyberterrorist also can be an angry employee or someone seeking revenge or justice for a perceived wrong.

The effects of a **cyberattack** can include physical damage and a general disruption of regular activities. It can also lower public confidence and create a climate of fear and mistrust.

Understand Data in the Cloud

Storing data on servers over the Internet, or in "the cloud," is a popular and economical way to store data, and can help protect against data loss from natural disasters and other causes. See **Figure 8-4**.

However, cloud storage has its drawbacks:

- Moving data across the Internet increases opportunities for theft or manipulation.
- The shift to cloud computing has also increased the demand on servers, storage devices, and networks, and increases our dependence on technology we don't own or control.
- If the Internet is inaccessible as a result of a power outage or another problem, or if your cloud storage provider has technical problems, your data could become unavailable.

Figure 8-4: Cloud computing

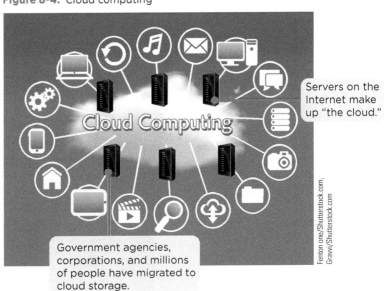

Servers on the Internet make up "the cloud."

Government agencies, corporations, and millions of people have migrated to cloud storage.

Be on Alert for Data Interception

Wireless networks are used by many people to send and receive data from mobile or other computing devices for personal and business activities. Protecting data from monitoring and theft at all potential points between its source and destination is critical for any organization. **Wireless sniffing** can intercept and analyze data transmitted over any network, and is a risk that can breach what otherwise might have been considered secured data. Data packets can be intercepted within a proximity of 300 feet or more. A data **packet** is a unit of data collected as a package so it can be transmitted in a network path. Packets are used for Internet Protocol (IP) on the web. A hacker only needs an inexpensive laptop computer, a wireless network card, free packet-sniffing software, and a vehicle to drive around in search of unsecured wireless access points to intercept your data.

Protect Your Data

Disasters of every type are bound to happen. Investing in prevention is better than trying to rebuild after an attack. The three most important steps you can take to protect your data are back up, back up, and back up! Other steps you can follow:

- Schedule regular backups, whether online or to a device that is protected against whatever might damage your primary device.
- Store backups in more than one location where they are safe from flooding, from other weather elements, and from theft.
- Back up your data when possible, and use online storage to guard against loss from disasters.
- Install an **uninterruptible power supply (UPS)** to provide battery backup for a short period.
- Educate classmates or colleagues about updating software and about updating and following security protocols. A knowledgeable team is less likely to jeopardize data security.
- Make sure your cloud provider uses strong encryption-based security and has a secure physical environment.
- Never share personal and sensitive information such as Social Security numbers, birth dates, maiden names, or address information unless you are sure whom you are giving it to.

Evaluate Email and Internet Risks

spam | address spoofing | clickbait | malware | virus | worm | Trojan horse | rootkit | spyware | ransomware | phishing | hoax | digital certificate | hotspot | Wi-Fi piggybacking | war driving | password manager | firewall | antivirus software | antispyware | wireless router | encryption

Hot Technology Now

Websites such as politifact.com, factcheck.org, and snopes.com provide warnings about hoaxes and fake news on Facebook, Twitter, and in spam emails. Before you pass on an email or retweet questionable events, facts, threats, or cures, check them out.

The only way to eliminate all risk on the Internet is never to go online—not a practical solution in our current society. Your best bet is to develop some habits that protect you and your data from malware, phishing, hoaxes, spam, and other tools designed to wreck your system or steal your money.

Figure 8-5: Threats on the Internet

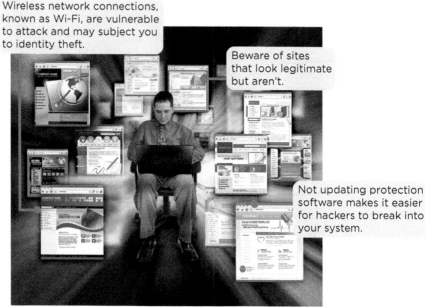

Wireless network connections, known as Wi-Fi, are vulnerable to attack and may subject you to identity theft.

Beware of sites that look legitimate but aren't.

Not updating protection software makes it easier for hackers to break into your system.

Angela Waye/Shutterstock.com

Define Spam, Address Spoofing, and Clickbait

Junk email, known as **spam**, can be annoying or even dangerous. The goal of a person sending spam is to have you click a link in a message; therefore, spam subject lines appeal to emotions such as compassion, trust, or curiosity. Some spam messages try to convince you that your computer already has a virus and instruct you to fix the problem by downloading software or clicking a link. That's when your computer gets infected.

Your Internet service or email provider and other businesses invest considerable resources to create spam filters that block spam, although junk email does inevitably sneak through. Spam makes up an estimated 80 percent of all email. Spam clogs the Internet and costs consumers an estimated $10 billion a year.

Address spoofing, a serious risk to email users, lures unsuspecting recipients to click a link to a harmful website. The sender uses a fake address masked by a familiar address, and provides a link that is supposed to be clicked. If clicked, the link will direct users to a site that can be used for illicit purposes, such as to steal data and personal information. For example, an email might arrive that appears to come from your local bank with a link to the bank. If you mouse over the link and look at the address in the status bar or in the popup window that appears, you will see that the actual link would take you to quite a different site. It is imperative that if your bank or any financial institution sends you mail with a link, do not click it; rather, search for the official website link online.

Clickbait describes a type of hyperlink on a webpage, social media post, or in an email that entices a visitor or recipient to click to continue reading an article or go to another page. Clickbait is a strategy used by some advertisers to lure users to their websites. The bait is often a catchy phrase such as "best tips for cooking shrimp EVER" or "you won't believe what this cat can do!" There is often a video or link that you are enticed to click to find the end of the sentence or content. Clickbait is common on social networks and doesn't always lead to malicious webpages, but frequently doesn't deliver on its promise of best tips ever or funniest videos; instead, it may lead you to a page of advertising for products you don't necessarily need or want.

Guard Against Malware, Viruses, Spyware

The term **malware** refers to viruses, worms, Trojan horses (or Trojans), and other software designed to disrupt a system or exploit data. **Viruses** can lurk undetected in your system, infect it, and spread when you distribute infected files—especially as email attachments. **Worms** are not the same as viruses; they spread by automatically sending themselves to everyone in your address book. **Trojan horses** and **rootkits** disguise themselves as useful programs or apps, but do damage when you run them; they often allow others to access your system or track and monitor your keystrokes. **Spyware** collects bits of data, such as your surfing habits; and can also scan your hard drive and change your default home page because it takes partial control of your system. Some cyberterrorists weapon of choice is **ransomware** which is malicious software that blocks access to a computer system until a sum of money, or ransom, is paid.

Avoid Phishing and Hoaxes

Just as the name implies, **phishing** involves casting "bait" in the form of an email or social media post, in the hopes that a few users will respond, so they can "reel you in." A phishing email or social media post looks genuine, but falsely claims that you must take immediate action. When you click a link in a phishing email and visit the fake site, it asks for your username and password sign-in or account information. After you fill in the form, thieves can access your account and use the data to obtain false accounts in your name. It has proven effective for scammers, even if the vast majority ignore it.

A **hoax** can be a fake coupon for a brand name store or item or an email that warns about a nonexistent virus in order to get you to click a link that installs malware.

Avoid Unsafe Sites

Regardless of how you reach a site, whether by typing a URL or by clicking a link on another page or in search engine results, you cannot assume that all websites are safe. Some websites "hook" you by falsely reporting that a website is unsafe. In reality, it is misleading you into clicking through a series of windows so you activate a scam antivirus program, which is actually malware.

If you participate in social media sites such as Facebook, YouTube, or Twitter, malicious users can easily hide malware in posts and links. Online gaming sites and online surveys can also hide malicious software. When you see a deal that seems too good to be true, it usually is.

If your browser and/or computer lacks security software—or if you haven't turned it on or updated it—you might never know that the website you're about to visit is dangerous.

Protect Digital Certificates

Digital certificates are used as identification cards to authenticate the website owner. Hackers steal copies of validly-issued digital certificates that companies use to validate documents and software applications. These stolen certificates can disguise malicious applications that can install on your Internet-connected computing device. Even stolen digital signatures can include Trojan horses. A hacker copies a company's hard drive that includes legitimate digital certificates from their vendors. Then the hacker replaces the legitimate certificates on their system with the stolen, infected digital certificates, which quickly attack the entire network with malicious software.

By the Numbers Now

What type of data is hacked the most? You might guess financial data, but identity theft accounts for 64% of all data breaches, adding up to a total of 621 incidents and theft of more than 294 million data records.

Protect Against Software Vulnerability

Hackers and scammers spend time finding and exploiting weaknesses in computers, devices, or web software. To protect yourself, your system, and your data, you must keep your security software up to date. Software updates often fix security issues, but if you don't install the updates, your computer continues to be vulnerable. Without updated software, smartphones can freeze up, prevent access to new features and functionality, and put your data at risk. In addition, be sure to install updates for your operating systems, application software, browser add-ons, and smartphone and tablet apps. Also, uninstall software that you don't use. See Figure 8-6.

Figure 8-6: Updating software

Update software on your computer.

Update apps and the OS on your smartphone when prompted.

Rawpixel.com/Shutterstock.com, Cristina Nixau/Shutterstock.com

Figure 8-7: Hotspots can be unsecured

RTimages/Shutterstock.com

Use Caution with Wireless Connections

Hotspots—areas in a wireless network where you can access the Internet—include coffee shops, airports, hotels, libraries, and other public places. Most hotspots (see Figure 8-7) are unsecured. While a wireless network can extend your reach online, the network and your computer are unprotected if the network is unsecured. You are only as secure as the weakest link in any network. Therefore, you should avoid passing sensitive data over unsecured networks. For example, do not do your online banking from a coffee shop's network.

Most homes now have wireless networks. If you live in an apartment complex, for example, a quick scan of your smartphone Wi-Fi settings screen will show you all the available nearby wireless networks, whether they are locked, and the signal strength. See Figure 8-8. A neighbor—or a stranger—can access your computer or device just by being in range of your unsecured Wi-Fi signal. Wi-Fi piggybacking occurs when someone taps into your unprotected Wi-Fi network. At a minimum, piggybacking can slow down your wireless connection.

Another way a hacker can gain access to your Wi-Fi network is by war driving, a practice in which someone searches for and maps unsecured Wi-Fi networks from a vehicle. After gaining access to your system, the hacker can pose as you online and download illegal content in your name.

Follow Guidelines to Protect Your Privacy

To protect your devices and data, use the following smart practices for every device or computer that connects to the Internet:

- Never open an attachment or click a link in an email or text from an unknown source.
- Don't install downloaded software that you have not first checked for malware.

- Keep your passwords in a safe and secure place. If you wrote them on paper, don't post the paper on your monitor, underneath your keyboard, or on your desk. If do must keep a written list, it's best to include only part of each password along with a clue that only you will know the meaning of. Don't keep passwords in a file on your computer.
- Use a software or hardware **password manager** such as LastPass and Dashlane to track and organize your passwords.
- If passwords are in a file, such as a password manager, you should add password protection to that file. Password managers usually store passwords encrypted. Therefore, you should create an extremely secure and strong master password, because it grants access to the other passwords.
- Never enter private information, such as your Social Security number, password, or account information, in a website you're not familiar with.
- Never include your Social Security number in an email message, and encourage any person or company emailing your tax or other financial documents to encrypt them.
- If you are concerned that your system may have been compromised, close the browser window immediately and run a scan using your security software.
- When in public, if you sign in to a Wi-Fi network that doesn't require a password, don't use the network for private or sensitive information.

Use Protection Software

Cybercriminals are creative and often successful in exploiting software and system weaknesses. To guard against cybercriminals, first make sure that you have installed firewall, antivirus, and antispyware programs. **Firewall** programs protect your system from intruders. See **Figure 8-9**. **Antivirus software** identifies malware that tries to install on your computer or device. **Antispyware** guards against spyware that attempts to install and then collect and transmit personal data from your system or device.

Figure 8-8: Available Wi-Fi networks

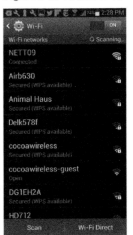

#security

Back up your smartphone periodically to a mobile cloud-based service such as iCloud for iPhones.

#security

Password-protect your home wireless router to protect from Wi-Fi piggybacking. Don't use the default network name or password that came with your router; instead, assign it a distinctive name and password.

Figure 8-9: Windows Firewall

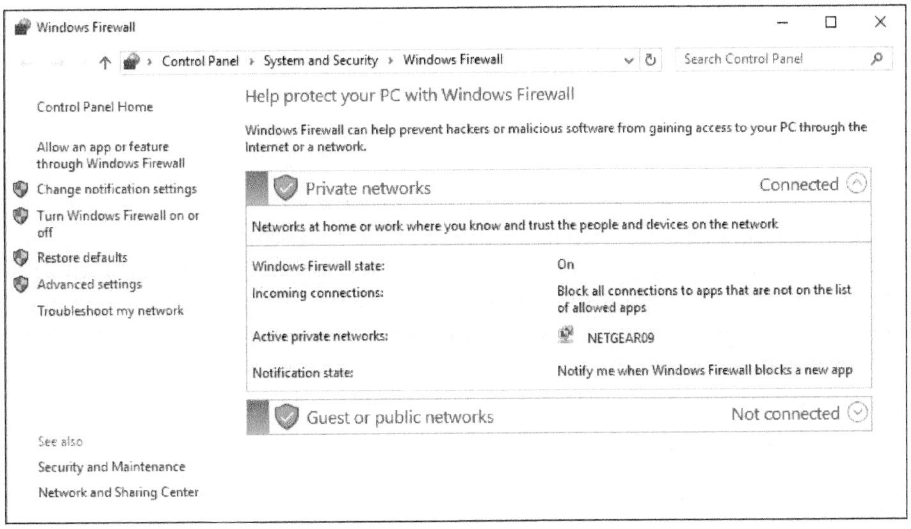

Windows Firewall	— □ ✕
↑ 📁 › Control Panel › System and Security › Windows Firewall	✓ 🔍 Search Control Panel 🔎

Control Panel Home

Help protect your PC with Windows Firewall

Windows Firewall can help prevent hackers or malicious software from gaining access to your PC through the Internet or a network.

Allow an app or feature through Windows Firewall

🛡 Change notification settings

🛡 Turn Windows Firewall on or off

🛡 Restore defaults

🛡 Advanced settings

Troubleshoot my network

🛡 Private networks	Connected ⌃

Networks at home or work where you know and trust the people and devices on the network

Windows Firewall state:	On
Incoming connections:	Block all connections to apps that are not on the list of allowed apps
Active private networks:	💻 NETGEAR09
Notification state:	Notify me when Windows Firewall blocks a new app

🛡 Guest or public networks	Not connected ⌄

See also

Security and Maintenance

Network and Sharing Center

Make sure your **wireless router**, the device that sends the signal to connect your wireless devices to the Internet, has encryption turned on. **Encryption** ensures that your data is scrambled as it travels between you and its Internet destination, so if a hacker were to intercept your message, he or she would see nothing but scrambled letters. Although no security is 100% safe, encryption can help.

Identify Financial Risks

electronic wallet

The Bottom Line

- If your financial transactions are not secure from hackers, phishing websites, and other online frauds, you can experience significant financial losses.
- Always make sure you're using a secure website whenever you conduct any online transaction; use smart practices for every computer or device you use.

When you shop, bank, or conduct any type of financial transaction online, you take the risk that your credit card number or other financial information could be stolen. Cybercriminals can steal sensitive data by intercepting it during transmission or by exploiting a weakness in the system.

Identify Unsecured Websites

Some websites are not what they appear to be. It's easy to be fooled into thinking you're visiting a secure website when in reality you've fallen victim to a website that only pretends to be legitimate. To ensure that you are using a secure website, look for https:// at the beginning of the URL or a padlock icon in the address bar. See **Figure 8-10**. If computer or network protection is weak, hackers can steal sensitive account information by intercepting transaction data when it's transmitted or stored.

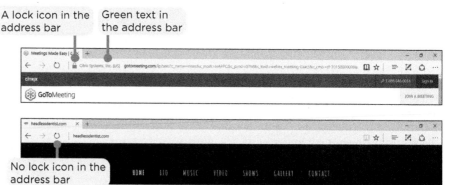

Figure 8-10: Secured vs. unsecured websites

A lock icon in the address bar

Green text in the address bar

No lock icon in the address bar

Source: GoToMeeting.com, headlessdentist.com

To help ensure safety when using the web, do the following:

- Be wary of any website that asks for your Social Security number or birth date before you can do business with it.
- Avoid shopping or conducting financial transactions on websites that look real but do not have https:// or a lock icon, or green text in the address bar.
- Check the spelling of a website URL (Starbuks rather than Starbucks) and any text on the homepage; websites with misspelled words are often fraudulent.

Identify Risks in Online Banking

Cybercriminals can take advantage of flaws in your security system and steal your banking and financial information. No matter which device you use to access the Internet, there are some simple rules you can follow to protect your data and information.

- Avoid typing sensitive personal or financial information when using a public wireless network.
- Do not enter sensitive or personal information in an email or after clicking a link in an email. Convincing phishing emails can appear to come from your bank or credit card company. No legitimate company will ask you for email sign-in or personal information.
- Delete suspect email that you receive, and call or email your bank if you have any questions.
- Do not unzip or open any unsolicited email or text messages. These can also contain fake forms, phony bills, or vouchers that can release malware on your device once you unzip or open them.
- Update your operating system, web browser software, and antivirus software when prompted.

#security

Keep an eye on your credit card accounts online instead of waiting for your monthly statement to check for fraud.

#security

Set up text or email notifications with your online bank account to notify you of suspicious purchases, significant withdrawals, or a low balance.

Hot Technology Now

PayPal, Venmo, and Stripe are services in which buyers and sellers, individuals or businesses set up an account that manages and secures money transfers.

Identify Risks in Online Shopping

Cybercriminals can take advantage of flaws in online shopping websites. Any choices you make or information you provide can be vulnerable to hackers. No matter which device you use to access the Internet, there are some simple rules you can follow to protect your data and information when shopping online.

- Avoid shopping at websites that don't have secure checkout procedures and clear privacy and return policies—or websites that lack contact information.
- Avoid making online purchases while using a public wireless network.
- Beware of web addresses that are spelled incorrectly or have extra words or numbers in them.
- Don't pay for online items with money transfers. Cybercriminals may offer a better deal if you pay for items with a money transfer. Almost certainly, you'll never receive the item you paid for.
- When you make an online purchase at a secure website, use a credit card, an **electronic wallet** such as Apple Pay, Android Pay, or a PayPal, Stripe, or Venmo account, that you can track if there is a problem. Electronic wallet devices and software process information for secure online purchases.

Protect Mobile Devices

Because mobile devices are easily lost or stolen, leaving a mobile device unlocked instantly exposes your data. Be sure to lock your smartphone when not using it to protect against someone using your mobile payment apps to transmit payment information from your smartphone to a nearby cashier reader. See **Figure 8-11**.

If you use your smartphone or mobile device for mobile payments, there are additional precautions you can take. Do not download apps from unknown or third-party stores unless you can verify their authenticity; many of these fraudulent apps often come loaded with malware. For security, use apps from a reputable source, such as your bank, credit card company, or retailer.

Follow Guidelines to Protect Financial Data

To protect yourself while using the Internet, be smart and be careful. By following these protection practices, you can greatly reduce the chances of losing your financial data to fraudulent activities:

- Make sure your shopping websites use https:// or lock icons; also make sure they are members of security organizations such as TRUSTe, VeriSign, or the Better Business Bureau by clicking the lock icon to view the digital certificate.
- Download electronic wallet software and security apps to use when you purchase items. You can also set up software that remotely erases information stored on a mobile device if it's lost or stolen.
- Get in the habit of logging out of your accounts, clearing the history in the web browser on all your devices daily, and keeping your operating system, browser, and security software up to date.
- Create multiple passwords and be sure that they are strong. The strongest passwords contain uppercase and lowercase letters, symbols, and numbers.
- Check your bank and credit card statements frequently for activity.
- Lock your mobile device and use the highest security settings on your home wireless network.

Secure Personal Information

identity thief | credit score | credit report | cyberbullying | cyberstalking | online identity | online profile | username | password | PIN (personal identification number) | authentication | biometrics | two-factor authentication | two-factor verification | two-step authentication | incognito browsing | InPrivate browsing | Incognito mode | InPrivate mode | pharming | router

What defines who you are to your bank? School? Credit card company? Employer? It's your personal information—facts about you that make you unique, such as your name,

Figure 8-11: Unlocking a smartphone

oatawa/Shutterstock.com

The Bottom Line
- Using your identity, thieves usually commit financial fraud. Prevent identity theft by safeguarding your personal information.
- To stay safe and maintain your privacy, it's important to limit the information you share online.
- Personal information is quickly and easily passed among friends, employers, and agencies through the Internet, so it is possible for this information to land in the wrong hands.
- Use settings in your browser and your home network router to safeguard your information.

birthdate, place of birth, parents' last names, and Social Security number. Your name alone might not be unique, but combined, these facts make it possible for you to carry out activities such as conducting business, getting loans, and applying for jobs. If your personal information is not secure, you could find yourself unable to accomplish these essential tasks.

Identity theft is the nation's fastest-growing crime. Unfortunately, its victims often don't find out about it until they have become victims of fraud. Your online profile on social media gives you many new ways to connect with others—and just as many ways to put yourself in potentially dangerous situations. In addition, websites track your browsing history, your identity, and other data. Use protection practices to help shield yourself from misuse of your information and to avoid putting yourself in harm's way.

Figure 8-12: Protect your online identity

IDENTIFY

Your online profile is compiled from many of your actions, including comments, postings, likes and shares, as well as the online coupons you use.

PROJEKTNOW/Shutterstock.com

By the Numbers Now

The first three digits of your Social Security number identify your geographical location when you applied for the number. The numbers with lowest digits were issued in the northeast, and the highest were issued on the West Coast.

Hot Technology Now

Check your credit report for free at sites such as annualcreditreport.com and creditkarma.com. Check at more than one site to be sure.

Avoid Identity Theft and Fraud

An **identity thief** obtains personal information from various online and real-world sources. Thieves might use online phishing messages or physical devices that read credit card or ATM numbers. They target your Social Security number, credit card and debit card numbers, PINs, passwords, and other personal information. They may steal from you directly, but the ultimate goal is to gain enough information to impersonate you without your knowledge. With your Social Security number, an identity thief can order a replacement birth certificate or driver's license. Even though this happens without your knowledge or permission, you will be responsible for every unpaid bill and financial crime committed in your name.

After identity thieves assume your identity, they can then commit various kinds of fraud. For example, an identity thief can easily impersonate you to employers, financial institutions, and even the police if he or she commits a crime in your name. Credit card fraud is also common. Thieves spend all the credit available on the fraudulent cards immediately and, of course, never pay the bills.

This kind of fraud has an instant and long-lasting effect on your **credit score**, the numeric score that affects your future ability to obtain credit. Having a damaged credit score causes problems in many aspects of your life. Education loans, car loans, and home loans become difficult to get, and job or rental applications are denied based on a bad **credit report**. Repairing your credit report after it has been damaged by fraud is a long and grueling process. Even though you did nothing wrong, you may still lose money.

Often, banks and credit card companies will compensate you for losses if you report fraudulent activity in a timely fashion. But, unfortunately, there are groups that illegally gather the information of people who have worked hard to keep their credit scores and reputation in good standing and sell these identities to others for profit. Once someone assumes your identity, it can take years of legal hearings to prove who you really are and straighten out the mess.

Because cyberterrorists, identify thieves, hackers, and spammers can pose significant threats to your physical, employment, and financial security, it is important to protect your bank and credit card numbers, and use verification processes and password protection systems to help protect your personal information.

Identify the Risks of Social Media

The numerous positive experiences you have interacting in social media and networking communities can be offset by privacy concerns if someone gains access to your information. People express themselves more boldly online knowing that posts or other communications can be anonymous. **Cyberbullying** involves humiliation, rumors, lies, taunts, or threats. Some of the cruelest cyberbullies have been preteen or teenage girls, but immaturity is no excuse. Make sure you and your family know how to recognize cyberbullying. School districts often develop policies and guidelines that address cyberbullying. Some states have extended a school's jurisdiction to act in cases that take place off campus or online. Cyberstalkers might harass and threaten coworkers, bosses, former love interests, or someone they disagreed with online. **Cyberstalking** often involves the same dynamics as other forms of violence—threats, power, intimidation, and control—and can escalate into real-world violence. To help protect yourself from stalkers, limit how much personal information you share online.

It's easy to overshare with people you think you can trust, and that's where problems begin. Someone can repost private details about you, including images and video, and within minutes, that information can be shared with people across the country and around the world.

Younger users may not know or care that they're divulging too much information to a predator, placing them in danger. Therefore, it's important for parents and peers to talk about what's appropriate to share. Content stays and is available on the Internet long after you might think it's been deleted or removed. Think about your posts, tweets, messages, photos, videos, comments, and status updates. Consider that in an instant, you've shared something about yourself or someone else that you can never take back.

Manage Your Online Profile

Your **online identity**, also called your **online profile**, consists of your photos, videos, purchases, public posts, comments, and information forwarded and reposted by your friends and by strangers. See **Figure 8-13**. When you click Share on Facebook, post a status, comment or update your LinkedIn profile, or post a photo on Instagram, you lose control of what goes online or shows up in search results.

Employers and other important decision-makers such as school admissions officers can and do check out your Internet "footprint." What you might consider a zealous response to a news story or just sharing a fun party photo can set off red flags if a potential employer or college admissions officer sees it. If you want to post more freely, you can consider creating a personal profile and a public profile on each of the social network sites. Employers screen applicants using social media, and they reject candidates that have lied about experience or qualifications, posted inappropriate content, or made negative comments about previous employers.

Avoid Storing Cookies

Just about every site you visit stores a cookie in your computer's browser. Cookies save your user preferences and identify you when you next sign in or visit. Cookies also can monitor your movements on a site and then send that information back to the website. A website can host ads from a third-party advertiser, which then places its cookie on your computer.

Hot Technology Now

Mobile apps like Snapchat share photos that self-destruct a few seconds after they are viewed, but there are many ways to capture the screen. Do not share anything that will affect your reputation.

By the Numbers Now

Almost 80% of potential employers admitted they use search engines like Google and Bing to screen their candidates. In addition, 35% of these employers eliminated a candidate from consideration based on information they found online.

#security

Search for your name on google.com and bing.com to see what information is available about you.

Figure 8-13: Social networks require online profiles

Andrey_Popov/Shutterstock.com

#security

There are two types of cookies. Temporary cookies are session cookies that are stored for a short time and then removed when the browser is closed. Permanent cookies are stored for a long time on your hard drive.

On the Job Now

Do not use your business email address for personal Internet usage. Set up a separate email for shopping online and using personal social media sites.

Unless you read the Privacy and Terms of Use statements on a website, you don't know how a business uses your history. Businesses also collect and track your personal information when you use something as simple as an online coupon. Advertisers combine details about your online and in-store shopping behaviors with other tracking data to form a personalized shopping profile.

Choose a Strong Password

Just as a username and password get you into your computer, your username and password are often the key to your online account information. Unlike most of your personal information and data, such as your bank and credit card numbers and Social Security number, you choose your username and password to create accounts at websites, banks, or wherever such information is needed. A **username** is an alphanumeric series of characters that you create to identify yourself on websites, banks, or other online places where you have an account. A **password** is a unique combination of characters or letters that you specify. When used in combination with your username, it grants you access to your account or website. Often the combination of username and password is required to get into any online account. If you forget your password or username, websites often can mail you a link that lets you set a new one to your email address or text message to the mobile phone number on record. A password is not a **PIN (personal identification number)**. A PIN typically is a three- to four-digit number that is either assigned by a bank or financial institution or selected by a user to get into accounts using an automated teller machine, or ATM.

Many people select usernames that are familiar and easy to remember. Since it is the combination of username and password that is the key to the information, you should create strong passwords. The stronger the password, the less likely that it will be easily guessed by another person who wants to access your accounts. So, you should follow some rules to ensure that your accounts are protected. See Table 8-1.

Table 8-1: Rules for creating strong passwords

Rule	Bad examples	Better examples
Passwords should have more than five characters; mix letters, numbers, and symbols as well as uppercase letters.	password1 12345	Mtwtf13579# DumFDP076
Do not use a password someone can guess, such as your name, pet's name, or birthday. If using a birthday or pet's name, include random numbers.	JenniferMarch1st1978 EmilyMay1998	Gatsby1129#45 123RoverDog456
Financial institution passwords should be especially strong; if using a common word, mix up letter case and numbers.	12poplar mybank123	PoPlAr345St!* Shekels5151$

#security

As visitors from other countries enter the United States, U.S. Customs and Border Protection collects biometric data including fingerprints and photos, which are checked against databases that track terrorists and undocumented or illegal immigrants.

Passwords can be difficult to remember, but you do not want to reuse the same password at several sites in case there is a breach. You can create similar passwords for several sites that do not have sensitive data, such as a photo site, but you should create a unique, strong password for your banking.

Use Two-Factor Authentication

How does a computer know who you are? If you meet someone face-to face, or even on a video conference, that person can see that you are you. But if you log into a computer from a remote location, the system needs a way of verifying your identity before granting access to sensitive information. The process of **authentication** is used to verify a user. There are three ways to verify your identity: 1) showing or swiping something you carry, such as a photo ID card; 2) entering information, such as a username, PIN, or a password; and 3) using a personal feature.

Biometrics is the use of personal features to identify a person. Biometric systems include fingerprint and hand scanners, facial recognition technology, and eye scans. Biometrics is used on many smartphones. For example, the Home button is also a fingerprint reader available to unlock a phone for an authorized user. See **Figure 8-14**.

Figure 8-14: Fingerprint reader on a smartphone

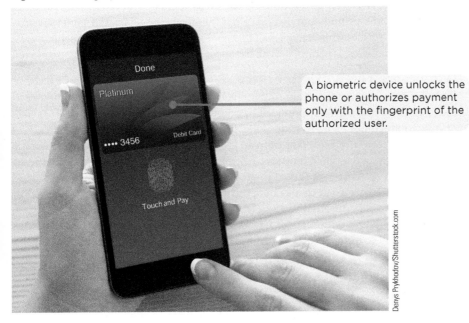

A biometric device unlocks the phone or authorizes payment only with the fingerprint of the authorized user.

Two-factor authentication, also called **two-factor verification** or **two-step authentication**, provides added security by requiring two distinct items for verification. These items can be a username and password, an ATM or debit card and a PIN, or a fingerprint and password. Some systems will let you access an account only after you verify a code that is sent as a text message to your cell phone number on record with the account. This code must then be entered into the site or sign-in screen and is good only for one-time use. Once verified, a user is authenticated or authorized to enter or have access to the device, place, or data.

Adjust Browser Security Settings

When browsing the Internet, you can take advantage of the security built into your browser to help keep your data and identity secure. Most browsers offer a way to surf the Internet without leaving a trace on the computer you used. In Chrome it's called **incognito browsing**. In Microsoft Edge, it's called **InPrivate browsing** (see **Figure 8-15**). By selecting use your browser's **Incognito mode** or **InPrivate mode**, your browser will not save your browsing history, temporary Internet files, form data, cookies, usernames or passwords. This is helpful when you browse in a public space such as a library. There is nothing left in the History file and cookies are deleted when you close the window.

Figure 8-15: InPrivate browsing in Edge

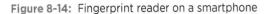

Check the security settings on your browser to be sure you have a level of security that meets your needs. There are safe site settings, phishing and pharming filters, and other features, such as the Smart Screen Filter in Microsoft Edge, and features in Google Chrome and other browsers that will help keep you safe.

Pharming is an illicit activity in which you are directed to a fake site to enter personal information. Once entered, the information is sold or transferred for illegal activity. Phishing is the gathering of information through fake email. You should never click any links that arrive in email claiming to come from your bank. Sure signs of a phishing email include misspellings and dire warnings that inaction will lead to some catastrophe. If you are unsure whether an email that appears to be from your bank, school, government, or employer is legitimate, call the apparent sender to confirm its authenticity.

Use Home Network Security
If you have a home network, your **router**, the hardware that connects your computer to the Internet, was most likely provided by your Internet Service Provider (ISP) as part of your contract. But it's up to you to keep the router safe and secure.

When you get a wireless router from an ISP, it comes with factory default settings. It is important that you follow the steps, often provided in the material from the ISP, to set up the router. As part of the setup process, you'll need to specify a network name and a password. Be sure to change both the name and password from their defaults to secure the network. The password will let you access the network from any computer, tablet, or smartphone within range. Create a strong password that is a series of characters, words and or numbers. Try to create a password that is easy for you to remember and to communicate to guests in your home, easy to type on a smartphone, but not easily guessed by a hacker.

Follow Guidelines to Protect Your Privacy
To help deter identity theft, shred financial documents, monitor your accounts, and protect personal information—and be wary if asked to provide it. These are some helpful guidelines you can follow:
- If you are a victim of identity theft, disconnect from the Internet, close suspect accounts, place a fraud alert on your credit reports, and file a police report and a complaint with the Federal Trade Commission at www.ftc.gov.
- If you're being harassed, bullied, or threatened online, report the abuse quickly.
- Reduce your Internet footprint by deleting old online accounts and increasing the privacy settings on your social network accounts.
- Don't share information via social media that would make you vulnerable. Pay particular attention to the images you share on any device.
- Learn how to configure your browser to block third-party cookies from certain sites and opt out of receiving emails or updates.

Maintaining privacy in an electronic world is a task that may seem overwhelming at first because it requires ongoing vigilance and your continued attention, but will pay off in increased personal safety and financial security.

Protect the Environment
electronic trash | e-trash | e-waste | green computing

Our lives today are full of electronic devices, and every year we get new ones and discard old ones. Because we're so used to electronic hardware, we don't usually think about what it takes to produce the device or what happens when we no longer need it and we must dispose of it. The volume of electronic waste is enormous and is having serious effects on the environment around the world.

Define Electronic Trash
Electronic trash, also called **e-trash** or **e-waste**, consists of discarded computers, cell phones, televisions, stereos, and the electronics from automobiles and appliances. See **Figure 8-16**. According to the U.S. Environmental Protection Agency (EPA),

#security

Just like phishing, "smishing" uses smartphone text messages as a scam. The text message may contain a link directing you to download a mobile app designed to steal your personal information or your digital wallet to drain your bank account.

The Bottom Line
- Green, or environmentally friendly, computing and recycling can reduce impact of electronic waste on the environment and ultimately reduce costs.
- Electronic waste and disposal is a critical global issue.

Americans generate millions of tons of electronic waste each year. The EPA has been effective with initiatives to educate the public and has put programs in place to facilitate the proper disposal and management of e-trash. You can learn more by visiting https://www.epa.gov/smm-electronics.

The United States exports much of its e-waste to countries such as China, Hong Kong, India, Nigeria, and Ghana, for disassembly, recovery and recycling of useful materials, and disposal. Countries in West Africa, like Ghana, also receive approximately 75 percent of European e-waste. E-waste presents a growing global health and environmental risk.

Figure 8-16: Discarding electronics

Identify Toxic Electronic Parts

You may not realize that the chips, circuit boards, disk drives, and plastics in your favorite products are toxic. They contain flame retardants and heavy metals such as lead, mercury, hexavalent chromium, and other toxic substances, in addition copper, iron, silicon, nickel, and gold. The process of recovering valuable metals from discarded electronics is hazardous and profoundly pollutes the environment in countries where environmental and worker safety laws are weak or not enforced. Metal recovery also requires a great deal of human labor, fuel, and chemicals to process because the e-waste must be burned or melted. When e-waste is burned or left in a landfill, harmful chemicals are released into the air or groundwater and soil, presenting a risk that people will develop serious health problems by coming into contact with these toxins.

On the Job Now

Data destruction of private and confidential information is vital to corporations and small businesses. Information such as Social Security numbers, credit card information, and medical records must be fully destroyed at the end-of-life of all equipment.

Address the Problem of E-Waste

Only recently have the nations that generate e-waste begun to construct agreements not to ship toxic waste to developing countries unless the countries have adequate waste management facilities. Whether these laws will be successful is still a question. Countries often allow illegal exports of toxic e-waste and ignore guidelines to recycle and reuse locally. Shipping to far-off countries puts e-waste out of sight, but it eventually affects everyone.

Regardless of the source of e-waste, most experts agree that manufacturers and consumers need to work together to address this growing problem. Some school districts, colleges, and universities have an e-waste recycling program. Many communities have passed legislation making it illegal to dispose of e-waste with the general trash.

#security

Go to twitter.com, search for @SAMTechNow, the book's Twitter account, and then follow @SAMTechNow to get tweets on your home page.

Practice Green Computing and Recycling

Green computing is designing, manufacturing, using, and disposing of electronic products in ways that are friendly to both people and the environment. See **Figure 8-17**.

- Look for products that have the Energy Star logo, indicating that the product was built using energy-efficient systems and reduced hazardous materials.
- Donate devices you don't want, rather than discarding them.
- Buy from manufacturers that accept and recycle their used products; then recycle your used electronics.

Being recognized as an e-Stewards recycler is the maximum certification a company or recycling business can receive from the international non-profit environmental watchdog, Basel Action Network. Recycle responsibly to practice green computing.

Figure 8-17: Recycle your electronics

Photographee.eu/Shutterstock.com

Chapter Review

Avoid Personal Health Risks

1. Define "ergonomics" and give one example of how you can create an ergonomic work environment.

2. List three problems you might have if your computer screen is not adjusted properly.

3. Explain how a person might get repetitive strain injuries.

Avoid Data Risks

4. Name three potential data risks and explain why it is important to have backups of your data.

5. Define the term "hacker" and explain how a hacker might compromise your data.

6. Explain three ways you can safeguard your data.

Evaluate Email and Internet Risks

7. What are two risks that you need to look out for when using the Internet?

8. Define "pharming," define "phishing," and give an example of how you can protect yourself from both.

9. Define and explain "clickbait" and "address spoofing."

10. Explain how malware can damage your data. Define the terms "virus" and "worm."

Identify Financial Risks

11. What should you look for in a bank's website before conducting any business on that site?

12. Define two methods for paying for goods or services on the Internet.

13. Name two ways you can protect your mobile devices.

Secure Personal Information

14. Define "identity theft" and explain why it can be so damaging. What personal information can a thief use to steal your identity?

15. What are the risks of participating in social networking, and how can you protect yourself from those risks?

16. What is biometrics? Give two examples.

17. What is a strong password? Explain the difference between a username, a password, and a PIN. Give an example of a password that would be a good choice for a bank account.

18. What is war driving? What is the best defense against it?

Protect the Environment

19. Define the term "e-waste."

20. Why is it bad for the environment to dispose of electronics in landfills?

Test Your Knowledge Now

1. An RSI that affects the wrist, hand, and arm is called _____ syndrome.
   a. Web-based
   b. social addiction
   c. carpal tunnel
   d. computer vision

2. _____ includes excessive use of online games, web surfing, texting, blogging, and shopping.
   a. Internet addiction
   b. E-commerce
   c. Web addiction
   d. Social networking

3. _____ creates a safe, healthy, and efficient working environment.
   a. Phishing
   b. Cybervision
   c. Pharming
   d. Ergonomics

4. _____ hard drives are more stable than magnetic hard drives, which can crash, resulting in lost data.
   a. Solid state
   b. Optical
   c. Flash
   d. Digital

5. People who break into computers and computer networks—often by exploiting weaknesses and preventable flaws—are called _____.
   a. cybers
   b. white hats
   c. hackers
   d. spammers

6. _____ is the premeditated disruption of computers and networks.
   a. E-commerce
   b. Cyberterrorism
   c. Cyberbullying
   d. Social networking

7. Some cyberterrorists use _____ to demand money to restore a system, blocking access to a computer system until a sum of money is paid.
   a. cloud storage
   b. Trojan horses
   c. ransomware
   d. digital certificates

8. _____ is also known as junk email.
   a. Spyware
   b. Phish
   c. Spam
   d. Malware

9. _____ collects your personal data on your surfing habits as your browse websites and can change your homepage.
   a. Spyware
   b. Spam
   c. Trojan horses
   d. Worms

10. A(n) _____ is used as an identification card to authenticate the owner of a website.
    a. spyware
    b. digital certificate
    c. electronic wallet
    d. worm

11. An email threat known as _____ sends you fake email so that you will click a link and submit your personal data on an illicit website.
    a. phishing
    b. spamming
    c. pharming
    d. worming

12. A(n) _____ is an area, often a public place, where you can access the Internet for free on your mobile device.
    a. Wi-Fi
    b. Internet zone
    c. hotspot
    d. router

13. _____ occurs when someone taps into your unprotected Wi-Fi network and uses it without your knowledge.
    a. identify theft
    b. cyberbullying
    c. cyberstalking
    d. Wi-Fi piggybacking

14. Which of the following should you install to protect your home network?
    a. firewall
    b. browser
    c. router
    d. digital certificate

15. A hyperlink on a webpage or social media post that entices a visitor or recipient to click to continue reading an article is called _____.
    a. malware
    b. clickbait
    c. hotspot
    d. spyware

16. Use _____ to avoid having your browser track your online actions.
    a. phishing
    b. Incognito mode
    c. biometrics
    d. clickbait

17. _____ is the use of personal features, such as a fingerprint, to identify a person.
    a. Biometrics
    b. InPrivate browsing
    c. Netiquette
    d. Ergonomics

18. Which of the following is commonly used for authentication at a banking website?
    a. username
    b. username and password
    c. strong password
    d. Social Security number and birthdate

19. _____ computing is designing, manufacturing, using, and disposing of electronic products in ways that are friendly to both people and the environment.
    a. Green
    b. Electronic
    c. E-trash
    d. Cyber

20. Electronic trash, or _____, consists of discarded computers, cell phones, televisions, stereos, and the electronics from automobiles and appliances.
    a. e-waste
    b. green waste
    c. cyber trash
    d. spyware

21. In the space next to each image below, write the letter of the phrase that describes it.
    a. unsecured website
    b. biometric device
    c. BSoD
    d. ergonomics
    e. form of ID

___
zimmytws/Shutterstock.com

___
AlexLMX/Shutterstock.com

___
Source: headlessdentist.com

___
Denys Prykhodov/Shutterstock.com

___
Maluson/Shutterstock.com

Try This Now

1: Proper Ergonomics with Smartphones and Laptops

Note: This assignment requires a smartphone with a camera, or any digital camera, or a laptop computer with a webcam.

With smartphones and laptops being commonplace in our world today, researchers are examining the ergonomic impact of these devices. Whether you are using a desktop computer, laptop, or tablet, you can place considerable strain on your body.

    a. Research the proper ergonomics of using a smartphone. Write a list of five ergonomic guidelines that you should consider when interacting with a smartphone to avoid repetitive injuries.

    b. Research the proper way to sit while using a laptop or computer. Sitting in front of any computer device, use what you have learned and have someone take a picture of you sitting properly in front of the device. Insert the image in the same document as the list of guidelines.

    c. Search the web for an image of a well-rated standing desk for an office and place this image in the same document with a description and model of the desk.

    d. Submit the document to your instructor.

2: Urban Legends

Urban legends are stories based on hearsay and passed along as being true. Internet hoaxes, such as email scams, blog, Reddit, or Facebook postings containing misinformation about medical facts, news events, or modern folklore are common. The website snopes.com is a validated source for debunking these false rumors and urban legends.

    a. Open a browser and open the site snopes.com.

    b. Tap or click the Hot 25 link. (If that link is not available, click a similar link.)

    c. Open the links and read about three recent hoaxes.

    d. Think about why these may have been written and who might believe that they are true. What damage might a hoax such as this do to those who might believe it?

    e. Write three paragraphs providing an overview in your own words of each of these scams.

    f. Submit the document to your instructor.

3: Secure Browsing

Note: This assignment requires a browser that has been updated in the last year.

Modern browsers provide many security features to make your surfing experience safe and secure. Research your favorite browsers security features.

    a. Research the use of private browsing capabilities within your favorite browser.

    b. Write a paragraph about the purpose of private browsing.

    c. Open the private browsing feature in any browser. Open three tabs, each containing your favorite websites, and take a screen shot. Place the screen shot in the same document as the paragraph written in step b.

    d. Write a second paragraph of other security features in your favorite browser.

    e. Submit the document to your instructor.

Critical Thinking Now

1: Reducing Your Digital Footprint

Your digital footprint starts the day that you compose your first text message or sign in to a social network. Your digital footprint begins a data trail of interactions which leads to future employers reading your online profiles. Research the topic of managing your digital footprint. Create a listing in Microsoft Word of eight best practices for maintaining a positive digital footprint, in your own words. Google your own name and determine how many of the results are directly related to your actions online. Write a paragraph about what type of information is often found when students Google themselves.

Facebook Impersonation

2: Facebook Impersonation

Barbara received a Facebook friend request from a good friend, Pam. It seemed odd, because she was already very active on Facebook, but Barbara accepted the request. A private message started out with a simple hello, how are you, but quickly progressed to Pam talking nonsense about obtaining cash from a new student loan. As this conversation seemed odd, Barbara called her friend Pam on the phone—sure enough it wasn't her friend Pam that she'd been communicating with on Facebook. Somebody had stolen Pam's name and profile photos, copied her work history, friended their friends, and were now trying to lure them into a scam.

Research the privacy basics of Facebook and write at least 100 words summarizing the policy in your own words. In addition, list several ways that Facebook users can avoid being impersonated online.

3: Local E-Waste Recycling

After reading this chapter, you should have a heightened awareness about the importance of recycling your electronic devices. Are you aware that throwing away e-waste in your household garbage could be illegal, as well as unethical, in many parts of the world?

a. Research green computing and proper disposal of a computer.
b. Write a paragraph about steps that you should take before disposing of a smartphone or laptop.
c. Write another paragraph of locations in your town or city that can assist with the disposal of e-waste. Be sure to mention the name, address, and policies of two facilities.

Ethical Issues Now

Snapchat provides a social community that connects millions of members around the world. When it comes to posting on Snapchat, it seems anyone is susceptible to oversharing.

a. Research the topic of oversharing on social media. In your own words, write a total of 10 comments summarizing dos and don'ts about sharing on Snapchat.
b. Research why people overshare on Shapchat. Write at least 100 words about why people feel compelled to share images that they would never share in a room filled with their peers.

Team Up Now—Mind Mapping: Cyber Attacks

Each week the media covers the potential or actual hacking of companies, political campaigns, and government agencies.

a. Each team member should research an incident of corporate hacking that has been in the recent news. Each team member should write at least 150 words using Word or a common word processor, about the security infringement. Be sure to mention whether consumers were personally affected by the hacking incident.
b. Share your research documents on the hacked companies with the other team members. As a team, create a mind map about cyberattacks. A mind map is a graphical representation of ideas and concepts. Open the website https://bubbl.us and watch the videos to learn how to create a mind map. As a team, create and share a mind map about your thoughts of cyberattacks. The assigned mind map should include a central idea and at least 25 subtopics with important connections between ideas.
c. Share the research essay documents and mind mapping link with your instructor.

Key Terms

address spoofing
antispyware
antivirus software
authentication
biometrics
black hat
Blue Screen of Death (BSoD)
carpal tunnel syndrome
clickbait
cloud storage system
computer vision syndrome
credit report
credit score
cyberattack
cyberbullying
cybercrime
cyberstalking
cyberterrorism
cyberterrorist
digital certificate
electronic trash
electronic wallet
encryption

ergonomics
e-trash
e-waste
firewall
green computing
hacker
hacktivist
hoax
hotspot
identity thief
incognito browsing
Incognito mode
InPrivate browsing
InPrivate mode
Internet addiction
magnetic hard drive
malware
online identity
online profile
packet
password
password manager
pharming

phishing
PIN (personal identification number)
ransomware
repetitive strain injury (RSI)
rootkit
router
solid state hard drive
spam
spyware
strong password
Trojan horse
two-factor authentication
two-factor verification
two-step authentication
uninterruptible power supply (UPS)
username
virus
war driving
white hat
Wi-Fi piggybacking
wireless router
wireless sniffing
worm

Communication

Liam is studying abroad in Sydney, Australia. He enjoys sharing his experiences with friends and family back home via his blog.

Communicating through Skype, Facebook, Twitter, Instagram, and email has dramatically shortened the distance between Liam and his friends and family.

Monte Rego Images/Shutterstock.com

For his first study abroad experience, Liam Stuart is studying in Sydney, Australia. Checking in with his academic advisor, parents, and friends back home allows him to share what he is learning in his oceanography classes and in his new routine. His laptop has communications software, an internal microphone, and a webcam. He can connect with his friends and family online, all with a single tap on his touch screen.

Define Digital Communications

webinar | digital communications | podcast | blog | wiki | online social network | communications system | protocol | TCP/IP | wireless fidelity (Wi-Fi) | 3G | 4G | Long-Term Evolution (LTE) | WiMAX | 802.16 standard | communications software | cell phone | mobile phone | smartphone | carrier | cell tower | cellular network | base station | cell | subscriber identity module (SIM) card | tablet | phablet

When you send a photo and short text message to a friend from your smartphone, post a description of a restaurant meal on a blog, or learn how to edit a video while attending a **webinar** (an online educational web conference), you are using **digital communications**, which involve transmitting information from one computer or mobile device to another.

Figure 9-1: Using digital communications

From your point of view, digital communications seem simple: you type a text message, press Send, and you're done.

Behind the scenes, a global communications system transmits your message instantaneously.

When the message arrives, your recipient uses a messaging app to read the message.

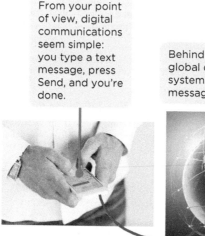

EpicStockMedia/Shutterstock.com, dgbomb/Shutterstock.com, lzf/Shutterstock.com

#communication

Smartphones use Wi-Fi in addition to 3G (3rd generation) and 4G (4th generation) cellular networks.

Describe Common Types of Digital Communications

To connect with other people, you probably use some type of digital communication. Suppose you're planning a trip to Denmark. You might use the following types of digital communications.

- Use email, instant messages, or text and video messages to send and receive digital messages while preparing for your trip.
- Share links to websites through your smartphone or computer to research places to visit and hours of operation.
- To listen to travel tales from other visitors to Denmark, you could download **podcasts** (audio files distributed on the web) to your smartphone or media player, or you could visit a blog about Denmark. A **blog** (web log) is an informal website of time-stamped articles written in a journal format.
- Visit a website such as TripAdvisor or Yelp to read reviews of travel destinations, things to do, restaurants, and hotels in Denmark to help you plan your trip.
- If you are traveling with a group, you could contribute to a **wiki**, a collaborative website where group members can communicate with each other.
- During your trip, you can update friends back home by posting photos, videos, and messages using an **online social network**, a website where members share information.

By the Numbers Now

The newest Wi-Fi standard is 802.11ac, which can reach the speed of 1 gigabit per second (Gbps). The next standard, 802.11ax, is being developed to achieve a speed of 10 Gbps.

Define Communications Systems

If you want to send a message to someone, you use a **communications system**, which sends electronic data from a source to a destination. Along the way, the data can pass through devices that convert it to electrical, sound, light, or radio signals. See **Figure 9-2.**

Figure 9-2: Using a communications system

Modem converts the message to electronic signals.

Communications channel, such as a cable TV line or fiber optic cable, transmits the signals.

Receiving device, such as another modem, converts the signals into an email message.

Destination device, such as a server, accepts the message.

Your computer or mobile device is the communication source.

Server repeats the process to send the message to your classmate's computer or mobile device.

Maxx-studio/Shutterstock.com, saginbay/Shutterstock.com, Norman Chan/Shutterstock.com, gladcov/Shutterstock.com, pryzmat/Shutterstock.com, indigolotos/Shutterstock.com

Identify Communications Standards

To make sure that devices can communicate with each other, they follow communications standards, or **protocols**. These protocols specify the method and speed that devices use to transmit data. **TCP/IP** is a network protocol that defines how to route data across a network. TCP/IP stands for Transmission Control Protocol (TCP) and Internet Protocol (IP). Because all servers on the Internet follow TCP/IP rules, TCP/IP is currently the most widely used communications protocol.

Computers and devices that communicate using radio waves across a medium distance of 100–900 feet use **wireless fidelity (Wi-Fi)**. Most Wi-Fi devices today use the 802.11n and 802.11ac standards. A laptop might use Wi-Fi to connect to a wireless router and TCP/IP to communicate over the Internet.

Cellular networks use **3G** (third generation) and **4G** (fourth generation) wireless communications standards. 3G communications can handle about 2 Megabits per second (Mbps) of data, which allows you to browse the web, exchange email, and download videos, for example. 4G communications are designed for speeds between 100 Mbps and 1 Gbps, which surpasses the speed of the average wireless broadband Internet connection. 5G communications are expected around 2020 with speeds of 1–10 Gbps.

To communicate across longer distances, mobile devices can use **Long-Term Evolution (LTE)**, a standard for high-speed wireless communication. LTE is usually marketed as 4G LTE and competes with the less common **WiMAX**, also known as the **802.16 standard**.

Use Communications Software

Communications software helps your computer connect to a network and then work with communications standards to manage transmitting and receiving data. One type of communications software is usually part of a computer's or mobile device's operating system or is provided with networking devices you purchase. See **Figure 9-3**.

Besides communications software built into an operating system, some application software lets users communicate with each other. For example, you can use email software to send and receive email messages, use messaging software on your smartphone, or use web-based software for a webinar.

Communications software works with communication protocols and devices so that all you have to do is enter a message on a computer or mobile device and select a Send command to communicate with people around the world.

Use Cell Phones

A **cell phone**, short for cellular telephone, also called **mobile phone**, is a portable phone that uses wireless cellular technology to send and receive phone signals. The Pew Research Center recently found that about two-thirds of Americans own a **smartphone**, a cell phone with many features of a computer, including Internet access and an operating system that can run apps.

Cell phones connect users to each other wirelessly through voice calls and text messages. These basic phones might also be able to connect to the Internet, but with limited capabilities. In contrast, smartphones connect users to the Internet and its vast

#communication

Airborne drones carrying LTE network equipment into the skies restore cellular networks when disasters such as hurricanes strike.

#communication

To save money on your smartphone plan and avoid roaming or international calling charges, connect to a Wi-Fi network and make free voice calls on Google Voice.

Figure 9-3: Communications software

Windows provides a quick way to connect to a wireless network.

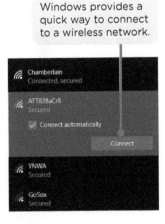

#communication

Because cell phone technology does not require the infrastructure investment of traditional phones, such as poles and telephone wiring, people in developing countries can use mobile phones to communicate, access information, and explore opportunities.

Figure 9-4: Cell towers in a cellular network

Kai19/Shutterstock.com

Hot Technology Now

Smartphones, tablets, and phablets all share the ability to take photos and videos and send them through networks to websites, social networks, and other Internet locations.

On the Job Now

Businesses, which often use hard-wired phones, demand clear and reliable communications through phone systems that include voicemail, conference-calling, call transfer, and line extension features.

Figure 9-5: Using a tablet with a cellular network connection

Kaspars Grinvalds/Shutterstock.com

amount of information and services. People use smartphones to make phone calls, exchange text messages, engage in social media, follow the news and weather, navigate by car and public transit, find information on websites, use productivity apps, and more.

To access online content and interact with others with a cell phone, you contract with a **carrier**, a company that provides voice and data services, similar to using an ISP to connect to the Internet. When you use your phone, it converts your voice or data into an electrical signal and transmits it via radio waves to the nearest **cell tower**, a raised structure with antennae and electronic communications equipment. The network of cell towers around the world relays the radio wave to the receiving phone, which converts the radio wave into an electrical signal and then into sound or data again. See **Figure 9-4**.

Carriers offer a wide range of plans, which determine the services you are purchasing, such as voice plans that include voice and text messaging only or data plans, which connect you to the Internet through a 4G network, for example. The contract you sign sets the terms of the service plan and the purchase of the cell phone. Some carriers subsidize some or all of the initial cost of the phone as long as you commit to a contract, typically for two years. Other carriers offer lower monthly charges with no contract, but require you to pay more upfront. Contracts can also set limits on the amount of data you use and charge extra if you exceed the limit. Because cell phone contracts vary widely, consider your needs and carefully read the terms and conditions of the contract before you commit to it.

Access Cellular Networks

A **cellular network** is a communications network linking many base stations that each cover a limited geographical area. A **base station** is a set of equipment that sends and receives radio signals, and is usually attached to a cell tower. The geographical area a base station covers is called a **cell**. Its coverage varies from a few feet to 20 miles, depending on the location of obstacles that can block or interfere with radio signals.

Smartphones include built-in features that connect to cellular networks. How your smartphone makes the connection depends on your cellular carrier and service plan. Typically, the phone connects automatically to your carrier's fastest available data network. In other cases, you might need to insert a **subscriber identity module (SIM) card**, which is card containing an integrated circuit that uniquely identifies the phone, or choose settings for a specific carrier.

While smartphones are designed primarily for voice communications, a **tablet** is a mobile device larger than a smartphone and has a touch-sensitive screen that accepts input from a digital pen, a stylus, or your fingertips. Tablets are designed more for data and information. (A **phablet** is a mobile device with a size between that of a smartphone and tablet.) Like smartphones, tablets are designed to connect to networks, though they are usually Wi-Fi networks, such as a home wireless network that shares a broadband connection to the Internet or a wireless network that provides hotspots for connecting in a public spaces.

Some tablets also offer wireless connections to cellular networks. Because these tablets include extra hardware for making cellular connections, they cost more than other tablets. As with smartphones, you sign up for a service plan from a compatible carrier so you can use the tablet on a cellular network.

If you are a tablet user, the advantage of using cellular connections is that they are easier to find than Wi-Fi hotspots when you are on the go. See **Figure 9-5**. On the other hand, most cellular plans limit your data usage, while Wi-Fi connections do not. It is therefore more practical to use your tablet for data-intensive activities such as streaming movies or music when it is connected to a Wi-Fi network, not a cellular network.

Define Email

email system | email service | email server | email message | store-and-forward technology | email client | router | email account | email provider | local email client | Post Office Protocol (POP) | webmail | Internet Message Access Protocol (IMAP) | Simple Mail Transfer Protocol (SMTP) | email address | domain name | email attachment | archiving

To keep in touch with a friend while you're on the go, communicate with your instructor, or send messages to family members, you can use email (short for electronic mail). For businesses and organizations, email is the standard for written communication.

Figure 9-6: Email requirements

To use email, you need an email account...

...an email application (also called an email client)...

...and a connection to a network such as the Internet

nmedia/Shutterstock.com, Source: Google, Source: Apple, Anton Balazh/Shutterstock.com

Use Email Systems

Any computer or mobile device that can access the Internet can connect with an **email system**, which consists of the computers and software that provide **email services**. The main computer in an email system is an **email server**, which routes **email messages** through the Internet or a private network. See **Figure 9-7**.

Figure 9-7: Using email services

1. Set up an account on an email server, which provides an electronic mailbox for you.

2. The email server retrieves your incoming messages and places them in your mailbox.

3. You use email software to send and receive messages.

4. The email server uses the Internet to send outgoing mail to other email servers.

indigolotos/Shutterstock.com, nmedia/Shutterstock.com, EDHAR/Shutterstock.com

Email uses **store-and-forward technology**. When you send an email message, it travels to a server that stores and then forwards the message along to the recipient.

You use email software to send and receive messages. Popular email software includes Gmail, Outlook, Yahoo! Mail, and private services, such as your school's email services or network email services such as through Office 365.

Describe the Email Communication Process

If someone asked you how to send an email message, you'd probably tell them to use an email app (also called an **email client**) to compose a message and then select the Send button or menu option. But what happens after you select Send?

1. Your email program uses your Internet or network connection to send the message to your email server.

2. Depending on the destination, the email server determines the best route for the message, which often involves sending the message to a series of network devices called **routers**.

3. The last router in the series sends the message to your friend's email server.

4. That email server stores the message in your friend's mailbox.

5. When your friend checks for messages, the email server transfers the message to an email program so it can display the message on your friend's computer.

Define Email Accounts

If you want to send and receive email, you need an **email account**. To sign up for an email account, you contact an **email provider**, which might be your Internet service provider, a school, an employer, or a website such as Yahoo! Mail or Google.

If you sign up with an ISP, your employer, or your school, you can use a **local email client**, which is installed on your computer or mobile device, to send and receive email. This type of email uses **Post Office Protocol (POP)**, a protocol that downloads messages from an email server for permanent storage on your computer.

You can also set up an account through an online service such as Gmail, and then access your email using a web browser, a system known as **webmail**. This type of email uses **Internet Message Access Protocol (IMAP)**, a protocol that leaves messages on the server, allowing you to access and read email from any device. When you use IMAP, you download a message only when you choose to do so, so you can read messages more quickly than when you use POP.

POP and IMAP are protocols for receiving email messages. **Simple Mail Transfer Protocol (SMTP)** is the protocol for sending all types of email messages.

Create Email Addresses

When you sign up for an email account, your email provider assigns you an email address or asks you to create one. An **email address** has three parts, shown in **Figure 9-8**.

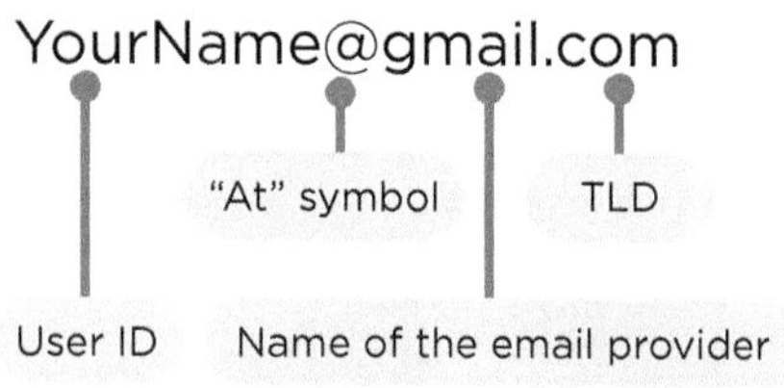

- **User ID**: Typically, this is your name or nickname. Every email address must be unique, however, or email servers couldn't route messages correctly. That's why you see user IDs such as BobJohnson738.
- **"At" symbol**: The @ divides the user ID from the name of the email provider, also called the **domain name**.
- **Domain name**: Although you can often select the user ID, you can't select the domain name because it identifies the email server. The domain name has two parts: the server name, such as Gmail, which is usually the name of the email provider, and the top-level domain (TLD), such as com or net. The server name and TLD are separated by a dot, or a period.

An email address reveals information about the owner. For example, EdMason@gmail.com is probably an address for someone named Ed Mason using a Gmail account. If you're planning to use your email address for job searches or other professional matters, choose a user ID that appears professional. Your email address should not contain your birth year, such as jillsmith98@outlook.com, or any other personal information.

Create Email Messages

Email software displays messages in a two-part form, shown in **Figure 9-9**.

- **Message header**: This part includes the email addresses of the recipients, including those who should receive a courtesy copy (cc). It also includes a subject line to describe the message topic. In addition, the message header can include a blind courtesy copy (bcc) line, which you use to send a message to someone without displaying his or her email address to the other recipients.
- **Message body**: Keep the message itself short. Provide longer text or supplemental information in a separate file, which you can attach to the message. End the message with a signature, which can be your name on its own or with other information, such as your company and phone number.

Figure 9-8: Parts of an email address

YourName@gmail.com

"At" symbol   TLD

User ID   Name of the email provider

#communication

Could your email address be affecting your job hunt? For example, don't use BobBeerGuzzler as the user ID in your email address if you want to be considered for a professional position.

Figure 9-9: Parts of an email message

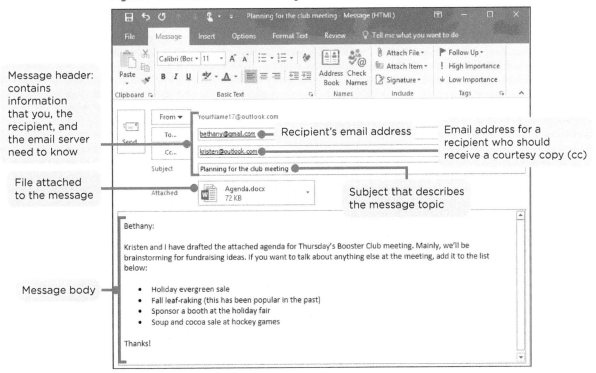

Message header: contains information that you, the recipient, and the email server need to know

File attached to the message

Message body

Recipient's email address

Email address for a recipient who should receive a courtesy copy (cc)

Subject that describes the message topic

Identify Typical Features of Email Software

Email software can be located on your computer or on a web server (for webmail). Such software provides the form for the message and includes buttons for formatting text, setting a priority for the message, and attaching files.

A file, such as a photo or document, you send with an email message is called an **email attachment**. If you receive a message with an attachment, you can save the attachment on your computer or open it to view its contents.

When you send an email message, your email address is included as the return address so your recipients can respond to your message by using the Reply or Reply All feature. Reply sends a response only to the original sender, while Reply All sends a response to the sender and anyone who received courtesy copies, but not blind courtesy copies. After you receive an email message, you can forward it and its attachments to other recipients.

Email software also includes built-in folders for managing messages. For example, the Inbox folder is for messages you have received and the Sent Items folder is for messages you have sent. Most email software also provides a Trash or Deleted Items folder for storing messages you want to delete. To prevent the accidental loss of important messages, you usually keep the messages in the Trash folder until you permanently delete them. You can also create your own folders to help organize messages by topic.

If you want to remove older messages without deleting them, you can archive the messages. **Archiving** moves email messages, usually those older than a specified date, to a file or folder separate from your active email.

Define Electronic Messaging

real-time messaging system | instant messaging (IM) | synchronous communication | contact list | presence technology | online chat | asynchronous communication | Short Message Service (SMS) | Multimedia Messaging Service (MMS) | emoticon | emoji | message board | Internet forum | thread | address book

Electronic messaging is a popular technology for communicating with others, especially when exchanging short messages. See **Figure 9-10** on the next page.

Each message technology has particular benefits (see **Table 9-1** on the next page) and can include text, links, photos, audio files, graphics, and video.

 #communication

To protect your computer from possible viruses, email systems often block files attached to email messages if they have an .exe, .jar, .scr, .cmd, .com, .lib, or .bat file extension.

 **By the Numbers Now**

Email attachments typically have a size limitation. For example, Gmail allows message attachments no larger than 25 MB.

The Bottom Line
- Types of electronic messages you can exchange include text messages, live chat, and forum postings.
- To exchange some types of messages, everyone who is communicating must be online at the same time, while other types involve one person posting a message that someone reads later.

Figure 9-10: Types of electronic messages

A student exchanges instant messages with a friend so they can meet before class.

A consumer joins a chat room where car owners are discussing the pros and cons of a particular car.

A rental agent receives a text message on her smartphone with information about an apartment.

A video game player visits a message board to learn strategies and tips for winning the game.

Table 9-1: Communicating through messaging and chatting

Service	Purpose	Benefits
Text messaging	Send short text messages, usually over cellular networks using mobile phones. You can also send text messages through the web using a desktop or mobile computer.	Send messages to a person or groups quickly.
Chatting	Real-time communication through the Internet between two or more people who are online at the same time.	Have a conversation in real time without using voice. Send links to share information on the web instantly.
Multimedia messaging	Send photos, video, or links to websites with your messages using desktop or mobile devices.	If your computer or mobile device has a camera, you can share your screen and send images and video directly from that device.

Exchange Instant Messages

A system that lets people exchange short messages while they're online is called a **real-time messaging system**. Real-time messaging is called **instant messaging (IM)** for short. Some systems include voice and video options, so you can speak to and see someone online using a microphone and camera built into your computer. Real-time messaging systems are primarily **synchronous communications**, which means that everyone who is communicating must be online at the same time.

You use instant messaging to exchange typed messages with people on your **contact list**, which consists of other IM users you've selected or approved. You can send and receive IMs using a computer, tablet, or a mobile phone and messaging software.

IM uses **presence technology**, which lets one computing device identify the status of another. As a result, you can see when people on your contact list are online. Because IM is a form of quick, casual communication, it is also called **online chat**. IM is a good way to exchange short messages. You might consider using IM if you are running late to meet a friend or want to know what to pick up for dinner;

#communication

Gmail has a built-in online chat feature. To use it, sign in to Gmail, click a link labeled "Start a chat" or something similar, and then enter the name, email address or phone number of the person you want to chat with.

you can send and receive text messages instead of making phone calls. You can also use chat when you need help using software or other products. You usually can visit a company's website and find a box labeled "Chat," where you can exchange messages with a technical support expert. For example, if you are having computer or cellular problems, use a browser to go to the company website (att.com), and then click the Chat Available button when it appears to open the Chat with window. See **Figure 9-11**.

Figure 9-11: Getting help from online chat

Start a chat with an expert who can help you select a smartphone.

AT&T (and other services) ask you to sign in before starting a chat.

Source: att.com

Exchange Text Messages

In contrast to synchronous communications such as instant messaging, **asynchronous communications** involve one person posting a message that someone reads later, as with a text message or forum. **Table 9-2** compares synchronous and asynchronous communications.

Table 9-2: Comparing communication types

Communication type	Requirements	Benefits	Examples
Synchronous communications	Participants must be online at the same time.	Takes place in real time, similar to a phone conversation.	Chat groups, web conferencing, and VoIP
Asynchronous communications	Does not require participants to be online at the same time.	One person can post a message that can later be accessed by one or more recipients.	Email, social networking posts, and text messaging

Text messaging, also called texting or **SMS (Short Message Service)**, is an asynchronous service because it delivers and stores messages until participants decide to view them. Text messaging is similar to IM, except that you typically use it on smartphones, not desktop or mobile computers.

- When you send pictures or video clips along with a text message, you are using the **Multimedia Messaging Service (MMS)**, which is based on SMS.
- You can send messages from your mobile device to another mobile device or to an email address.
- You also can sign up for a website or app to send messages to your mobile device to alert you to breaking news, weather events, or sports scores, for example.
- In addition to text, you can include emoticons and emojis in a message. An **emoticon** is a group of characters or an image that expresses an emotion, such as a colon and closing parenthesis for a smiley face. An **emoji** is an image that expresses an idea or concept, such as a picture of clapping hands to mean congratulations.
- Keep in mind that text messages are short and informal, more well-suited to a simple exchange of comments with a friend than a professional conversation. However, it is appropriate to send short, informational text messages at work when an issue is urgent, needs to be resolved quickly, or requires an immediate response. Avoid using text messages at work for bad news or important decisions, and always use professional language. Emojis, for example, are not appropriate in a professional context.

Use Message Boards and Forums

A **message board**, also called an **Internet forum**, is an online discussion site where people with a common interest participate in a conversation by posting messages. A forum temporarily saves messages and often uses a moderator to approve messages

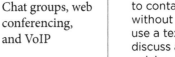 **#communication**

In general, choose the electronic communication type best suited to your situation. For example, to contact someone immediately without disturbing others nearby, use a text message. To converse, discuss a topic, or receive a quick response, use a phone call. To keep a record of exchanged messages, perhaps with attached documents, use email. Of these, email is likely to generate the slowest response.

 By the Numbers Now

WhatsApp is the most popular messaging app in 58% of the countries in the world, according to cnet.com. On a smartphone, you can install WhatsApp to chat without incurring any messaging costs.

 Hot Technology Now

Chat instantly with a group of business colleagues or classmates without installing any software using the website simplemeet.me.

before they are posted for others to read. A **thread** or threaded discussion includes the original message and all the replies. For example, technology companies host forums so that users can get help from experts and other users. Groups such as sports teams, political organizations, and news websites also have message boards to exchange ideas and information.

Use and Share Calendars

Another way to communicate briefly with others is through personal information apps such as electronic calendars and address books. Calendar apps including Google Calendar and iCal let you keep track of appointments and events and communicate with others who need to know the schedule or events in the calendar. Most email software such as Outlook also includes a calendar feature. You can invite others to an event through the calendar. To schedule an appointment or event, you usually select the date on the calendar and then enter details, including the start and end times, location, invitees, notes, and time zone, if necessary. See **Figure 9-12**, which shows the calendar in the Windows 10 Mail app.

You can use calendar software to maintain two or more calendars, such as one for work events and another for personal activities. To view the calendars side by side, you select the calendars, and the software displays each one in a different color. In Outlook, you can also combine the calendars to show the events from each calendar in a different color.

Figure 9-12: Scheduling an event

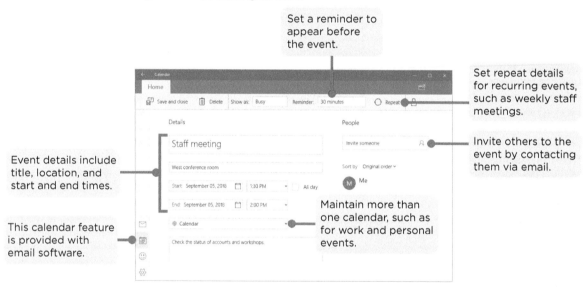

Set a reminder to appear before the event.

Set repeat details for recurring events, such as weekly staff meetings.

Event details include title, location, and start and end times.

Invite others to the event by contacting them via email.

This calendar feature is provided with email software.

Maintain more than one calendar, such as for work and personal events.

To coordinate and communicate activities, you can share calendars with other people. Most calendar software includes a Share feature that lets you enter the email address of the person you want to share your calendar with. That person receives an email invitation to view your calendar, but cannot make changes to it unless you allow them to do so.

By subscribing to a public calendar, many users can access the same events. For example, your soccer club might create a calendar showing practice times and game times and locations. As long as the public calendar meets the standards of your calendar software, you can use your calendar software to read the entries on the public calendar, though you typically cannot add or change entries. Popular calendar standards include CalDAV and iCalendar, which are the types used by Google and Yahoo! calendars, and iCal, which is for the Mac, iPhone, and iPad.

Set Notifications

Most email software can notify you whenever you receive a new message. If you retrieve email on your phone or tablet, a notification can appear on your lock screen. In software such as Outlook, you can set rules for receiving these notifications.

For example, if you want to respond to certain people, such as a family member or client, immediately, you can set a rule that shows email notifications only from specified senders. You can also use other conditions to set rules, such as for messages marked as important or those with certain words in the Subject line. See Figure 9-13.

Figure 9-13: Creating a rule for email notifications

When you receive email from this sender, Outlook will alert you.

Choose how you want Outlook to alert you.

Create Rule ✕

When I get e-mail with all of the selected conditions

☑ Liam Stuart

☐ Subject contains | Studying in Australia

☐ Sent to | yourname@outlook.com | ▼

Do the following

☐ Display in the New Item Alert window

☐ Play a selected sound: | Windows Notify Em | ▶ | ■ | Browse...

☐ Move the item to folder: | Select Folder | Select Folder...

OK | Cancel | Advanced Options...

Calendar software and the calendar feature in email software also let you set up notifications for appointments and reminders. Recent operating systems such as Windows 10 and macOS Sierra also include notification features for appointments, events, and reminders.

When you create an appointment or event, you can set a reminder to display a notification one minute or longer before the event. The notification appears as an on-screen message and is signaled with a sound or vibration depending on your preferences.

Manage Contacts

Most email software provides a tool for keeping track of your contacts, including email correspondents. You can usually store names, email addresses, street addresses, several phone numbers, and other personal information, such as anniversaries and birthdays, in an **address book**, a central location for storing contact information. An address book is associated with a specific email account, so you can maintain more than one address book.

When you create an email message to someone stored as a contact, a full-featured email app such as Outlook or Gmail suggests the email address after you type a few characters in the To line.

Use Podcasts and Online Conferences

podcast | feed | video podcast | streaming media | Really Simple Syndication (RSS) | Rich Site Summary (RSS) | web conference | webinar | video conference | video chat | webcast | Voice over Internet Protocol (VoIP) | Internet telephony

People use communications technology to learn and share information on news and about topics using podcasts, RSS feeds, web conferences, webinars, and video conferences. See Figure 9-14 on the next page.

Use Podcasts

If you miss a lecture or your favorite comedian's stand-up act, you might be able to catch it on a podcast. A **podcast** is an audio or video file stored online and distributed by downloads or through feeds. A **feed** is basically a service that you subscribe to so you can receive frequently updated web content. If you subscribe to a feed, you automatically receive notifications of new podcast episodes as they are produced. If you don't subscribe, you can still access podcast episodes online.

#communication

You can often import contact information you maintain at social networking sites such as Facebook and Google+ into the contacts feature of your email app.

The Bottom Line

- You can download podcasts, which are audio or video files, and play them on your computer, tablet, smartphone, or portable media player.
- To collaborate with others online, you can have a web conference or a webinar.

Hot Technology Now

Download Apple's Podcasts app for iPhone and iPad to enjoy free audio and video podcasts on topics such as technology, business, TED talks, yoga, hobbies, and more.

Figure 9-14: Using podcasts and online conferences

A traveler downloads a podcast to catch up on local news and events while traveling.

A soccer fan subscribes to an RSS feed to keep up with the latest scores and matches.

A businesswoman uses a web conference to discuss her company's sales strategy with out-of-town colleagues.

Unable to attend a class in person, a student attends a webinar instead.

Dmitrijs Dmitrijevs/Shutterstock.com, leedsn/Shutterstock.com, Andrey_Popov/Shutterstock.com, michaeljung/Shutterstock.com

Examples of podcasts include music, radio shows, news stories, classroom lectures, political messages, and comedy routines. **Figure 9-15** shows how to subscribe to an iTunes podcast. A **video podcast** is a file that contains video and audio, and is usually offered as part of a subscription to a podcasting service. After you download an audio or a video podcast, you can listen to it or watch it at any time.

Figure 9-15: Subscribing to an iTunes podcast

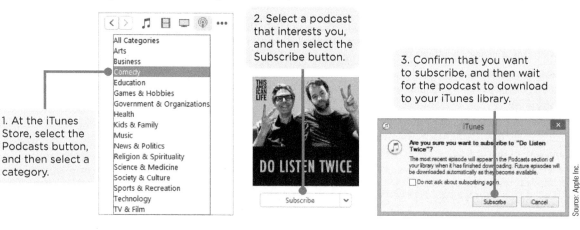

1. At the iTunes Store, select the Podcasts button, and then select a category.

2. Select a podcast that interests you, and then select the Subscribe button.

3. Confirm that you want to subscribe, and then wait for the podcast to download to your iTunes library.

Source: Apple Inc.

You can download a podcast as a file and listen to it or watch it at your convenience or you can stream the media file. With **streaming media**, you start playing the content right away without having to wait for the entire file or broadcast to download to your computer.

Subscribe to RSS Feeds

In addition to podcasts, feeds provide other web content, such as news stories or blogs, delivered directly to your browser or email software. The technology for feeds is called **Really Simple Syndication** or **Rich Site Summary (RSS)**, a data format for distributing online content.

#communication

You can subscribe to podcasts using apps such as iTunes or Podcasts so that podcasts "come to you" when you refresh, update, or sync your mobile device.

RSS content is often free, though you need to subscribe to the feed at the website offering the content you're interested in. Websites with feeds often display the Feeds icon on its webpages. See **Figure 9-16**. To read the content, first install an RSS feed reader such as Feedly (feedly.com) or add the tool to your browser. For example, you can add RSS Feed Reader to Google Chrome using the Chrome Store.

To subscribe to the feed, click the Feeds icon or a Subscribe link on the webpage.

Attend Web Conferences and Webinars

Suppose you're working on a business project with a team that includes people in different cities or countries. To collaborate on the project, you can have a **web conference**, a meeting that takes place on the web.

Web conferences typically are held on computers or mobile phones. Participants use web conferencing software to sign into the same webpage. One user acts as the host and shares his or her desktop with the group. During the online session, the host can display a document that participants see at the same time. If the host edits the document, everyone sees the changes as they are made.

To send typed messages to each other, participants can use a chat window. Finally, participants might also join a conference phone call or use microphones and speakers attached to their computers to speak to each other.

A **webinar**, short for web-based seminar, is a type of online conference in which a presenter gives a lecture, demonstration, workshop, or other type of instructional activity. Some webinars involve one-way communication, in which the presenter speaks and demonstrates and the audience listens. Other webinars are more interactive and collaborative, especially if they allow polling to survey the audience on a topic or if they let participants ask and answer questions.

Webinars and web conferences often include slide show presentations and videos. Some include electronic whiteboards, where participants can record and save notes, and provide tools for activities such as brainstorming and problem solving.

Hot Technology Now

One way to subscribe to RSS feeds is within email software such as Microsoft Outlook 365. Unlike browsers, email software updates the feed when you sync or receive email messages.

Hot Technology Now

Share your screen with up to 10 friends or colleagues during a free collaborative webinar using websites such as join.me.

Attend Video Conferences

Similar to a web conference, a **video conference** allows people at two or more locations to meet electronically using a network such as the Internet to transmit video and audio data. To participate in a video conference, you need to have a video camera, microphone, and speakers or headphones attached to your computer. Because video conferences let many people from different geographic locations meet electronically, they are different from video phone calls, which connect only two people online. A video conference always allows participants to see and hear each other, while a web conference does not.

Video chat is a face-to-face conversation held over a network such as the Internet using a webcam, microphone, speakers, display device, and special software. Video chat is used in businesses and education for **webcasts** (video broadcasts of an event transmitted across the Internet). It is also a popular way for people to stay in touch with friends and relatives who live far away.

You can use smartphones for video chatting as well as desktop, laptop, and tablet computers with an Internet connection, microphone, and webcam. You cannot have a video chat over a landline phone. Video chatting software lets you control the images that appear onscreen, voice and sound volume, and other features. Chatters without a webcam can participate in the chat, but won't be seen on screen by other chatters.

#communication

Skype is a Windows 10 app for making video and voice calls. To use it, set up a Skype account. Add contacts by searching for them using their email address or Skype account name. Click the contact to call that person, and then click the camera icon to make a video call or the phone icon to make a phone call. You can leave a message if the person is offline.

Use Voice Over IP

Voice over Internet Protocol (VoIP) refers to voice communications over the Internet, and is sometimes called **Internet telephony**. In the past, voice communications traveled only along phone lines. Communications or telephone companies charged for phone calls, usually on a minute-by-minute rate, based on the distance or time of the call. With the Internet, voice can travel through the same network lines that carry webpages and other Internet services. Just as you pay for email services, not each message you

send, you also pay for VoIP services, not each phone call you make. In fact, many Internet service providers (ISPs) now offer phone services; if you have a phone number through your ISP, you are using VoIP.

- VoIP providers include Vonage, Skype, Grasshopper, and Google. Often calls from one country to another are included in your monthly Internet fee.
- VoIP allows you to receive calls on your computer from landline or cell phones and to place calls from your computer to these phones.
- You can use different devices to make VoIP calls as long as the device has a speaker and a microphone. Devices can include landline phones, smartphones, laptops, tablets, and even desktop computers.
- If you have a webcam, VoIP technology lets you include video in your calls.

Use Blogs and Wikis

blog | blogger | blogging software | blogosphere | vlog | blog aggregator | microblog | live blog | wiki | blogware | content management system | post | pageview | About page | tag | label | hashtag

If you like to keep up with the latest social, family, and career news, as well as share information with others, you can take advantage of the power of the web by using blogs and wikis. See **Figure 9-17**.

Use Blogs

Suppose you spend your free time learning how to make desserts. In fact, you're thinking of becoming a pastry chef. How can you tell the world about your experiences? Start a blog. A **blog**, short for web log, is a webpage listing journal entries with commentary and information, usually about a particular interest. The author of a blog, also called a **blogger**, uses **blogging software**, available at sites such as Blogger.com, to create and publish entries.

Blogs can contain text, photos, video clips, and links to additional information. See **Figure 9-18**. If a blog isn't private, all you need is the web address to access it. Otherwise, you need permission from the blogger to read entries. Because a blogger can post at any time and doesn't need to be online when readers are, a blog is considered asynchronous communication. Visitors can read and comment on the blog entries but cannot change them.

Identify Types of Blogs

In the **blogosphere**, which is the worldwide collection of blogs, blogs vary by media, length, and purpose. Many blog authors post entries consisting of mostly text, though authors of video blogs, or **vlogs**, such as YouTube mainly post video clips, and authors of photo blogs mainly post photos. **Blog aggregators** such as Flipboard and News 360 locate information from many online sources, including blogs.

A **microblog** allows users to publish short messages, usually between 100 and 200 characters, for others to read, making it a combination of text messaging and blogging. For example, Twitter allows messages up to 140 characters. News media use microblogs to broadcast short messages, including headlines, to their readers. Cities and other municipalities use microblogs to send wireless emergency alerts through cellphones and systems, such as Nixle, including alerts about traffic, severe weather, and missing persons, for example.

- Businesses create blogs to communicate with employees, customers, and vendors.
- Personal blogs often focus on family life, social life, or a personal interest or project, such as building a house or planting a garden.
- Other blogs can include commentary on news and politics and are an outlet for citizen journalists, members of the public who report on current events. Citizen journalists often produce **live blogs**, which are blogs that comment on an event while it is taking place, usually in the form of frequent short updates.

Blog posts are dated and then listed in reverse-chronological order on the site.

Blogs can contain text, photos, and links to additional information.

The Roaming Kitchen blogger posted this entry about making hot chocolate.

Click the Read More link to continue reading this post.

Click a tag (a topic link) to display other blog posts on this topic.

Six people have commented on this post; click the link to read the comments or leave one of your own.

Source: theroamingkitchen.net

A sales clerk at an electronics store loves gadgets, so he starts a blog to let his friends know about the latest smartphones and tablets.

Create Blogs

To create, edit, and maintain a blog, you use blogging software, also known as **blogware**. This type of software is classified as a **content management system**, software that lets a group of users maintain and publish content of all kinds, but especially for websites. Blogware provides graphics, photos, standard text, and tools for web publication and comment posting and moderation.

Popular blogware includes Blogger and WordPress. Google runs Blogger as a service that publishes blogs with time-stamped articles, or **posts**. A blog consists of separate pages, which are webpages displaying a single post. Your home page lists many posts with the most recent ones at the top of the list. To create a blog in Blogger:

1. Sign into Blogger using a Google account, and then select the New Blog button.

2. Enter a title and web address for the blog, and then select a template, which provides basic design elements such as colors, fonts, and graphics.

3. Use Blogger's tools to write and publish a post, add images and videos, customize the design, and view the activity on your blog, such as the number of **pageviews**, which indicates the number of times your blog has been viewed in a browser.

After creating a home page, you should create an **About page**, which is where you describe yourself, list any relevant experience or skills, and insert a photo and display name. If you assign your blog to one or more categories, which characterize your content in general, the category list appears on the About page. Anyone on the web can learn more about you and your blog by visiting your About page.

To attract an audience to your blog, you include tags and links to other webpages. A **tag** (also called a **label**) is a key term associated with a post. For example, if you publish a post on how to decorate a cake, one tag might be "cake decoration," so that people looking for steps for decorating a cake can find your blog post.

A recent graduate is moving across the country for a new job and is recording her experiences in a video blog.

Use Microblogs

Twitter, Tumblr, and Instagram are examples of microblogging websites where you can post short text messages, links, photos, and videos from a smartphone or other computing device. Microblogs help you keep track of topics that interest you and let you repost content from other users. Most also notify you if another user reposts your content. All of the content is for public consumption.

Another student is using a microblog to exchange information with future graduates about careers and employers.

The most successful microbloggers post content at least once a day, including personal updates or observations, brief opinion statements, links to online content, reactions to events, and other types of short information. To receive posts from microbloggers, you follow them. New messages appear as soon as they are posted, which makes microblogs popular for people participating in the same activity, such as watching a sporting event. Like blogs, microblogs provide a way to categorize posts into topics or conversations so that other people can easily search for other posts about those topics. Instead of tags, microblogs use **hashtags**, a type of tag that starts with a hash symbol (#) and does not allow spaces. For example, #StudyAbroad-Sydney, indicates that the post is of interest to users who are studying or want to study in Sydney. Social networking sites such as Twitter, Facebook, Google+, and Instagram also use hashtags.

Use Wikis

A **wiki** is a collaborative website that members of a group can access and edit using a web browser. If you want to change something posted on the wiki, you typically select an Edit button or link and then make the change so other users can see it. All group members can make changes to the wiki, which is one thing that makes a wiki different from a blog: readers of a blog can comment on, but not modify, a blogger's posts.

Identify Types of Wikis

If you've ever used a search engine to look up a definition of a term or the meaning of a phrase, you've probably visited Wikipedia, one of the largest wikis on the web. Wikipedia is a free online encyclopedia with millions of articles. About 126,000 users contribute to Wikipedia by writing, editing, and reviewing articles. You can edit articles by creating a Wikipedia account and then signing in. See **Figure 9-19**.

#communication

Wikis get their name from the Hawaiian phrase "wiki wiki," meaning "quick," because wikis let you collaborate online quickly and easily.

Figure 9-19: Reading and contributing to a wiki

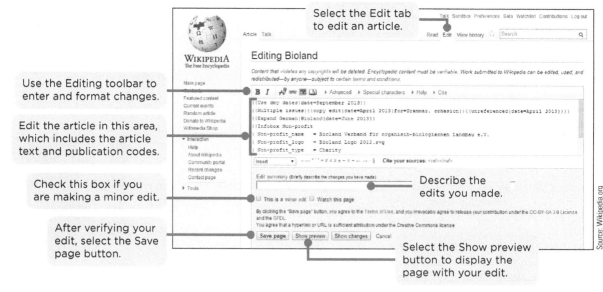

Hot Technology Now

Wikispaces Classroom (wikispaces .com) is designed as an online workspace where students can communicate and work as teams.

Wikipedia is open to the public, but some wikis restrict access to members only. For example, students and teachers often use private educational wikis to collaborate on projects. Researchers use wikis to share findings, offer and receive suggestions, and test their work. Businesses also use wikis, especially when employees are not all in the same physical location. As with blogs, people use wikis to share their knowledge, experience, and point of view.

Define Social Networks

social network | profile | clip | group | community | Timeline | Facebook friend

A **social network** is a website that links people via the Internet to form an online community. Facebook, Instagram, Google+, and LinkedIn are examples of social networks. To join a social network, you provide a name and password and complete an online form to create a virtual identity, or **profile**, which includes information you choose to describe yourself.

You can expand your profile to describe your interests and activities and invite friends to visit your page. Friends can leave messages for you, and you can keep in touch with them by including links to your blog or wiki and by sharing media such as photos and videos.

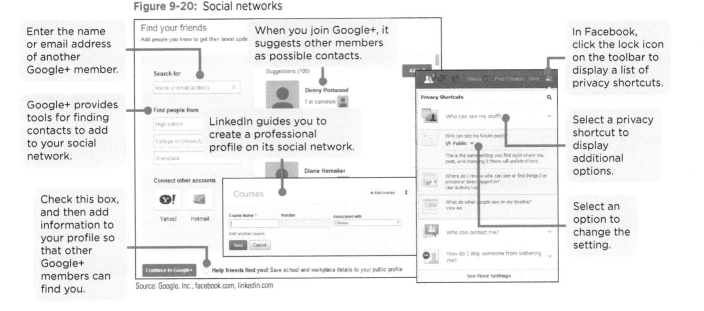

Figure 9-20: Social networks

Enter the name or email address of another Google+ member.

Google+ provides tools for finding contacts to add to your social network.

Check this box, and then add information to your profile so that other Google+ members can find you.

When you join Google+, it suggests other members as possible contacts.

LinkedIn guides you to create a professional profile on its social network.

In Facebook, click the lock icon on the toolbar to display a list of privacy shortcuts.

Select a privacy shortcut to display additional options.

Select an option to change the setting.

Source: Google, Inc., facebook.com, linkedin.com

Identify Types of Social Networks

Posting messages and finding friends on Facebook is perfect for some people, but what if your main interest is sharing photos or videos? There are social networks for that. On photo-sharing sites such as Instagram, Imgur, Flickr, Photobucket, and Shutterfly, you can post photos and then organize them into albums, add tags, and invite comments. On Instagram, followers "LIKE" photos. Popular Instagramers can have tens of thousands of followers and are Internet sensations building businesses from their social profiles and posts. Organizations and businesses use social networks like Instagram to build brand loyalty and a customer base.

Video-sharing sites such as YouTube and Vimeo provide a place where you can post short videos called **clips**. You can set up a post so that anyone, or only people you invite, can view or comment on your clip.

Other social networks focus on the types of connections you can expect to make on the site. For example, on a professional networking website, such as LinkedIn, you keep in touch with colleagues, clients, employers, and other work-related or business contacts. In addition, sites such as LinkedIn provide skills training, endorsements, and tools for hiring freelancers.

LinkedIn is a valuable social network for businesses, especially those who want to market a product or service. Businesses can do so by creating a company page, building connections to customers and clients, and keeping the page up to date. To take a more active approach, businesses can join groups, post answers to user questions, advertise, and write articles.

By the Numbers Now

To view the 1.3 billion faces of Facebook, click to see profile pictures at app.thefacesofface-book.com.

On the Job Now

If you are considering a job in education, visit teachertube.com to find educational resources including videos and presentations.

Use Social Networks

One reason everyone seems to belong to a social network is that joining is so easy. All you need is a web browser and a computer, smartphone, tablet, or other device connected to the Internet.

To use social networking:

1. Join a social network and create a profile.

2. Use the site's privacy settings to determine how much personal information you want to share and with whom.

3. Create a network by inviting people to "follow you", "be your Friend" or "join your network or circle."

Social networking sites usually provide tools described in Table 9-3.

Table 9-3: Social networking tools

Tool	Description
Edit Profile	Personalize your posts and comments, such as by adding a photo to your profile.
Find Friends or Followers	Search for members who share your interests and compile a list of contacts from other sources such as your email address book.
Create Group	Form a group or community, which is a collection of people who share a particular background or interest. Groups can be public (open to anyone), or private (restricted viewing and access, where you have to accept a request to join).
Check In	Use the Check In feature to identify your current location so that you can meet nearby friends and family members or keep track of your travels.
Timeline	Display personalized content from your profile and posts. In Facebook, the Timeline lists posts with the most recent content at the top of the list.
Friends or Contacts	On Facebook, contacts are called Facebook friends; you can display a list of friends by selecting the Search box, and then selecting My Friends. You can also designate some friends specifically as family or as close friends—these are the contacts you keep in touch with the most.
News Feed or Network	Read about the activities of your contacts. On Facebook, this feature is called News Feed. On LinkedIn, it's called Network, and on Google+, it's called home stream.

#communication

In Facebook, change your privacy settings to limit who can see your posts. Change the setting to review all content that tags you before the content is posted.

Exchange Messages on Social Networks

If you have something to say, you can find a quick way to say it on a social network. Most social networking sites let members post messages on the pages of other members, which is ideal when they are not online at the same time. Select privacy settings to determine who can send you a message and who can post on your Timeline or tag you in other posts. For each post, you can decide whether the post is visible to the public, to only your friends and friends of friends, or only within your friends' network. If you are online at the same time as another member, you can use a chat feature to exchange text messages or engage in a video chat to see and speak to another member.

Some social networks let you broadcast text, photos, video, and other content as you post it. For example, you can use Hangouts on Air in Google+ to let the public or selected members know what you're thinking and doing.

Businesses participate in social networks to encourage consumers to connect to their company by posting messages with questions, comments, and ratings.

Evaluate Social Networking

Social networking can threaten your privacy. You reveal personal information when you join and use a social network, and your online activity may be tracked or used by people seeking to advertise or do harm. If you use social networks, evaluate the risk and the potential benefits of interacting with other people online. For example, by using the Check In feature on many social networks, you broadcast that you are not home at the same time you identify your whereabouts. Businesses count on the check-in feature to promote their museum, activity, restaurant, hotel or other place.

In general, the security tools you use to keep your computer safe, such as antivirus software, protect your system while you're participating in a social network. The main safety concern is privacy. Once your content is posted, you lose control of it; for example, a photo or comment can make its way across the world and be replicated millions of times in a flash. A big part of social networks is sharing personal details, but remember that those details could be available to other audiences you may not have intended, including current and future employers.

- Write and act professionally on social networks, and post only comments and images that are appropriate for a full range of contacts, from friends to employers.
- Consider how much information you're willing to share online, and adjust your privacy settings accordingly.
- All social networks have privacy policies. Read each policy so you know how the website itself uses your personal information.

On the Job Now

Marketing a business using Facebook, LinkedIn, and Twitter has an enormous potential. Set up a strategy to market new products, connect with your customers, and offer special services or discounts to your social network followers.

Follow Internet Etiquette Guidelines

etiquette | netiquette | emoticon | flaming | cyberbullying | cyberstalking | online reputation

When you're meeting friends, interacting with family, and working with colleagues, you're guided by rules for acceptable behavior, or **etiquette**. Even if much of your communication is now online, you still need to follow similar dos and don'ts that help make your online interactions civil and productive.

When you abide by the rules of **netiquette**, short for Internet etiquette, you follow a set of guidelines for acceptable online communication:

- Treat others as you want them to treat you. If you wouldn't say something to a person's face, don't write in an electronic message.
- Be polite in your online communications. Avoid wording that might seem offensive, passive-aggressive, suggestive, or argumentative. Take care when using humor or sarcasm, which can be misinterpreted easily.
- Take a neutral stance on controversial subjects, especially political ones.
- Read your messages before sending them and correct errors in spelling, grammar, and tone.
- Consider email as public communication, because people might forward your message to others without your knowledge.

The Bottom Line
- Knowing the rules for online communication means you can express yourself without being misunderstood.
- Following the rules helps you develop beneficial personal and professional relationships and engage in online conversations that are constructive, friendly, and enjoyable.

Follow Guidelines for Professional Messaging

Originally, text messaging and chat were a new way to take advantage of emerging technology to exchange messages among friends. Because they're now valuable business tools as well, you need to follow the professional guidelines listed in Table 9-4 when sending IMs at work or participating in company chat rooms.

#communication

Rule #1 for netiquette: Remember that a human being is on the other side of your communication.

Table 9-4: Guidelines for professional messaging

Message element	Examples	Guidelines
Abbreviations	TTFN BRB	Abbreviations such as LMK ("let me know") or BRB ("be right back") are too informal for professional communications.
Emoticons		An **emoticon** is a symbol for an emotional gesture, such as a smile or frown that you create using keyboard characters or insert as an image. Emoticons are very informal, so you should use them only in casual messages.
Personal information	"I've never told anyone this, but I really don't like our boss."	Avoid revealing personal information in Internet forums. You can't verify the identities of the participants, and you don't know how they might handle personal information.

Yayayoyo/Shutterstock.com, Teguh Mujiono/Shutterstock.com

On the Job Now

Never use shorthand abbreviations such as LOL when writing to a customer or client. Apart from sounding too casual, you risk the possibility of people thinking you are simply too busy to write to them properly.

#communication

Go to twitter.com, search for @SAMTechNow, the book's Twitter account, and then follow @SAMTechNow to get tweets on your home page.

Follow Guidelines for Blogs

If you participate in blogs as someone who posts entries or makes comments, you should be aware of blog guidelines for both roles:

- As a blogger, you're publishing information online that others might rely on to make decisions. Make sure the information you post is accurate and up to date.
- Acknowledge any connections you have with companies and people you endorse. If you review travel destinations, for example, and a hotel gives you a free vacation, disclose that information when you post a review of the hotel.
- As a commenter, read the commenting guidelines on the blog, which usually encourage you to use good judgment and basic courtesy.
- In particular, don't engage in flaming, which is posting hostile or insulting comments about another online participant.

Guidelines for Personal Social Networking

The fundamentals of netiquette apply to social networks just as they apply in other online communications:

- Respect other participants.
- Introduce yourself and get to know other members before adding them as friends. Show consideration for their time by keeping your messages short and focused.
- Before posting a comment, ask yourself how readers will react to it. If it is offensive, don't post it.
- Do not post annoying or unwelcome messages or other information that may be considered harassment, or cyberbullying.
- Do not use social networks to monitor or keep track of a member's activities or whereabouts, which could be considered cyberstalking.
- Protect your online reputation, which is information about you that others can find on the Internet. Make sure your posts won't embarrass you someday.

Guidelines for Professional Social Networking

Businesses are turning to social networks as a productive way for employees to connect with each other and with customers. If you are using a social network on the job, keep in mind the dos and don'ts listed in Table 9-5 to build professional relationships and convey an image appropriate for your organization.

Table 9-5: Dos and don'ts for using social networks in business

Do	Don't
Create a profile for your professional connections apart from your personal ones. In the professional profile, use your full name and a photo of yourself (not a pseudonym or photo of your pet, for example).	Invite visitors to play games or join other activities that could waste their time.
Offer information that visitors to your page will find valuable. Understand who visits your page (such as colleagues or clients), and adjust the content for these visitors.	Post anything that you don't want a future or current boss, colleague, client, or other professional contact to read.
Learn about the people who want to follow you or be your friends. Doing so is good business and helps you avoid an embarrassing connection.	Publish posts or comments when you are not yourself, such as when you are tired or angry.
Post photos, messages, and videos that reflect your professional image and appropriate online reputation.	Publish posts or comments about controversial subjects that others might find offensive.

Chapter Review

Define Digital Communication

1. Name four types of digital communication.
2. What is a communications system?
3. What is the difference between a Wi-Fi network and a cellular network?

Define Email

4. Describe the five steps involved in sending an email message.
5. What is the main difference between the two types of email accounts you can use?
6. Explain the two main parts of an email message.

Define Electronic Messaging

7. What is a real-time messaging system? Give an example of such a system.
8. What is presence technology and how is it used in electronic messaging?
9. Which three features does email software often provide besides working with messages?

Use Podcasts and Online Conferences

10. Describe how you might use a podcast and feed.
11. What is the difference between a web conference and a webinar?
12. Define Voice over IP (VoIP). Explain how it differs from cellular phone technology.

Use Blogs and Wikis

13. What is a blog and what kind of content does it provide?
14. What is a wiki and what kind of content does it provide?
15. In what circumstances would you use a microblog?

Define Social Networks

16. What is important about your profile on a social network?
17. Describe four types of tools a social network typically provides.
18. Identify and describe the risk should you be aware of when deciding to use social networks.

Follow Internet Etiquette Guidelines

19. What are three rules for Internet etiquette?
20. Name three actions to avoid when participating in a social network for professional purposes.

Test Your Knowledge Now

1. A(n) _____ sends electronic data from a source to a destination.
   a. communications system
   b. email address
   c. protocol
   d. netiquette

2. _____ networks use 3G and 4G wireless communications standards.
   a. Wi-Fi
   b. Cellular
   c. TCP/IP
   d. VoIP

3. Computers and devices that communicate using radio waves across a distance of 100 to 900 feet use _____.
   a. TCP/IP
   b. LTE
   c. radar
   d. Wi-Fi

4. The main computer in an email system is an email _____, which routes email messages through the Internet or a private network.
   a. server
   b. account
   c. client
   d. network

5. A service that uses the _____ protocol leaves email messages on the server, allowing you to access and read email from any device.
   a. Temporary Mail Storage Protocol (TMSP)
   b. Post Office Protocol (POP)
   c. Internet Message Access Protocol (IMAP)
   d. Simple Mail Transfer Protocol (SMTP)

6. In an email address, the _____ identifies the email server.
   a. domain name
   b. user ID
   c. account name
   d. @ (at) symbol

7. Instant messaging uses _____, which lets you see when people on your contact list are online.
   a. synchronous communications
   b. presence technology
   c. asynchronous communications
   d. profile technology

8. Real-time messaging is also called _____ messaging.
   a. instant
   b. wiki
   c. micro
   d. forum

9. _____ communications involves one person posting a message that someone reads later, as with a text message or forum.
   a. Asynchronous
   b. Synchronous
   c. Instant
   d. Atypical

10. A _____ is an audio or video file stored online and distributed by downloads or through feeds.
    a. protocol
    b. podcast
    c. blog post
    d. video chat

11. On an Internet forum, a _____ includes the original message and all the replies.
    a. feed
    b. thread
    c. stream
    d. wiki

12. _____ refers to voice communications over the Internet.
    a. RSS
    b. VoIP
    c. MMS
    d. IM

13. A _____ allows users to post short messages, usually between 100 and 200 characters, for others to read.
    a. short blog
    b. vlog
    c. microblog
    d. webcast

14. Blogs publish time-stamped articles, also called _____.
    a. tweets
    b. feeds
    c. timelines
    d. posts

15. All group members can make changes to a(n) _____, while readers of a blog can comment on, but not modify, a blogger's posts.
    a. profile
    b. microblog
    c. wiki
    d. RSS feed

16. A _____ network is a website that links people via the Internet to form an online community.
    a. social
    b. real-time
    c. messaging
    d. blogosphere

17. To join a social network, you provide a name and password and complete an online form to create a virtual identity, also called a _____.
    a. profile
    b. circle
    c. hashtag
    d. friend

18. "Treat others online as you want them to treat you" is an example of _____.
    a. cyberbullying
    b. netiquette
    c. flaming
    d. online reputation

19. Using a social network to monitor or keep track of a member's activities or whereabouts is called _____.
    a. presence awareness
    b. social monitoring
    c. phishing
    d. cyberstalking

20. Your _____ is information about you that others can find on the Internet.
    a. user ID
    b. hashtag
    c. online reputation
    d. privacy policy

21. In the space next to each statement below, write the letter of the term that defines it.
    a. feed
    b. webmail
    c. blog
    d. hashtag
    e. profile

    _____ An informal website of time-stamped articles written in a journal format

    _____ A service that you subscribe to so you can receive frequently updated web content

    _____ A system for accessing your email using a web browser

    _____ A name and password you provide to create a virtual identity

    _____ A way to categorize posts into topics or conversations on a microblog

Try This Now

1: Your Online Image Speaks Volumes

A majority of business communications take place online. Making a strong impression digitally is just as important as a face-to-face meeting.

   a. Considering that most communication is formal, list five general netiquette rules to follow when creating formal email communications.
   b. During a video conference you are meeting a customer for the first time. List five guidelines to create a very positive impression.
   c. Record the rules and guidelines in a document, save the document, and then submit it to your instructor.

2: Conducting Research Using YouTube

A free Gmail account is necessary to complete this assignment.

YouTube has hundreds of thousands of free educational and entertaining videos at youtube.com. As you research a topic for a class project, you can focus your search within the educational portion of YouTube to make sure you are using an academic source.

    a. Open a browser and then visit youtube.com. Sign into YouTube.com with a Gmail account and search for HoloLens.

    b. Watch four HoloLens videos on youtube.com that are not listed as ads. Write one or two sentences summarizing each of the four video topics.

    c. Locate the Browse channels tool on the YouTube site. Search for channels with technology products such as technology companies, online magazines, and your favorite technology products. Subscribe to three different channels. Open each channel and take a screenshot of each of the three pages showing the recent videos on that channel. Add the screenshots to the Word document.

    d. Save the document and submit it to your instructor.

3: Business Marketing Plan for Facebook

Marketing a local business on Facebook could help that business be a success. Instead of posting random Facebook comments, your employer has requested that you create a digital Facebook marketing plan.

    a. Research the creation of a marketing plan for Facebook. Create a one-page, double-spaced document written in your own words that serves as a Facebook marketing plan for any small business.

    b. Provide three links of Facebook business pages that create an exceptional business connection to customers.

    c. Save the document and submit it to your instructor.

Facebook Plan

tanuha2001/Shutterstock.com

Critical Thinking Now

1: Apple Product Support Blog

Companies want to foster the two-way communication between customers and company representatives. Using product support blogs, customers can find product information quickly on their own or they can ask a direct question. Apple has a product support blog for their product line located at the website discussions.apple.com/welcome. Open the website in any browser and navigate through the product pages. In a document of at least 150 words, write an overview of what this product support blog offers to customers.

2: Massive Open Online Courses (MOOCs)

The term "MOOC" can be defined as an online course aimed at an unlimited audience with open access via the Internet. Some MOOCs provide a social platform that provides the class with a way to communicate and ask the professor questions. Research the topic of MOOCs. In a document of at least 100 of your own words, describe MOOC communications. Open the website www.edx.org, a MOOC that partners with MIT, Harvard, Berkeley, and others. Take a screenshot of the course topics offered and place the screenshot in the Word document. If you were to take a course from EdX, locate and take a screenshot of the course that would interest you. Explain why you are interested in the course. Place the screenshot and your response in the Word document and submit to your instructor.

3: LinkedIn Profile

As you prepare for searching for a job, you need to create a digital professional presence on LinkedIn. Write a list of 10 dos and five don'ts regarding how to best market yourself on LinkedIn.

Ethical Issues Now

The right to be forgotten is now being observed in the European Union and Argentina for those who feel misrepresented by search results that are no longer accurate or relevant. For instance, people and companies can ask search engines such as Google to delink information about old financial matters. If the search engine approves the request, the information remains online at the original site, but no longer is listed under certain search engine queries.

Right to Be Forgotten

Evan Lorne/Shutterstock.com

    a. With the realization that incorrect or old information can affect your professional career, research the topic and then write 150 words stating your opinion about the right to be forgotten.

    b. As a search engine company, the removal of the "forgotten information" is time consuming and expensive, and introduces a legal liability. Write 100 of your own words explaining how the search engine companies should allocate resources to remove the links requested for deletion.

Team Up Now—Sharing Your Desktop with Your Team

Discuss a date and time that you can connect with your team online using join.me, a free technology for teams of up to nine people. The join.me website provides desktop sharing, voice communication, and online chat on a Windows or Mac platform. Establish one person as the team leader, the person who will share a desktop with the other team members and will begin the session at join.me. Open a browser and then go to join.me. The team leader must first start the free trial meeting and send out an email or a text message to the team sharing a nine-digit number. The other team members should type the nine-digit number into the "join meeting" text box to begin viewing their team leader's desktop.

    a. When everyone on the team has arrived in join.me, each team member should search for other screen sharing platforms used in business today for video conferencing such as Skype for Business and Google Hangouts. Discuss what features each of these products offer.

    b. Collaborate to research how screen-sharing and video conferencing tools could be productive in the business place. Create a list of 10 business activities or features of business screen-sharing tools that your team locates during your research using join.me.

    c. Take a screenshot with all the team members' names listed and submit the list and screenshot to your instructor.

Key Terms

3G
4G
802.16 standard
About page
address book
archiving
asynchronous communication
base station
blog
blog aggregator
blogger
blogging software
blogosphere
blogware
carrier
cell
cell phone
cell tower
cellular network
clip
communications software
communications system
community
contact list
content management system
cyberbullying
cyberstalking
digital communications
domain name
email account
email address
email attachment
email client
email message

email provider
email server
email service
email system
emoji
emoticon
etiquette
Facebook friend
feed
flaming
group
hashtag
instant messaging (IM)
Internet forum
Internet Message Access
   Protocol (IMAP)
Internet telephony
label
live blog
local email client
Long-Term Evolution (LTE)
message board
microblog
mobile phone
Multimedia Messaging Service (MMS)
netiquette
online chat
online reputation
online social network
pageview
phablet
podcast
post
Post Office Protocol (POP)

presence technology
profile
protocol
Really Simple Syndication (RSS)
real-time messaging system
Rich Site Summary (RSS)
router
Short Message Service (SMS)
Simple Mail Transfer Protocol
   (SMTP)
smartphone
social network
store-and-forward technology
streaming media
subscriber identity module
   (SIM) card
synchronous communication
tablet
tag
TCP/IP
thread
Timeline
video chat
video conference
video podcast
vlog
Voice over Internet Protocol (VoIP)
web conference
webcast
webinar
webmail
wiki
WiMAX
wireless fidelity (Wi-Fi)

Information Literacy

Shawna is taking a challenging healthcare class. Online research helps her to find the most recent medical studies for her clinical exam reports.

Internet, Shawna
at her own pace
nbarrassment,
atch videos,
r almost any

iStockphoto.com/Wavebreakmedia

Keeping an "A" average in her healthcare class is important to Shawna. With her tablet, she is discovering how to use the Internet to find the latest medical studies. Using free academic websites such as khanacademy.org and wolframalpha.com, Shawna can learn how to research her clinical exam reports at 2 a.m. or any other time of day.

Find Online Information

surface web | public web | visible web | restricted site | deep web | hidden web | invisible web | database | dark web

The Bottom Line

- The surface web is huge, but it does not include sites that require a membership or subscription.
- News sites supply us with breaking stories as they are happening, but they often don't give us in-depth analysis.
- You can rely on scholarly sites for accurate, in-depth information that has been researched and reviewed by experts.

The web is a vast library of information contained in more than one billion sites. With so many sites, it can be difficult to know if the information you find is reliable. To find what you need on the web, you should understand the types of resources the web provides.

Find Information on the Surface Web

Suppose you need to give a presentation on green technology for a course you're taking. You would probably start by using Google to search for green technology and then look over the results. The websites listed in the results are on the **surface web**, which includes sites that are freely available to the public and can be searched by standard search engines. The surface web is also called the **public web** or the **visible web**.

General search engines such as Google can access nearly eight billion webpages, which is one of the benefits of the surface web. However, open websites can come and go, so you can't rely on them as permanent sources of information. Furthermore, surface web content changes frequently and has not always been reviewed or evaluated by experts. You need to know how to determine whether the information you find on the web is dependable and useful.

Figure 10-1: Finding reliable information on the web

In ancient Egypt, the Library of Alexandria's goal was to collect all the knowledge in the ancient world.

Today, we are attempting to collect all of the modern world's knowledge on the web. But the web is so vast that no one is certain how many sites it contains.

Search tools can help you search the web to find information. You can then evaluate the information to see if it fills your needs.

leoks/Shutterstock.com, Angela Waye/Shutterstock.com, jannoon028/Shutterstock.com

By the Numbers Now

As of this writing, the top five most visited news websites according to TopTere include, in order, The New York Times, Huffington Post, The Daily Mail, Forbes, and Fox News. The TopTere rankings are updated monthly.

Access Restricted Sites

Suppose you're in your school library and want to gather information for your presentation on green technology. When you use the library's online system to search for green technology, the results are significantly different from Google's. The websites in the library's search results are **restricted sites** because they require a subscription or other type of paid membership. See **Figure 10-2**. Restricted sites require you to sign in with a username and a password before you can access some or all of material on the site. These sites are part of the **deep web**, also called the **hidden web** or the **invisible web**.

Search engines can't access some pages on these restricted sites because they're part of **databases** (collections of information) such as library catalogs or article collections

Figure 10-2: Restricted site

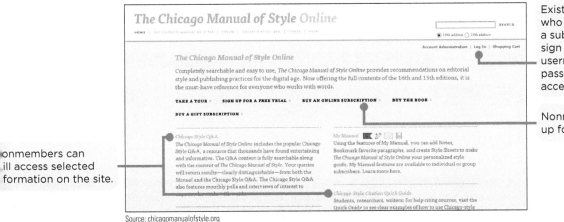

Existing members who have paid for a subscription can sign in with their username and password to gain access.

Nonmembers can sign up for a new subscription.

Nonmembers can still access selected information on the site.

Source: chicagomanualofstyle.org

that require passwords or subscriptions for searching. The number of restricted sites is estimated to be many times larger than the number of sites on the surface web.

Benefits of the deep web are that identified experts develop most of the resources, so they are fairly reliable, and that most resources are part of permanent collections. Publishers and libraries make agreements with search engines so the public can access their restricted sites.

However, a part of the deep web is used for illegal activities. The **dark web** is also not reached by search engines, and includes hacking groups, traffic in hoaxes, scams, terrorism, and illegal drugs, pornography, and animal trade.

Use News Sites

During a major event such as a weather disaster or national election, you can go to news sites and news apps to get quick, often instant, information.

- **Television, radio, and other media** provide up-to-date information on their websites, including videos and photos.
- **Print newspapers** and magazines also provide online versions of their articles.
- **News apps** are apps that you can install on your tablet or smartphone; most television and radio stations and print newspapers have news apps.

The day of a major event, news sites report facts as they occur, such as the spread of a flood or the number of votes recorded. Information is incomplete because the event is ongoing. Shortly after a major event, news sites report the results and provide details, such as the amount of damage a tropical storm caused. Sometimes you can view today's content for free but need to subscribe to the site to look at back issues or other special features.

Although news sites are excellent resources for facts and immediate reactions to current and recent events, they don't typically offer in-depth analysis and perspective, which take more time to develop.

Find Information on Scholarly Sites

A few weeks after a major event such as an election, news sites stop covering the event because it's no longer new. Instead, scholarly sites provide access to articles and books that analyze the event and place it in historical perspective.

Some scholarly sites are search engines that let you access electronic databases of scholarly publications. For example, ScienceDirect lets subscribers search the full text of thousands of scientific journals. The publisher shown in **Figure 10-3** on the next page publishes journals in architecture and design, business and management, and chemistry and physics, among other fields.

Scholarly sites include information that's been written and thoroughly researched by experts, double-checked for accuracy, and reviewed by other experts. These sites also have citations, including publication name, date, and author, to help you evaluate them. Scholarly sites are reliable resources for in-depth, complete information on almost any topic.

On the Job Now

According to the U.S. Department of Labor, the median pay for a news reporter, correspondent, or broadcast news analyst is around $37,700 per year.

Hot Technology Now

One of the most popular apps for iOS, Android, and Windows is a news magazine named Flipboard. The free app provides a well-designed magazine format that displays your selection of news sources and social networks in one location.

Hot Technology Now

Popular academic sites include scholar.google.com, wolframalpha.com, and khanacademy.com. KhanAcademy provides thousands of free tutorial videos on academic subjects.

Figure 10-3: Website of a scholarly journal publisher

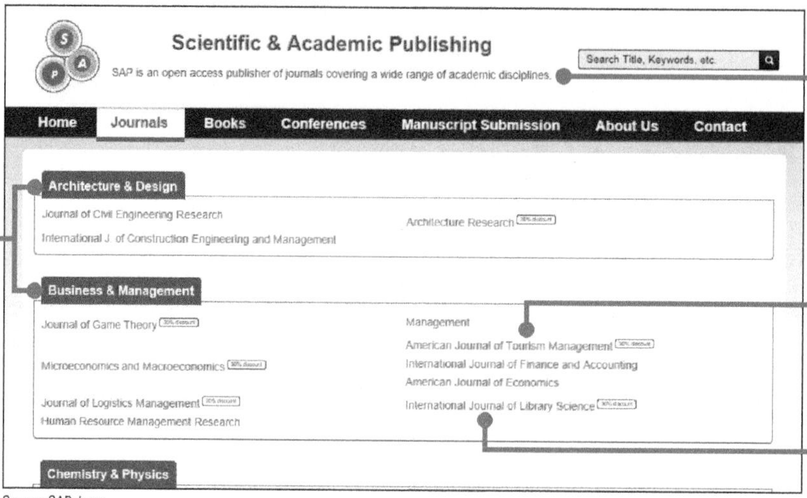

Site description indicates the journal publishes scholarly works.

This academic publishing site produces journals in selected fields of study.

Editorial board reviews the content to ensure accuracy.

Journals are written for experts in the field.

Source: SAPub.org

Search for Information

keyword | word stem | search operator | hit | filter | Creative Commons | sponsored link | search engine optimization (SEO) | public domain

The Bottom Line

- To improve the quality of the information you find using a search engine, you can narrow your search results by using search operators, customizing search results, and customizing browser settings.
- Using search engine tools can help you go directly to the information you need.

Just about anyone with a computer knows how to use a search engine to look up information on the web. But with billions of webpages available and more being added every day, you need to develop strategies to be search savvy. See **Figure 10-4**.

Develop Search Strategies

Let's say you need to give a presentation on the future of computing and have heard about an augmented reality (AR) headset, which gives users a view of the world enhanced by a computer. How do you begin researching this technology?

Before you start using a search engine, write down one or more questions you are trying to answer. Next, examine the questions to select a search phrase, which contains **keywords**, words that best describe what you want to find. The keywords you choose should make the search phrase unique and specific. Avoid using a search term that has more than one meaning, such as "AR," which could display results for augmented reality, the state of Arkansas, and other topics.

When you enter a search term in a search engine, it looks for webpages that contain the keywords you specify.

Figure 10-4: Searching for information

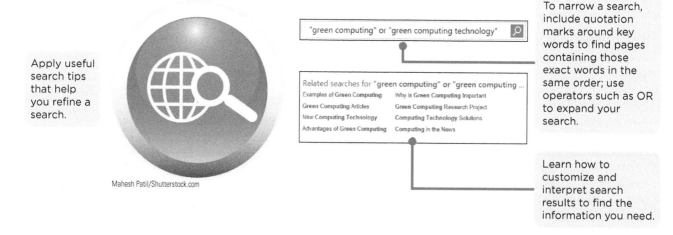

Apply useful search tips that help you refine a search.

To narrow a search, include quotation marks around key words to find pages containing those exact words in the same order; use operators such as OR to expand your search.

Learn how to customize and interpret search results to find the information you need.

Mahesh Patil/Shutterstock.com

Follow Search Guidelines

Google averages over 3.5 billion searches per day, which is a staggering number of searches. How can you search more effectively to improve your chances of finding what you want?

Start by refining your search term. Use a **word stem** (the base of a word, without -ed or -ing endings) to broaden a search. Use **search operators**, which are characters that help you focus your search. Table 10-1 lists some common search operators.

Table 10-1: Common search operators

Use this operator	To indicate	Example
" " (quotation marks)	Pages containing that exact phrase with words in the same order	"computer jobs"
+	AND	computer + jobs
| (vertical bar)	OR	computer | jobs
- (hyphen)	NOT	computer -jobs
˜ (tilde)	Pages that include synonyms	˜computer jobs

Many websites have tools for searching their pages. Google lets you search a site more thoroughly. Start the search term with **site:** followed by the site address and keywords to completely search that website. For example, if you wanted to search for information on SAM on the Cengage.com site, you could use the following (with no space after "site:"):

site:www.cengage.com sam

Browsers often have tools that let you search the page you are viewing. Microsoft Edge, for example, has a Find on page feature.

Another Google feature lets you search for related sites. To search for sites related to Netflix, you could type the following (with no space after the colon):

related:netflix.com

Evaluate Search Results

Suppose you're curious about flexible computer screens on mobile devices, which let you zoom and scroll a page by twisting the device. Enter **flexible computer screen** in a search engine, and the results could include millions of pages.

To find the information you're seeking, learn from your search results, as shown in Figure 10-5:

Hot Technology Now

The site venngage creates infographics, short for information graphics, which are visual representations of information, data, or knowledge intended to present information clearly. To search for information contained in infographics, use the site www.infographiqs.com.

By the Numbers Now

To convert currency such as U.S. dollars to another currency such as Great Britain pounds, type **150 USD to GBP** in the Google search box.

#infoliteracy

If you are using a search engine to find a salsa recipe that does not contain onions, type **salsa recipe -onions**.

Figure 10-5: Refining searches with filters and related terms

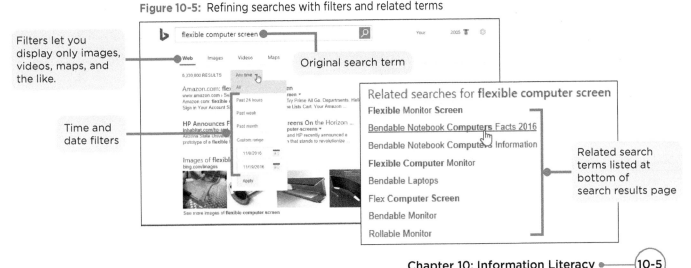

Filters let you display only images, videos, maps, and the like.

Time and date filters

Original search term

Related searches for **flexible computer screen**

Flexible Monitor Screen
Bendable Notebook Computers Facts 2016
Bendable Notebook Computers Information
Flexible Computer Monitor
Bendable Laptops
Flex Computer Screen
Bendable Monitor
Rollable Monitor

Related search terms listed at bottom of search results page

1. Search engines place the most relevant results, or **hits**, on the first few pages. Examine those results for clues about refining your search.

2. For many found sites, Google provides a list arrow next to each found URL that lets you find similar sites to further focus your search.

3. Most search engines include **filters** for finding certain types of results, such as images or news, or pages posted in a certain date range, such as within the last 24 hours. The Google advanced filtering page lets you search by "usage rights" to locate only graphics that are covered by Creative Commons licenses. **Creative Commons** is an organization that provides free, standardized copyright licenses to encourage legal sharing of creative material. You'll learn more about Creative Commons at the end of this chapter.

4. Finally, check the bottom of a search results page for suggested search terms related to the one you entered.

As you view web results, it's important to know that not all results are equal. Some search results are **sponsored links**, which are hyperlinks to paid advertising content related to your search text. Sponsored links may appear above, within, or near actual results. When users click a sponsored link, the search engine earns money from the advertiser. If you are not shopping for a product or service related to your search terms, use only nonsponsored links.

In addition to sponsored links, advertisers use **search engine optimization (SEO)** techniques to increase the likelihood that their pages will appear closer to the top of search results, where more users will see them. Such techniques may include editing page content and code so that they are more relevant to certain keywords used in a search. Finding relevant keywords helps ensure that the right visitors are drawn to their site. SEO techniques change over time as search engines modify their methods for ranking sites, and as developers use new strategies to improve their site rankings.

Customize Search Results

When you use a search engine, do you sometimes want to list more results per page so you can avoid opening new results pages? Or do you find the results pages cluttered with too many links?

You can change the preferences in your search engine to customize the results, as shown in **Figure 10-6**, which shows Google search settings.

Figure 10-6: Customizing Google search settings

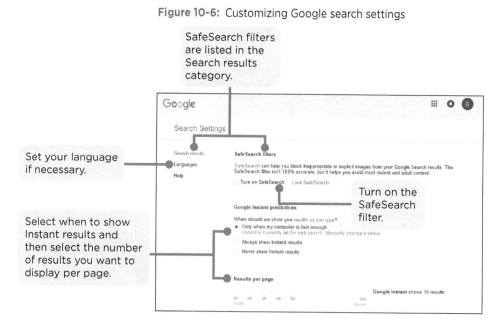

SafeSearch filters are listed in the Search results category.

Set your language if necessary.

Turn on the SafeSearch filter.

Select when to show Instant results and then select the number of results you want to display per page.

1. In Google, click the **Google Settings button** and then click **Search settings** to display the Search settings you can change, including the Results per page; in Bing, click the **Preferences** button and then click **Settings**.

2. Bing and Google let you identify your location to search for webpages relevant to your area.

3. Some search engines also let you personalize content by limiting the results to pages you have or have not already visited.

4. If offensive content turns up in your results, Bing and Google let you turn on the SafeSearch filtering to remove as much explicit content as possible.

5. Bing and Google have specialized image searches that let you locate the image you want more quickly. You can specify the image size, color, type (photo, clip art, drawing), region, file type, or Creative Commons usage rights.

Use Search Engine and Browser Tools

If you're getting stumped in your online searches or want more direct access to basic information, search engine and browser tools can help.

1. Most search engines provide definitions of words and phrases. For example, type **define cybercafe** as a search term to find a quick definition of "cybercafe."

2. In a more direct way, you can calculate numbers and convert measurements. For example, enter **8 kilometers in miles** at Ask.com to figure out if you can walk the distance.

3. If you're researching a topic and want to learn about new articles, blog posts, or other online information as it becomes available, set up a Google Alert to receive emails with links to relevant pages. You can also use Cortana, the Windows 10 virtual assistant, to set up an Academic Card to notify you of conference updates, news updates, and new papers in a scholarly field of study you choose.

4. To see a sampling of a book's text, use the book's title as your search term in Google, and then click Books in the search bar. If the book is in the **public domain**, which means the copyright has expired or otherwise doesn't apply, you can click Read to read the free e-book.

5. The Microsoft Edge browser that comes with Windows 10 has several tools to make your searches more productive and useful. See **Figure 10-7**. Annotation tools such as a highlighter, pen, and comment box let you call attention to and highlight website content. A clip tool lets you copy any webpage region for pasting

By the Numbers Now

Ninety percent of people look at only the first page of Google results.

On the Job Now

In the search box of the U.S. Department of Labor website (dol.gov), enter any job title to find the occupational outlook for that field.

Figure 10-7: Microsoft Edge browser tools

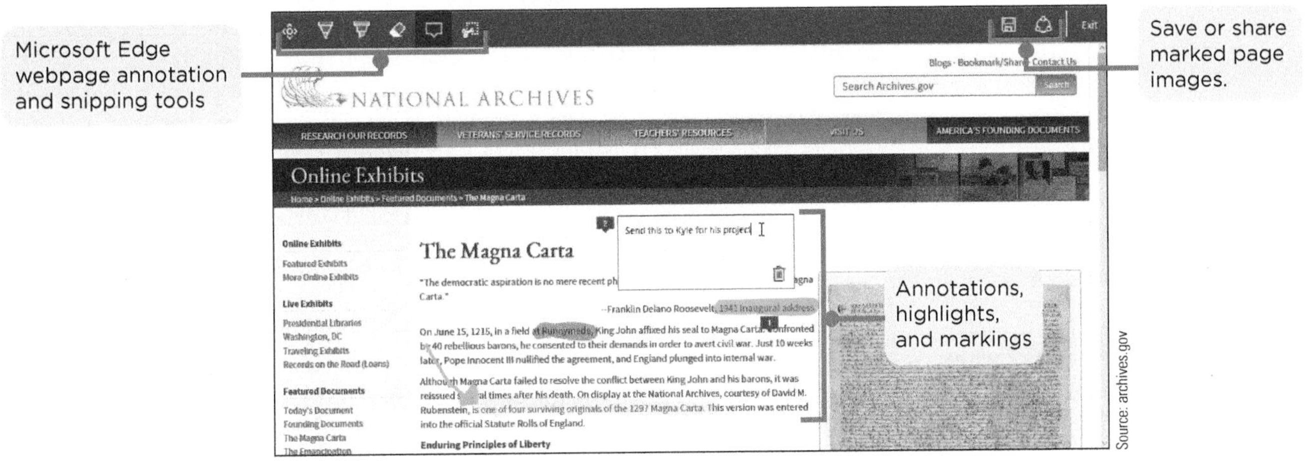

Microsoft Edge webpage annotation and snipping tools

Save or share marked page images.

Annotations, highlights, and markings

Source: archives.gov

elsewhere. You can save annotated webpages as Favorites or as a reading list, or send them to the OneNote note-taking program. Reading view lets you view webpage content without ads. In the Hub, you can track favorites, your reading list, your browsing history, and downloads. You can also share webpages using email, OneNote, Twitter, a Reading list app, or other selected apps.

6. The Microsoft personal digital assistant, Cortana, is now part of the Edge browser, so you can right-click a webpage word or phrase and select "Ask Cortana" for more information. Cortana may spontaneously offer to help as you shop online by supplying coupons, business contact info, or useful app links on related websites.

Evaluate Online Information

CARS checklist | credible | accurate | reasonable | support | credit line

On the Internet, anyone can publish anything to a website, a blog, or a social media site, regardless of whether the information is true. Recent years have seen a spike in misleading or outright false "news" and hoaxes that are shared as fact on social media. Even well-known figures and news outlets have shared such sites, adding to the influence of "fake news" in national and world affairs. These sites persist because they earn money for creators and advertisers each time someone clicks a link to their site. At a time when over half of Americans use social media as their primary news source, web users must be able to distinguish between truth, half-truths, satire, and outright fiction. If you use the Internet for research, be skeptical about the information you find online. Evaluate a webpage before you use it as an information source. See **Figure 10-8**.

Figure 10-8: CARS checklist

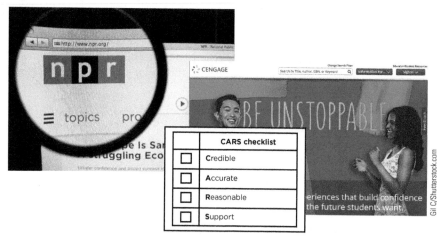

Evaluate the Credibility of Online Information

When someone is providing you information face to face, you pay attention to clues such as body language and voice tone to determine whether that information is **credible**, or believable. Obviously, you can't use that same technique to evaluate the credibility of a webpage, so you need another way to establish the page's credibility.

For example, suppose you are researching targeted web ads and find a page you want to use.

1. **Identify the author.** Look for a link such as About us or Background, and then click it to learn about the person or organization responsible for the webpage.

2. **Check the author's credentials.** Look for a title, such as President or Senior Editor. If you find biographical information, read it to learn whether the author has a degree in a field related to the topic. You also can use a search engine such as Google or the professional networking site LinkedIn to search for the author's name and see whether the information qualifies the author as an expert on the subject.

The Bottom Line

- Recent years have seen a spike in "fake" news and hoaxes that spread quickly around the web, making it more important than ever to verify information before or sharing using it.

- To evaluate online information, apply the **CARS checklist** to ensure that the information is credible, accurate, reasonable, and supported.

- Look at potential online sources critically—a site with errors, a bad design, or an unclear navigational structure may be unprofessional and therefore unreliable.

#infoliteracy

Be careful to distinguish between a webmaster and an author when citing a website as an information source. A webmaster designs and updates an author's writings but is not the source of the content.

For posts on social media, examine the account and see how long it has been in existence. An account that has only been around for two months may or may not be a reliable source.

Evaluate the Accuracy of Online Information

You're attending a classmate's presentation on the history of the personal computer, and he mentions that Bill Gates invented the first PC for home use in 1980, citing an online resource. You know it was actually Steve Wozniak and Steve Jobs in 1976. That inaccuracy makes you doubt the quality of the rest of the presentation.

Always remember that anyone can publish a webpage, whether he or she verifies the information, passes along rumors, or takes wild guesses at dates and other facts. Some sites have a kernel of truth, which is then distorted to intentionally mislead readers. To make sure your online information sources are **accurate**, do the following:

- **Verify facts and claims**. Accurate information is also detailed and comprehensive, not vague, general, or incomplete. Reject an information source if you learn that it left out important facts, qualifications, or alternatives. Consult an expert or use fact-checking sites such as snopes.com and factcheck.org to find professionally researched information.
- **Evaluate the information source**. Check site URLs, which may contain slight modifications of legitimate sites, use unusual domain names, or use long URLs. Be suspicious of an organization that has no history, physical location, or staff. Check to see if the source has a bias and evaluate the information with the bias in mind.
- **Check the date** the information was published or updated. For many topics, especially technology, you need current information. See **Figure 10-9**. Outdated facts or images will cause readers to doubt your authority.
- **Check photographs** to see if they have been taken from other sites, intentionally modified to mislead or to promote a point of view. Use tineye.com to see how it has been previously used or if modified versions exist.

Evaluate the Reasonableness of Online Information

Along with credibility and accuracy, consider how reasonable an online information source is. **Reasonable** means fair and sensible, not extreme or excessive. To evaluate reasonableness, start by identifying the purpose of the webpage. Is the page designed to provide facts and other information, sell a product or service, or express opinions? A page that provides information should do so objectively. Look for the following:

- **More than one point of view**. Evaluate how the author balances them.
- **Emotional, persuasive, or biased language**, which is often a sign that the author is not being fair or moderate. Even opinions should be expressed with a moderate tone.
- **Conflict of interest**. For example, if the page reviews a certain brand of smartphone and the author sells those types of phones, he or she has a conflict of interest.

Some sites are intended to be satirical and are sometimes shared as fact. Others are known to have poor reputations and regularly publish outlandish stories and dire predictions under the guise of information. Still others are the result of inaccurate reporting. If information seems unreasonable, check for multiple reputable sources to validate a site's claims.

Evaluate the Support for Online Information

Suppose you read an intriguing claim on a webpage: a poll found that most people consider computer professionals to be highly ethical. But the page doesn't link to the poll itself or mention other sources that support this claim. Therefore, the page is failing the final criterion in the CARS checklist: **support**.

To evaluate a webpage's support, look for the following:

- **Links or citations** to reputable sources or authorities. Test the links to make sure they work.
- **Other pages and print material on the topic**, to see if they cite the same sources.
- **Quotations** from experts.
- **For photos or other reproduced content**, a **credit line** should appear somewhere on the page that states the source and any necessary copyright information.

#infoliteracy

Check the domain in a site's URL when you want to use the site as a reference. In some cases, the domain shows where the page originated. For example, a site ending in .de was posted in Germany.

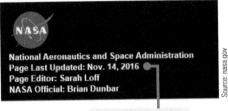

Hot Technology Now

To verify a fact, check multiple sites such as scholar.google.com or wolframalpha.com, which cite well-respected sources.

Figure 10-9: Checking the Last Updated date on NASA website

Recent date helps ensure accuracy.

#infoliteracy

As you investigate a topic, view the sites you research with healthy skepticism, as you would an infomercial, until you carefully verify the source and purpose of the site.

On the Job Now

Many media companies have fact checkers on staff to meticulously research and confirm all facts before publishing them.

An information source that simply states a belief or conclusion without support is basically expressing an opinion, not offering documented information.

As you evaluate web sources, consider your own viewpoint and how it can influence your choices. If you agree with a particular claim, that might make you more likely to accept it without thoroughly checking its supporting information.

Follow Evaluation Guidelines

When evaluating an online information source, you often can trust your initial reactions to a webpage. For example, if the page contains typos and grammar errors, the author didn't take the time to review, edit, and polish the writing. An authoritative resource usually does.

Consider the design of the webpage itself. If the page is difficult to navigate, search, or read, it's not as useful as a well-designed page. The page should be error-free, and any graphics, photos, video clips, or animations should enhance the content, not clutter the page. See Figure 10-10.

Figure 10-10: Poorly designed webpage

Finally, apply these same evaluation tips and the CARS checklist to your own writing, whether online or not. When you organize the material you've gathered and communicate it to others, you switch from being a consumer to being a producer of information. That means you have a responsibility to make sure the information you provide is credible, accurate, reasonable, and has support.

Use Search Tools

general search engine | spider | crawler | index | query | subject directory | specialty search engine | social search tool

Searching the web for just the right information can be time consuming and tedious—and you may wonder if you're searching in the right places. You can improve your searches by using online search tools. See Figure 10-11.

Describe How Search Engines Work

You're working on a presentation about web design and need to know the common navigation patterns for websites. How can you find this information quickly?

You'd probably start a **general search engine** such as Google, Bing, or Yahoo! and enter a search term or phrase such as **website navigation patterns**. Within seconds, the first page of search results lists a dozen webpages that might contain the information you need.

The Bottom Line

- In your searches, you can use general search engines, such as Google, and subject directories to find just the information you want.
- Specialty search engines and social media tools can lead you to valuable information sources other than websites.

Figure 10-11: Online search tools

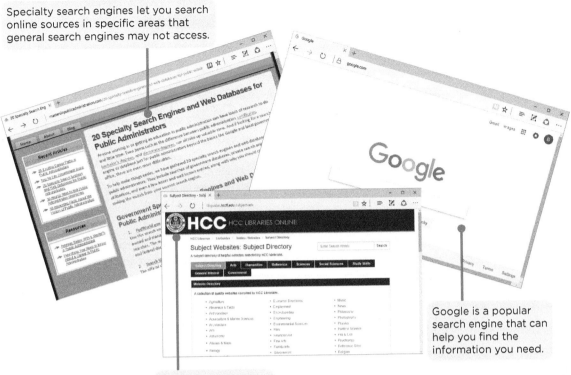

Specialty search engines let you search online sources in specific areas that general search engines may not access.

Google is a popular search engine that can help you find the information you need.

Subject directories can help narrow your search by subject.

You may wonder how a general search engine chooses the results you see. When you perform a search, a general search engine does not search the entire Internet. Instead, it compiles a database of information about webpages. It uses programs called **spiders** or **crawlers**, software that combs the web to find webpages and add new data about them to the database. These programs build an **index** of terms and their locations.

When you enter a search term, or **query**, a general search engine refers to its database index and then lists pages that match your search term, ranked by how closely they answer your query.

Use Subject Directories

Search engines are great when you already have an idea of what you want to find, such as pages predicting the future of the web. But what if you want a narrower view of what's available on the web, focused on a particular subject? You can use a **subject directory**, which is a catalog of webpages organized by subject.

Like a catalog in the library, a subject directory is the work of people (usually subject-matter experts) who can evaluate the content of a website and classify it. Subject directories offer a limited number of webpages and help you discover new topics and content. Libraries, colleges, and universities often create subject directories. Figure 10-12 on the next page shows a subject directory on the Library of Congress website. To use it, you select a general category, such as Maps, and then drill down to websites about that topic.

Use Specialty Search Engines

Suppose you're interested in alternative energy and want to research wind power. When you use a general search engine to search for wind alternative energy, the results include millions of webpages, many for commercial businesses. Where do you go to find academic information for your research? Try using a **specialty search engine**, which lets you search databases, news providers, podcasts, and other online information sources that general search engines do not always access.

Figure 10-12: Library of Congress subject directory

Links to subject areas lead to other links and source material in that area.

Source: loc.gov

Hot Technology Now

To find your local news at Bing, open bing.com/news. Type **local** followed by the name of your city or town, as in **local Toledo**.

On the Job Now

To create a free, professional online newspaper from sources such as Twitter, Google+, Facebook, YouTube, and RSS feeds, go to the site paper.li, which is free for personal usage. You can customize your topic to tap into the constant flow of information.

A search tool's ability to search databases is important, because much of the information on the web is stored in databases. To access database information, you need to use a special search form and may need to enter a username and password. For example, Google Scholar searches scholarly literature from many disciplines and includes articles, books, theses, and abstracts.

Other specialty search tools let you find information published on certain types of sites. For example, use Google News or Alltop to find news stories and Podcast Search Service to search podcasts.

Search Social Media Sites

Like most students, you probably spend time using social media, such as social networks, which let you connect with others. Suppose you had a memorable online discussion about climate change and want to know what others think about the topic. You can use a **social search tool** such as Social Searcher and Google Social Search to search blogs, microblogs, comments, and conversations on social media sites.

Social media search tools are designed for finding subjective content, such as comments, reviews, and opinions. Some social media search tools such as SocialMention let you search one or more social networks, blogs, and other sites at the same time.

General search engines, including Google and Bing, also provide social search tools. For example, when you're signed into Facebook, you can use Bing to ask friends for advice or to see which friends liked an event you attended. Social networks such as Facebook, Foursquare, and Twitter have tools for searching data shared by members. Facebook includes six reaction buttons—Like, Love, Haha, Wow, Sad, and Angry—to respond to posts, articles, videos, and other web information.

Use Search Tools for Research

If you've searched for information using a variety of search tools and still can't find what you're looking for, don't despair. Consider using innovative approaches to finding information. Some search sites help you refine research topics, shown in Table 10-2.

Table 10-2: Additional search tools

Search tool	What it does
Wolfram Alpha	Answers factual questions directly, without listing webpages that might contain the answer
Blinkx	Finds videos or other multimedia; uses speech recognition to match the audio part of a video with your search term
Ask a Librarian	Connects you to librarians at the Library of Congress and other libraries; allows you to engage in an online chat or submit your question in an online form
TinEye	Does a reverse search for submitted images, rather than keywords, to locate the original image and match it with other indexed images

Use Information Ethically

ethics | plagiarism | citation | citation style | paraphrase | intellectual property rights | copyright | digital rights management | public domain | fair use doctrine | Creative Commons (CC) | licensor | licensee

Just because it's easy to copy the material from Internet sources doesn't mean you should. To use online information ethically, cite sources and avoid plagiarism, a serious academic offense. You should also know about intellectual property rights, the public domain, and the fair use doctrine.

Define Ethics

Because the Internet provides easy access to other people and to information, you should carefully consider how you use that information. When you use the Internet for research, you face ethical decisions. **Ethics** is the set of moral principles that govern people's behavior. Many schools and other organizations post codes of conduct for computer use, which can help you make ethical decisions while using a computer.

Figure 10-13: Ethical use of online information

A copyright is a way of protecting the rights of intellectual property owners.

Know how to cite works or apply fair use guidelines to avoid **plagiarism**, which is using the work or ideas of others and claiming them as your own.

The Internet is full of information, images, videos, music, and other material that you can easily copy using your computer. But you must make ethical decisions about how you can and should use that information.

Wilm Ihlenfeld/Shutterstock.com, koya979/Shutterstock.com, chanpipat/Shutterstock.com

Cite Sources

Ethically and legally, you can use other people's ideas in your research papers and presentations, but you must cite the source for any information that is not common knowledge. A **citation** is a formal reference to a published work.

Thorough research on technology and other topics usually involves books, journals, magazines, and websites. Each type of information source uses a different **citation style**. Instructors often direct you to a particular citation style, such as MLA, APA, or Chicago. You can find detailed style guides for each style online. Some software, such as Microsoft Word, helps you create and manage citations and then produce a bibliography, which is an alphabetical collection of citations. See **Figure 10-14** on the next page.

By the Numbers Now

If a photographer created a photo after March 1, 1989, it is copyrighted until 70 years after the photographer dies.

Figure 10-14: Citing sources in Microsoft Word

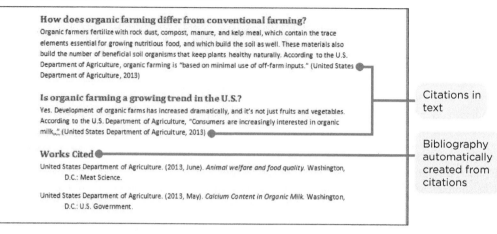

How does organic farming differ from conventional farming?
Organic farmers fertilize with rock dust, compost, manure, and kelp meal, which contain the trace elements essential for growing nutritious food, and which build the soil as well. These materials also build the number of beneficial soil organisms that keep plants healthy naturally. According to the U.S. Department of Agriculture, organic farming is "based on minimal use of off-farm inputs." (United States Department of Agriculture, 2013)

Is organic farming a growing trend in the U.S.?
Yes. Development of organic farms has increased dramatically, and it's not just fruits and vegetables. According to the U.S. Department of Agriculture, "Consumers are increasingly interested in organic milk,.." (United States Department of Agriculture, 2013)

Works Cited
United States Department of Agriculture. (2013, June). *Animal welfare and food quality*. Washington, D.C.: Meat Science.

United States Department of Agriculture. (2013, May). *Calcium Content in Organic Milk*. Washington, D.C.: U.S. Government.

Citations in text

Bibliography automatically created from citations

Avoid Plagiarism

If you use the content from a Wikipedia article but change some of the words, do you have to cite the source for that material? Yes, you do. Otherwise, you are guilty of **plagiarism**, which is using the work or ideas of someone else and claiming them as your own.

To avoid plagiarism, cite your sources for statements that are not common knowledge. Even if you **paraphrase**, which means to restate an idea using words different from those used in the original, you are still trying to claim someone else's idea as your own. Cite sources when you borrow ideas or words to avoid plagiarism.

Observe Intellectual Property Rights

If you copy a photo from the Internet and use it in a report, you might be violating the photographer's **intellectual property rights**, which are legal rights protecting those who create works such as photos, art, writing, inventions, and music.

A **copyright** gives authors and artists the legal right to sell, publish, or distribute an original work; and it goes into effect as soon as the work exists in physical form.

If you want to use a photo in your report, you need to get permission from the photo's owner. Contact the photographer by email, and explain what you want to use and how you plan to use it. If a copyright holder gives you permission, keep a copy of the message or document for your records. The holder may also tell you how a credit line should appear. Acquiring permission protects you from potential concerns over your usage and also protects the copyright holder's intellectual property rights.

Some online resources, such as e-books, newspapers, magazines, and journals, are protected by **digital rights management**, which are techniques such as authentication, copy protection, or encryption that limit access to proprietary materials. It is a violation of copyright law to circumvent these protections to obtain and then use the materials. Only use materials to which you have legal access, and then follow accepted usage laws for any information you obtain.

Use Content in the Public Domain

Some work is in the **public domain**, which means you can use it freely because it is not subject to copyright. This applies to material for which the copyright has expired and to work that has been explicitly released to the public domain by its owner. Many websites provide public domain files free for you to download. Much information on U.S. government sites is in the public domain, although you must attribute the information and be aware that the sites might contain copyrighted information. See **Figure 10-15.**

Figure 10-15: Copyright information on the U.S. Department of Agriculture site

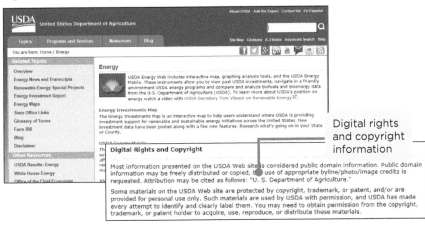

Digital rights and copyright information

For any online source, if you don't see a copyright symbol, look for a statement that specifically defines the work as being in the public domain. For quotations and other cited material, the United States **fair use doctrine** allows you to use a sentence or paragraph of text without permission if you include a citation to the original source.

Use Creative Commons Content

With all the billions of pages of Internet content available today, it can be hard to know what is legal to use and what's not. Most people are not legal experts, so how can you know what you can use and how you can use it? If you make your writing, photographs, or artwork available online, how do you specify to others how they can use that content?

Creative Commons (CC) is a nonprofit organization that aims to help **licensors**—those who create content—keep copyright to their materials while still allowing others to use, copy, or distribute their work under conditions the licensors choose. For example, you can choose whether to allow commercial use of your poem, or allow derivative works, such as translations or adaptations. People who use content that carries a Creative Commons license, called **licensees**, must follow CC license rules on giving credit for works they use and displaying copyright notices.

CC licenses are based on copyright law and are legal around the world. The licenses themselves have three formats: one that is intended for those with a legal background; one written in plain language that can be understood by nonexperts (like most licensors and licensees), and one that can be read by computers, which make it possible to search for CC-licensed material in search engines like Google Advanced Search or photo sharing sites like Flickr. The CC system is helping to build a large and ever-growing pool of "digital commons," a collection of content that users can legally copy, distribute, and build upon.

For example, the information in this Creative Commons section was adapted from https://creativecommons.org/share-your-work/licensing-considerations/. The plain-language license for its website material says that "You are free to: Share — copy and redistribute the material in any medium or format; Adapt — remix, transform, and build upon the material for any purpose, even commercially. Under the following terms: Attribution — You must give appropriate credit, provide a link to the license, and indicate if changes were made. You may do so in any reasonable manner, but not in any way that suggests the licensor endorses you or your use." You can find the license outlining the permitted uses of Creative Commons website content at https://creativecommons.org.

#infoliteracy

Go to twitter.com, search for @SAMTechNow, the book's Twitter account, and follow @SAMTechNow to get tweets on your home page.

Chapter Review

Find Online Information

1. What are the three major types of websites?

2. What do you call a collection of information, such as a library catalog? Why can't general search engines access them?

3. Name one benefit and one disadvantage of the deep web.

4. How do scholarly sites differ from news sites?

Search for Information

5. What do search operators allow you to do? Name three search operators and explain how you would use each one in a search.

6. Name two ways you can refine your search results.

7. What can you find at the bottom of a search results page, and how can they help you?

8. What is public domain material? Give one example.

Evaluate Online Information

9. Briefly describe the CARS checklist and how you would use it in searching the Internet.

10. How might you establish that a web source is credible?

11. Name two tools you might use to look for a website author's credentials.

12. Name three types of support that a website might provide.

Use Search Tools

13. How does a general search engine locate information?

14. What does a web spider do?

15. If you wanted to find what other people think about an important world issue, what kind of tool would you use, and what kinds of sites would it examine?

16. Describe a subject directory and give one example.

Use Information Ethically

17. Define "ethics," and explain how ethical principles can guide you in your use of Internet material.

18. What is the purpose of intellectual property rights?

19. What is the purpose of Creative Commons licenses, and what three forms do CC licenses take?

Test Your Knowledge Now

1. A website that requires a subscription or membership is called a _____.
   a. surface site   c. new site
   b. restricted site   d. scholarly site

2. Which search operator would you use to locate pages with an exact phrase, in the same order?
   a. +   c. -
   b. " "   d. ~

3. When you perform a web search, what do you call the most relevant results?
   a. queries   c. citations
   b. hits   d. filters

4. Which of the following would you use to broaden a search?
   a. " "   c. site:
   b. a word stem   d. -

5. Checking a site author's credentials is one way to establish a site's _____.
   a. reasonableness   c. credibility
   b. accuracy   d. support

6. Which of the following is *not* part of the CARS checklist?
   a. reasonable   c. copyright
   b. accurate   d. support

 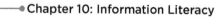

7. Which of the following is one way to establish a site's accuracy?
   a. Check the site's date.
   b. Identify the author.
   c. Look for the author's credentials.
   d. Look for just one point of view.

8. What part of the web is used for illegal activities?
   a. news sites
   b. the dark web
   c. the public domain
   d. subject directories

9. Which of the following lets you use a sentence or paragraph of text without permission if you include a citation to its source?
   a. Creative Commons
   b. Citation style
   c. CARS checklist
   d. Fair use doctrine

10. Which of the following operators lets you search for pages that include synonyms for your search term?
    a. ~
    b. -
    c. +
    d. " "

11. Which of the following sites does a reverse search for submitted images?
    a. Wolfram Alpha
    b. Alltop
    c. TinEye
    d. Yahoo!

12. A specialty search engine lets you search _____.
    a. databases, news providers, and podcasts
    b. multimedia sites
    c. blogs, microblogs, comments, and conversations on social media sites
    d. a catalog of webpages organized by subject

13. What do you call a collection of information, such as a library catalog or article collection, that requires passwords or subscriptions for searching?
    a. the deep web
    b. the public domain
    c. database
    d. a subject directory

14. Text that is *not* subject to copyright is found in _____.
    a. Wikipedia
    b. citations
    c. the public domain
    d. ethics

15. Which of the following searches lets you find sites that mention either onions or radishes?
    a. onions ~ radishes
    b. onions + radishes
    c. onions | radishes
    d. "onions + radishes"

16. MLA, APA, and Chicago are examples of _____.
    a. citation styles
    b. the fair use doctrine
    c. intellectual property rights
    d. copyrights

17. Plagiarism is best defined as _____.
    a. a citation style
    b. using another's work and claiming it as your own
    c. moral principles that govern our behavior
    d. the act of citing sources

18. Which of the following helps you find certain types of search results, such as images or news?
    a. search engine alert
    b. webpage filter
    c. the CARS checklist
    d. a citation

19. Which of the following are websites that are reliable sources for in-depth, complete information?
    a. private sites
    b. news sites
    c. search engine sites
    d. scholarly sites

20. Which of the following is *not* a way to customize search results?
    a. Identify your location.
    b. Turn on the SafeSearch filter.
    c. Limit the number of results per page.
    d. Use a spider.

21. In the space next to each image below, write the letter of the phrase that describes it.
    a. tools to annotate webpages
    b. citation
    c. a method to verify web information
    d. setting filters
    e. helps ensure up-to-date information

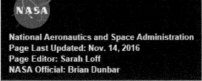

Source: archives.gov

According to the U.S. Department of Agriculture, "Consumers are milk..." (United States Department of Agriculture, 2013)

Source: nasa.gov

Try This Now

1: Advanced Googling

To become a Google power user, practice the following special searches at Google.com. For each search, take a screenshot of the results page. Place the screenshots in a single Word document, and then submit the document to your instructor. Open a browser, open the site google.com, and then use the following search terms:

   a. Type **population** and the name of your town or city (example: **population Scottsdale, AZ**), and then press Enter.
   b. Type the largest city near you, press Enter to display the search results, and then click Tools. Click the Any time list arrow, and then select Past week.
   c. Search on the name of a current technology company and click the News link.
   d. Search on a famous place in the world that is your dream vacation location and click the Images link. Using the Search tools, select the Size: Large, Color: blue, Type: Photo, and Usage rights: Labeled for reuse.
   e. Search on the name of any major sports team in season now (example: **Miami Dolphins**) and then click the Videos link.
   f. Search on any math problem (example: **3*7 +(sqrt 8)**), and make sure the All link is selected.
   g. Enter **define** followed by any word (example: **define antiestablishment**).

2: Technology Trends Social Media Newspaper

You can create an online paper in minutes by selecting custom topics from millions of social media posts and web articles published each day. Open a browser and then open the site paper.li.

   a. Create a free account at paper.li.
   When you create a paper.li account, you authorize the website to access content in your Twitter, Facebook, or any email address. Paper.li publishes content from these accounts to create an online newspaper. If you do not agree to these terms, return to the paper.li home page, click the Watch the video link, and then watch the video to learn about how paper.li works. Complete steps b and c to take a screenshot of a completed newspaper and paste the image in a Word document. Below the screenshot, write at least 100 words describing how paper.li works.
   b. Create a free online paper based on technology news topics that interest you. Give your paper a unique name and choose to create a weekly edition.
   c. Take a screenshot of your online newspaper. Paste the screenshot in a Word document, and then submit the document to your instructor.

3: Free Math Tutor at Khan Academy

Learn for free at Khan Academy in subjects such as math, art, computer programming, chemistry, biology, history, and medicine. Open a browser, and then open the site khanacademy.org.

   a. Sign in with your Facebook user name or your email address.
   b. Click the Subjects list arrow and then locate a math topic and select a level appropriate for you.
   c. Select an activity and then click subject links to watch three complete Khan Academy videos. Each video provides a link for a Tips & Thanks comment below the video. In this comment box, type a comment describing your impression of each of the three videos.
   d. Take a screenshot of each video with your comments. Paste the three screenshots in a single Word document.
   e. Save the document and submit it to your instructor.

Critical Thinking Now

1: Browsing with Microsoft Edge

Note: This assignment requires you to use the Microsoft Edge browser.

   Using the Microsoft Edge browser, take a screenshot of each scenario listed below. Place the screenshots in a single Word document, and then submit the document to your instructor.

   a. Open the Best Buy site or a similar site for which Cortana provides coupons. (If Cortana cannot find coupons, close Edge, click the Ask me anything box on the taskbar, and then click the Notebook icon. In the Notebook list, click Shopping, and then click the All shopping cards option to turn on coupons.) Take a screenshot with the coupon pane opened. Write one paragraph about whether you would change your browser to Edge to use the Cortana coupons.

b. Open your favorite news site and open an article. Click the Reading View button (if nothing happens or the Reading View button is unavailable, select another news site). Take a screenshot of the news story in the Reading View. Write one paragraph about how the Reading View could cut down on distractions while conducting research.

c. Open the website Bing.com, search for a college or university, and then select Images. Click the Make a Web Note icon to open the Annotations tools. Use the Pen tool to circle the three best pictures on the results page in any bright color. Take a screenshot of the annotated webpage. Write one paragraph about other ways that the Annotation tools might be helpful.

2: Wearable Devices

Use either bing.com or google.com to search for information about three wearable devices that you would consider using. Take a screenshot of each of the three results pages and paste the screenshots in a Word document. Research the pros and cons of each wearable device. Write at least 150 words about your conclusions in selecting a wearable device.

Wearable Devices

Halfpoint/Shutterstock.com

3: Research Plagiarism Software

Because anyone with an Internet connection has unlimited access to online information, schools, publishers, and other organizations must discourage plagiarism by setting clear standards for original work.

a. Check on your school's website, read your student handbook, or interview an instructor or administrator at your school to learn about its plagiarism policy. Write a paragraph in a Word document about your school's penalties for plagiarism.

b. Research a plagiarism-checking software called Turn It In. Use Word to write a 100-word document about how this software detects plagiarism and submit it to your instructor.

Ethical Issues Now

Note: This assignment requires a Gmail account.

Smartphones can passively track where you have been using Google's Timeline feature with location awareness.

a. Open google.com/maps/timeline using your smartphone or computer. Does this site show places you've been in the world? This site has an opt-in setting. If you have Location History turned on, the Timeline uses locations reported by your mobile device and allows only you to see the information.

b. Write 150 words about how Google Timeline works and what you think about a website using this private data. Submit the Word document to your instructor.

Team Up Now—CARS Checklist for Validating Sources

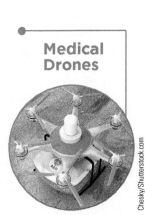

Medical Drones

Chesky/Shutterstock.com

Before you can cite a source, you must determine if a website is credible, accurate, reasonable, and has the proper support. Using the search engine scholar.google.com, each member of the team should research the topic of "drone use in the medical field." Each team member should select a different site that explains drone use in the medical field. Using the CARS checklist, each member must document the website URL and answer the following questions:

a. Credible: What evidence was provided to make the argument persuasive? Are there enough details for a reasonable conclusion about the argument?

b. Accurate: What date was the information published? Would any of the content be considered vague? What are your general impressions of the validity of this site?

c. Reasonable: Based on the author's statements, what was the tone of the article? Would you consider any portion to be slanted or biased?

d. Support: What are the sources of the site? Does the author provide contact information so that you can ask questions? Does the site link to other credible sites? List if possible.

Share your results with your team and submit the combined information to your instructor.

Key Terms

accurate
CARS checklist
citation
citation style
copyright
crawler
Creative Commons (CC)
credible
credit line
dark web
database
deep web
digital rights management
ethics
fair use doctrine

filter
general search engine
hidden web
hit
index
intellectual property rights
invisible web
keyword
licensee
licensor
paraphrase
plagiarism
public domain
public web
query

reasonable
restricted site
search engine optimization (SEO)
search operator
social search tool
specialty search engine
spider
sponsored link
subject directory
support
surface web
visible web
word stem

Digital Media

William is taking Music Appreciation 101 this semester as an online course. He has been listening to popular genres of American music, including blues, jazz, country, rock, rap, and pop.

The Music Appreciation instructor posted many samples of music on the course's website so students can play them on any computer platform.

William also uses YouTube to watch and listen to music videos and premiere performances.

iStockphoto.com/g-stockstudio

William Lucas is surprised by how much he is enjoying an eclectic mix of music from Bach to Frank Sinatra in his music appreciation class, including artists that were never part of his playlist before, such as Conway Twitty, Elton John, and Louis Armstrong. Armstrong is right: It *is* a wonderful world! William's assignment today is to watch and listen to early jazz musicians on YouTube, such as Scott Joplin and Bessie Smith.

In this Chapter

Define Graphics

graphic | digital graphic | bitmap image | pixel | vector image | download | clip art gallery | JPEG | GIF | PNG | TIF | BMP | SVG | license filter | digital camera | geotagging | graphics tablet | scanner | graphics software | paint software | image-editing software | drawing program | photo-editing software | computer-aided design (CAD) software | 3-D CAD software | resolution | resolution dependent | megapixel | compression | lossy compression | lossless compression | meme

A **graphic** is an image or picture. A **digital graphic** is an image you can see, store, and manipulate on a computer, tablet, smartphone, or other digital device. You can obtain graphics from external sources such as the web, or you can create your own.

Define Image Types and Formats

Digital graphics can be used for a variety of purposes. See **Figure 11-1**.

Figure 11-1: Types of graphics

Graphics can be color or black and white, and may incorporate text.

Illustrations convey concepts and ideas.

Computer-aided design (CAD) software creates highly detailed 3-D images.

Graphics can range from plain to complex; vector images are based on simple shapes.

Courtesy of Judy Walker Design, Courtesy of Peter Clemens, miumiu/Shutterstock.com

#digitalmedia

Android, iOS, and Windows apps on mobile phones typically display .png files, which have small file sizes due to their high compression rate.

Digital images fall into two main types: **Bitmap images** assign colors to the smallest picture elements, called **pixels**. **Vector images** are based on simple objects that can be grouped and layered to create a graphic. Bitmap and vector images are created and stored in a variety of file formats. Each file format is suited for particular uses. Do you need a two-color button for a webpage? Vacation photos for posting on Facebook? A highly detailed photograph that will appear in print? Each of these uses has different requirements. You can select from the file types shown in **Table 11-1**.

Download Graphics

If you want to add a picture to your document or presentation to illustrate a key point, you can **download** it, which means to transfer it from the Internet to your computer. The Internet provides a rich source for graphics. **Clip art galleries** contain collections of illustrations and photos, such as openclipart.org. Websites such as Shutterstock and Fotolia maintain large inventories of photographs and other graphics, which you can download for a fee.

Table 11-1: Common graphics file formats

Graphic file format	File extension	Details
JPEG	.jpeg or .jpg (Joint Photographic Experts Group)	A bitmap format used by many digital cameras; images have rich colors and are widely used, but discard some data to reduce file size, which can affect quality; widely used on the web
GIF	.gif (Graphics Interchange Format)	A bitmap format used for simple web graphics and short web animations; limited to 256 colors; supports transparency; small file size makes it good for websites
PNG	.png (Portable Network Graphics)	A bitmap format used for web graphics, especially on smartphones; good quality even when highly compressed; supports 16 million colors; better quality and smaller file size than GIF
TIF	.tif or .tiff (Tagged Image File Format)	A bitmap format used for high-quality photos and graphics; but extremely large file size TIF images better suited for print rather than web use
BMP	.bmp (Bitmap)	The Windows bitmap format; also called paint or raster images; does not compress well and files are very large; not widely used in web design today
SVG	.svg (Scalable Vector Graphics)	A vector format developed by the World Wide Web Consortium (W3C); allows interactivity and animation

Search engines such as Google and Bing help you find links to websites containing graphics relating to specific topics. To help you find images that you can use legally, Google and Bing let you search using a license filter. A **license filter** lets you search for pictures that you can use, share, or even modify for personal or commercial use. However, when you download any graphic from an external source, be sure to double-check the license and follow any restrictions on using it.

Create Graphics
If the graphic you need is not readily available, why not create it yourself? You can create graphics using hardware devices such as those shown in **Figure 11-2**.

Figure 11-2: Creating graphics using hardware devices

Digital cameras

Scanner

Graphics software

Graphics tablet

Courtesy of Barbara Clemens, Source: Samsung Galaxy 7, Source: NikonUSA.com, PRILL/Shutterstock.com, thampapon1/Fotolia LLC, ifong/Shutterstock.com, Source: Corel.com

A **digital camera** creates a digital image of an object, person, or scene. Almost all smartphones contain high-quality digital cameras and are increasingly popular for creating digital photographs. The latest smartphone cameras such as the iPhone 7 have 12-megapixel resolution and a built-in gyroscope for image stabilization, and work well in

On the Job Now

If you need to purchase the rights to a professional photo to use in a project, consider using shutterstock.com, fotolia.com, istockphoto.com, or gettyimages.com.

Hot Technology Now

Create graphic images for free at sumopaint.com.

Hot Technology Now

To create a professionally designed layout for a document, Facebook cover, blog graphic, or presentation, check out a free design website at canva.com.

On the Job Now

According to the United States Department of Labor, a graphic designer creates visual concepts, by hand or using computer software, to communicate ideas that inspire, inform, or captivate viewers.

Figure 11-3: Tagging photos

Joanna's Cat.JPG
JPG File

Tag photos with search terms

Date taken:	11/24/2016 5:20 PM
Tags:	Nani; Hawaii; cats; animals
Rating:	☆ ☆ ☆ ☆ ☆
Dimensions:	2160 x 2508
Size:	1.16 MB
Title:	Portrait of Nani
Authors:	Bill
Comments:	Sent to Joanna 11-28
Availability:	Available offline
Camera maker:	NIKON CORPORATION
Camera model:	NIKON D3300
Subject:	Portrait of Nani

Rate photos using stars

Courtesy of Barbara Clemens

Figure 11-4: CAD software drawings

ArchMan/Shutterstock.com, Kotkoa/Shutterstock.com

low-light settings. They can also identify a picture's geographical location, a feature known as **geotagging**, and can automatically post photos to online locations, such as your Facebook page or your OneDrive. High-end digital cameras have these features and more.

You can use a **graphics tablet** to create drawings with a pressure-sensitive pen. Architects, mapmakers, designers, and artists use graphics tablets. In addition, Windows 10 now includes the Windows Ink Workspace with a Sketchpad and Screen sketch. Many newer laptop computers, such as the Surface Book, allow you to draw on the screen using these features with a digital pen.

A **scanner** converts a printed document into a bitmap file by dividing the image into a grid of tiny cells and assigning colors to each cell. Scanners vary in size and shape and include flatbed, sheet-fed, pen, and handheld types.

In addition to capturing images with hardware devices, you can use a variety of popular **graphics software** to create your own graphics or modify existing ones. You can create images with **paint software** such as Microsoft Paint using brush tools and paint palettes that simulate water colors, pastels, and oil paints. Paint and other **image-editing software** let you modify existing images. For example, you can rotate an image on its axis, change its colors, or modify lines and other shapes.

Drawing programs, such as CorelDRAW, let you create simple cartoon-like images. Some programs let you layer graphics one on top of the other to create collages. You can use more advanced programs such as Adobe Illustrator to create sketches, logos, typography, and complex illustrations for web or print use. You can use **photo-editing software**, such as Adobe Photoshop, to enhance and retouch photographs. For example, you can add special effects such as reflections or a sepia tone, correct problems such as red-eye or poor lighting, or remove unwanted parts of an image. You can also edit photos on a smartphone using a variety of free mobile apps such as Snapseed, VSC, and Adobe Lightroom. You can tag photos with keywords and rate them so that you can easily find them later, as shown in **Figure 11-3**.

Use Computer-Aided Design

Some graphics require more sophisticated software. Architects, scientists, designers, engineers, and others use **computer-aided design (CAD) software** to create highly detailed and technically accurate drawings. With CAD software, drawings can be shared, modified, and enhanced with exceptional speed and accuracy. See **Figure 11-4**.

Interior designers use CAD software to model proposed room designs. Clothing designers can experiment with fabrics and patterns. Architects use CAD to design buildings and create floor plans. Engineers and scientists use **3-D CAD software** to create wireframe drawings of objects, which they can rotate to view from multiple angles. You can also overlay materials on CAD designs to see the visual and technical impact of different materials.

Lastly, some CAD software even generates material lists for building designers to pass on to the construction teams.

Define Resolution and Compression

When using graphics in your work, you should be aware of how certain properties affect the way graphics look. **Resolution** refers to the clarity or sharpness of an image: the higher the resolution, the sharper the image. Bitmap graphics are **resolution dependent**, which means image quality deteriorates as size increases. Vector graphics keep the same quality as their size increases.

On a digital camera, resolution is typically measured in **megapixels**, or millions of pixels. The higher the number of megapixels, the higher the resolution of your photos, and the larger the picture files. However, high-resolution photos and other complicated graphics can be difficult to copy, download, or send as email attachments, due to their large file size.

Compression makes graphics files smaller by reducing the number of bits a file contains. JPEG files use **lossy compression**, which means some of the original file data is discarded during compression. Fortunately, the "lost" data is generally not noticeable. TIF, PNG, and GIF files can be compressed using **lossless compression**: when uncompressed, the files contain all of their original data.

Use Graphics Effectively

You can use graphics to improve your work as follows:

- Stories and articles become more interesting and memorable with dramatic or informative **photos**.
- **Illustrations** and **drawings** can convey ideas and concepts better than words alone can.
- **Product photos** are essential on shopping websites.
- **Graphic logos** on corporate documents and websites help increase brand awareness.
- **Graphical buttons and icons** help to execute commands, display menus, or navigate documents or screens.
- Simple **cartoons** can add humor to your work.

No matter the context, graphics add functionality and fun to documents and webpages.

Hot Technology Now

A **meme** is a humorous graphic or video, often with text, that is copied or imitated and spreads virally over the Internet.

Hot Technology Now

The site colorhunter.com matches the colors in an uploaded image to a color palette so you can identify the colors and use them in a professional document or webpage.

Define Digital Audio

digital audio | Voice over IP (VoIP) | voice-over | audio input device | headset | sound recorder software | digitize | analog sound wave | sampling | sampling software | MP3 | AAC | M4P | WAVE | WAV | AIFF | WMA | synthesized sound | MIDI (Musical Instrument Digital Interface) | speech synthesizer | phoneme | text-to-speech software | speech recognition software | speech-to-text software | sound card | micro speaker | audio software | skin | stand-alone player | live audio feed | streaming audio | audio capture and editing software | music production software | mix

The Bottom Line

- Audio hardware and software let you record or synthesize digital sound files in a variety of file formats.
- You can play digitized sound files on your computer, edit them, and use them on websites and in presentations.

If you listen to music using your computer or mobile device, you are listening to digital audio. **Digital audio** is any type of sound that is recorded and stored as a series of 1s and 0s. Digital audio can enhance any presentation or movie. You can listen to digital audio in the form of audio books, using sites such as Audible, where you can listen to a book as it streams from the Internet, or download it for offline listening. In addition, you can stream or download audio podcasts, which may include news stories, music, lectures, or radio shows. See **Figure 11-5** on the next page.

Identify Audio File Formats

Audio files can be stored in a variety of formats, each with a specific purpose. For example, different audio formats are used for storing music, audio recordings such as Audible books, and podcasts. You can recognize the different audio file formats by looking at the file extensions. **Table 11-2** on the next page summarizes common audio file formats.

Record Sound

You may want to record yourself performing a song or reading a **voice-over**, or voice narration, to add to a slide presentation. You can easily record voice-overs and save the recordings for playback on a computer, but you need the following hardware and software:

1. You need an **audio input device** such as a microphone or headset. A **headset** combines speakers and a microphone into one device.

2. You also need **sound recorder software** to capture the sound from the input device.

3. Finally, you need to **digitize** the captured sound, which means to convert it to a format your computer can read.

Sound is produced when vibrations, such as a drumstick hitting a drum pad, cause pressure changes in the surrounding air, creating **analog** (continuous) **sound waves**. A process called **sampling** converts the analog sound waves into digital sound. **Sampling software** breaks the sound wave into separate segments, or samples, and stores each sample numerically. The more samples taken per second, the higher the sound quality and the larger the file. See **Figure 11-6** on the next page.

Hot Technology Now

To convert images or audio files from one type to another type, such as from WMA to MP3, you can use a free website such as zamzar.com.

Hot Technology Now

One of the most popular programs available for recording sound is called Audacity (audacity.sourceforge.net). Audacity is a free, open source, cross-platform program that works on Macs, Windows, and Linux computers.

Figure 11-5: Using digital audio

You can record and play digital audio files using any computer or mobile device.

You can edit sound files using audio-editing programs.

When you Skype with far-flung family and friends, you are using **VoIP (Voice over IP)** technology, which enables people to speak to each other over the Internet.

Andresr/Shutterstock.com, Maridav/Shutterstock.com, ArtFamily/Shutterstock.com, iStockphoto.com/Track5

Table 11-2: Common audio file formats

File format	File extension	Compressed?	Notes
MP3	.mp3	Yes	Common format for music and audio books
AAC and M4P	.aac and .m4p	Yes	Apple uses these formats for iTunes downloads
WAVE or WAV (Waveform Audio)	.wav	No	Files are large; good to excellent sound quality
AIFF (Audio Interchange File Format)	.aiff or .aif	No	Files are large; good to excellent sound quality
WMA (Windows Media Audio)	.wma	Yes	Played using Windows Media Player; also copy-protected

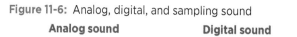

Figure 11-6: Analog, digital, and sampling sound

Analog sound **Digital sound** **Sampling sound**

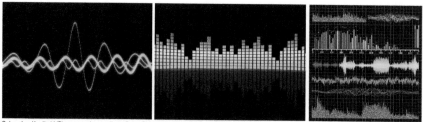

Sebastian Kaulitzki/Shutterstock.com, Ilona Baha/Shutterstock.com, Eliks/Shutterstock.com

Once you capture and digitize sound, you can save it as an audio file and then play it back or edit it as you wish.

Use Synthesized Music

Some digital audio files are recordings of actual sounds; other sounds, known as **synthesized sounds**, are created artificially by computers and special software. The term **MIDI (Musical Instrument Digital Interface)** refers to a system for creating and storing synthesized music. MIDI files do not contain sound; rather, they contain instructions for generating specific sounds, including pitch, volume, and note duration.

A computer reads these instructions and encodes the resulting MIDI "music." MIDI music files have .mid, .cmf, or .rol filename extensions. MIDI files are much more compact than digital audio files; they take up less storage space and are easier to transmit. However, MIDI files do not produce high-quality vocal sounds. They lack the "tonal" qualities associated with real-life, high-quality music, so they can sound artificial to the trained ear.

Use Synthesized Speech

In addition to music, computers can synthesize speech. **Speech synthesizers** break words into individual sound units, called **phonemes**. Synthesizers string these phonemes together to create words and phrases. **Text-to-speech software** then generates the corresponding sounds from the phoneme sequences to create synthesized speech.

Synthesized speech is widely used in mobile communications and call centers. To make computers accessible to the visually impaired, synthesized speech reads aloud from the screen. Text-to-speech technology also lets you type text into your computer, create a sound file, and then play it back, post it on a website as a podcast, or email the sound file.

Use Speech Recognition Software

Speech recognition software, or **speech-to-text software**, does the reverse of text-to-speech software by translating spoken words into text. **Speech recognition software** analyzes speech and converts the sounds into phonemes. The phonemes are then matched to words in a digital dictionary and written as text on the screen.

Using speech recognition technology, you can activate computer commands or browse the web using your voice instead of a keyboard and mouse. If you use this technology with word processing software, you can even create a report by speaking into your computer's microphone.

Play Sounds and Music

Playing sounds on a computer or digital device requires special hardware and software. A **sound card**, shown in **Figure 11-7**, is a circuit board that gives the computer the ability to process sound.

Speakers play sound and can be built-in or attached as peripheral devices to your computer, either by a cable or wirelessly. Add-on speakers, which often offer higher-quality sound than built-ins, used to have bulky profiles. But today's portable **micro speakers** come in a range of sizes, some as small as an inch or two in height and width. They connect to your smartphone, tablet, or other devices using a wireless Bluetooth connection, and can double as speakerphones for phone calls or similar audio communications. If you're in an environment such as an office or library, where speakers are not practical, you can use a headset or headphones to keep the sound private.

You also need software to play sound. **Audio software** is included on portable media players such as iPods and smartphones and often offers features such as file-shuffling and volume control; some audio software even has **skins**, visuals to go along with the sounds.

When playing certain types of audio files on a desktop or laptop, such as MP3 files, you need a **stand-alone player**. For Windows computers, Windows Media Player, Groove Music, and Google Play Music are popular apps for playing stand-alone audio files such as downloaded songs.

You can play audio directly from the Internet by connecting to **live audio feeds** for live sports events, shows, or even police, fire department, and air traffic control feeds using a web browser or a media player. For prerecorded content, you can listen to

Figure 11-7: Sound card

DeSerg/Shutterstock.com

content using **streaming audio**, which downloads and plays small amounts of music from the Internet as the remainder is downloading. Streamed music is not stored on your computer. Popular music streaming services include Pandora, Spotify, Sound-Cloud, Groove Music, and iHeartRadio. Some streaming services are free, and others are paid; the free services usually feature advertisements.

Edit Sound Files

You can edit, copy, and share digital audio files using **audio capture and editing software**. You can enhance audio by removing background and other unwanted noises or pauses, deleting or reordering entire sections, and adding special effects.

Music production software such as Apple Garage Band lets you record, compose, mix (combine), and edit music and sounds. See **Figure 11-8**. You can create sounds of multiple instruments, change tempos, add notes, or rearrange a score to produce a unique arrangement.

Figure 11-8: Editing a sound file in Garage Band

Each sound track appears in the timeline with controls for each one.

Controls for the selected sound track appear in the Audio region.

Waveforms for selected sound

Software "instruments" are listed in this panel.

Courtesy of Garage Band

While many music production programs are geared toward consumers, full-featured audio software such as Adobe Audition lets professionals edit sound for commercial websites, podcasts, presentations, and even TV shows and movies.

Finally, audio-editing programs and features are often integrated into video-editing software because sound tracks are integral to video.

Define Digital Video

video | digital video | HD (high-definition) video | Ultra HD video | digital video camera | camcorder | smartphone | webcam | video card | media player | viral video | streaming video | video conferencing | video-editing software | transition | codec | Moving Pictures Experts Group (MPEG) | MP4 | on-demand content | live video streaming | set-top box | smart TV

You probably use video often for entertainment, school, and work. **Video** combines moving images and sound and can be live or prerecorded. Video can range from home slide shows on your home computer to feature-length high-definition Hollywood movies. See **Figure 11-9**.

Capture Video

A **digital video** is a series of image frames displayed quickly enough for us to perceive them as continuous motion. Digital videos can come from a digital video camera, video-enabled smartphone, DVD, or digital video recording (DVR) device. DVDs and DVRs are used less frequently as time goes on. Much video today is

The Bottom Line
- You can create digital videos using a digital video camera, and play them back on a computer or other device with the appropriate hardware and software.
- You can edit a digital video file to adjust its length and appearance, and to add special effects, text, graphics, and audio.

Figure 11-9: Uses for digital video

You can use video to communicate in real time with other people. Businesses often use video conferences to conduct meetings on a network or the Internet.

It's easy to create videos using a video camera or smartphone.

Video is an important way of presenting content on the web for individuals and companies.

In many programs, you can edit video—even Microsoft PowerPoint lets you embed and play videos and make basic changes.

Blend Images/Shutterstock.com, Gaudilab/Shutterstock.com, Video courtesy of Barbara Clemens, dolphfyn/Shutterstock.com

HD (high-definition) or Ultra HD video (which has four times the pixels of HD), both of which produce a much sharper picture than standard definition video.

A digital video camera, camcorder, or smartphone (see Figure 11-10) captures full-motion images and stores the images in a file on the camera or phone. Action camcorders are compact, waterproof, and weather-resistant, making them ideal for live action. They are used in activities such as sailing, surfing, skiing, and extreme sports.

Digital video files are large: when you transfer a video from a digital video camera to your computer or storage media, you could need 1 to 30 GB of storage for each hour of video, with HD video requiring storage space in the upper end of the range.

A webcam is a digital video camera that captures video and sends it directly to a computer. Webcams are often built into laptops, tablets, and smartphones. They can also be attached to any computer through a USB or FireWire port.

You can view desktop videos using popular software such as Windows Media Player, Movies & TV, or Apple QuickTime Player. Many people watch videos using the YouTube app on mobile devices.

Play Video

To watch video on a computer, you need special hardware and software. The hardware is built into computers, tablets, or smartphones and includes a screen, speakers, and a video card—a circuit board that lets your computer process video.

You also need software called a media player. Most tablets and smartphones also include the software to display video. Video technology changes so quickly that you need to update your media player and related software frequently.

Access Video on the Web

Fast Internet connections have made watching videos on computers and mobile devices almost as popular as watching television. You can watch videos on many websites, whether the videos are posted by individuals, by web developers, or as advertising on websites. People use websites such as YouTube, Vimeo, Vine, and Snapchat to share personal videos; you can also watch commercial movies and TV through YouTube.

Figure 11-10: Digital video camera and smartphone

Olinchuk/Shutterstock.com, Jaros/Shutterstock.com

#digitalmedia

Windows 10 includes the Movies & TV app, which lets you download and play movies and TV shows (for free or a rental fee), or play other video files stored on your computer.

By the Numbers Now

Ultra HD (4K) televisions play Ultra HD videos on screens with an ultra-wide ratio of 21 × 9, which display vivid, detailed images that rival those shown in feature-length movies.

A **viral video** is a video that has been shared millions of times over social media in a short period of time.

One way to store and present video from the web is as individual video files, such as movie clips that you must download completely before playing them. Another method is **streaming video**, which transfers a segment of a video file from the web to your computer, letting that segment play while the next segment is being sent. You'll learn more about streaming video later in this chapter.

Video conferencing, or face-to-face meetings using computers, is increasingly used on the web as a way of reducing business travel costs and bringing friends and family together over long distances. Microsoft Skype lets users stay in audio and video contact using Windows and Mac computers as well as Windows, iOS, and Android smartphones. With Google Hangouts, you can have group conversations with live video calls using computers as well as Apple and Android devices.

Edit Video Files

Video-editing software makes it possible for anyone with a home computer to enhance and customize video. You can transfer video files from a camcorder for editing on your computer. You can also shoot and edit video using your smartphone. Most video-editing software shows the video as a timeline with separate tracks for video and sound. **Figure 11-11** shows a video being edited in Adobe Premiere. Lightworks and Apple iMovie are popular personal video-editing programs. More fully featured

Figure 11-11: Editing video

Editing tools

Playback controls

Video appears on a timeline

Source: Adobe, Inc.

video-editing programs include Apple Final Cut Pro and Adobe Premiere. You can also edit video on your smartphone using apps such as Adobe Premier Clip, GoPro App, Revu for iOS, and Magisto for Android. Some apps allow you to delete unwanted footage or rearrange or copy scenes to produce a professional-looking video. You can also add voice and music over existing scenes to narrate a scene or create a mood.

Transitions are graphics that help a viewer know when one scene ends and another begins. You can use video-editing software to insert transitions such as fades and swipes between scenes.

Videos can consume a lot of storage space—up to 30 GB per hour of video. For this reason, many users save the files in compressed format and store videos on external hard drives after editing.

Use Video Codecs

When you edit video, it's in an uncompressed, or raw, format. After editing, you use a **codec** (compressor/decompressor) to convert the video into other formats and reduce file size for distribution. **Moving Pictures Experts Group (MPEG)** is a popular video compression standard, with a widely used codec called MPEG-4 or **MP4**. Other popular codecs include Apple QuickTime, DivX, and Windows Media Video. Video files may use filename extensions such as .mkv, .mts, and .mov.

With the variety of digital video media, viewing and editing software, and distribution methods available today, you can create and distribute just the video you want.

Stream Videos

You can access video content on your computer via streaming video, which lets you watch or listen to the content as it arrives from the web, while later portions are being downloaded. For **on-demand content** such as TV shows, the original media file is stored on the media distributor's server, and is sent to your computer for viewing. Because the file is stored online, you can watch it multiple times. Examples of streaming services include Netflix, Hulu, Amazon Prime video, HBO Go, Chromecast, Roku, and YouTube. In contrast, with **live video streaming**, often used for sports events, the content is sent out live, as it happens, and is available only once.

In addition to viewing streaming video on your computer, you can view it on your television set. You need additional hardware, including a **set-top box** (such as Apple TV, Roku, Google Chromecast, or Amazon Fire TV), Blu-Ray player, or game console, which lets you view the Internet content (including social media sites such as Facebook and LinkedIn) on your TV. Increasingly, **smart TVs** are incorporating the Internet abilities of set-top boxes, including streaming media and social media. (You'll learn more about social media later in this chapter.) See **Figure 11-12**. The Microsoft Edge browser has a Cast media to device features, which broadcasts whatever is displayed in your browser onto your smart TV or set top device.

#digitalmedia

Many people are "cutting the cord" to their cable and satellite paid television subscriptions. You can create your own personal entertainment hub with smart TVs, Roku, Apple TV, or Chromecast, and Hulu and Netflix subscriptions to watch your favorite shows, movies, news, and sports.

Figure 11-12: Streaming media to your computer and TV

TV shows
YouTube
Pandora
Facebook

Set-top box or plug-in

Computer with media player or plug-in

SmartTV

The Bottom Line

- Animation is used in films and games, as well as in education, training, and business presentations.
- Three-dimensional animation is common in films and computer games, while 2-D and 3-D animation appear on the web.
- You can create animations using animation software.

Define Animation

animation | simulation | PowerPoint transition | 3-D animation | frames per second (fps) | in-betweening | animated GIF | SWF format | plug-in | HTML5 | wireframe drawing | rendering | animation software

If you have played a video game lately or watched an animation-enhanced film such as *Finding Dory*, *Brave*, *Avatar*, or *Frozen*, then you've experienced **animation**, the art of bringing an object to life by giving it the appearance of motion or activity. See **Figure 11-13**.

Figure 11-13: Uses for digital animation

Animation gives life to inanimate objects to create appealing entertainment.

Animation is used in special effects for movies, as well as entire animated films, with animated characters.

Animation is often created by repeating an image with slight variations in each frame...

...where the variations create the illusion of motion or life when you view the frames in rapid succession.

Music4mix/Shutterstock.com, lineartestpilot/Shutterstock.com, Crisan Rosu/Shutterstock.com

Figure 11-14: Using simulation for training

Simulation is used to teach pilots new techniques for flying a plane.

flun/Fotolia LLC, ifong/Shutterstock.com

Use Animation

Although we commonly think of animation as being used for entertainment in films and games, animation has other uses. For example, animation can teach medical students a procedure. **Simulations** are sophisticated computer animations that are useful for training and teaching in many fields, particularly in areas in which learning can be dangerous or difficult. See **Figure 11-14**.

A popular use of simple animations is in PowerPoint or Prezi presentations, in which you can animate slide text and objects. **PowerPoint transitions**, the way one slide moves to another, are a type of animation. You can also embed a graph from a spreadsheet program such as Microsoft Excel and animate the bars to emphasize important trends.

Use 3-D Animation in Films

Special effects for movies, as well as entire animated films, are produced using **3-D animation**. Digitally animated films, such as *Moana* and the *Frozen* series, are examples of how sophisticated 3-D animation has become. When you're watching animation, you're actually seeing many **frames per second (fps)**, with an image in each frame. For example, television uses 30 fps, many videos use 24 fps, and 3-D computer games often display 60 fps. 3-D animation in films is done during the production phase, while the film is being shot, and then incorporated into the final footage.

Animation is created using a sequence of bitmap images in which one or more objects are changed slightly between each image. Not surprisingly, this technique is called **in-betweening**. You can create the in-between bitmaps manually or let a computer create them.

Use Animation in Games

Animated special effects in computer games, such as massive battle scenes, are created using a sequence of bitmap images with objects moved or changed between each rendering. Whereas animation in films is done ahead of time and then incorporated into the rest of the film, 3-D computer game animation is produced as you're playing. See **Figure 11-15**.

This real-time animation consumes an incredible amount of computer resources. At 60 frames per second, your computer must handle more than 1 billion bits of information every second just to display a 3-D image in 32-bit color. The computer also has to track the movements of each player, using even more resources. Because of these requirements, serious gamers use computers with powerful processors, such as the Intel Core i7, which allow faster performance. You will learn more about gaming later in this chapter.

Use Animation on the Web

When you view a webpage and objects move, you are viewing animation. Animation is frequently used on websites to enhance text as well as images. One popular animation method is an **animated GIF**, a series of slightly different bitmap images displayed in sequence to achieve animation effects.

For many years, Adobe Flash was used to create static or animated graphics in the **SWF format**, which was designed for web use. But Flash required users to download a **plug-in**, a component added to your browser, to play videos. Flash also became a target for malware developers. Currently, most web animations are created with **HTML5**, the latest version of the Hypertext Markup Language that is built into browsers. HTML5 features high-quality playback without the need for additional plug-in software, and is now becoming the standard for web animation development. Adobe Flash has been replaced by Adobe Animate CC, which incorporates HTML5.

Compare 2-D and 3-D Animation

Animation can be 2-D or 3-D. Three-dimensional animation is more complex than 2-D animation because the artist must first create the 3-D graphic, and then create 24 to 60 versions of the graphic for each second of animation.

To create a 3-D animation, you start with a 2-D object and then add shadows and light. Next, you define the texture of each surface of the object, which determines how the object reflects light. One way to create a solid 3-D image is to apply highlights and shadows to a **wireframe drawing** (a 3-D object composed of individual lines) in a process called **rendering**. See **Figure 11-16**.

Although the process sounds complicated, animation software can make it more manageable.

Use Animation Software

With a personal computer and readily available software, anyone with a little training and some skill can create animations. **Animation software** includes Adobe After Effects, Adobe Animate CC, and Microsoft Silverlight. Professional-level animation software such as Autodesk Maya and NewTek LightWave is expensive and has a steep learning curve.

HTML5 includes support for creating and displaying animation and is being used by Apple on its iPhone, iPad, and other products.

Figure 11-15: Real-time animation in 3-D computer gaming

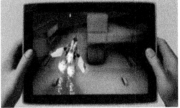

One02/Fotolia LLC

Figure 11-16: 3-D rendering

Wireframe drawing

Rendering adds highlights and shadows

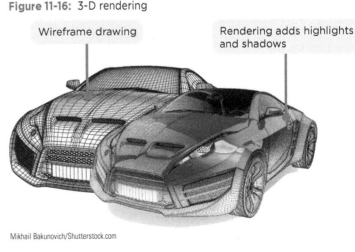

Mikhail Bakunovich/Shutterstock.com

Use Gaming Systems

video console | game console | software development kit (SDK) | augmented reality (AR) | hologram | motion-sensing game console

The Bottom Line

- Most sophisticated video gaming requires video or game consoles, but many others can be played on computers, tablets, and smartphones.
- Mobile gaming, played on smartphones or small consoles, uses scaled-down versions of computer games.
- Augmented reality (AR) is poised to revolutionize gaming by allowing users to interact with virtual objects and characters in the context of actual room objects.

Digital electronics and gaming are interactive media that engage players. Today's video games use high-end graphics, sophisticated processors, and the Internet to create environments that rival reality and bring together players from around the world. Games account for most software sales, currently totaling nearly $100 billion in annual revenue. Computer and video games include role-playing, action, adventure, education, puzzles, simulations, sports, and strategy/war games.

Set Up a Gaming System

Most games are played on **video consoles** with special controllers. A popular choice for video gaming is a **game console** such as the Microsoft Xbox, Nintendo Wii, or Sony PlayStation. These use handheld controllers as input devices, a television screen or computer monitor as a display device, a hard drive, and memory cards or optical discs for storage. See **Figure 11-17**.

On consoles that connect to the Internet, you can play with multiple players online and stream TV or movies. Large-scale multiplayer games such as Halo, Doom, Overwatch, Uncharted, and World of Warcraft operate on multiple Internet servers, with each server able to handle thousands of players.

However, many games can be played on computers, tablets, or smartphones that use a keyboard, mouse, touchpad, or touchscreen to input commands. Simple games may come with the operating system of a computer; they can also be downloaded from free from an app store. Hardware for handheld game consoles, tablets, and smartphones is built into the devices. Some devices use memory cards, cartridges, or miniature optical discs to store games.

Participate in Mobile Gaming

Some game consoles are self-contained devices that fit in one hand. These handheld consoles are designed for single-player or multiplayer video games. See **Figure 11-18**. Many use memory cards to store games; others use a cartridge or a miniature optical disc for storage.

Mobile computing and smartphones have put the world of gaming right in the palms of many hands. Phones often come with scaled-down game versions to introduce them. Popular games such as Pokémon Go can "go viral" and become overnight sensations. Some games, such as Words with Friends, are designed to be played by people with similar smartphones or on social networks. Game apps are a growing market, but many people feel that game apps can't offer the same experience as game consoles.

View Gaming Graphics

Today's video games feature startlingly real graphics. Gaming graphics are created by graphic artists and technical illustrators, who use advanced software and graphics tablets to generate complex images. Windows, Android, and macOS offer **software development kits (SDKs)** for games, with tools for creating 2-D and 3-D drawings, as well as game-playing interfaces, multiplayer control, and more.

Although most computer games are viewed on a 2-D screen, developers are designing 3-D graphics, which appear to have height, width, and depth, making many computer games look surprisingly real.

The next generation of computer gaming uses **augmented reality (AR)**, a technology that combines elements from the physical world with elements generated by a computer, such as images, sound, and video. See **Figure 11-19**.

Figure 11-17: Gaming hardware

Display device

Storage device

Input device

Source: Samsung.com

Figure 11-18: Handheld gaming console

The controls, the screen, and the speakers are built into the device.

The screens are small—3 to 5 inches.

rangizzz/Shutterstock.com, Memo Angeles/Shutterstock.com

Users experience augmented reality using hardware such as monitors and head-mounted display devices. Microsoft HoloLens is a headset with built-in processors, sensors, and cameras. See **Figure 11-20**. It uses **holograms**, projected images that appear three-dimensional, to allow players to superimpose virtual objects and characters onto scanned images of real-world objects in the room, and have the two interact. For example, in one of the first HoloLens games, Young Conker, a squirrel character appears to interact with actual room objects, moving with the user's gaze. The user completes different levels of challenges involving physical movement and interaction, collecting objects, and avoiding hazards along the way. In the game Fragments, the user explores the virtual space to solve a crime, looking for clues and interacting with virtual characters who may appear to be seated in an actual chair in the room.

Figure 11-19: Augmented reality

Identify Gaming Trends

Game consoles are also being used for activities other than entertainment. For example, doctors can practice their fine motor skills on surgery simulators using **motion-sensing game consoles**. Physical therapists use virtual reality gaming techniques to challenge and motivate young patients who have difficulties with physical movements. Wearable sensors and monitors can sense degrees of movement and energy expenditure in tasks such as reaching and balancing. Attaining physical goals can be reflected by reactions in the virtual world.

One software manufacturer is using gaming concepts to enhance e-commerce by creating a virtual shopping experience with 3-D stores. You can browse aisles, view product labels, and even compare products side by side.

The use of augmented reality in gaming is expected to expand as more game developers find new applications for HoloLens capabilities. Although AR headsets will also have to overcome possible limitations on weight, heat generation, and the possibility of motion sickness for users, the possibilities for hologram use in gaming are just beginning to be discovered.

Figure 11-20: Microsoft HoloLens augmented reality headset

Andrew Burton/Getty Images News/Getty Images

Use Social Media

social media | social networking | blogging | microblogging | media sharing | content sharing | collaborative project | social bookmarking | social news | file sharing | virtual social world | crowdfunding | crowdsourcing

Since the early days of the web in the 1990s, computer users have seized on social media as a way to interact with each other using text, pictures, sound, and video. The dawn of tablet computers and mobile devices such as smartphones has only spread the reach and influence of social media. See **Figure 11-21** on the next page.

Define Social Media

Social media refers to the many ways computer users share information and interact using the Internet. See **Figure 11-22** on the next page. The information they share ranges from stories, photos, news, and opinions to complete diaries, daily life updates, professional networking and job searching, as well as sophisticated games.

Social media differs from other forms of communication because it is:

1. **Immediate**: Traditional forms of personal and business communication take time: Letters have to travel through the mail; newspapers and books have to be published, distributed, and sold. Communication using social media can take place almost immediately: a Facebook update can prompt reactions within seconds.

> ### The Bottom Line
> - Social media allows people to share information with others around the world, instantaneously.
> - Different types of social media let you network with others, publish your ideas, share media, work collectively, share links, news, and files, and play interactive games in virtual environments.
> - While social media has many benefits, it entails some risks; users must decide if, and how, they want to participate.

Figure 11-21: Types of social media

Whenever you read or post a message on Facebook, write an online product review, or play an online game with others, you are participating in social media.

Blogs let you publish online diary entries.

$99,832 USD

Raised of $150,000 Goal

11 hours

Crowdfunding sites raise money for projects or causes.

Media sharing sites let you share photos and videos.

CONTRIBUTE NOW ▸

iStockphoto.com/Erik Khalitov, iStockphoto.com/fazon1, iStockphoto.com/william87, Source: Indiegogo.com

Figure 11-22: Using social media

rvlsoft/Shutterstock.com, weedezign/Shutterstock.com

2. **Widespread**: Since their beginnings in the 1990s, social media websites have exploded in popularity worldwide. According to a recent estimate, one in four people around the world uses social networking—more than 1.7 billion users. In the United States alone, over 70 percent of computer users participate in social networking.

3. **Interactive**: Traditional media outlets such as television, newspaper, and radio are "one-way streets," with little opportunity for users to respond. With social media, interactivity is common and expected. A user posts a photo or a video on a sharing site hoping to get a response from others. In fact, almost all traditional media outlets, such as TV and radio, have social media sites where users can post reactions and contribute content.

Social media helps us form online communities with users with similar interests around the world.

Identify Types of Social Media

Social media has evolved into many forms, which are summarized in Table 11-3. You can choose the types of social media in which to participate, depending on your interests.

Table 11-3: Types of social media

Type	Lets you	Includes	Examples
Social networking	Share ideas, opinions, photos, videos, websites	Personal and business networking, chat, video chat and video conferencing, instant messaging, online dating, social memorials	Facebook, LinkedIn, Snapchat, Google+, Microsoft Skype, Google Hangouts
Blogging and microblogging	Create and update an online journal that you share with readers	Personal journals, essays, expert advice, information on special areas of interest	Twitter, Blogger, WordPress, Tumblr
Media sharing and content sharing	View and distribute pictures, videos, audio files	Photo and video sharing, podcasting, news sites, online learning, distance learning	YouTube, Break, Dailymotion, Flickr, Photobucket, Picasa
Collaborative projects	Read, add, and discuss articles about topics of interest	Online encyclopedias, forums, wikis, message boards, news groups	Wikipedia, WikiAnswers, Wikia
Social bookmarking and social news	Tag (mark) and search websites; share websites, articles, news stories, media	Tagging; knowledge management	Delicious, Reddit, Digg
File sharing	Send and receive files from others on an Internet location	Free or paid access to file storage locations on the Internet	Egnyte, ShareFile, Hightail, Dropbox, WeTransfer
Virtual social worlds	Play games with others; create a simulated environment	Virtual reality games	World of Warcraft
Crowdfunding	Raise funds for a project, cause, or business	Websites that let anyone contribute; site takes a percentage of funds raised	GoFundMe, Indiegogo, Kickstarter, Startsomegood

While placing websites into categories can help organize your thinking about social media, a website might span more than one category. For example, you can share YouTube videos on Facebook, and you can post comments on blogs.

Gather Support with Social Media

Social media has become a major way for individuals and organizations to gather knowledge, support, or contributions from a worldwide audience. Such support might include physical labor, data collection, research, or financing.

Crowdsourcing entails using the Internet and the "intelligence of the crowd" to accomplish a task or solve a problem for the benefit of all. Project leaders put out a public request on the Internet, sometimes called an "open call," and motivated people respond. Examples of crowdsourcing include the following:

- **Community projects**, such as a beach cleanup, or electronic petitions to accomplish a change in a community
- **Creative projects**, in which people contribute ideas such as designing a new public building or a new state license plate

- **Skill-based projects**, in which people donate skills such as editing, translation, scanning, or data transcription to create or improve publicly available data (such as census information, databases, or historic newspapers)
- **Location-based projects**, such as wildlife counts, language use surveys, or a recent NASA project that asks citizen astronomers to help locate asteroids that may pose a threat to earth

A particular type of crowdsourcing is **crowdfunding**, in which individuals come together on the Internet to provide funding that will support others in an endeavor. See Figure 11-23 for an example of a successful crowdfunding project on Kickstarter. com. Other popular crowdfunding sites include Indiegogo and Crowdfunder.

On the Job Now

If a business does not have the talent in house to handle a new project, CrowdSource (crowd-souce.com) provides a managed workforce for hire.

Figure 11-23: Successful Kickstarter campaign

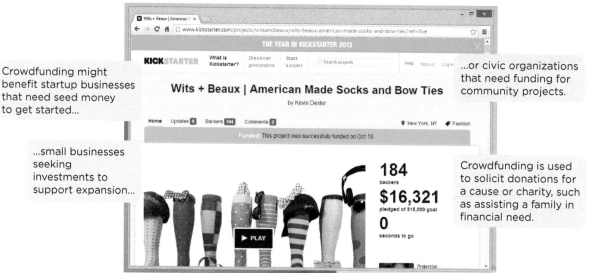

Source: Kickstarter, Inc.

Use Social Media in Business

Social media is widely used not only for social networking between individuals, but for businesses. In contrast to traditional avenues for advertising, social networking sites such as Facebook, Twitter, and Tumbler let businesses reach a wide audience quickly, at low cost.

Many businesses have social media pages, which they use to foster connections with their users and increase brand awareness. Businesses regularly use them to share photos, videos, and updated information with their customers and potential customers. The speed and immediacy of social networking helps businesses be flexible in their offerings by "getting the word out" quickly and learning customer reactions in real time, helping them make effective business decisions.

In addition to free sites, businesses can also opt for paid options on social networking sites, to further extend their reach. They can target customers of a specific age, location, or interest group. Most customers expect businesses to have social media sites, and they use them frequently for communication. Social media sites are essential for businesses to build relationships with customers.

Evaluate Social Media

Opinions of social media vary widely: some people use it regularly and can't imagine life without it; others are suspicious and avoid it completely. Is social media a positive force in our lives or a negative one? There is support for both sides.

Pros: On the plus side, social media is accessible; it's an inexpensive way for people to reach a wide audience. Communications can be immediate, and they're easy to change. Businesses can communicate easily with customers and hear their reactions. News organizations use social media to post breaking news and to receive contributions of news items from their audience. Social media can help people overcome isolation so they feel informed and connected.

Cons: On the minus side, the quality of social media content can vary widely because it lacks the expert oversight of traditional media (editors or managers, for example). Security and privacy are also important concerns:

- It's not always possible to control who can access personal data posted online.
- New online acquaintances might misrepresent themselves using false identities.
- Users need to exercise care regarding the type of information they post; for example, future employers may form unfavorable opinions of job candidates who have posted unprofessional images and language in the past.
- Some users are uncomfortable that businesses can track our browsing and shopping habits so they can target us with customized advertising.
- Other people become addicted to social media, at the expense of personal relationships.

In the end, it's up to individual users and businesses whether the benefits of social media outweigh the risks. But social media use will likely continue its growth for the foreseeable future.

 #digitalmedia

Go to twitter.com, search for @SAMTechNow, the book's Twitter account, and then follow @-SAMTechNow to get tweets on your home page.

Chapter Review

Define Graphics

1. Name two graphic file formats that can produce large file sizes.
2. Name the four main ways you can create a graphic yourself.
3. What kind of software lets scientists and engineers create highly detailed and technically accurate drawings?

Define Digital Audio

4. What does MIDI stand for? Briefly describe its use.
5. Briefly describe how a speech synthesizer works.
6. What kind of software is Apple Garage Band, and why would you use it?

Define Digital Video

7. What kind of digital video camera captures video and sends it directly to a computer?
8. What hardware and software does your computer need to play video?
9. Name two kinds of streaming media, and give an example of the kind of program you might view with each one.
10. Name two programs you might use for video conferencing and the type of hardware that is compatible with each one.

Define Animation

11. What kind of animation is useful for training and teaching, particularly when learning can be dangerous or difficult?
12. Briefly describe in-betweening and how it is used in animation.
13. Name three software products that let you create animations.

Use Gaming Systems

14. Xbox 360 and Nintendo Wii are examples of what kind of hardware?
15. Name three types of input devices used to control movement and player actions in computer games.
16. Name the Microsoft product that lets you experience augmented reality and briefly explain how it works.

Use Social Media

17. Name three ways that social media differs from traditional communications, and give examples of each one.
18. On what type of social media site would you maintain a personal journal to share with others?
19. If you wanted to raise funds online for a new business you plan to start, what type of site would you use?
20. List three reasons businesses use social media.

Test Your Knowledge Now

1. Which of the following is a highly compressed bitmap graphic format used for web graphics?
   a. BMP
   b. PNG
   c. TIF
   d. GIF

2. _____ is a photo-editing software product you can use to correct red-eye.
   a. Adobe Photoshop
   b. Microsoft Paint
   c. CorelDRAW
   d. Microsoft Office

3. What type of graphic keeps its quality as its size increases?
   a. bitmap
   b. JPEG
   c. vector
   d. BMP

4. Which of the following is a copy-protected audio file format used by Apple iTunes?
   a. MP4
   b. WAV
   c. WMA
   d. RA

5. What converts analog sound waves into digital sound?
   a. sound recorder software
   b. sampling software
   c. a synthesizer
   d. an audio input device

6. Which of the following converts speech into text on a computer screen?
   a. text-to-speech software
   b. speech synthesizer
   c. speech recognition software
   d. MIDI files

7. To edit videos, you can use video-editing software such as _____
   a. Apple iMovie.
   b. Vimeo.
   c. YouTube.
   d. Apple Garage Band.

8. To convert a video to another format to reduce its file size, you would use a _____
   a. camcorder.
   b. media player.
   c. codec.
   d. plug-in.

9. A _____ lets you view Internet content on your television.
   a. media player
   b. set-top box
   c. codec
   d. video card

10. A series of image frames displayed quickly enough for us to perceive them as continuous motion is called _____
    a. digital audio.
    b. digital video.
    c. skins.
    d. streaming video.

11. How many frames per second (fps) does a typical 3-D computer game use?
    a. 60
    b. 24
    c. 30
    d. 200

12. Animation in 3-D computer games is created _____
    a. during the production phase.
    b. in "real time," as you're playing
    c. using PowerPoint transitions.
    d. using simulations.

13. A series of slightly different bitmap images displayed in sequence on the web is called a(n) _____
    a. animated GIF.
    b. wireframe drawing.
    c. hologram.
    d. simulation.

14. Which of the following is an example of a game console?
    a. digital camera
    b. Xbox 360
    c. Halo
    d. SDK

15. Which of the following lets you play games using augmented reality?
    a. SDK
    b. HoloLens
    c. Nintendo Wii
    d. animation software

16. Which of the following lets you interact with virtual objects superimposed on images of real objects?
    a. Nintendo Wii
    b. augmented reality gaming
    c. video consoles
    d. Doom

17. Which of the following is a large-scale multiplayer game?
    a. Overwatch
    b. Sony PlayStation
    c. SDK
    d. Autodesk Maya

18. Which type of social media site would you use to share ideas, photos, videos, and opinions?
    a. collaborative projects
    b. social networking
    c. social bookmarking
    d. file sharing

19. Which of the following is not a feature of social media?
    a. immediate
    b. interactive
    c. solitary
    d. widespread

20. What type of social media site would you use to gather volunteers for a town cleanup project?
    a. crowdsourcing
    b. crowdfunding
    c. file sharing
    d. blogging

21. In the space next to each image below, write the letter of the phrase that describes it.
    a. Set-top box
    b. Digital sound
    c. HoloLens
    d. Analog sound
    e. Sound card

_____ Source: Apple, Inc.   _____ Ilona Baha/Shutterstock.com

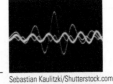

_____ Sebastian Kaulitzki/Shutterstock.com

_____ Andrew Burton/Getty Images News/Getty Images

_____ DeSerg/Shutterstock.com

Try This Now

1: Free Market Social Philanthropy

Free market social philanthropy sites such as GoFundMe and Fundly provide customizable websites that represent you and your story, then share it to collect online donations. People give money more efficiently to a vast array of personal causes using this crowdfunding model. Sites like GoFundMe typically take a 5 percent cut of the money raised on the site.

    a. Research the most common types of causes posted on philanthropy funded sites. Write 100+ words about these causes.

    b. Research news stories about how this type of site changed a life for the better and a story of how people were fooled by some's story. Write a paragraph about each of the two stories.

2: Leverage Social Media for a Small Business

Social media for a small business is no longer optional; it is integral to its success. By having a presence on social media, businesses make it easier for their customers to create brand loyalty.

    a. Research marketing a small business on social media and in your own words create a list of eight best practices for a local business.

    b. Search for one of your favorite brands at Twitter.com. Copy and paste the last eight postings that the company posted recently. Write a paragraph summarizing the purpose of your selected brand's connection with their customers.

    c. Submit the document to your instructor.

3: Professional LinkedIn Social Presence

The professional social media site LinkedIn is helpful for career networking. LinkedIn allows you to search for volunteer and paid internship positions in addition to full-time positions. Open a browser and then open the site LinkedIn.com. Create a professional profile to begin making connections with people that can recommend you for a position.

    a. Your profile should list your career interests, education, job experience, skills, technology experience, and expertise.

    b. After you complete your profile, share it with your instructor by adding a connection.

Critical Thinking Now

1: Professional Image Palette with Color Hunter

Creating a professionally designed color palette can give a polished look to a webpage, Word document, or PowerPoint presentation. Search for a colorful picture of your hometown online at bing.com or google.com using the image search feature, and then download the image to your local computer. Open the site colorhunter.com and upload the image to create a free color palette based on the hues and tones of the image. In a Word document, display the picture and a screenshot of the palette from Color Hunter. Write a paragraph of at least 100 words on the topic of how a color palette based on a company's logo or hometown event could be used within professional documents.

2: Augmented Reality Gaming

Pokémon Go is a popular game that has a GPS-enabled map of the player's real-world surrounding. The app opens up the smartphone's camera, showing the Pokémon as an augmented reality creature seemingly moving in the real world. Research how augmented reality is changing gaming.

AR Gaming

iStockphoto.com/George Clerk

    a. What are the five augmented reality games that are being developed or presently available? Explain the topic of each game.

    b. What are the five most popular games for virtual reality? Explain the topic of each game.

3: Social Networking Personal Safety

Facebook, Twitter, Pinterest, LinkedIn, and other social networks have become an integral part of online lives. Social networks are a great way to stay connected with others, but you should be wary about how much personal information you post. Research the best practices for staying safe while using social media and in your own words, list the 10 best practices for social networking in your personal life.

Ethical Issues Now

Snapchat and the Ethics of Copyright

The Digital Millennium Copyright Act covers many of the copyright laws for Internet postings. The most common infraction of this set of laws is the posting of other people's images and videos on sites such as the Snapchat app.

a. Research the Digital Millennium Copyright Act. In at least 100 of your own words, briefly explain what this set of laws covers.

b. Research the Terms of Service for Snapchat. In at least 100 of your own words, briefly explain what the website allows when you post to Snapchat.

c. If you own copyright to your own image or video and post it to Snapchat, people can legally watch this video. Would it be legal for your audience to copy your Snapchat image or video to watch later if they have a very slow Internet connection in their apartment? What do the Snapchat Terms of Service say about this action?

Team Up Now—Record a Podcast (Audio Blog)

Record a Podcast

TED Summary Audio Podcast

Note: This assignment requires the use of a headset or built-in microphone for audio recording.

Many companies create free audio and video podcasts about new products to post on websites or to make available for download. Search ted.com videos about a topic that interests your team. Then create an audio podcast on the same subject. You may use any audio recording technology for this assignment on a computer or smartphone. If you do not have audio recording software, download a free copy of Audacity for a Windows, Mac, or Linux computer at the site audacity. sourceforge.net.

a. Before you record a podcast, it is best to write a script. As a team, decide on a ted.com video to watch. Write a script of at least 250 words about this Ted talk.

b. Split up the script in equal parts by topic and record the audio for your commercial podcast summarizing the Ted talk.

c. Save the audio file in the format requested by your instructor. Submit the script and audio podcast to your instructor.

Key Terms

3-D animation
3-D CAD software
AAC
AIFF
analog sound wave
animated GIF
animation
animation software
audio capture and editing software
audio input device
audio software
augmented reality (AR)
bitmap image
blogging
BMP
camcorder
clip art gallery
codec
collaborative project
compression
computer-aided design (CAD)
   software
content sharing
crowdfunding
crowdsourcing
digital audio
digital camera
digital graphic
digital video
digital video camera
digitize
download
drawing program
file sharing
frames per second (fps)
game console
geotagging
GIF
graphic
graphics software
graphics tablet

HD (high-definition) video
headset
hologram
HTML5
image-editing software
in-betweening
JPEG
license filter
live audio feed
live video streaming
lossless compression
lossy compression
M4P
media player
media sharing
megapixel
meme
microblogging
micro speaker
MIDI (Musical Instrument Digital
   Interface)
mix
motion-sensing game console
Moving Pictures Experts Group
   (MPEG)
MP3
MP4
music production software
on-demand content
paint software
phoneme
photo-editing software
pixel
plug-in
PNG
PowerPoint transition
rendering
resolution
resolution dependent
sampling
sampling software

scanner
set-top box
simulation
skin
smart TV
smartphone
social bookmarking
social media
social networking
social news
software development kit (SDK)
sound card
sound recorder software
speech recognition software
speech synthesizer
speech-to-text software
stand-alone player
streaming audio
streaming video
SVG
SWF format
synthesized sound
text-to-speech software
TIF
transition
Ultra HD video
vector image
video
video card
video conferencing
video console
video-editing software
viral video
virtual social world
voice-over
Voice over IP (VoIP)
WAV
WAVE
webcam
wireframe drawing
WMA

A Changing World

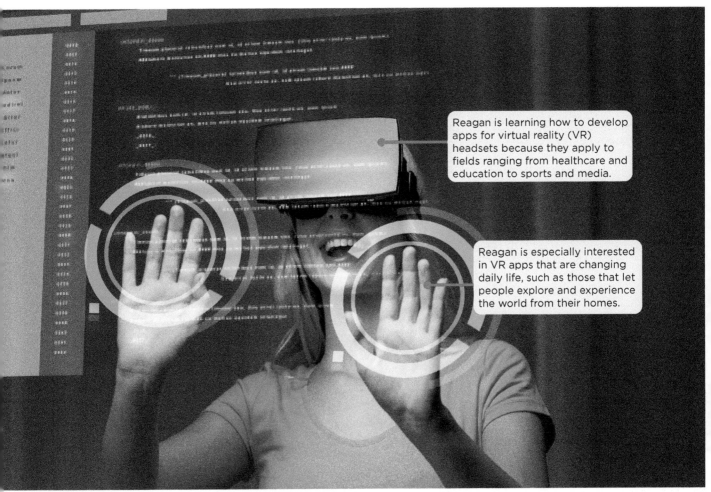

Reagan is learning how to develop apps for virtual reality (VR) headsets because they apply to fields ranging from healthcare and education to sports and media.

Reagan is especially interested in VR apps that are changing daily life, such as those that let people explore and experience the world from their homes.

Syda Productions/Shutterstock.com

Every new development in technology brings with it new career opportunities, and the fields of augmented reality and virtual reality are no exception. Reagan Ryan is taking a class on developing Android apps for virtual reality headsets. She is dedicated to creating apps that help everyone avoid stress and lead more fulfilling lives.

Use Automated Technology

embedded computer | smart device | automated technology | device mesh | adaptive system | telematics | smart card | Internet of Things (IoT) | smart grid | near field communication (NFC) | radio frequency identification (RFID) tag | drone | unmanned aerial vehicle (UAV) | home automation | chip-and-PIN technology | kiosk

The Bottom Line
- Automated devices and systems are designed to run automatically, with little or no user intervention, simplifying tasks that people once performed.
- Automated technology relies on small, limited-purpose computers embedded in devices such as vehicles, thermostats, and appliances.

Fifty years ago, people imagined that future inventions would include talking cars that drove on their own and refrigerators that tracked what you ate that day. These examples of automated technology are available today. They rely on **embedded computers** and are often called smart devices. See **Figure 12-1**.

A **smart device** is an appliance, vehicle, environmental system, wearable or mobile computer, or any other machine that includes electronics, software, sensors, and network connectivity to collect and exchange data. You can often use a mobile device such as a smartphone or smart watch to control smart devices, though many are designed to run automatically, making them **automated technology**. Smart devices are part of the **device mesh**, a mix of devices and technology that you use to access apps, services, and information or interact with other people and organizations.

Figure 12-1: Automation in daily life

Cruise control systems are automated to maintain speed.

An automated refrigerator can signal when food is no longer fresh.

Programmable home thermostats monitor the temperature and can be part of the Internet of Things (IoT).

Riders on mass transit systems can use a smart card with an embedded computer chip instead of a ticket or token.

Ye Liew/Shutterstock.com, Source: Samsung, auremar/Shutterstock.com, Source: Nest Labs

Use Automated Motor Vehicles

Perhaps you've heard about cars that can park themselves. What's next? Cars that can drive on their own. Companies such as Volvo, Tesla, and Apple are developing self-driving, or autonomous, cars that use embedded computers to control acceleration and braking, sensors to detect surroundings, and a global positioning system (GPS) to navigate. See **Figure 12-2**.

Although fully self-driving cars are years from mass production, automated features use embedded computers to improve the safety and efficiency of all automobiles manufactured today:

- An embedded computer monitors engine emissions in your car and adjusts settings such as idle speed to keep the emissions as low as possible.
- Cruise control systems use embedded computers to maintain speed.
- **Adaptive systems** can detect if your car is following another car too closely or moving into the path of another car and adjust the speed or steering to maintain a safe distance.

- Airbag sensors can detect the severity of a collision and inflate the airbag accordingly, which reduces airbag injuries.
- Some cars use **telematics**, a wireless communication technology, to provide systems such as roadside assistance and remote vehicle tracking.

Figure 12-2: Self-driving car

CLOUD BASED 3D DIGITAL MAP

Rooftop sensor, cloud connection, and a GPS help to navigate this self-driving car.

Source: Volvo Car Corporation

Emergency vehicles also use automated technology to enhance emergency services and reach their destinations safely and quickly. For example, an ambulance can use embedded computers to control traffic signals and communicate with medical staff to improve treatment on site and in the emergency room.

Use Automated Public Transportation

Americans are using public transit more now than they have in over 60 years. One reason for the move is that embedded computers are helping to make public transportation convenient, efficient, and safe. For example, on smart buses, drivers use touch screens to check traffic, communicate with people waiting for rides, collect fares, and provide travel information to riders waiting for the bus.

In addition, mass transit systems use smart cards instead of tickets or tokens. About the size of a credit card, a **smart card** contains an embedded computer chip to manage payments and deposits and to provide security.

Public transportation vehicles can communicate with embedded computers in road signs to reduce traffic congestion, display the safest speed limits for the conditions, and transmit warnings to drivers.

Public transportation is part of the trend moving toward self-driving vehicles. One example is Olli, an electric-powered, 3-D printed, self-driving bus. Riders use an app on their mobile devices to summon Olli, similar to requesting a ride with an app such as Uber or Lyft. Olli is equipped with sensors that collect data about traffic, road construction, and other variables, allowing it to make quick decisions to keep riders safe.

Use Smart Home Appliances

Washing machines that launder clothes using the most efficient amount of electricity and water, and ovens you can turn off from smartphones are examples of smart home appliances. As part of the **Internet of Things (IoT)**, they use sensors to collect data and embedded computers to reduce energy consumption and enhance daily living.

In some home appliances, an embedded computer controls how much energy the appliance is using. If the appliance is connected to the **smart grid**, an automated network linking your meter to the local utility, you can set the machine to run when

#changingworld

Slow response times of emergency vehicle services due to traffic and weather conditions cause many heart attack emergency calls to end in tragedy. The ambulance-drone can save lives with an onboard, integrated defibrillator. The goal is to improve existing emergency infrastructure with a network of ambulance drones.

Hot Technology Now

Apps such as Uber connect you with a driver at a tap of a button. You can share your location to request a ride and receive a fare estimate in seconds. Uber is the first company to deploy driverless car rides and truck deliveries.

electricity rates are at their lowest. Other appliances can send messages to your mobile device, such as alerting you when a dryer's cycle is complete. Appliance technicians can also use embedded computers to remotely troubleshoot mechanical problems.

You can use a mobile or other smart device to control many appliances and other automated systems. For example, Amazon Echo and Google Home are voice-activated speakers that respond to your requests to turn on and control entertainment devices, provide information such as traffic conditions, manage home automation features, and communicate with other smart devices. See Figure 12-3.

Figure 12-3: Amazon Echo smart speaker

Voice-activated smart speakers respond to your requests to control other devices.

Source: Amazon

Use Automated Stores

Embedded computers in appliances such as refrigerators and ovens are only half the story. The other half is embedded technology in supermarkets and other stores.

Near field communication (NFC) is a short-range wireless technology that works with smartphones and **radio frequency identification (RFID) tags**, which are programmable computer chips embedded in paper or plastic. If a grocer includes an RFID tag next to a product on the shelves, you can hold your smartphone near the tag to send a coupon or detailed nutritional information to your phone.

Another shopping technology uses a robot-controlled grocery cart that stores your shopping list, tracks your purchases, and helps you find items anywhere in the store. With these technologies, you can fill a shopping cart from home, pay for the products using a smartphone, and then arrange to have the goods delivered to your door—avoiding the store completely. To avoid shopping altogether, you can use an online service such as Blue Apron or Fresh Direct, which deliver meal-ready ingredients and recipes to your door.

Other stores let you shop online and schedule deliveries or arrange for in-store pickups. In the near future, your purchases might be delivered by a **drone**, also called an **unmanned aerial vehicle (UAV)**, which is a small aircraft without a pilot that can navigate by remote control or on its own.

Automate Homes

Buyers have always balanced cost, location, and size when searching for a new home. Now they can consider an additional factor: home automation. **Home automation** involves controlling systems such as heating, cooling, and security to increase comfort, quality of life, and even health.

Using sensors and embedded computers, you can set up a home automation network and communicate with it from a control pad or mobile device. For example, you can set music to start playing as party guests arrive, lock or unlock doors remotely, and turn off lights in empty rooms. See **Figure 12-4**.

Home automation systems are especially valuable for older people who want to live independently. They can coordinate smart refrigerators that track nutrition, smart ovens that simplify cooking tasks, and monitors that detect when someone needs help.

Use ATMs and Kiosks

Using an automated teller machine (ATM) to withdraw cash from a bank account is nothing new. You insert a card with a magnetic stripe, enter a personal identification number (PIN), and then indicate the amount of cash you want to receive. Recent innovations are improving card security. Cards using **chip-and-PIN technology** store data on an embedded chip instead of a magnetic stripe, which is much more difficult to copy. In some cases, you don't need a card at all. You set up a banking transaction from a home computer or mobile device, and then scan a code on your smartphone to complete the transaction.

New technology also makes the machines more personal. For example, using one type of ATM, you can interact with a bank teller by videoconference.

Banks aren't the only businesses that have automated customer interactions. Machines called **kiosks** enable self-service transactions in busy locations such as airports and hotels, so you don't have to wait in line to check in for a flight or a room. Healthcare providers can also install kiosks or tablets for patients, who can use them to check in and enter information such as insurance numbers.

Perform Daily Living Tasks Online

online banking | mobile banking | mobile payment | mobile wallet | e-learning | asynchronous course | synchronous course | live blogging | on-demand media | electronic retail (e-tail) sales | mobile commerce (m-commerce) | digital citizen

Your grandparents probably spent much of their day outside their home. They managed their finances at their local bank, picked up a paper at a newsstand, went to a theater to see movies, and shopped along a downtown street or in a mall. Now you can perform all of these activities from home using a computer and an Internet connection.

Figure 12-4: Home automation

Home automation app lets owners control home systems inside or outside the house.

Hot Technology Now

The Nest thermostat is a device you can use to control your home's heating and cooling systems and lower the cost of your energy bill. You can use any computer or mobile device to manage the Nest.

The Bottom Line

- You can manage most of your daily living tasks, including keeping up with news, finances, entertainment, and shopping, using websites and online tools.
- If job or home responsibilities prevent you from enrolling in traditional classes, you can extend your education using online resources.
- As digital citizens, users have a responsibility to use technology effectively.

Figure 12-5: Managing daily living tasks

E-learning is formal education in which students connect to instructors, information, and other students online.

Track your bank balances and conduct financial transactions online.

Research products and services online, and then make a purchase from any Internet-connected device.

Find and read news articles and opinions online, in some cases, even as events are happening.

Manage Finances Online

Most people use computers in some way to manage their finances. For example, you might use financial software to balance your checkbook and track your income and expenses. Banks and other financial institutions also let you do **online banking** and **mobile banking**, in which you use a computer or mobile device connected to the Internet to manage your bank accounts. For example, you can use a smartphone to take a picture of a check and then submit the picture to your bank to make a deposit. If you use a **mobile payment** service (also called a **mobile wallet**) such as Apple Pay or Android Pay, you can use a mobile device instead of cash, check, or debit or credit card to pay for goods and services. Online wallets, also called electronic wallets, such as PayPal work in a similar way, except they are available on all types of computers.

At many websites, you can plan for retirement, maintain a budget, and calculate mortgage payments. The Internal Revenue Service (IRS) and state governments have websites where you can file your federal and state tax returns. If you want to invest in the stock market, you can use online investing tools to buy and sell stocks and bonds without using a broker.

Access Online Education

Suppose you want to enroll in a career-training program, but your current job or family responsibilities prevent you from taking traditional classes. A popular solution is online education, also called **e-learning**, short for "electronic learning." E-learning is a type of formal education in which students connect to instructors, information, and other students using a computer and the Internet.

Some courses are **asynchronous courses**, which means that instead of receiving instruction live from a teacher, you connect to educational content such as recorded demonstrations and lectures to participate at your own pace. Others are **synchronous courses**. The instructor holds a class that you and other students attend virtually in real time. The teacher speaks, plays videos, and shows presentations. When you ask a question, you receive an immediate response from the instructor. In both types of online education, you interact with other students using blogs and wikis to hold discussions, collaborate on projects, and brainstorm.

People interested in less formal types of e-learning can use educational websites such as Khan Academy, Lynda.com, and Skillshare. These websites present video tutorials and provide self-assessments, help you develop business, software, technology, and creative skills, and prepare you for standardized tests.

Access Online News and Information

Fifteen or twenty years ago, most people learned about world events through television or newspapers. The web has changed how we access news in the following ways:

- **Type of information**: The web has changed the kind of information provided in news reports. TV newscasts feature amateur videos from video-sharing sites to cover events such as weather disasters. Newspapers quote bloggers who post eyewitness accounts of events, an activity called **live blogging**.
- **Access to information**: As a news consumer, you can use the web to access almost every newspaper and magazine in the world. If you run across an article you find important or funny, you can share it with your friends on social networks. In fact, referrals from social networks are the fastest-growing source of traffic for news websites.
- **Contribute to information**: On hybrid websites that combine news and blogging, you can develop and refine news reports by commenting on them and posting contributions.
- **Receive information**: Websites focused on time-sensitive information, such as news, weather, and sports, send headlines and other notifications directly to your computer or mobile device.

Access Online Entertainment and Media

As with news and information, the web has transformed entertainment and media by delivering it online. **On-demand media** is popular because you can view or listen to it at any time rather than according to a set schedule. For example, you can do the following:

- Download digital books and magazines and then use an e-book reader or tablet to read them.
- Stream TV shows, movies, and music online, instead of downloading them.
- Subscribe to podcasts of radio programs or other audio content, and then listen to them at your convenience.

The web is making entertainment more personal in other ways. For example, using an online music service, you can create a personal radio station by listening to songs and then voting for the ones you like or dislike. You can also let the app suggest new songs based on your preferences. See **Figure 12-6**.

Shop Online

Do you like to research products and services online before you buy them? If so, you are part of the trend in **electronic retail (e-tail) sales**. E-tail websites are helpful to consumers looking for bargains. These sites provide product descriptions and reviews and let you compare features and prices of similar products. You can make purchases online or save items in a wish list for you or others to purchase later.

Another shopping trend is **mobile commerce (m-commerce)**, which involves using wireless mobile devices such as smartphones and tablets to make retail purchases of almost any product or service. Instead of carrying cash or bank cards, you can use your mobile device to scan a graphic code and then authorize a payment from a connected account. A new type of m-commerce are Amazon Dash buttons, which are small proprietary Wi-Fi connected devices you touch to reorder products such as household supplies. See **Figure 12-7**.

Amazon Go extends m-commerce into the store itself. Before entering an Amazon Go store, you activate the Amazon Go app, find and take the products you want, and then leave, with no checkout necessary. Amazon charges your account and sends you a receipt.

Become a Digital Citizen

When you use information technology, especially the Internet, regularly and effectively, you become a **digital citizen**. In addition to skills and knowledge, such as using mobile devices and apps proficiently to perform tasks, digital citizenship means using technology ethically and responsibly and being aware of upcoming changes so that everyone can use technology productively.

According to digitalcitizenship.net, digital citizenship has nine elements including digital access, commerce, communication, literacy, etiquette, law and ethics, rights and responsibilities, security, and health and wellness. All of the elements involve making appropriate decisions about using technology. For example, if you often use a video chat app such as Skype, be willing to train or adapt to people who do not have or use that tool when you communicate with them.

Use Intelligent Workplaces and Classrooms

enterprise computing | social enterprise | telecommute | BYOD | computer-aided manufacturing (CAM) | machine-to-machine (M2M) | telemedicine | mobile health (mHealth) | ingestible | digital divide | WhiteFi | learning management system (LMS)

Innovations in workplaces and classrooms are making it possible for all types of people to work and learn more productively. In many cases, people use these innovations to work and learn independently or remotely, away from a central physical location.

Use Enterprise Computing

Have you dreamed of starting a career in a major corporation and working your way up to the executive suite? If so, you aspire to be part of an enterprise. Enterprises have special computing needs because they employ hundreds or thousands of people in many locations.

Figure 12-6: Online entertainment

Source: Spotify

By the Numbers Now

Of all shoppers considering a major purchase, 81% conduct online research before making the purchase decision.

Figure 12-7: M-commerce

James W Copeland/Shutterstock.com

Press an Amazon Dash button to reorder consumer products.

The Bottom Line
- Technology is changing the way enterprises and manufacturing companies do business.
- Technology is also changing how healthcare, transportation, and education services are delivered to people who need them.

Figure 12-8: Working and learning online

A recent college graduate starts a new job with a major corporation, but spends three days a week working from home.

Following directions from a surgeon on a video conference, a medical team prepares to treat a patient who lives far from a surgical hospital.

A factory foreman supervises robots on the assembly line from the safety of his office as they perform dangerous manufacturing tasks.

Elementary school students use computer simulations to learn how a cold virus develops and spreads.

spotmatik/Shutterstock.com, Nataliya Hora/Shutterstock.com, iStockphoto.com/Blend_Images, Hurst Photo/Shutterstock.com

On the Job Now

Most employees prefer not being stuck at their desk with a desktop computer. Mobile computing provides the flexibility employees like and makes telecommuting easy.

Figure 12-9: Mobile devices on the shop floor

Monkey Business Images/Shutterstock.com

Enterprise computing refers to the computer network a business uses to let employees communicate with customers, vendors, and other employees. For example, an airline has software that customers can use to book air travel and check flight information, employees use to produce payroll and track sales, and vendors use to deliver services such as in-flight meals. To make that communication easy and familiar, businesses work with the **social enterprise**, which uses short blog posts and collaboration tools instead of email and in-person meetings.

Because they can connect to the enterprise network from anywhere, employees who need flexible work schedules can **telecommute**—an arrangement that lets them work from home and conduct business using the phone and the Internet.

When they do come to the office, employees increasingly are bringing their own computing devices, a trend called **BYOD** for "bring your own device." Employees strongly prefer using their own mobile devices to desktop computers issued by the information technology (IT) department of their employer. If employees take advantage of workplace storage options such as SharePoint and Google Drive for Business, they can store documents and data in one place but access it anywhere and with any device.

Use Technology in Manufacturing

When you think of a factory, you probably imagine a chaotic place full of industrial dangers where people work on an assembly line to produce identical products. That type of manufacturing is becoming a thing of the past. New and future factories are bright centers of innovation, primarily due to **computer-aided manufacturing (CAM)**.

Manufacturers use CAM to streamline production and ship products out the door more quickly. With CAM, robots perform work that is too dangerous, detailed, or monotonous for people. In particular, they play a major role in automotive manufacturing. For example, robots typically paint the bodies of cars and trucks on an automotive assembly line because painting is complex, difficult, and hazardous. Pairing robotic systems with human workers also improves quality, productivity, cost efficiency, and competitiveness. A Mercedes E-Class car that took 61 hours to build on a traditional assembly line in 2005 now takes only 30 hours and fewer workers when robotics are added to the line.

Computers and mobile devices on the shop floor also make it possible to order parts and materials from the warehouse just in time to assemble a custom product according to the customer's specifications. This streamlined approach is called just-in-time manufacturing. See **Figure 12-9.**

Finally, using **machine-to-machine (M2M)** communications, a company's computers can monitor assembly lines and equipment to keep them running safely and efficiently.

Use Technology in Healthcare

Every job in healthcare involves computers, whether patients receive care in a hospital, clinic, or their own homes. Physicians use computers to monitor patients' vital signs and to research symptoms and diagnoses. Surgeons use computer-controlled devices to provide precision during operations such as transplant surgeries.

If you live in a remote area and need to see a specialist, your doctor might use telemedicine to confer with the specialist. **Telemedicine** involves holding a video conference with another healthcare professional.

Mobile health (mHealth) is a growing trend. Doctors and nurses typically use smartphones and tablets to access electronic health records (EHRs), which are electronic versions of patients' medical histories. EHRs can be stored in the cloud where patients and members of a health team can easily access the records. Patients also can use mHealth devices to monitor their conditions and treatments, reducing their dependence on overburdened healthcare systems. For example, one mHealth application tracks prescription information and reminds patients to take medications by sending text messages to their mobile devices.

Medical monitoring technology is another area of recent innovation. You can wear an electronic bracelet that collects your vital signs and sends the data to a specialist for analysis. People with diabetes may soon be able to wear special contact lenses with embedded microchips to monitor their glucose levels. Embedded microchips also help people use paralyzed limbs and control eye pressure during cataract surgery. Smart pills, also called **ingestibles**, contain tiny sensors that help people remember to take medications regularly and in the right dosages. Some ingestibles contain micro cameras and replace invasive procedures such as colonoscopies.

3-D printing is revolutionizing healthcare and helping to reduce costs. For example, experts have used 3-D printed skin on burn victims and 3-D printed airway splints for babies whose lungs are prone to collapsing. Besides its use for prosthetic devices, healthcare professionals are using 3-D printing to create flexible casts that heal bones 40 to 80 percent faster than traditional casts. They are also creating 3-D printed pills in shapes that improve a drug's release rate.

Use Technology in Transportation Services

You've heard of the global economy. A product such as a soccer ball is developed in one country, manufactured in another using materials from three other countries, and then sold around the world. The global economy needs high-tech transportation services to run efficiently.

If you work in the transportation industry, you use handheld computers to scan codes on packages or containers full of products before loading them on a vehicle, train, ship, or plane. See **Figure 12-10**. A computer automatically routes the packages to their destinations as efficiently as possible. You can track the progress of a package using almost any computing device.

If you're driving a truck or other vehicle, you use an onboard navigation system with GPS, which communicates with satellites to determine your exact location. The entire transportation industry relies on GPS to navigate from one location to another quickly and safely.

Self-driving long-haul trucks also rely on GPS for navigation in addition to robotics for mechanical control. For example, the autonomous trucks tested by Otto, a startup company owned by Uber, use technology that works only on the highway, controlling trucks so they maintain a safe following distance and change lanes only when necessary. After a driver maneuvers a big rig onto the interstate, the autonomous technology takes over so the driver can complete online forms and catch up on communications with the main office.

Advocates of autonomous vehicles argue that driverless cars and trucks save lives, lower the cost of travel and transporting goods, and provide independent transportation

Hot Technology Now

A free app named ZocDoc finds available appointment times with local doctors based on zip code.

Figure 12-10: Electronic shipping

Handheld computer scans the code on a package.

Kzenon/Shutterstock.com

for people with disabilities. Ford, for example, plans to produce fully autonomous vehicles for ride sharing by 2021 to "improve safety and solve social and environmental challenges for millions of people," according to Mark Fields, Ford president and CEO.

Use Technology in Elementary Education

Imagine a group of fifth graders tracking the path of an electron in a water molecule or solving urban traffic problems. Computer games and simulations in the elementary classroom make such investigations possible, helping students visualize processes that are otherwise hard to see.

Schools are also using special social networking tools designed for education to promote school events, work cooperatively on group projects, and prevent bullying. As the cost of mobile devices declines, schools are adopting them to help close the **digital divide**—the gap between those who can access digital information, especially on the Internet, and those who cannot.

Methods of bridging the digital divide include permitting mobile devices to connect to the Internet using **WhiteFi**, short for "white space fidelity," or unused TV and radio frequencies, which avoid expensive investments in infrastructure. The Gates Library Initiative places computers in libraries around the world and provides training on request.

Use Technology in Higher Education

Look in the backpack or hand of the average college student and, chances are, you'll find a smartphone or tablet. Besides using these mobile devices for social networking and texting, you can take advantage of recent innovations to further your education. For example, you can visit websites such as Academic Earth and connect to resources such as iTunes U to watch video lectures, demonstrations, and performances by world-class professors.

Instructors can use a **learning management system (LMS)** to set up web-based training sites where students can check their progress in a course, take practice tests, and exchange messages with the instructor and other students. In fact, SAM offers many of these features. See **Figure 12-11**.

Hot Technology Now

The educational site Merlot.org provides free learning content and apps for online courses.

Figure 12-11: Learning management system

SAM is a web-based training site where students can check their progress in online activities and take practice tests.

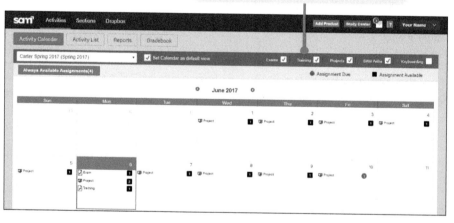

Hot Technology Now

Learning management systems are software applications for the delivery and reporting of coursework. In the higher education market, popular providers include Blackboard, Moodle, Kannu, and Desire2Learn.

Some schools provide these systems in the cloud, which means they are installed on a server so that students can access the systems at any time using their web browsers. Schools can then enhance the systems more frequently and easily, keeping pace with commercial software.

Explore Artificial Intelligence

artificial intelligence (AI) | conventional AI | computational AI | expert system | heuristic | neural network | data mining | robotics | robot | natural language processing | speech recognition | digital assistant | chatbot | virtual reality (VR) | augmented reality (AR) | digital twin

It was big news when a computer named Deep Blue beat the reigning world chess champion, and even bigger news when a computer named Watson beat two all-time champions on the television game show Jeopardy! These are only two examples of **artificial intelligence (AI)**, a branch of computer science devoted to increasing the intelligence of machines. See **Figure 12-12**.

Figure 12-12: Artificial intelligence

Self-propelled vacuum cleaners are robots that use AI to navigate rooms.

A computer named Watson used AI to beat two all-time champions on Jeopardy.

Personal digital assistants use AI to respond to spoken commands.

Personal investment software uses AI to help investors select stocks and bonds.

John Kasawa/Shutterstock.com, Bloomicon/Shutterstock.com, Source: IBM, dennizn/Shutterstock.com

Define Artificial Intelligence

Computers with AI can collect information to make decisions, reach conclusions, and combine that information in new ways, which is a form of learning. They also can communicate using language. AI applications fall into two broad categories: conventional AI and computational intelligence, as shown in **Table 12-1**.

Table 12-1: Categories of AI

Type	Definition	Example
Conventional AI	Takes advantage of a computer's ability to use logic or statistics and probabilities to solve a problem	Search engine suggesting a search term after you enter a few letters
Computational AI	Performs cycles of tasks and learns from each cycle	Financial system that helps investors select the best stocks or bonds

Use AI Software

When you visit the doctor seeking treatment for a skin rash, you trust that the doctor has enough expertise to tell the difference between a common rash and something more serious. To make an accurate diagnosis for more complicated medical problems, your doctor might use an **expert system**—conventional AI software programmed to follow rules specified by an expert in the field.

Expert systems use **heuristics**, or experience-based learning, to solve problems, just as people do. For example, if it's a hot summer day and your rash is red and itchy, an expert system would evaluate those conditions and conclude that you might have a heat rash.

In contrast, software that relies on computational intelligence can learn for itself. **Neural networks**, for instance, use technology to simulate how our brains generate paths from one neuron to another when gaining knowledge. Neural networks are well-suited to recognizing patterns such as those in sounds and symbols, which leads to speech recognition and reading. **Figure 12-13** compares an expert system with a neural network.

Figure 12-13: Expert systems and neural networks

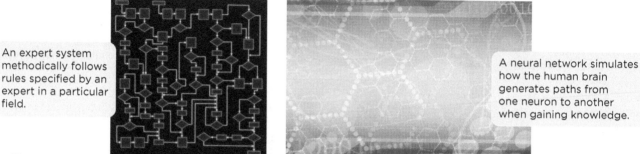

An expert system methodically follows rules specified by an expert in a particular field.

A neural network simulates how the human brain generates paths from one neuron to another when gaining knowledge.

maxstockphoto/Shutterstock.com, wongwean/Shutterstock.com

#changingworld

You interact with AI in your daily life when a site such as amazon.com suggests products that you might like. To make these suggestions, Amazon uses data mining to compare your shopping profile to those of other shoppers.

Hot Technology Now

Open YouTube and search for "Double Robotics" to view a robot that provides face-to-face interaction for telecommuters, remote workers, and students.

Figure 12-14: Robotics

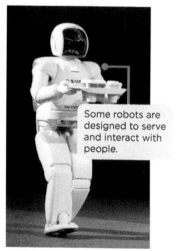

Some robots are designed to serve and interact with people.

catwalker/Shutterstock.com

Instead of diagnosing a condition using heuristics, a neural network could use **data mining**, a search technique that organizes and analyzes data in a meaningful way, to quickly analyze a mountain of data and recommend the best treatment.

Use Robotics

Robots seem to be everywhere: on the factory floor, in the operating room, and even collecting soil samples on Mars. **Robotics** is the area of AI that focuses on practical uses for **robots**, which are machines that can move automatically.

Researchers have designed robots that roll, walk, and glide. Many types of robots have been used on factory floors for decades. Some robots interact with people by recognizing speech and interpreting gestures and facial expressions. See **Figure 12-14**.

For the most part, robots' accomplishments are limited by their programming. A robot vacuum such as the Roomba can clean the floor but not learn which rooms need cleaning the most frequently. However, a new generation of robots is being developed that mimics the way people can sense, learn, and adapt as they perform tasks. For example, such robots can serve as receptionists in hospitals, assist the elderly, and clean office buildings.

Use Natural Language Processing

When you say, "Where can I find lunch around here?" to a smartphone, how does it understand your request? The answer is **natural language processing**, a type of AI that computers can use to understand natural human languages, such as English.

Natural language processing makes speech recognition possible. With **speech recognition**, a computer can understand and react to spoken statements and commands. Using speech recognition tools on a mobile phone, for example, you can say, "Call Reagan Ryan," and have the phone dial the number for Reagan Ryan as specified in its contacts list. Mobile devices and other types of computers use **digital assistants** as personifications of their speech recognition tools. Digital assistants complete electronic tasks in response to voice commands.

Speech recognition software uses AI to gather the sounds of your speech, compare them to a large library of words, phrases, and sentences, and then make a best guess about what you said. To enjoy the full benefits of speech recognition software, you must train it so it understands your speaking style and terms you use often.

Similar to a digital assistant, a **chatbot** is an app that uses AI to simulate conversation with users, especially over the Internet. Companies including Microsoft and Facebook are replacing frustrating phone trees with chatbots that deliver automated customer support, e-commerce guidance, and information. Chatbots offer a personalized, responsive type of communication that users enjoy and are much less expensive than call centers for companies to operate.

Use Virtual Reality

Have you played a super-realistic online game that lets you explore worlds and interact with digital beings? If so, you have enjoyed immersive virtual reality. **Virtual reality (VR)** is a computer-simulated, 3-D environment that you can explore and manipulate. **Augmented reality (AR)** is a type of VR that uses an image of an actual place or thing and adds digital information to it. For example, a map that shows the location of nearby transit stops or a football broadcast that shows a first-down marker is using augmented reality.

Although VR developers work mostly with digital graphics and animation, they use artificial intelligence when creating virtual creatures that make decisions and change their behavior based on interactions with others.

Outside of games, science and medicine use VR for training and research. For example, medical students can use VR to practice their emergency medical skills. NASA uses VR to simulate space flight and the environment of other planets. NASA also uses VR along with AI to train a robot that performs repairs, for example. In fact, VR is most helpful exploring outer space, the depths of the oceans, and other hard-to-reach places.

VR and AR also have wide-ranging commercial and industry applications. For example, some Lowe's home improvement stores have HoloLens headsets customers can wear to design a virtual kitchen or bathroom by selecting items from the Lowe's catalog or another online resource and displaying them as 3-D images in the virtual space of their headsets. See **Figure 12-15**.

#changingworld

Chatbots could replace 1-800 numbers, offering customer support experiences without the hassle of waiting on hold, enduring lengthy phone conversations, and using annoying phone button selection trees.

Hot Technology Now

Skype for HoloLens lets your friends and family see what you see in your HoloLens headset. They can draw on their screens to place holograms and images in your view. You might use this technology to follow a friend's instructions to set up a wireless network or repair a leaky faucet.

Figure 12-15: Commercial use for virtual reality

Customer sees a simulation of a kitchen in her HoloLens goggles and selects items to redesign the room.

HoloLens goggles

Source: Lowe's Innovation Labs

Fields such as the military and aerospace use **digital twins**, digital copies of physical objects. The twin is a virtual replica of an object such as an airplane, including its design specifications, materials, and behavior. An aircraft manufacturer could use the digital twin during development to conduct rigorous tests that might uncover deficiencies or lead to breakthrough performance enhancements.

Use Green Computing

green computing | vampire device | e-reader | e-writer

When you buy a computer, experts tell you to look for one with a large hard drive, lots of memory, and a powerful processor. Considering the high cost of electricity and the global need to conserve resources, you also should look for a computer that saves energy.

The Bottom Line
- Green computing means using computers and mobile devices in environmentally responsible ways.
- Following green computing practices reduces energy consumption and conserves resources.

Figure 12-16: Green computing

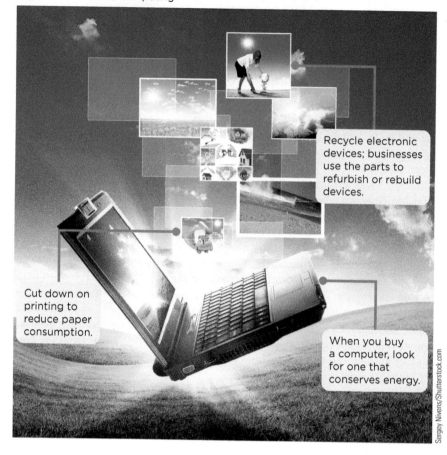

Recycle electronic devices; businesses use the parts to refurbish or rebuild devices.

Cut down on printing to reduce paper consumption.

When you buy a computer, look for one that conserves energy.

Sergey Nivens/Shutterstock.com

If you're concerned about how much energy computers consume and how much waste they contribute to the environment, you're not alone. Companies that create and use computers realize that **green computing**, the environmentally responsible use and manufacture of computers and their components, makes business sense because it saves money and resources.

Manufacturers are making an effort to build energy-efficient computers and use recyclable cases and packaging. They are also reducing the amount of toxic chemicals in components such as display devices to make them easier to recycle.

You can help reduce energy consumption by unplugging **vampire devices**, which are those that draw power even when they are turned off or in standby mode, such as computers, chargers, and home electronics. Conserve resources when you can. For example, reading documents on-screen instead of printing them can save tons of paper over time.

Recycle Electronics

As a conscientious consumer, you probably take advantage of recycling programs for paper, glass, and plastic. You also can recycle computer equipment, though doing so is more complicated than placing an old monitor in a recycling bin.

- **Recycling centers**: Some community and private recycling centers accept electronic equipment, but many charge a fee because they must safely extract the hazardous materials the equipment contains.
- **Device manufacturers**: The companies that manufacture electronic equipment often collect and recycle their products, and some reclaim parts that they can use to refurbish other products.
- **Creative reuse**: People make mobiles and wind chimes from old CDs, mosaics from keyboard keys, jewelry from computer parts, and clocks from hard drives.

Recycle Ink and Toner

Laser and inkjet printers that quickly produce high-quality text can benefit businesses and consumers alike. But they also generate an enormous amount of e-waste. In North America, people discard over 350 million ink and toner cartridges per year in landfills. These cartridges can take up to 450 years to decompose.

Instead of throwing away your ink and toner cartridges, recycle them. Most printer manufacturers provide postage-paid shipping boxes so you can return the cartridges for recycling. Manufacturers also refill used cartridges and resell them at reduced rates. Refilling cartridges consumes less energy than manufacturing new ones. If you buy recycled cartridges to begin with, you are reducing e-waste and energy consumption at the same time. See **Figure 12-17**.

Figure 12-17: Recycling ink and toner

Source: HP

Reduce Paper Consumption

Has a store clerk recently asked whether you want a printed receipt? Forgoing printed receipts is part of a larger move toward a paperless society, which provides and stores information electronically instead of on paper.

Right now, the United States uses about 85 million tons of paper each year, which is more than one billion trees' worth of paper. Paper mills also contribute significant amounts of pollution to the environment. To combat this, businesses and organizations are cutting down on paper consumption. For example, the U.S. government is phasing out paper checks for Social Security and other benefit programs.

Digital alternatives let you decrease your personal paper use. For example, **e-readers** let you read paperless books, and **e-writers** make it possible to write paperless notes, draw sketches, and even make doodles.

#changingworld

Consumers save paper by paying most of their bills online, sending email instead of handwritten letters, and accepting receipts as instant messages for most transactions.

Donate Computer Equipment

Instead of letting old PCs or cell phones collect dust in a back room or leak toxic chemicals into a landfill, donate the device to a school, church, or community program. Secondhand stores often accept electronic equipment if it's in good working order.

Refurbishers repair newer computer equipment and sell it or distribute it to groups that need it. Some recyclers accept donations of older computer equipment, break it down, and then use the parts to create inexpensive devices. To aid refurbishers, include the keyboard, mouse, and other peripherals along with the original documentation or other printed information. Before donating a computer or mobile device, protect yourself from identity theft by wiping the hard disk to remove all of its data. Deleting files does not thoroughly remove data. Use a special disk-wiping program to make sure the job gets done properly.

Identify Technology Jobs

information technology (IT) department | resume | web portfolio | certification | certification exam

Whether you want to work for a major corporation or a small startup business, you can find ample job opportunities in the computer field. You can take advantage of community and online resources to pursue careers in the computer industry.

The Bottom Line

- Careers in technology fields are among the highest paying and in the most demand of all employment fields.
- To prepare for a career in technology, you need training and possibly certification.

Figure 12-18: Technology careers

A recent graduate used his degree to secure a position as a software engineer, one of the fastest-growing occupations in the computer field.

A freelance designer enrolled in a program on website design and is now starting her career at a global company.

A former computer technician visited the online job boards until he found an exciting job with an innovative software publisher.

michaeljung/Shutterstock.com, wavebreakmedia/Shutterstock.com, EDHAR/Shutterstock.com

Technology jobs include the following:

- **Enterprise**: To manage computer systems and their software, medium and large businesses usually have an **information technology (IT) department**. As a member of an IT department, you might set up computer equipment, design and maintain systems, train and assist other employees, or develop security practices.
- **Manufacturing**: If you work for a company that manufactures computer equipment, your job could range from assembling computer parts to engineering new products.
- **Data**: Data scientists comprise a recent breed of technology professional that gathers structured and unstructured data and uses skills in math, statistics, and programming to organize the data to find trends, solve problems, and spur insights.
- **Software**: In the software field, you might write programming code, test programs, design an application, or develop an exciting new computer game.
- **Sales**: If you work for a company that sells computers, you present hardware and software that meets a buyer's needs.

Conduct a Job Search Online

Are you happiest tinkering with a faulty circuit board or sluggish printer? Do you design webpages or write user guides for your friends? Do you delight in solving technology problems for other people? If you answered yes to any of these questions, you should look for a job in the computer field.

1. Start your job search by learning about specific types of technology jobs that suit your skills. Websites such as the one for the Bureau of Labor Statistics describe hundreds of jobs, including those in the computer field. See Figure 12-19.

2. Look in many places for job openings, including local notices, your school's career placement office, and web resources. Web resources include online newspapers, company websites, and job-search sites.

Figure 12-19: Technology careers

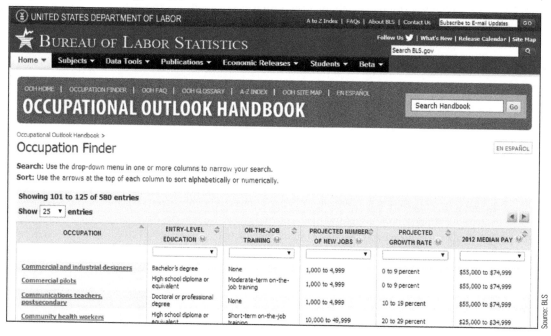

Prepare Resumes

After scouring the web, talking to friends, and reading want ads, you've found a few jobs you're qualified for and maybe even one that looks like your dream job. Now what? Prepare your **resume**, a summary of your education, work experience, skills, and accomplishments. An effective resume is clear, concise, accurate, and easy to read.

Resumes you submit electronically, such as by posting on a website or sending as an email attachment, probably will be scanned electronically. That means you need to focus on content, not formatting. Ask friends and career advisors to review your resume and offer suggestions for improvement.

Consider creating a **web portfolio**, which is a hypertext version of your resume that includes links to samples of your work, such as webpages you designed or programs you wrote.

Prepare for a Career in Technology

Perhaps you have a part-time job selling mobile devices or training people in how to use applications. This kind of experience can prepare you for a career in the computer industry. Most likely, you need additional formal education.

A technical college, also called a trade school or career college, teaches you specific skills in programming, networking, or security, for example. You generally can complete a technical college program and receive a certificate or an associate's degree within two years of full-time studies.

To earn a bachelor's degree, you can attend a four-year college or university and study computer information systems, computer science, or computer engineering. As in many other fields, the more advanced your degree in a specific field, the better your chance of success.

Earn Certification

Once you're armed with an associate's, bachelor's, or advanced degree in a technology field, how can you stand out from other job seekers? You can earn **certification** in a particular area, such as software, hardware, operating systems, networking, or databases.

To become certified, you demonstrate your mastery of technology skills and knowledge by taking and passing an exam. A **certification exam** is an objective test offered by an authorized testing company. Most people prepare for a certification exam through self-study, online classes, or instructor-led training.

Keep in mind that certification alone usually is not enough to qualify you for a job in the computer industry. However, certification can improve your chances for employment, enhance your position in the workplace, and increase your salary potential.

On the Job Now

Post your resume on LinkedIn.com to network with your colleagues, classmates, and friends.

On the Job Now

Most businesses consider that MOS (Microsoft Office Specialist) certification demonstrates mastery of the most recent version of Microsoft Office.

#changingworld

Go to twitter.com, and then search for @SAMTechNow, the book's Twitter account, and follow @SAMTechNow to get tweets on your home page.

Chapter Review

Use Automated Technology

1. What is a smart device? What role does it play in a device mesh?
2. What is an embedded computer? Give two examples of embedded computers.
3. Describe a benefit of adaptive systems in an automotive vehicle.
4. What types of automated technology are used in home appliances, public transportation, and stores?

Perform Daily Living Tasks Online

5. What is a mobile payment service? Describe how you might use the service.
6. What is e-learning? In what circumstances might you use e-learning?
7. What is m-commerce and what advantages does it offer?
8. What does it mean to be a digital citizen?

Use Intelligent Workplaces and Classrooms

9. What is a social enterprise and why might businesses want to use it?
10. How do manufacturing companies use computer-aided manufacturing (CAM)?
11. Describe recent innovations in healthcare technology that involve patient monitoring.
12. How is technology changing the transportation industry?

Explore Artificial Intelligence

13. Briefly explain and then give an example of conventional AI and of computational AI.
14. What is robotics? Give an example of how robotics is used today.
15. What is natural language processing?
16. Describe scientific, medical, and retail applications for VR.

Use Green Computing

17. What are vampire devices and how should you deal with them?
18. Describe three ways you can recycle electronic equipment.
19. What should you do before donating a computing device to an organization?

Identify Technology Jobs

20. What types of responsibilities do employees in IT departments have?
21. What is certification and why might you want to earn it?

Test Your Knowledge Now

1. A(n) _____ car uses embedded computers to control acceleration and braking, sensors to detect surroundings, and a global positioning system (GPS) to navigate.
   a. augmented reality
   b. self-driving
   c. adaptive
   d. digital

2. A washing machine that launders clothes using the most efficient amount of electricity and water and an oven you can turn off from a smartphone are part of the _____.
   a. Web of Things
   b. Internet of appliances
   c. world of AI
   d. Internet of Things

3. A(n) _____ contains an embedded computer chip to manage payments and deposits and to provide security.
   a. ATM card
   b. smart card
   c. token
   d. drone

4. _____ is a short-range wireless technology that works with smartphones so that you can receive detailed nutritional information about products in a supermarket, for example.
   a. Short-range communication (SRC)
   b. Computer-aided manufacturing (CAM)
   c. Near field communication (NFC)
   d. Computer-aided shopping (CAS)

5. A(n) _____ is a small aircraft without a pilot that can navigate by remote control or on its own.
   a. drone
   b. kiosk
   c. device mesh
   d. clone

6. When you connect to educational content such as recorded demonstrations and lectures and learn at your own pace, you are participating in _____.
   a. telematics
   b. an asynchronous course
   c. m-learning
   d. artificial intelligence

7. _____ websites provide product descriptions and reviews and let you compare features and prices of similar products.
   a. On-demand
   b. M-tail
   c. E-tail
   d. Chip-and-PIN

8. _____ is popular because you can view or listen to it at any time rather than according to a set schedule.
   a. Live blogging
   b. On-demand media
   c. The Internet of music
   d. Telemusic

9. _____ means using technology ethically and responsibly and being aware of upcoming changes so that everyone can use technology productively.
   a. Online education
   b. Digital citizenship
   c. Smart automation
   d. Mobile commerce

10. Employees who need flexible work schedules can _____, an arrangement that lets them work from home and conduct business using the phone and the Internet.
    a. use synchronous learning
    b. telecommute
    c. data mine
    d. telework

11. Using _____ communications, a company's computers can monitor assembly lines and equipment to keep them running safely and efficiently.
    a. robot
    b. machine-to-machine (M2M)
    c. radio frequency identification (RFID)
    d. asynchronous

12. Smart pills, also called _____, contain tiny sensors that help people remember to take medications regularly and in the right dosages.
    a. sensibles
    b. reminder pills
    c. ingestibles
    d. micro pills

13. The gap between those who can access digital information, especially on the Internet, and those who cannot is called the _____.
    a. virtual divide
    b. Internet gap
    c. digital divide
    d. information rift

14. A system that performs cycles of tasks and learns from each cycle is using _____.
    a. adaptive technology
    b. e-learning
    c. conventional AI
    d. computational AI

15. Expert systems use heuristics, which are _____, to solve problems.
    a. types of databases
    b. experience-based rules
    c. computer-to-computer communications
    d. opinions

16. _____ language processing is a type of AI that digital assistants use to communicate with people.
    a. English
    b. Natural
    c. Machine
    d. Foreign

17. Computers and chargers that draw power even when they are turned off or in standby mode are examples of _____ devices.
    a. green
    b. vampire
    c. power
    d. neural

18. Eliminating printed receipts is part of a larger move toward a(n) _____, which provides and stores information electronically.
    a. recycled society
    b. social enterprise
    c. electronic revolution
    d. paperless society

19. To manage computer systems and their software, medium and large businesses usually have a(n) _____ department.
    a. social networking
    b. enterprise
    c. information technology
    d. green computing

20. To _____ in a technology field, you take and pass an objective exam offered by an authorized testing company.
    a. create a resume
    b. apply for a job
    c. earn certification
    d. research a career

21. In the space next to each term below, write the letter of the phrase that defines it.
    a. home automation
    b. embedded computer
    c. neural
    d. e-learning
    e. e-writer

    _____ A type of network that controls systems such as heating, cooling, and security to increase comfort, quality of life, and health

    _____ A tiny special-purpose computer included as a component in a larger product

    _____ Formal education that involves students connecting to instructors, information, and other students using a computer and the Internet

    _____ A device that makes it possible to create paperless notes and sketches

    _____ A type of network that uses technology to simulate how our brains generate paths from one neuron to another when gaining knowledge

Try This Now

1: Augmented Reality

Augmented reality devices such as the HoloLens headset display the real world supplemented by holograms and additional sensory input such as sound and GPS data. AR is growing quickly and changing our lives.

   a. Search YouTube for a current video about Skype with HoloLens. In a Word document, insert the URL of the video and then write an overview of the video in your own words in a paragraph format.

   b. Search YouTube for a current video about HoloLens gaming. In the same Word document, insert the URL of the video and then write an overview of the video in your own words in a paragraph format.

   c. Search YouTube for a current video about HoloLens and a company named Vuforia. In the same Word document, insert the URL of the video and then write an overview of the video in your own words in a paragraph format. Save the document and submit it to your instructor.

2: Self-Driving Cars

Self-driving cars can be a controversial topic because they have many pros and cons.

   a. Investigate five benefits of self-driving vehicles. Create a document that contains a complete sentence about each benefit.

   b. Investigate five negative aspects of self-driving vehicles. Add a complete sentence about each negative aspect.

   c. Using YouTube.com, search for three videos about self-driving trucks. Place the three URLs of the videos in the Word document and add a paragraph describing each video.

   d. What are your thoughts about self-driving vehicles? Add at least three sentences to the Word document stating your opinion. Save the document and submit it to your instructor.

3: Online Job Search

Years ago, job searches were conducted primarily with the Help Wanted ads in a newspaper. Today, posting your resume online, searching jobs sites, and online networking connects an employee to an employer.

   a. Identify five online job search engines. Search each of the five job sites for openings in a position that interests you. Take a screenshot of the search results page from each of the five job sites and record the URLs of the sites.

   b. Place the screenshots in a single Word document. After each screenshot, insert the URL of the site and then write a paragraph about each online job search engine for a total of five paragraphs. Compare the ease of use, results, and layout of the site. Save the document and submit it to your instructor.

Critical Thinking Now

1: Google Home and Home Automation

Devices such as Google Home and Amazon Echo can control the lights, provide information, and even assist in making a grocery list. Search YouTube for three videos about devices such as Google Home or Amazon Echo. In a Word document of at least 150 words, discuss different features and supported app partners and share the three URLs of the videos, and then submit the document to your instructor.

Source: Google

Home Automation

2: Internet of Things Simplifies Life

The Internet of Things is changing our quality of life. Open a browser and then open bing.com/videos. Search for "Internet of Things life simplified" and watch at least five videos on the topic. In a Word document, insert the URLs of the five videos and then write a short paragraph providing an overview for each video. How do you see IoT changing your personal life? Write a paragraph in response.

3: Trending Technology Jobs

Every job uses technology to some extent, but fields that are dedicated to technology are booming. Research the fastest-growing technology jobs. Locate the seven technology jobs with the most growth potential and then rank them in a list. Write seven short paragraphs that explain each job.

Ethical Issues Now

Recently, Moshe Vardi, a computational engineering professor at Rice University, predicted that computer intelligence was growing so quickly that most human jobs would be automated by 2045. Research the topic of artificial intelligence and the workforce.

Artificial Intelligence

a. If software could wipe out most of the job market overnight, how would this affect our lives? Write at least 100 words expressing your reaction in a Word document.

b. If artificial intelligence masters driving personal vehicles, ambulances, trucks, Uber transportation, and delivery trucks, how would our lives change? Write at least 100 words expressing your opinion in a Word document.

c. If chatbots can mimic a text-to-speech engine that replaces most customer service agents, should a company's ethics board consider not using the software because of the effects on the work force? Write at least 100 words expressing your opinion in a Word document.

Team Up Now—Remote Business Meetings

Telecommuting, remote workforces, and outsourcing are increasing all over the world. Even if you work with a team that is technically based in the same physical office, it's becoming more common that participants prefer to communicate in a virtual manner instead of in person, due to time constraints. To research this topic, each team member should use the term "remote business meetings" in a search engine.

Based on your team's findings, assign each person to research a best practice in conducting remote business meetings. Each team member should write a paragraph about his or her findings.

As a team, research five positive aspects and five negative aspects of remote business meetings. Next, research Marissa Mayer's opinion of telecommuting. Write a paragraph on whether your team agrees or disagrees with Ms. Mayer.

Share your results with your team and submit the combined information to your instructor.

Key Terms

adaptive system
artificial intelligence (AI)
asynchronous course
augmented reality (AR)
automated technology
BYOD
certification
certification exam
chatbot
chip-and-PIN technology
computational AI
computer-aided manufacturing (CAM)
conventional AI
data mining
device mesh
digital assistant
digital citizen
digital divide
digital twin
drone
e-learning
electronic retail (e-tail) sales

embedded computer
enterprise computing
e-reader
e-writer
expert system
green computing
heuristic
home automation
information technology (IT) department
ingestible
Internet of Things (IoT)
kiosk
learning management system (LMS)
live blogging
machine-to-machine (M2M)
mobile banking
mobile commerce (m-commerce)
mobile health (mHealth)
mobile payment
mobile wallet
natural language processing
near field communication (NFC)

neural network
on-demand media
online banking
radio frequency identification
   (RFID) tag
resume
robot
robotics
smart card
smart device
smart grid
social enterprise
speech recognition
synchronous course
telecommute
telematics
telemedicine
unmanned aerial vehicle (UAV)
vampire device
virtual reality (VR)
web portfolio
WhiteFi

Index

A

AAC audio file format, 11-6
About page, 9-15
absolute reference, 4-10
accuracy, online information, 10-9
Action Center, 3-32
active window, 3-12
activity trackers, 1-5
adaptive programming
methodology, 2-9
adaptive systems, 12-2
address bar, 5-5
address book, 9-11
address bus, 1-14
address spoofing, 8-6
administrator accounts, 3-33
adware, 6-19, 7-21
aggregator sites, 5-22
agile programming
methodology, 2-9
AI. See artificial intelligence
AIFF audio file format, 11-6
algorithms, 2-7
alignment, text, 4-7
all-in-one desktop computer, 1-3, 6-4
ALU (arithmetic logic unit), 1-14
analog sound, 11-6
analog sound waves, 11-5
AND operator, 5-12
Android, 3-18—19
animated GIF, 11-13
animation(s), 4-15
  definition, 11-12
  in films, 11-12—13
  in games, 11-13
  software, 11-13
  2-D vs. 3-D, 11-13
  on Web, 11-13
antispam software, 2-17
antispyware, 2-17, 8-9
antivirus software, 2-17, 8-9
application help, 2-16
application service providers
(ASPs), 5-18
application software
  databases. See database
    software
  definition of, 2-2, 2-6
  graphics. See graphics
    software
  presentation. See presentation
    software
  spreadsheets. See spreadsheet
    software

  system software and, 3-2
  word processing. See word
    processing software
application software programs, 4-2
apps, 2-2, 2-11, 4-2
  accessing, 4-2—3
  development, 4-4—5
  drawing, 4-19—20
  features of, 4-3
  painting, 4-19
  photo-editing, 4-20
  types of, 4-3—4
  update, 4-5
app stores, 2-11, 4-23
App Tab, 5-7
AR (augmented reality), 11-14, 12-13
archive files, 3-23
archiving, 9-7
arguments, 4-10
arithmetic logic unit (ALU), 1-14
artificial intelligence (AI)
  computational, 12-11
  conventional, 12-11
  definition of, 12-11
  natural language processing,
    12-12—13
  robotics, 12-12
  software, 12-11—12
  virtual reality, 12-13
ASCII, 1-15
Ask a Librarian search tool, 10-12
ASPs (application service
providers), 5-18
assemblers, 2-10
assembly language, 2-9
asynchronous communications, 9-9
asynchronous courses, 12-6
ATMs, embedded computers, 12-5
audio
  digital, 11-5
  editing sound, 11-8
  file formats, 11-5
  playing sound, 11-7—8
  recording sound, 11-5—7
  speech recognition, 11-7
  streaming, 11-8
  synthesized music, 11-7
  synthesized speech, 11-7
  Websites, 5-14—15
audio capture and editing
software, 11-8
audio input device, 11-5
audio software, 11-7
augmented reality (AR), 11-14, 12-13
authentication, 7-23, 8-14

authentication methods, 7-24
authentication technologies,
2-13, 2-15
automated motor vehicles, 12-2—3
automated technology, 12-2

B

backing up, 2-18, 3-23, 6-9—10
BAN (body area network), 7-4
bandwidth, 7-10
banking, online, 5-22, 8-10
banner ads, 5-15
barcodes, 5-23
base station, 9-4
basic input/output
system (BIOS), 1-17
B2B (business-to-business)
e-commerce model, 5-21
B2C (business-to-consumer)
e-commerce model, 5-20
behavioral health risks, 8-2—3
benchmarking, 1-14
beta, 2-10
binary codes, 1-15, 2-9
binary number system, 1-15
biometric devices, 7-23, 7-24
biometric input device, 1-8
biometrics, 1-8, 5-22, 8-15
BIOS (basic input/output
system), 1-17
bit, 1-15
bitmap, 4-18
bitmap graphics, 5-14
bitmap images, 11-2
BitTorrent, 7-12
black hat, 8-4
Blinkx search tool, 10-12
blog(s), 5-17, 9-2
  creating, 9-15
  definition of, 9-14
  etiquette, 9-20
  microblogs, 9-15—16
  types, 9-14—15
Blog aggregators, 9-14
blogger, 9-14
blogging, 9-14, 11-17
blogosphere, 9-14
blogware, 9-15
Blue Screen of Death (BSoD), 8-4
Bluetooth, 6-6, 7-3
Bluetooth standard, 7-6
BMP graphics file format, 11-3
body area network (BAN), 7-4